This book is essential reading for anyone wishing to gain a comprehensive grasp of how pluralistic forms of American consumer culture were born, flourished, dissipated, and in some cases, were reinvigorated. Starting before the birth of the nation, Terry Witkowski offers a palatable and penetrating look at seven broadly defined eras of consumer culture history. His choice to compare the developments of consumer culture across three threads—the meaning consumers attribute to goods and services, gender-role discourses as they pertain to household and macro-marketing phenomena, and resistance to consumerism—make for a compelling and coherent narrative. Chockablock with compelling images, this book is sure to remain a vital reference.

Cele C. Otnes, *Investors in Business Education Prof. of Marketing, University of Illinois at Urbana-Champaign, USA.*

A History of American Consumption provides a much-needed overview of how consumption came to occupy such a central place in the consumer culture of the US. Richly illustrated and meticulously researched, this book makes an important contribution to the growing area of historical research in marketing.

Jonathan Schroeder, *William A. Kern Professor of Communications, Rochester Institute of Technology, UK.*

A History of American Consumption

The United States has been near the forefront of global consumption trends since the 1700s, and for the past century and more, Americans have been the world's foremost consuming people. Informed and inspired by the literature from consumer culture theory, as well as drawing from numerous studies in social and cultural history, *A History of American Consumption* tells the story of the American consumer experience from the colonial era to the present, in three cultural threads.

These threads recount the assignment of meaning to possessions and consumption, the gendered ideology and allocation of consumption roles, and resistance through anti-consumption thought and action. Brief but scholarly, this book provides a thought provoking introduction to the topic of American consumption history informed by research in consumer culture theory.

By examining and explaining the core phenomenon of product consumption and its meaning in the changing lives of Americans over time, it provides a valuable contribution to the literature on the subjects of consumption and its causes and consequences. Readable and insightful, it will be of interest to scholars and advanced students in consumer behavior, advertising, and marketing and business history.

Terrence H. Witkowski is Professor of Marketing and Director of the International Business Program at California State University, USA. Educated at Northwestern University, UCLA, and UC Berkeley, he has published over 120 scholarly works.

Routledge Studies in the History of Marketing
Edited by Mark Tadajewski and Brian D. G. Jones

It is increasingly acknowledged that an awareness of marketing history and the history of marketing thought is relevant for all levels of marketing teaching and scholarship. Marketing history includes, but is not limited to, the histories of advertising, retailing, channels of distribution, product design and branding, pricing strategies, and consumption behaviour – all studied from the perspective of companies, industries, or even whole economies. The history of marketing thought examines marketing ideas, concepts, theories, and schools of marketing thought including the lives and times of marketing thinkers.

This series aims to be the central location for the publication of historical studies of marketing theory, thought and practice, and welcomes contributions from scholars from all disciplines that seek to explore some facet of marketing and consumer practice in a rigorous and scholarly fashion. It will also consider historical contributions that are conceptually and theoretically well-conceived, that engage with marketing theory and practice, in any time period, in any country.

1 **On The Origins of Self-Service**
Franck Cochoy

2 **The Foundations of Marketing Practice**
A history of book marketing in Germany
Ronald A. Fullerton

3 **Pioneering African-American Women in the Advertising Business**
Biographies of MAD Black WOMEN
Judy Foster Davis

4 **A History of American Consumption**
Threads of Meaning, Gender, and Resistance
Terrence H. Witkowski

A History of American Consumption

Threads of Meaning, Gender, and Resistance

Terrence H. Witkowski

Routledge
Taylor & Francis Group
LONDON AND NEW YORK

First published 2018 by Routledge

2 Park Square, Milton Park, Abingdon, Oxfordshire OX14 4RN
52 Vanderbilt Avenue, New York, NY 10017

Routledge is an imprint of the Taylor & Francis Group, an informa business

First issued in paperback 2019

British Library Cataloguing in Publication Data
A catalogue record for this book is available from the British Library

Library of Congress Cataloging in Publication Data
Names: Witkowski, Terrence H., 1970– author.
Title: A history of American consumption / Terrence H Witkowski.
Description: 1 Edition. | New York : Routledge, 2018. | Includes bibliographical references and index.
Identifiers: LCCN 2017019467 (print) | LCCN 2017022310 (ebook) | ISBN 9781315676524 (eBook) | ISBN 9781138936911 (hardback : alk. paper) | ISBN 9781315676524 (ebk)
Subjects: LCSH: Consumption (Economics)–United States–History. | Consumer behavior–United States–History.
Classification: LCC HC110.C6 (ebook) | LCC HC110.C6 W58 2018 (print) | DDC 339.4/7–dc23
LC record available at https://lccn.loc.gov/2017019467

ISBN: 978-1-138-93691-1 (hbk)
ISBN: 978-0-367-87441-4 (pbk)

Typeset in Times New Roman
by Wearset Ltd, Boldon, Tyne and Wear

To Sherri, John, and Edward with love

Contents

Figures

Preface and Acknowledgments

The idea of writing a book on American consumption history had been on my mind for some time, but more as an item on my academic bucket list than as an actual project. The situation changed when I contributed a chapter entitled "A History of Consumption in the United States" to *The Routledge Companion to Marketing History*, edited by D.G. Brian Jones and Mark Tadajewski (Witkowski 2016b). After reading the manuscript, Brian invited me to submit a proposal for a book length version to the Routledge Studies in the History of Marketing, a new series he and Mark also were editing. So I wrote a proposal, which was supported by the reviewers, the series co-editors, and the Routledge editorial staff, and signed the contract. Thank you all for your confidence in my work and in my ability to complete an endeavor of this nature.

My interest in studying marketing and consumer history developed early in my academic career. By the time I had finished my doctoral dissertation at U.C. Berkeley in 1980, which was a survey of the alcohol field and the attitudes this interest group held toward alcohol advertising and its regulation, I had become disenchanted working with quantitative data or, more precisely, working with SPSS and mainframe computers. In those days, users entered data on 80-column cards using a keypunch machine. At the front of their "job," they punched other cards to control the program and perform the analyses. One would hand a heavy box full of cards to an operator who then fed the batch into a card reader. The cards and the paper line printout would be available later, sometimes overnight. One little typo or misfiled card and the whole process had to be repeated. This was very discouraging. To make matters worse, I was rather indifferent toward applying and developing theory in a positivistic research sense, especially in the service of managerial decision-making, and tended to be an academic loner preferring to work without co-authors and to call my own, idiosyncratic, shots. These predilections did not bode well for success in the marketing field and although I liked research and writing, my academic career had hit a big, mostly self-imposed obstacle. What kind of research in marketing or consumer behavior could be qualitative, relatively atheoretical, and the product of one person working alone? The answer, of course, was historical research.

As an undergraduate I had majored in History at Northwestern University. My major GPA was a bit below my overall GPA, and given my lack of foreign language skills, I saw no academic future in history and instead chose to attend business school, first at UCLA (M.S. in Management with a Marketing emphasis), and then at U.C. Berkeley (Ph.D. in Business Administration with a Marketing emphasis). Yet, I still liked history and so in the spring of 1982 I presented a little paper, "Getting Women to Smoke: Cigarette Advertising in the 1920s," at the annual meeting of the Popular Culture Association. A few more short papers followed including "Marketing Silver in the Eighteenth Century" given at the Second Workshop on Historical Research in Marketing, hosted by Michigan State University, April 28–30, 1985. Professor Stanley C. Hollander, a leading retailing scholar and marketing historian, organized this and subsequent biennial meetings, which eventually became incorporated as the Conference on Historical Analysis and Research in Marketing (see www.charmassociation.org). Stan had a fine sense of humor and came up with the designation because he liked the acronym, CHARM. More important to me personally, he became a very supportive mentor of mine. I missed the 1987 meeting, but returned in 1989 and have been active ever since including serving as program chair in 2003, local arrangements chair in 2005 and 2015, and CHARM president for two terms (2005–2009).

My first historical journal article, "Colonial Consumers in Revolt," was published in the *Journal of Consumer Research* in September 1989. I believe Stan was one of the reviewers of this piece, as was historian and consumer culture theorist Grant McCracken, whose name was revealed to me inadvertently. Stan and Grant's helpful opinions and then JCR editor Rich Lutz's nurturance at this crucial juncture in my career was and is most appreciated. I should also mention the very positive influence around this time of Alan Andreasen, who was the chair of my department from 1987 to 1990. Alan's good research sense and strong work ethic, not to mention his sage comments on my JCR manuscript, definitely inspired me. In 1989 I also published a history article in the summer issue of the *Journal of Marketing Education* and since then have contributed history articles to a number of different journals in marketing and consumer research, most of which are listed in the references.

The roots of this book also tap into my collecting of Americana. By nature, I am a collector. As a boy I dabbled with stamps, then coins, and finally antique firearms and edged weapons. Later I developed interests in nineteenth-century American silver and pewter, stoneware and historical Staffordshire pottery, Audubon and Currier and Ives prints, and early California paintings. Collecting demands historical knowledge and I became a serious student of material culture who, in turn, applied some of this learning to scholarly research and writing. Collecting small pieces of Americana also led to furnishing our house with reproduction Queen Anne, Chippendale, and other early American furniture in mahogany and cherry and mostly built from high-end, mail order kits that I personally assembled, finished, and varnished. With collectibles surrounded by sympathetic furniture, the next step was architectural and in 1992 my wife, Sherri, and I added a second story to our Southern California ranch house that transformed the whole assemblage into something approximating a federal New England home. I am a pretty good woodworker and finish carpenter and over the years have added moldings and other traditional touches to the walls and ceilings. I suppose the next phase in cultural consistency would be to wear period attire, but I already have acquired enough commodity fetishes and am not yet into re-enacting. So my everyday clothing remains academic modern.

My late parents, Henry and Natalie Witkowski, had similar decorative instincts and I remember when, after a visit we made to Colonial Williamsburg in 1959, they began to furnish our Cape Cod style lakeside home in northern Illinois with early American furniture and accessories. Most were purchased from a local Ethan Allen store. These pieces were not close reproductions like mine, but rather very loose interpretations of past styles in maple. Created at the post World War II tail of the colonial revival movement, they were meant to convey tradition and homeyness for the mass market. I remember them all as part of the setting of my happy childhood so greatly shaped by the love of my parents who indulged my collecting by giving me reference books and display cabinets for Christmas presents. In the very first, 2009, issue of the *Journal of Historical Research in Marketing*, their devoted son published a little article about them and a bookstore they operated in Chicago from 1938 to 1947. I was born in 1948.

The Civil War centennial, 1961 to 1965, fired my collecting and historical interests and thus provided still another influence on this book. This anniversary received massive coverage in the media at the time and further fueled my historical imagination and collecting passions. On an Oldsmobile road trip to the East Coast with my parents in the summer of 1963, we stopped at Gettysburg, Pennsylvania, the site of the most significant combat of the War. The battlefield was impressive, as were the various monuments erected in subsequent years in memory of the Union and Confederate troops who fought and died for their respective causes, and for each other. Later that year my dad twice drove me to The Powder Horn, an antique gun shop in Wilmette, Illinois. I had saved enough money from gifts and part time work to buy two breech loading percussion carbines, a Sharps and a Smith, made during the Civil War years. I did not return to Gettysburg until the summer of 2001. Accompanied by Sherri and our then young sons, John and Edward, I was as excited as I had been on my first visit. For good measure, we also visited the Civil War battle sites of Antietam, Harpers Ferry, and Fredericksburg. Thanks, family, for indulging dad's history mania!

My first full time position was as an Instructor in the Department of Advertising at the University of Texas, Austin from 1978 to 1982. I started ABD (all but dissertation) and took two years to finish my dissertation, so tenure was out of the question. However, I am grateful for UT's patience with me. Plus, Sherri was one of my students and we married in 1982. California State University, Long Beach, my academic home since August 1982, provided crucial writing assistance in the form of sabbatical leave during Spring Semester 2016. "The Beach" as we call it has been a good match for my professional skill set and I appreciate the generally supportive atmosphere over the years. Historical work in marketing and consumer research does not have a broad following in business schools in the U.S. and may be looked down upon by top shelf institutions transfixed by the quantitative models and arcane theorizing of high social science.

Long Beach, California
July 2017

1 Writing American Consumption History

This introductory chapter provides some conceptual and methodological grounding for researching and writing American consumption history. It examines a few basic concepts of consumption and consumer culture, some issues and literature in consumption historiography, types of data sources for consumption history, approaches to the analysis of material artifacts, the topic of historical periodization, and the structuring and scope of this book. The next chapter discusses the history of the field of consumer research, as well as consumer culture theory perspectives on meaning, gender, and resistance that are the threads that inform and guide this history.

Consumption and Consumer Cultures

Consumption history is about what consumers have done in the past, but also an account of what they and critical observers (e.g., theologians, social commentators, politicians, and activists) have thought, felt, and said about consumer behavior. Consumers in this book are to be considered people (i.e., end-users of goods and services), not companies or governments, and their consumption behavior entails a broad range of acquisition, use, and recycling or disposal activities. In modern economies, acquisition largely results from shopping and buyer behavior in a commercial marketplace. This requires personal income. However, the United Nations Human Development Programme reminds us that much consumption is collective and non-material (HDR 1998). People also consume a wide variety of goods and services from sources outside the market including nature (e.g., hunting, fishing, gathering), unpaid work (e.g., domestic activities, self-production), and public provisioning (e.g., food stamps, subsidized water, sanitation services). In the distant past, nature and unpaid work undoubtedly accounted for much consumption.

The meanings of the terms "consumption" and "consumer" have changed over time. Historian Lawrence Glickman (2009) showed how in eighteenth-century America to consume meant essentially "to use" or "to use up" something. Purchasing was seen as a separate activity. In the nineteenth century, consumption became understood, like it is today, to include the buying of both goods and services and to be the driving force of economic activity. The word "consumer" began to be used in its modern sense in the 1820s. In the twentieth century, the consumer was identified as a separate class of social actor that in the aggregate constituted the target market for sellers, but also needed protection from the vagaries of the market.

Historians and consumer culture theorists have long debated the meaning of the interrelated terms "consumer society," "consumerism," and "culture of consumption." Two perspectives will suffice for our purposes. First, Kathleen Rassuli and Stanley Hollander (1986, 5) argued that a culture of consumption required four conditions:

1 People (or some very substantial segment of the population) consume at a level substantially above that of crude, survival-level subsistence.
2 People obtain goods and services for consumption through exchange rather than self-production.
3 Consumption is seen as an acceptable and appropriate activity.
4 People, in fact, tend to judge others and perhaps themselves in terms of their consuming lifestyles.

As Russell Belk (1996) observed, the choice of the word "crude" to characterize subsistence hunting and gathering was potentially biased, but the last two requirements of this definition do highlight the importance of belief and value systems in addition to basic economic conditions.

Second, in his fine and learned book, *Consumer Culture and Modernity*, Don Slater (1997, 24–32) identified a number of features of a modern consumer society. These signposts included the following (Slater's statements in italics):

1 *Consumer culture is a culture of consumption.* This is Slater's way of saying that the values of consumption prevail in consumer cultures and inexorably spread into numerous domains of social action.
2 *Consumer culture is the culture of a market society.* In other words, we generally consume goods and services made and distributed by others primarily within a capitalist system.
3 *Consumer culture is, in principle, universal and impersonal.* This observation reaffirms the idea of "mass consumption" where buyers are usually unknown to sellers. Everyone, in theory, has the right to consume and "all social relations, activities and objects can in principle be exchanged as commodities" (Slater 1997, 27).
4 *Consumer culture identifies freedom with private choice and private life.* This statement embodies the arguably mythical, but heavily promoted notions of "consumer sovereignty," a "democracy of goods," and the consumer as "voter," "judge," and "jury" (Schwarzkopf 2011).
5 *Consumer needs are in principle unlimited and insatiable.* Ever growing demand, once considered a social or moral pathology in some cultures, and a status marker reserved for elites in others, becomes normalized and a prerequisite for progress in consumer cultures (see, e.g., Campbell 1987; Mukherji 1983).

6 *Consumer culture is the privileged medium for negotiating identity and status within a post-traditional society.* Here, fixed social orders – often reinforced by sumptuary laws regulating food, clothing, and luxuries – are swept away and identity becomes a function of consumption.
7 *Consumer culture represents the increasing importance of culture in the modern exercise of power.* Symbols, especially brands, conveyed by advertising, packaging become preeminent in consumer culture.

Historically, America did not become a consumer culture in Slater's full sense until the twentieth century, but as will be shown several of these features became apparent by the mid-eighteenth century, at least within some colonial circles, and these and other criteria became increasingly widespread over time. This is why it may be more appropriate to use the plural "consumer cultures" when referring to the past, just as it would be when alluding to different societies in the present.

Consumption Historiography

History is a branch of knowledge dealing with past events, as well as with the evolution of ideas within their larger societal contexts. Sometimes, academics in marketing and consumer research regard history as a methodology. This view is mistaken. History is a subject area in the same sense as advertising, retailing, and services marketing are topics of study. Although historical data can be used to investigate theories developed by the social sciences, history as a discipline is very much concerned with addressing historical questions. So, when discussing methods for researching the past, the appropriate term is historiography, which refers to the principles, theories, and methodologies of historical writing. Note that the term "history" also refers to a chronicle or narrative of the past and that the term "historiography" too has a second meaning, as a body of literature. This section reports on some relevant literature, mainly that created by academics in marketing and consumer research, and is then followed by a further look into some methodological issues.

In the fields of economic, business, and marketing history, the majority of research concentrates on past practices and events, but a sizeable minority examines the evolution of economic, business, and marketing thought (Witkowski and Jones 2006). Similarly, historical studies of consumption patterns focus on past behavior and happenings, whereas investigations of market ideologies over time relate to the field of intellectual history or how thinking about consumers and consumption has evolved. An example of the latter was Merle Curti's (1967) "The Changing Concept of 'Human Nature' in the Literature of American Advertising." Based on an analysis of articles published from 1888 to 1954 in *Printers' Ink*, a pioneering advertising trade journal (see Figure 1.1), Curti documented a shift from envisioning the consumer as a rational, self-interested actor to one moved more by emotions and non-rational drives. Ronald Fullerton's (2007) "Psychoanalyzing Kleptomania" offered another exemplar of intellectual history in consumer research. Descriptions of consumer theft and shoplifting

Figure 1.1 *Printers' Ink*, October 19, 1892. Founded in 1888 by early adman George P. Rowell (1838–1908), this cover referred to a dispute with retailer John Wanamaker (the fox) who had been appointed Postmaster General in 1889 and who charged *Printers' Ink* (the game bird) a higher postage rate than he did for his own trade publication, *Book News* (the center chicken).

behaviors have been stable for 200 years, but explanations have ranged from "lesions of will" in the nineteenth century to Freudian notions of sexual significance and Adlerian inferiority complexes in the twentieth century to contemporary emphases on chemical imbalances treatable by pharmaceuticals.

A review of the methods literature in consumption and consumer culture historiography should begin with Ronald Savitt's (1980) "Historical Research in Marketing," published in the *Journal of Marketing*. Savitt argued that historical research should be conducted according to the philosophies of positivism and empiricism: "Historical research must retain the objectivity of the scientific method, following its structure as closely as possible" (Savitt 1980, 54). His outline of historical research included seven activities: (1) problem definition, (2) literature review, (3) formulation of hypotheses, (4) research design, (5) data collection, (6) hypothesis verification, and (7) theory development. Contributing to theory is not the only and perhaps not even the most important justification for historical work in marketing and consumption, but researchers trained in the social sciences have taken this purpose seriously. Savitt's article helped stimulate renewed interest in history among marketing academics and consumer researchers.

The 1987 meeting of the Association for Consumer Research (ACR) featured five presentations on consumer historiography. Of this group, Ronald Fullerton's (1987) "Historicism: What It Is, and What It Means for Consumer Research," has had a great influence on my own thinking. The German historical school, in a challenge to logical positivism, was skeptical of law-like generalizations and cumulative social knowledge. Its proponents argued that societies are constantly in flux and that theories having credence in one time period may no longer be so relevant at a later date (Fullerton 1987). Events were considered "historical individuals" and so researchers should focus on concrete social phenomena. Stated differently, the focus of historical research should be on addressing particular historical issues and questions, not on building universal theories (Smith and Lux 1993). Thus, some professional historians have identified more with the humanities, whereas others have leaned toward the social sciences. In practice, a given study might serve either historical or theoretical ends or both simultaneously in various proportions. Indeed, historical inquiry sometimes is based upon the perspective of a particular theory, such as neo-Marxism or feminism.

Also among the 1987 ACR papers were "Historiography, Scientific Method, and Exceptional Historical Events" by Fuat Firat, "An Historical Perspective Framework to Study Consumer Behavior and Retailing Systems" by Erdogan Kumcu, "Comparative History as a Research Tool in Consumer Behavior" by Kathleen Rassuli and Stanley Hollander, and "Insights into Consumer Behavior from Historical Studies of Advertising" by Richard Pollay. Firat (1987) compared different traditions in historiography – specifically, the French Annales school of history, hermeneutic interpretation, and Marxist analysis – and explored their philosophical implications. Kumcu (1987) approached the study of consumer history as an alternative to logical positivism as a paradigm for understanding change in retailing systems. Rassuli and Hollander (1987) discussed data sources for comparative consumer history and proposed a model accompanied by examples for conducting this type of research. Pollay (1987) championed the potential of historical methods through reviews of Curti's (1967) article and the then recently published books by Roland Marchand (1985) and William Leiss, Stephen Kline, and Sut Jhally (1986).

Two years later in "The Relevance of Historical Method for Marketing Research," a chapter in the ACR-sponsored book, *Interpretive Consumer Research*, Marilyn Lavin and Thomas Archdeacon explored the relationship between interpretive (qualitative) and scientific (quantitative and deductive) approaches. Lavin and Archdeacon (1989) implicitly criticized Savitt's (1980) model as too narrow and, for good measure, took a potshot at German historicism, which they depicted as "a philosophically dubious viewpoint" (60).

In "Historical Method in Consumer Research: Developing Causal Explanations of Change," Ruth Anne Smith and David S. Lux (1993) deployed historical research in order to explain change in consumer behavior. Their conceptual model of historical methodology consisted of two stages: (1) Research Design, which includes question framing and research procedures, and (2) Historical Analysis, which entails investigation (discovery of facts), synthesis (construction of causal statements and writing an explanatory narrative), and interpretation or the "implications of the narrative for the research question" (605). The following year, I added my own two cents with "Data Sources for American Consumption History: An Introduction, Analysis, and Application," a chapter in *Explorations in the History of Marketing*, the sixth supplement in the series *Research in Marketing* (Witkowski 1994). Among various topics, I discussed colonial probate records and household furnishings as potential data sources, and conducted a little experiment using material culture methodology, which I will revisit later in this chapter.

Three chapters in the *Handbook of Qualitative Research Methods in Marketing*, edited by Russell W. Belk and published in 2006, contributed to the historiography of consumption. Linda Scott, Jason Chambers, and Katherine Sredl (2006) in "The Monticello Correction: Consumption in History" explored issues related to who should be the subject of historical inquiry – elites and rich people or the everyday variety – and issues related to presentism, letting preconceptions from the researcher's time influence views of the past. Richard Elliott and Andrea Davies (2006) in "Using Oral History in Consumer Research" explained this retrospective interview method and then presented some findings regarding the evolution of brand consciousness and consumer culture in the UK. In "Qualitative Historical Research in Marketing" (Witkowski and Jones 2006), my good colleague Brian Jones and I covered a range of practical topics including selecting a topic, source materials and their assembly, analysis and writing, and preparing manuscripts for marketing journals. Marketing and consumer research are social science driven fields and thus have different requirements than journals catering to academic historians. For example, historians generally have not been very transparent about research methods and, aside from discussions of sources, their writings do not include detailed accounts of methodology (Fullerton 2011).

In 2011, the *Journal of Historical Research in Marketing* featured a primer on oral history methodology "A Life Course Perspective of Family Meals Via the Life Grid Method" by Robert Harrison, Ann Veeck, and James Gentry. Later that year, the Journal put out an entire special issue on "historical methods and historical research in marketing." Several articles are very relevant to researching and writing the history of consumer culture. Ron Fullerton's (2011) autobiographical article on "Historical Methodology" drew upon his background as a professionally trained historian. He advocated strongly for consulting primary sources (evidence created during the period under consideration), understanding the past on its own terms, reading data critically, and giving high importance to interpretation and coherent story telling. In "Voices Passed," Andrea Davies (2011) critically examined oral history, the reconstruction of the bygone events and feelings from interviews with surviving eyewitnesses. This method remains contested among historians who observe that individual recollections of events are unreliable and interact with public, group, and family memories. Rick Pollay (2011) in "Biographic and Bibliographic Recollections," told how his collecting of advertising and promotional ephemera led first to original content analyses of evolving cultural values and ultimately to his becoming an expert witness in tobacco litigation.

In fusing his collecting passion with serious historical research, Rick has been a person after my own heart. Other collector/scholars who have contributed to consumption history include Janet L. Borgerson and Jonathan E. Schroeder. They have repurposed their collecting of Peter Pauper Press books from the 1950s and 1960s into a chapter on collecting, and have leveraged their collection of vinyl record albums and covers from the same era into several papers, Consumer Culture Theory conference presentations, and a book (Borgerson and Schroeder 2002, 2006, 2017). For more than a century, collectors and dealers have stimulated much art history research and decorative arts scholarship. Originally focused on objects and their makers, by the 1980s these studies of material culture increasingly were exploring consumer culture issues (Martin 1993).

On a final historiographical note, Brian Jones and I published an article, "Historical Research in Marketing: Literature, Knowledge, and Disciplinary Status," in *Information & Culture: A Journal of History* (Witkowski and Jones 2016). In it we discussed how the literature in marketing history has grown, in part because of the dedication of key scholars who organized conferences, arranged for special issues, and launched journals. We also demonstrated how marketing history writing has developed some distinguishing features – explicit literature reviews, data borrowing, multiple types of primary sources, and methodological transparency – that reflect the social science background of many writers and, accordingly, meet the expectations of editors and reviewers for marketing journals. Since much consumer research has become closely identified with the marketing field, what applies to marketing history generally applies to the writing of consumption history, this book in particular.

Data Sources for Consumption History

Historians distinguish between primary and secondary data sources. Primary sources are forms of evidence produced during the historical period under investigation or, in the cases of autobiography and oral history, produced somewhat later by people who had participated in the events in question. Secondary sources, on the other hand, consist of the literature (historiography in the second sense) about the period, such as books and articles, written at an even later date.

Respectable consumer histories can be developed entirely by mining the existing secondary literature. Among a number of possible examples were my account of colonial American consumers and the nonimportation movement (Witkowski 1989) and, more recently, Karl Moore and Susan Reid's (2008) discussion of 4000 years of brand history. Nevertheless, professional historians will argue persuasively that the best and most exciting historical research comes from having a strong set of primary evidence and being fully conversant with it (Fullerton 2011). Poring over primary data allows the historian to get into the mindsets of past consumers and see the world through their eyes. Most consumer culture history writing will entail a mix of primary and secondary data sources (see, e.g., Karababa and Ger 2011). For earlier periods, original data may be scarce, scattered, and quite difficult to locate and thus requires greater reliance on secondary sources. Even when primary evidence is plentiful, consumer historians should be familiar with the secondary literature and any debates over interpreting primary sources it may have spawned. There is no need to repeat analytic errors already identified by other scholars.

The major categories of primary sources include (1) numerical data, (2) written records, (3) artifacts, (4) visual images, and (5) memories elicited through oral history interviews. A particular piece of evidence can straddle more than one category. Probate records, for example, consist of text and numbers. Print advertising, one of the most frequently consulted primary sources, usually includes both body copy and visual content. Paintings, prints, and photographs contain images, but are also physical objects, often with provenance – their history of sales and ownership.

A wide variety of quantitative data are relevant to writing consumption history. Often aggregated or macro rather than at the individual level, numerical data can be taken from secondary sources, such as government reports from, say, the U.S. Bureau of the Census, or created by the researcher, such as through content analyses of advertising (Belk and Pollay 1985; Pollay 1985). Historians of early America have frequently consulted probate records, which included wills, inventories, and accounts of administration. According to Gloria Main (1975, 90):

> The first directed the disposition of property. The second itemized and evaluated the forms of that property. The third furnished reports to the court on the disposition of property in intestacy cases and also in those cases where the will provided an insufficient guide to the legal settlement of the estate.

Inventories constitute the vast majority of all surviving probate records. Colonial era appraisers, usually neighbors of the deceased, compiled lists of items, sometimes on a room-by-room basis, and assigned values expressed in pounds, shillings, and pence. The number of goods and their value tells us about the decedent's standard of living and, in the assortment of goods, about the consumer lifestyle. Only one-third to one-half of all inventoried estates left wills, while accounts of administration survive for less than one-third of cases (Main 1975).

As a data source for consumption history, probate records have much to recommend them. Great numbers of them were originally created and they are now available in various media. Inventories covered a broad range of people and described a great variety of consumer goods. Thus, they lend themselves to quantitative research. However, many different currencies prevailed at various times and places – early Maryland inventories even expressed values in terms of pounds of tobacco (Main 1982) – and need to be converted into a common denominator. Furthermore, estate inventories did not necessarily typify community consumption patterns because of unavoidable age and nonresponse biases (Shammas 1978). Decedents tended to have been older than living neighbors and, consequently, may have had the time to accumulate more possessions. Also, appraisers did not inventory all estates, especially those of the mobile young and the very affluent, and when acting neighborly may have deliberately omitted some items to protect surviving widows and children who, in turn, may have hidden articles for their own reasons. The claims of creditors kept such practices within reasonable bounds (Main 1982). Finally, the obsession with inventories eventually petered out: "As a general rule, coverage declined with time, leveling off to 40 percent in Massachusetts by the Revolution and during the nineteenth century" (Main 1975, 98).

Academic historians consult written or textual sources far more than any other type of primary data and some have (mistakenly) argued that they are the only trustworthy evidence (Thompson 1988). Students of material culture use them as external evidence to validate or deny hypotheses about artifacts (Prown 1982). Typical forms applicable to researching consumption history include the following, listed from the most public to the most personal.

1 Public records such as tax lists, probate documents, and court proceedings.
2 Articles and letters in newspapers and magazines, trade publications, and scholarly journals.
3 Advertising, handbills, trade cards, catalogs, and other promotional ephemera.
4 Nonfiction travel accounts, cookbooks, and housekeeping manuals.
5 Novels, poetry, and other published fiction.
6 Private business records such as account books and invoices.
7 Personal writing in the form of letters and diaries.

Even relatively recent articles in scholarly journals can be used as primary sources. For example, Lizabeth Cohen (2003) cited *Journal of Marketing* articles from the 1950s and 1960s as evidence of increasing social segmentation after World War II. In this book, some contemporary (at this writing) *Journal of Consumer Research* articles are used as data sources.

As data sources, written documents possess both strengths and weaknesses. On the plus side, they exist in great numbers for most periods of American history and thanks to the Internet and diligent archivists have become increasingly accessible at a distance. Some forms, such as letters, literature, and diaries, can give insights into people's inner thoughts and feelings about buying and using things. However, written records of all types are often incomplete, difficult to read if penned by hand, and occasionally contradictory. Researchers should always be on the lookout for the occasional fake document and, more commonly, for possible selective perception and retention on the part of the source. Indeed, the person or persons who wrote an account may have had reason to deliberately distort the truth. Since the dominant classes in a society traditionally have produced most of the writing, their reports might stress privileged consumers and luxury consumption. Elite American writers, mostly males until the twentieth century, have tended to underrepresent the consumption experiences of common people, especially blacks and other minorities, recent immigrants, and women. Finally, literature can be an inefficient data source. As Kenneth Ames (1978, 23) once put it: "Although occasional passages may be illuminating, finding them is not easy." Amen.

Material artifacts – both those excavated in situ (found objects) and those that have been saved and have passed into museums and private collections (preserved objects) – can provide still additional information for writing consumption history. Found objects are recovered and studied by historical archaeologists, while preserved objects are the primary interest of art and architectural historians, decorative arts scholars, folklorists, and collectors. In the 1970s and 1980s, decorative arts scholarship expanded its disciplinary purview to address broader contexts including the practice and meaning of consumption. As Ames (1985, 79) then observed: "the field has been in transition from studying antiques or artistic objects as ends in themselves to studying those objects in order to understand society and culture."

Material artifacts for consumption history come in so many shapes and sizes that for purposes of discussion a classification system is desirable. Prown (1982) proposed the following list, which I have slightly revised, based on function and progressing from the more decorative to the more utilitarian.

1 Art (paintings, drawings, prints, sculpture, photography, film and video).
2 Diversions (books, toys, games, theatrical props, sporting accessories).
3 Adornment (jewelry, clothing, hairstyles, cosmetics, tattooing, piercing, and other alterations of the body).
4 Modifications of the landscape (home and garden architecture, town planning).
5 Applied arts (furniture, furnishings, décor).
6 Devices (machines, vehicles, musical instruments, implements).

Like written sources, artifacts have their advantages and limitations. Most important, they are graphic evidence and sometimes all that remains of what people actually used in their lives as consumers. "Objects created in the past are the only historical occurrences that continue to exist in the present" (Prown 1982, 3). In addition to experiencing the alluring aesthetic and haptic (touch) qualities of old things, a tangible connection with past lives is part of what attracts collectors and scholars. Because many kinds of artifacts were used by a broad cross-section of the population, they are potentially more representative data sources than words. Moreover, with the exception of works of art, objects are generally less self-conscious cultural expressions and, therefore, conceivably more truthful. Through their style, objects communicate tacit but fundamental values of a society (Prown 1980, 1982).

On the other hand, they do not reveal beliefs, attitudes, values, and meanings as directly as do written records. Equally important, artifacts suffer from their own problems of representativeness. Found objects from the American past are generally restricted to certain materials, such as ceramics, glass, or precious metals that can survive many years of exposure or burial on land or under water. Leather, wooden, and base metal consumer goods rarely last under these conditions and textiles hardly at all unless the climate is very dry. Aside from the pure chance of being the one item out of many to survive, preserved objects were typically saved because they possessed special attributes. They may have been made from the highest quality components, particularly artistic in execution, or originally owned by distinguished, affluent persons and families. More common and often cruder artifacts tended to have deteriorated more rapidly with use and were discarded as junk. Their survival rate is much less than that of high-style objects. To make matters worse for the consumption historian, preserved objects may have been altered over time, either innocently for reuse (e.g., re-sewing a dress for a daughter) or with the intent to deceive (e.g., adding fake engraving to increase value on the collectors' market), and no longer are the same evidence as they once were when first produced and consumed. These historical accretions remind us that objects live in the present as well as in the past.

Images can reveal things about past consumption that cannot be conveyed by other data sources (Belk 1986; Witkowski 1994, 1996, 2004). They can show visually what buyers and sellers and their merchandise and accoutrements actually looked like. They can depict color, form, movement, and other details people once took for granted and failed to mention in texts (Burke 2001). Through narrative content and allegory, images can express social attitudes and, hence, validate or challenge written sources such as diaries, letters, newspaper accounts, or probate records (Witkowski 1994). In *Eyewitnessing: The Uses of Images as Historical Evidence*, author Peter Burke (2001) points out that unlike written documentary evidence, where usually only the investigator has had an opportunity to visit an archive and read the sources, when images are reproduced in research reports, both authors and readers have access to the data and can examine it together.

However, images can be misleading. Past artists and other image makers selected only certain subjects and rendered the world the way they personally perceived or remembered it, what Burke (2001) aptly described as their "painted opinion." Artists also created within the expectations of their patrons and audiences. Consequently, art can sometimes be a better guide to past social attitudes and cultural conventions than to the exact nature of people, things, and consumer behavior. American genre painters, for example, sometimes distorted actual behavior in order to instruct or entertain the viewer and drew upon stock social characters that fulfilled the expectations of their patrons (Hills 1974; Johns 1991; Williams 1973). Works of art have aesthetic qualities and polemical content that can elicit powerful, possibly biased, emotional responses in the researcher. Art must be read carefully and the analyst needs to distinguish a contemporary reading from a historical or period reading. For example, viewers today may find it difficult to appreciate nineteenth-century sentiment because its character and language of expression have changed (Bolton-Smith and Truettner 1973). The challenge is to recreate the "period eye."

Visual understanding of consumption history can be gained by blending approaches and interests from art history with concepts and methods from the fields of visual culture and postmodern theory. Art history has long been concerned with elements intrinsic to images, such as their shape, line, color, texture, and composition. The term "style" refers to how these elements are treated by individuals and artistic movements (Barnard 2001). Art historians have also examined the lives of the artists, using biography to gain insight into the intentions and meanings behind visual representation. However, much current art historical writing, like research in the closely related field of material culture, focuses less on the artists and their works per se, than on using images and artifacts as analytical points of departure for raising questions about the original audiences, owners, and society and culture that produced and received them (Fernie 1995; Prown 1982). In effect, fine and decorative art objects are used as evidence for investigating larger historical questions. This book draws upon and analyses visual data sources in several periods, especially genre paintings from the 1850s, poster campaigns from World War II, and advertisements and photographs from the late nineteenth to early twenty-first centuries.

The images discussed above are all static, but motion pictures and television along with documentary films and videos are potentially rich, but underutilized data sources for consumption history. In America, nickelodeons showing short films flourished from 1905 to 1915, by which time feature length movies dominated. Themes of materialism and how goods do not bring happiness have been at the heart of many films, above all Orson Welles' 1941 masterpiece *Citizen Kane*, although others, such as Ingmar Bergman's *Fanny and Alexander* (1982), suggest that "possessions can make the world magical and add childlike joy to life" (Belk 1986, 18). The first documentary film, *Nanook of the North* (1922), recorded a staged version of Inuit life near Hudson's Bay (Belk 2011). More recent documentaries that address issues in American consumption, such as Michael Moore's *Bowling for Columbine* (2002), Morgan Spurlock's *Supersize Me* (2004), PBS's *The Merchants of Cool* (2004), and Al Gore's *An Inconvenient Truth* (2006), may become valuable data sources for future historians. These entertainment and documentary media share many of the strengths and weaknesses of static visual images and have some drawbacks of their own. They have an ephemeral quality, are usually produced by non-academics, and have a strong point of view rather than the usually more balanced approach of scholarly writing (Belk 2011).

Donald Ritchie in *Doing Oral History* (1995, 1) offers a succinct definition of our fifth type of primary source: "Simply put, oral history collects spoken memories and personal commentaries of historical significance through recorded interviews." Researchers typically capture this data with audio/video equipment, although some situations still require note taking. Interview techniques can range from being very unstructured and free flowing to obtaining open-ended answers to a specific list of questions, such as the life grid method where questions about events are reused as cues to elicit recall of consumption patterns (Harrison, Veeck, and Gentry 2011). After a session is finished, recorded words are then transcribed verbatim save minor editing to clarify, to remove false starts or repetitions, and to insert punctuation. Although time-consuming, transcription facilitates interpretation since most people can read and reread print faster than they can listen to and comprehend an audio or video recording. Further, given potential problems in where to store taped or digital audio recordings and how they might be accessed in the future when technology changes, a written version helps preserve the findings.

A few sniffy historians have dismissed oral history as little more than the collection of sentimental memories from old people. They have a point: "some interviewee's remarks are self-serving; they remember selectively, recall only events that cast themselves in a good light, and seem to always get the better of opponents" (Ritchie 1995, 92). Human memories start from the perspective of one person and are fallible, although most forgetting takes place soon after an event has occurred. Oral history informants have been characterized as being "special" people – survivors, more successful, and self-confident (Gluck 1987). Oral historians frequently encounter informant nostalgia, where the past is remembered as better than it was lived, and thus need to press for more candid and critical responses (Ritchie 1995).

All in all, however, interview data are probably no more subjective or less representative than any other pieces of evidence and they have special advantages of their own. For one, respondents can be selected to ensure that many different points of view are being voiced. Oral history is democratic in its desire to gather information from a variety of social actors, including the more quiescent part of the population who may not produce any written documents. Also, oral interviews can elicit recollections of inner feelings and states of mind that are frequently absent from or disguised by written records. Finally, the interviewing process allows the astute investigator, in effect, to cross-examine informants and thereby reveal sources of bias. Paul Thompson (1988) describes a phenomenon among the elderly known as a "life review" – a sudden flood of memories, a desire to remember, and a willingness to be candid and less concerned about fitting one's story to the expectations of an audience.

Oral interviews are especially useful as data sources for consumption history because they usually entail ordinary people recalling everyday experiences. The field of consumer research has made use of interview data for many decades and since the 1980s has seen a resurgence of interest in more or less unstructured questioning and small samples. Historians of American consumption also have utilized interviews in the sense of deliberately collected field data. For example, Ronald Hill, Elizabeth Hirschman, and John Bauman (1997) based their account of Great Depression consumers partly on oral data originally collected by academics, journalists, and writers between 1933 and 1935 under the direction of Harry Hopkins, director of the Federal Emergency Relief Administration. Ellen Hogan and I created new oral data by asking elderly California women to recall their consumer experiences during World War II (Witkowski and Hogan 1999).

All primary sources have strengths and all have weaknesses. They need to be read critically because various authors of historical data (past number crunchers, writers, diarists, artists, artisans, and oral informants) had different points of view. When multiple sources are used, they can validate one another, as did the letters and the photographs from Great Depression America examined in Hill, Hirschman, and Bauman (1997). In other cases, different data sources may contradict one another. Needless to say, the Internet has made a great deal of primary source material easily accessible to consumer culture historians.

Given its broad scope, this book's account of American consumption history and some of its cultural themes draws heavily from secondary works including books, chapters, and journals articles in American economic, social, and cultural history, as well as historical research published in the fields of business and retailing history and marketing and consumer behavior. However, it is also based upon analyses of primary sources including written documents and with a special emphasis upon material artifacts and visual images.

Analyzing Artifacts

E. McClung Fleming (1974) described a model for analyzing objects using two conceptual tools – a classification of basic properties and a set of operations performed on those properties. An object's properties are its history, material construction, design, and functions, either intended or unintended. The operations include *identification* (a factual description), *evaluation* (judgments of quality), *cultural analysis* (the relationships linking an object to its culture), and *interpretation* (the relationships of the artifact to the analyst's culture). Whereas identification and evaluation are within the long tradition of connoisseurship, cultural analysis and interpretation introduce methods of material culture. Fleming reminds us that interpretation varies according to the personal and cultural characteristics of investigators and their audiences.

Another advocate of the material culture approach, Yale University art historian Jules David Prown, has argued persuasively that stylistic changes denoted shifts in cultural values. In "Style as Evidence" (1980), he showed how the popularity of neoclassical motifs after the Revolutionary War signified the diffusion of Enlightenment thought in America. Two years later, in "Mind in Matter: An Introduction to Material Culture Theory and Method," Prown (1982) proposed an intriguing three-stage method for object analysis. The intent of his method was "the quest for cultural belief systems, the patterns of belief of a particular group of people in a certain time and place" (6). This approach is deterministic since it assumed that the properties of an artifact (the effect) correspond to the mental patterns (the cause) of the producer and of his or her culture. Prown also contended that the methodology of material culture rests on premises shared by theories of linguistic structuralism and semiotics. That is, people structure their world through forms as well as through language. In turn, these forms "transmit signals which elucidate mental patterns or structures" (6).

In the first stage of object analysis, *description*, the investigator records what can be observed of the object itself, that is, the internal evidence. This includes physical measurement, description of constituent materials, and an analysis of content and configuration or style. The second stage, *deduction*, entails an interaction between the object and the perceiver. Here, the investigator experiences the object with the physical senses, apprehends it intellectually, and perhaps responds emotionally. In the third stage, *speculation*, the analyst reviews information gathered in prior stages and then formulates hypotheses. External evidence in the form of written sources is then located and analyzed to verify the questions posed by the material artifacts.

I once applied Prown's methods to the study of four brass candlesticks (Figure 1.2) in the family collection (Witkowski 1994). First, I described them in terms of their dimensions (7 to 8¼ inches in height and 4¼ to 5 inches in base width), weight (about one pound each), material composition (brass, an alloy of copper and zinc), style (rococo or "Queen Anne"), and condition (worn with

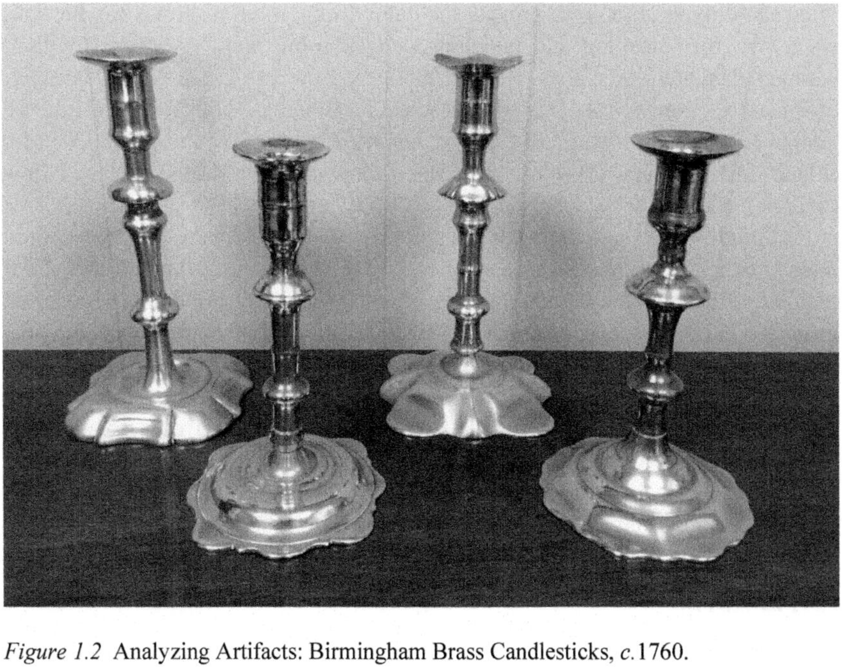

Figure 1.2 Analyzing Artifacts: Birmingham Brass Candlesticks, *c.* 1760.

Source: Author's collection.

evidence of minor old repairs). Despite a lack of identifying marks, the above findings indicated likely manufacture in Birmingham, England, *c.*1760 (see Burks 1986). The provenance of these particular objects was unknown, but exporters sent great quantities of Birmingham brass candlesticks to colonial America so these particular examples represent a type of household good possibly used in the third quarter of the eighteenth century. In Prown's next stage, deduction, I experimented with candlelight in order to further link myself, both intellectually and emotionally, with a hypothetical original user. The burning candles produced far less light than do modern lamps, but did illuminate our house reasonable well. They gave the effect of tranquility, but also of dancing shadows and a bit of mystery. The eight-inch candles dripped and smoked a bit and were consumed within about six hours. Based on these observations, I formulated three hypotheses: (1) the low light levels led colonial consumers to prefer very shiny, reflective surfaces and objects; (2) the dripping and smoking required frequent maintenance activities both during and after use; and (3) rapid product consumption necessitated the purchase or home production of large supplies of candles.

External evidence in the form of books, diaries, and letters reported by Elizabeth Garrett (1983, 1990) confirmed all three hypotheses. If they could afford such objects, early American households favored highly polished mahogany furniture with shining brass hardware, numerous reflectors and mirrors, glossy fabrics, bright gold trim, and glittering jewelry. Depending on their ingredients – those made from tallow were the poorest quality – candles ran, smoked, dripped on clothing, smelled awful, and required snuffing the charred end of the wick as often as 40 times an hour to prevent the flame from guttering. Brass candlesticks needed regular cleaning and polishing, a task some families allotted to their younger daughters or nieces. Finally, many consumers dipped or molded their own candles, a messy task saved for the cooler months. "The Reverend Edward Holyoke, president of Harvard College, recorded in his diary on March 22, 1743, 'Made 112 Baybery Candles,' and the following day, 'Made 62 lbs. tallow candles'" (Garrett 1983, 410).

Although Prown said the analyst should carry out each stage in sequence, my prior knowledge of candlesticks, candles, and their uses made this difficult. Consequently, the hypotheses stemmed as much from dimly remembered external evidence (Burks 1986; Garrett 1983, 1990) as they did from my own creative induction. Moreover, the modern candles I used probably performed differently from ones made in the past and our modern California home, even with its early American furnishings and ambience, surely had properties (room dimensions, building materials) much unlike colonial originals. This authenticity gap may have affected the experiment. Still, doing research through historical reenactment can be good fun and teach us much about past American consumption.

Periodization

This history of American consumption begins in the early seventeenth century with the settlements at Jamestown, Virginia (1607) and Plymouth, Massachusetts

(1620) and extends until the present day. The narrative focuses upon the experiences of English and European settlers and immigrants and to a lesser extent Africans, Asians, and other peoples who came to North America during the past 400 plus years. Consumption by Native Americans after settlement is briefly touched upon. Space limitations exclude consideration of early consumption in areas influenced by the Spanish. Given these parameters, an important and sometimes rather vexing decision is how to structure the narrative through periodization.

The reporting of past events – including the individuals, groups and societies involved and their various discourses about consumption – can be arranged chronologically, topically, geographically, or in some combination of the three (Hollander *et al.* 2005; Witkowski and Jones 2006). Finding an appropriate periodization scheme for writing a history of American consumption is challenging. Sometimes the choice is based on little more than narrative convenience, such as the way chapters of a novel help to convey a storyline. Marketing and consumer historians have succumbed to the expediency of dividing history into decade long segments with two exemplars being the classic account of marketing thought by Robert Bartels (1962) and the content analysis investigating the "good life" in twentieth century advertising by Belk and Pollay (1985). Ideally, significant external events and relevant consumption turning points should be used (Fullerton 2011; Hollander *et al.* 2005). For example, the American home front economy during World War II, with its full employment, high wages, rationing and price controls, was a much different environment for consumers than the subsequent years of postwar prosperity and burgeoning mass consumption. So the end of the War in 1945 would mark a logical division. However, other milestone dates in American political history, such as the signing of the Declaration of Independence in 1776 and the end of the Civil War in 1865, have less relevance for accounts of consumption.

Writers of American history have utilized a great many different periodization schemes depending upon the topic, the length of time covered, perceived coherence, and other good reasons. This book consists of seven broadly defined eras whose divisions mark important turning points. Being somewhat obsessive about such matters, selecting the most logical periods has caused me some consternation and on more than one occasion I shifted dates around. The history will begin with the colonial years from the early 1600s to 1790, then proceed into the nineteenth century to 1865, enter the "Gilded Age" from 1865 to 1900, cover the twentieth century up to 1930, describe the Great Depression and World War II from 1930 to 1945, retrace the immediate postwar period and continue through the social and economic turmoil of the 1960s and 1970s, and, lastly, assess the years 1980 to the present. These periods have different lengths ranging from about 180 years for the colonial era to just 15 for the Depression and World War II. Shorter periods may induce greater volatility and variability in the data (Witkowski and Jones 2006), but great changes and events may be precisely the reason why a historical period is conceived in the first place.

As Grant McCracken (1988) reminds us, the history of consumption has not been a steady, inexorable march toward modernity, but rather has been punctuated by a series of consumer "revolutions," episodes when marketing institutions, social relations, and consumer culture changed more quickly and with greater public awareness than at other times. Don Slater (1997) identifies several such eras in his backwards telling of the history of consumer culture. In the 1980s, neo-liberal ideology celebrated individual, private consumption and was, in part, a reaction to perceived 1950s' conformism, mass consumption, and mass production. Earlier, in the 1920s, an ideology of affluence had emerged that associated everyday consumption with modernization. Yet, some of these ideas can be traced to the Victorian boom of the 1850s through 1870s where modernization and private, bourgeois domesticity gained respectability (Slater 1997).

Periodization is a useful, even necessary, tool for narrating history, but it can have a dark side. Periodization schemes in marketing and consumption history, even though based upon flawed concepts or incomplete data, sometimes enter the literature and then persist despite new strong evidence to the contrary. The most problematic example of this situation has been Robert Keith's (1960) article, "The Marketing Revolution," first published in the *Journal of Marketing*. Based on his experience at Pillsbury, Keith theorized four eras in marketing history. In the "production era" starting in 1869 at Pillsbury, manufacturing was the preeminent concern with marketing an afterthought. The sales era commenced in the 1930s when the company began to emphasize its consumer advertising and channels of distribution. In the 1950s Pillsbury entered the "marketing era" when it established a brand manager system to focus on the consumer. By 1960, Pillsbury had embarked on the fourth era, "marketing control," where in Keith's (1960, 38) words "We are moving from a company which has the marketing concept to a marketing company."

Introductory marketing textbook writers adopted Keith's model and, in a lame attempt to introduce a bit of historical content, uncritically applied it to American marketing as a whole. This practice continued into the first decade of the twenty-first century (Jones and Richardson 2007). However, the notion that marketing was relatively unimportant until the 1930s simply did not stand up to more serious historical scrutiny. In the 1980s two well-researched papers in marketing history, one using American examples (Hollander 1986), and the other mobilizing U.S. and international findings (Fullerton 1988), both debunked Keith's scheme. Companies made serious marketing efforts throughout the nineteenth century and as far back as the eighteenth century. Through a content analysis of Canadian trade journals from the 1890s, Brian Jones and Alan Richardson (2007) added still more evidence of vigorous early marketing. The persistence of the myth of the marketing revolution can be attributed to its memorability and pedagogical simplicity, but also to sloppy scholarship, plagiarism of previous texts, and ignorance of historical research (Jones and Richardson 2007). Hollander *et al.* (2005) mention further pitfalls of periodization. Reductionism occurs when writers compress "a complex set of events into a single catchphrase or catchword. Under the pressure of such reductionism, periodization often omits important events or variables that would otherwise result in a more accurate account of history" (Jones and Richardson 2007, 23). The "gay nineties" (1890s) were not so happy for African Americans or poor European immigrants. Compounding this problem is bias introduced by presentism, the tendency to envision history as moving from a less desirable past (the production era) to a more desirable present (marketing orientation).

In the realm of consumption history, a less egregiously flawed, but still troubling periodization scheme was introduced by Robert O. Herrmann (1970) and then adopted by Philip Kotler (1972). Herrmann (1970) characterized consumer unrest in the United States as cresting in three different periods: the early 1900s, the 1930s, and the 1960s. In all three eras rapidly rising prices combined with visionary leadership (e.g., Ralph Nader in the 1960s) were important causal factors. As will be shown in later chapters, this view has some merit, but overlooks a great deal of important history. Consumer boycotts and other organized actions took place in the colonial period and throughout the nineteenth century (Friedman 1999; Glickman 2009; Witkowski 1989). But even if we limit analysis to events after 1900, overlooking the 1955–1956 bus boycott by African Americans in Montgomery, Alabama, which in my opinion was one of the most important acts of consumer resistance in American history, bespeaks a serious failure in historiography. Herrmann's account of the consumer movement should have been more inclusive.

Summary

Consumption historians can choose from an abundance of fascinating research topics addressing purchase, use, recycling, and disposal activities over time in different places among various classes of consumers and products. Work on the evolution of consumption thought – a line of inquiry within the purview of intellectual history – can trace what commentators, fierce critics, aggressive apologists, and opinionated scholars have written and said about consumers and their possessions. Consumption historians need to familiarize themselves with the secondary literature on their chosen topic, and then engage as fully as possible with primary sources by seeking out one or more categories of numerical data, written records, artifacts, visual images, and memories elicited through oral history interviews. This process can be great fun and I personally have spent many happy hours searching online for visual data at the Library of Congress, the Smithsonian, and many other archives, favorite museums, auction catalogs, and Wikimedia Commons. Since 1980, a small band of business professors with an interest in researching the past have created an informative literature consisting of conceptual models of historical methodology, as well as a variety of ruminations on salient issues in marketing and consumption historiography. Periodization, the partitioning of historical narrative, can be shallow unless turning points have robust justification in terms of important events and cultural change. Choices of what an historical study should cover and what it should exclude have multiple determinants, some practical and some a question of epistemology, the theory of knowledge.

2 Consumer Culture Theory in Historical Perspective

Analytical concepts and themes from the research tradition known as consumer culture theory (CCT) have inspired and guided this history. Now an important part of the larger field of consumer research, CCT has addressed, through typically qualitative research methodologies, "the sociocultural, experiential, symbolic, and ideological aspects of consumption" (Arnould and Thompson 2005, 868). The CCT literature has emphasized the hedonic, aesthetic, and ritualistic dimensions of consumption, consumer identity projects, and marketplace cultures. All of these phenomena have existed in the recent past, and frequently in the more distant past, and, arguably, historical precursors have left a legacy for consumption in later periods, and thus continue to influence the present.

Although most CCT research has been situated in the investigators' own here and now, this work has acknowledged the contributions historical research can make to our understanding of consumption (Arnould and Thompson 2005). Some CCT researchers have been careful to provide a modicum of historical context to their otherwise contemporary theorizing, data gathering, and analysis. Craig Thompson and Gokcen Coskuner-Balli (2007), for example, briefly traced the roots of early twenty-first century community-supported agriculture in the U.S. to the organic food movement that appeared in the 1960s. Moreover, a small number of CCT researchers have made past consumption the focus of their work. My article, "Colonial Consumers in Revolt: Buyer Values and Behavior During the Nonimportation Movement, 1764–1776" (Witkowski 1989) was one of the first such efforts. Based on a rich trove of primary sources, Russell Belk (1992) explored the symbolism embodied in the possessions of Mormon pioneers during the period 1847 to 1869. Later, Eminegül Karababa and Güliz Ger (2011) provided a fine account of consumption outside the U.S. with their piece, "Early Modern Ottoman Coffeehouse Culture and the Formation of the Consumer Subject." However, the total amount of historical analysis within CCT research has been modest. Philosophical differences in research objectives create a tension between CCT and history. The purpose of most CCT research – including studies with some partial up to more extensive historical content – is to develop and advance theory. Stated differently, scholarly work in CCT asks and seeks to answer theoretical questions about consumption. The sizeable historical literature on consumer culture written by academics and independent scholars outside of schools and colleges of business sometimes draws from theory, and may even enhance it, but historians generally focus on addressing historical questions through an informed account of the past.

This book will follow three bundles of cultural threads found throughout American consumption history: (1) the threads of meaning transferred to goods and services, to their use, and to consumers themselves, (2) the threads of gender assigned to individual and household decision making, to purchasing behavior, and to products themselves, and (3) the threads of resistance to consumerism, to the goods of political antagonists, and to societally mandated prohibitions. Over time these threads gathered into broader discourses and have been expressed rhetorically and through individual and collective consumer actions. Studied intensely by intellectual and social historians, meaning, gender, and resistance also have been fundamental CCT concerns, as will be discussed in the sections below. Clearly, these particular groups of threads do not comprise an exhaustive list of consumer culture research topics with historical implications. They have been chosen from many other potential candidates for reasons of personal interest. Simply put, investigating meaning, gender, and resistance has dominated my own historical research in consumption since the early 1980s. These are the histories I know and love. It should be noted that the three groups of threads often have been entangled conceptually and historically. Both gendering and resisting consumption have provided important categories of meaning, and resistance itself frequently has been gendered. Later chapters will describe, for example, how American women very aggressively boycotted high priced meat in 1902 and bared a lot of leg protesting Japanese silk imports in 1937. Since the 1970s many American men seem to have invested firearms with partisan political and self-assertive identity meanings.

Before reviewing a selection of noteworthy CCT scholarship relevant to the threads of meaning, gender, and resistance, the next section establishes historical context by briefly recounting the development of consumer research as an academic field or discipline. This additional context moves the subsequent literature review in the direction of true intellectual history. Literature reviews and intellectual history are not the same. Ronald Fullerton and Girish Punj (2004, 9) put it this way:

> Intellectual history differs from literature reviews as conventionally done in the social sciences. The former assumes change in environments and influences over time. The latter present findings over time in a ahistorical manner, as if they had all occurred in similar social and cultural environments.

Consumer research and CCT have had several intellectual progenitors, a sample of which the disciplinary history to follow will describe.

A Disciplinary History of Consumer Research

As used in academics, the term "discipline" has had various connotations, mostly positive ones (Shumway and Messer-Davidow 1991). It has referred both to a bounded body of knowledge as well as to the specialized training and accepted methodologies necessary for producing that knowledge. In *The Structure of Scientific Revolutions*, philosopher of science Thomas Kuhn (1970, 182–187) described a "disciplinary matrix" consisting of four elements: (1) symbolic generalizations (theories or conventional wisdom), (2) metaphysical paradigms (beliefs in specific models), (3) values (what is considered important), and (4) exemplars (the best examples students learn in texts and from the periodical literature). Michel Foucault (1972, 224) characterized an academic discipline as "a system of control in the production of discourse" and stressed the important role exercised by gatekeepers. Synthesizing these views, accounting historian Alan Richardson (2008, 267) defined an academic discipline as "the organizational and cognitive structure of academic knowledge." In his view, disciplines contain institutional, cognitive, and psychological components. As institutions, disciplines form academic associations, hold regular conferences, and create specialist journals. Cognitively, they exist as a bounded body of knowledge, controlled by peer review, within larger systems of knowledge. The psychological component of a discipline is comprised of a critical mass of scholars who self-identify as members of the discipline. All of these viewpoints agree that disciplines are socially produced and resolutely defended and promoted by scholarly groups characterized by tribalism and traditions (Becher and Trowler 2001).

The roots of the consumer research discipline in America extend back to the late nineteenth century. At that time, economic theories and scientific aspirations greatly influenced academic research and writing on consumption and would continue to do so for many decades. In her review article, "The Development of the Field of Consumption," Hazel Kyrk (1939) singled out eight important early books: *Consumption of Wealth* (1901) by Simon Patten, *Welfare as an Economic Quantity* (1915) by George Watkins, *Social and Economic Standards of Living* (1925) by Theresa McMahon, *The Consumption of Wealth* (1928) by Elizabeth Ellis Hoyt, *Economic Principles of Consumption* (1929) by Paul Nystrom, *Consumption and Standards of Living* (1936) by Carle C. Zimmerman, and *Economics of Consumption* (1937) by Charles Wyand. Three years later Walter Matherly (1942) wrote another review article, "The Development of Consumer Economics," that listed additional specialized books on consumption and also discussed the coverage of consumption in introductory economic texts. A complete account of this literature is beyond the scope of this chapter. It is worth noting, however, that in their reviews of the consumption literature neither Kyrk nor Matherly mentioned Thorstein Veblen's (1899/1953) masterpiece, *The Theory of the Leisure Class*. An instructor at the University of Chicago while writing his original yet iconoclastic book, Veblen applied concepts from cultural anthropology to economic behavior. His vividly imagined concepts and memorable terminology received learned attention when first published and his book remains one of the most important ever written on the topic of consumption. Its biting social commentary will be revisited at greater length in Chapter 5.

Empirical studies of American families, their consumption activities, and their expenditures accompanied the economic theorizing, both mainstream and Veblenian. This type of consumer research was conducted by social workers employed by various governmental and civic organizations; by educators in schools and universities; and by analysts working for and with manufacturers, magazines, and advertising agencies. Perhaps the earliest budget study took place in Massachusetts in 1875 when Carroll Wright and the state Bureau of Labor Statistics surveyed the families of 397 workingmen to determine their income levels, expenditures by category (subsistence, clothing, rent, fuel, sundry), and savings (Stigler 1954). In 1902, progressive reformers coined the term "standard of living" as a yardstick for measuring the material welfare of industrial workers and their families. The term was sometimes applied to earned wages and income, but "increasingly became defined through consumer goods and the spaces established and maintained to contain these goods" (Moskowitz 2004, 4). In his extensive bibliography, under the category "Costs and Standards of Living Studies," Nystrom (1929) recorded 93 entries, most of which for research conducted within the United States. For example, in 1909 the Russell Sage Foundation commissioned a report, *The Standard of Living Among Workingmen's Families in New York City*, and ten years later the U.S. Bureau of Labor Statistics published a *Tentative Quantity and Cost Budget Necessary to Maintain a Family of Five in Washington, D.C. at a Level of Health and Decency* (cited in Strasser 1982, 113, 119). The progressive impulses behind such research will be discussed further in Chapter 6.

The best-selling book, *Middletown: A Study in Contemporary American Culture*, written by Columbia University sociologists Robert S. and Helen Merrell Lynd (1929), included findings on how middle-American consumers defined themselves and others. Based on systematic ethnographic research they and a team of researchers conducted in the mid-1920s in the small Midwestern city of Muncie, Indiana, the Lynds observed, among many things, the importance of home ownership to consumers and how people assessed their neighbors according to where they lived and what they owned. The Lynds conducted follow-up research in Muncie in 1935 during the middle of the Great Depression and published *Middletown in Transition: A Study in Cultural Contradictions* in 1937. Additional academic consumer research appeared in the *Journal of Applied Psychology* (see Chapter 6 for a discussion of L.R. Geissler's 1917 early brand study) and in *The Annals of the American Academy of Political and Social Science*. The May 1934 issue of the *Annals*, titled "The Ultimate Consumer. A Study in Economic Illiteracy," was entirely devoted to consumer topics. In business, meanwhile, some corporate experts of the 1930s referred to themselves as "consumption engineers" (Blaszczyk 2009, 100).

The home economics field contributed a great deal to the welfare of consumers and to the literature on consumption. In 1909, after ten years of holding meetings at Lake Placid, New York on the topics of home science and household economics, conference delegates under the leadership of chemist, educator, and sanitary engineer Ellen H. Richards (1842–1911) created the American Home Economics Association and *The Journal of Home Economics* to advance the teaching and study of homemaking arts and sciences (American Home Economics Association 1909). Consumer topics were important from the outset and in 1994 the organization renamed itself the American Association of Family and Consumer Sciences. Home economists hoped to help consumers cope with an increasingly complex market where comparing prices and quality of an expanding array of goods was difficult, especially under the relentless influences of high-pressure selling and clever advertising. Matherly (1942, 60) observed how "the books written by home economists stress matters of labelling, testing, grading and standardizing and are concerned primarily with methods and techniques of wiser spending." Electric appliance manufacturers incorporated key principles of home economics – rational consumption, increased efficiency, and reduced drudgery – into the ads they placed in *Good Housekeeping* magazine. The one from November 1916 in Figure 2.1 instructed women how they could save time and effort with Westinghouse irons and toasters (Paulson and Schramm 2017).

Women in home economics wielded great influence on the early development of consumer research. Two names stand out. Hazel Kyrk (1886–1957) was a leading consumption theoretician. One of the first women to receive a doctorate in economics from the University of Chicago, she taught at Oberlin College in Ohio before securing a faculty appointment at Chicago in 1925. Kyrk's new academic home, the department of home economics, fit her interests in household behavior and social reform. She later gained a joint appointment in economics and remained at Chicago until her retirement in 1952 (Figure 2.2). In addition to the above-mentioned *A Theory of Consumption* (1923), which came out of her doctoral dissertation, Kyrk also wrote *Economic Problems of the Family* (1933) and *The Family in the American Economy* (1953). Her first book investigated, among many other topics, how unequal distribution of income limited freedom of choice, and how standards of consumption changed and developed over time. Through her extensive writing, teaching, mentoring, and professional service, Kyrk had great impact on the field of family economics, but stressed economic concepts more than practical household management (Beller and Kiss 1999; Tadajewski 2014; van Velzen 2003).

Christine Frederick (1883–1970), Kyrk's more entrepreneurial contemporary, showed less theoretical inclination, but gathered a bigger following among the public at large. Frederick's career incorporated both educational and business interests and, like many home economists at the time, she aimed to educate scientifically trained female experts and to become a consumption coach for housewives. Frederick established the Applecroft Home Experiment Station at her Long Island home in 1912 as a place to carry out her home efficiency studies (Figure 2.3). She delivered lectures, testified before a U.S. House Judiciary Committee, and cultivated consulting relationships with advertisers. She wrote articles for the trade publication, *Printers' Ink*, and between 1912 and 1919 for

Figure 2.1 "Saving Steps and Making Strides," Westinghouse Electric Ware for the Home, *Good Housekeeping*, November 1917.

the *Ladies' Home Journal*. Frederick compiled her articles on efficient housekeeping and household engineering into books. Frederick was married to an advertising executive, and in 1912 she and her husband founded the New York League of Advertising Women (now known as Advertising Women of New York, Inc.). In 1929, Frederick published a successful business book, *Selling Mrs. Consumer*, and promoted herself as a surrogate for female consumers (Rutherford 2003; Scanlon 1995, 61–76; Strasser 1982, 214–219).

Other notable female consumer economists included Martha Van Rensselaer (1864–1932), Elizabeth Ellis Hoyt (1893–1980), and Margaret Gilpin Reid (1896–1991). Van Rensselaer co-founded the Department (later School and College) of Home Economics at Cornell University in 1904, served as President

Figure 2.2 Hazel Kyrk, undated (*c.*1930s?).

Source: University of Chicago Library, Special Collections Research Center.

of the American Home Economics Association from 1914 to 1916, and edited the home-making section of the *Delineator*, a mass circulation women's magazine, from 1921 to 1926 (Zuckerman 2014). Hoyt began her career in 1917 working for the National Industrial Conference Board on the cost of living index, then earned a Ph.D., and eventually spent most of her professional life at Iowa

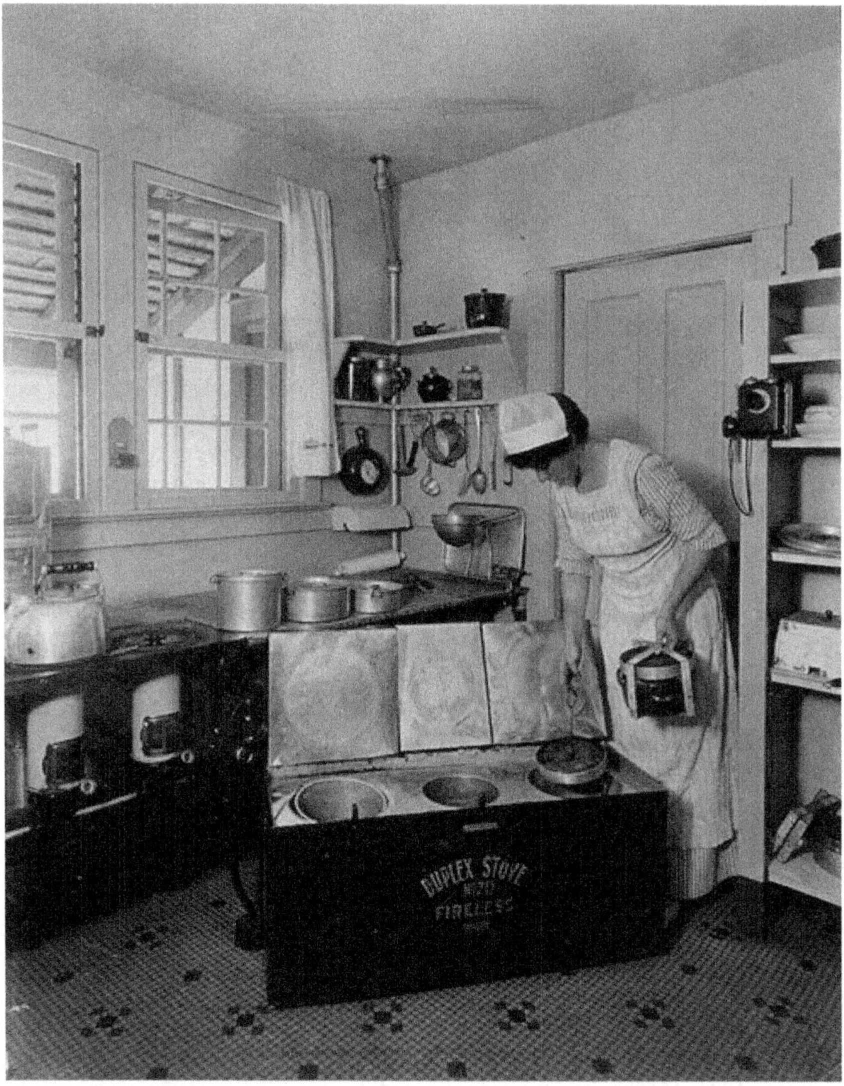

Figure 2.3 Christine Frederick, 1913. She is removing food from an oven in the kitchen of her Applecroft Home Experimental Station.

Source: Harvard University, Schlesinger Library on the History of Women in America.

State University. A prolific writer, Hoyt viewed consumption as a democratic process and emphasized how available time, energy, and money influenced consumption (Parsons 2014). Reid, who was a student of Hazel Kyrk, taught at Iowa State with Elizabeth Hoyt, worked for the federal government in the 1940s, and eventually took a position at the University of Chicago. Reid pioneered research on the economic contribution of non-market, household activities, excluding leisure activities and conspicuous consumption. The very male-dominated economics profession largely ignored Reid's formidable scholarship, along with the work of other academic women in her area. In 1996 the journal *Feminist Economics* devoted an entire issue to her research (Forget 1996; Yi 1996).

When it came to consumer research, the business field of marketing lagged behind these other social sciences. Marketing as an academic field began to split from mainstream economics starting in the 1902–1903 academic year when the universities of Illinois, Michigan, and California offered their first classes on distribution. The term "marketing" appeared in course titles a few years later and by 1920 a handful of teachable texts were available (Bartels 1962). However, the scholarly side of the discipline did not fully coalesce institutionally until 1936 when the American Marketing Association and its flagship publication, the *Journal of Marketing*, were cobbled together from predecessor organizations and journals (Witkowski 2010b).

Until after World War II, most marketing academics were trained in economics and hence approached consumer research from that discipline's point of view (Kassarjian 1994; Kassarjian and Goodstein 2009). One exception was Harvard University marketing professor Melvin T. Copeland (1884–1975) who emphasized consumer buying habits and motives over his long career (Copeland 1923; McNair 1957). In his classic article "Relation of Consumers' Buying Habits to Marketing Methods," published in the *Harvard Business Review*, Copeland (1923) laid out the famous distinctions between convenience, shopping, and specialty goods and then went on to theorize the progression of consumer attitudes from recognition to preference to insistence. The allied business fields of retailing and advertising had a more practical interest in consumer research, the latter incorporating buyer psychology early on. At the University of Minnesota, for example, psychologist Harlow Gale (1862–1945) started conducting experiments on attention to and attitudes toward advertising in 1895 (Eighmey and Sar 2007) and at Northwestern applied psychologist and later University President Walter Dill Scott (1869–1955) wrote *The Theory of Advertising* in 1903 and *The Psychology of Advertising* in 1908.

The interwar period saw an influx of people and ideas from Europe that would impart psychological grounding to American consumer research (Horowitz 2004; Kassarjian 1994; Kassarjian and Goodstein 2010). Hungarian born George Katona (1901–1981), for example, arrived in America in 1933 and quickly secured a position at the New School for Social Research in New York City. He did not believe economic theory sufficient to explain the business cycle and that knowledge of consumer sentiments was necessary to understand trends. He moved to the University of Michigan in 1946 where he conducted surveys of consumer finances and expectations (Figure 2.4) and published numerous books including *Psychological Analysis of Economic Behavior* (1951), *The Powerful Consumer* (1960), and *The Mass Consumption Society* (1964). Katona believed that rising consumer aspirations made for a healthy postwar economy and "questioned the puritanical and anti-materialistic streak in American culture, envisioning

Figure 2.4 George Katona and the Survey of Consumers, *c.*1946.
Source: Institute for Social Research, University of Michigan.

a society based on expanding wants and increasing pleasures" (Horowitz 2004, 73). Because his work was at a macro-economic level, it did not stir that much interest among business school consumer researchers who by the 1950s were developing an interest in micro-level social psychology (Kassarjian 1994).

Paul F. Lazarsfeld (1901–1976) came to the U.S. from Vienna, Austria in 1933 on a Rockefeller Foundation fellowship. He later worked for the Roosevelt Administration, directed the Radio Research Project funded by the Rockefeller Foundation, and eventually secured a position at Columbia University's Bureau of Applied Social Research (Figure 2.5). Lazarsfeld became a major figure in the study of mass communications. His early radio work investigated soap operas, audience listening habits, and the persuasive elements of the mass media, the last topic becoming of great interest during World War II because of the apparent success of totalitarian propaganda. His very important book with Elihu Katz, *Personal Influence: The Part Played by People in the Flow of Mass Communications* (1955), examined how the mass media influenced individual decision-making through the two-step flow of communication. Instead of directly influencing audiences, known as the one-step flow or "hypodermic needle"

Figure 2.5 Paul F. Lazarsfeld, *c.*1941.

Source: University Archives, Rare Book and Manuscript Library, Columbia University in the City of New York.

model, the authors argued that ideas from the mass media (including advertising messages) were relayed to people via opinion leaders who served as consumer gatekeepers and interpreters.

Ernest Dichter (1907–1991) also had decamped from Austria. Like Katona and Lazarsfeld, Dichter was Jewish and the rise of Nazism forced him to depart for New York in 1938. He had earned a Ph.D. in Psychology from the University of Vienna and, with the help of Lazarsfeld, launched a successful career applying an eclectic mix of Freudian psychoanalytic and other theories and methods to consumer research (Tadajewski 2006, 2013). Dichter conducted in-depth, qualitative interviews of consumers for advertising agencies and manufacturers and, in 1946, established his own company he dubbed the Institute for Motivational Research.

He wrote several books, including *The Psychology of Everyday Living* (1947) and *Strategy for Desire* (1960), and published articles in the *Harvard Business Review* and in other scholarly journals in marketing and business. Dichter avidly explored the sexual, irrational, and hidden drivers of consumer behavior, an approach that attracted somewhat prurient attention. His books celebrated the consumption of abundance and linked it to democracy and the American way of life (Horowitz 2004; Tadajewski 2013). He was popularized in Vance Packard's (1957) *The Hidden Persuaders*, testified, in 1961, to a U.S. Senate hearing on packaged goods, and even received investigative scrutiny from the FBI for possible communist associates (Tadajewski 2013). However, Dichter's work attracted ample criticism for being manipulative of consumers and for delimiting women's roles to those shoppers and housewives (Friedan 1963). By the early 1960s Dichter's theoretical and methodological position among consumer researchers was beginning to diminish (Tadajewski 2006). Consumer psychology, then increasingly drawing from cognitive theories and quantitative methods, and focusing on decision-making processes, had moved on (Horowitz 2004; Kassarjian 1994; Kassarjian and Goodstein 2010).

Mainstream marketing professors began to introduce psychology into their research, but the total published output was relatively small. I scrutinized the first 25 years of the *Journal of Marketing* (1936 to 1961) and counted just 21 articles that more or less focused upon consumer psychology. Examples included Seymour Banks (1950) on "The Relationships Between Preference and Purchase of Brand," Warren Bilkey (1953) on "A Psychological Approach to Consumer Behavior Analysis," Klein and Lansing (1955) on "Decisions to Purchase Consumer Durable Goods," James Bayton (1958) on "Motivation, Cognition, Learning: Basic Factors in Consumer Behavior," and Walter Woods (1960) on "Psychological Dimensions of Consumer Behavior." Interestingly, the motivation research theory and techniques applied by Ernest Dichter and other practitioners received good coverage in the *Journal of Marketing* during the 1950s. Some articles discussed different projective techniques (Haire 1950; Lysaker and Bradley 1957; Westfall, Boyd, and Campbell 1957; Zober 1956) and others debated the scientific rigor of motivation research (Rothwell 1955; Wells 1956; Wiebe 1958; Williams 1957).

Consumer research as discipline independent from marketing did not fully emerge until the 1960s and early 1970s. Several milestones in this development are worth noting. First, comprehensive models of consumer behavior were developed by Franco M. Nicosia (1966) in his *Consumer Decision Processes: Marketing and Advertising Implications*; by James Engel, David Kollat, and Roger Blackwell (1968) in *Consumer Behavior*; and by John Howard and Jagdish Sheth (1969) in *The Theory of Buyer Behavior*. These models explained purchasing behavior largely, though not exclusively, using psychological variables, but had little to say about consumption more broadly. Second, an influential book of readings, *Perspectives in Consumer Behavior* by Harold Kassarjian and Thomas Robertson (1968), presented an overview of the field that included essays on cognition, motivation and personality, social influence, social class, and culture. An interesting and readable text – Professor Hal Kassarjian assigned the first edition to my graduate consumer behavior course at UCLA in 1971 – *Perspectives* helped define the field primarily in terms of social psychology and, to a lesser extent, sociology and cultural anthropology, with just minor grounding in economics. It went through four editions, the most recent in 1991, each of which included a different mix of writings. Third, the Association for Consumer Research (ACR) formed in 1969 and ever since has hosted yearly conferences whose proceedings are now freely available on its website. The vision was of a truly interdisciplinary group not beholden to business schools and marketing departments (Kassarjian 1994). The organization has grown to approximately 1700 members and sponsors a variety of related conferences (ACR 2016). Fourth, the *Journal of Consumer Research*, launched in 1974 and currently published by Oxford University Press, quickly established itself as the leading outlet for scholarly research on consumer behavior. Intended to be interdisciplinary, the Journal was co-sponsored by nine other groups in addition to ACR. They included the American Economics Association, the American Home Economics Association, and the American Marketing Association. With the field of knowledge broadly defined, with teachable texts and books of readings, with a professional association, and with a dedicated journal, consumer research had become an established academic discipline.

By the middle of the 1980s, however, a number of consumer researchers expressed discomfort with the direction their field had taken. Reflecting on the state of the art at the time, University of Minnesota professor and former advertising executive William D. Wells (1991, iii) lamented how

> … the consumer had but disappeared from "scientific" consumer research. In the most prestigious journals, the method of choice was the controlled experiment: college student subjects made artificial responses to artificial stimuli in situations which had none of the annoying details of real life. Most of these experiments were about Theory, which in turn was about other theories, none of which had much to do with how mom buys bread.

Wells went on to criticize mathematical models, other numerical methods, and the seeming worship of quantitative, hypothesis testing, logical positivism. The majority of the literature, by and large, had reduced consumers to rational, information processors and the field had come to rely heavily on the theories and methods of cognitive psychology. This conceptualization of consumer behavior presumably served managerial desires to influence decision-making. However, the application of consumer research findings to marketing practice in the business world probably was limited.

Nonetheless, some researchers had long been exploring cultural approaches to consumption much different from cognitive, information processing inquiry. As far back as the 1930s, embryonic interpretive studies had investigated the experiential, social, and cultural sides of consumer behavior (Tadajewski 2006). Later, Northwestern University marketing professor Sidney Levy (1959) wrote a path breaking article, "Symbols for Sale," for the *Harvard Business Review* (within which, by the way, he discussed both meaning and gender) and subsequently contributed, among many other culturally oriented writings, "Interpreting Consumer Mythology: A Structural Approach to Consumer Behavior" (Levy 1981). Other notable works in this vein included "Hedonic Consumption: Emerging Concepts, Methods and Propositions" where Elizabeth Hirschman and Morris Holbrook (1982) theorized about multisensory, fantasy, and emotive product experiences. Having more to say on the subject, they followed up with a companion article on "The Experiential Aspects of Consumption: Consumer Fantasies, Feelings, and Fun" (Holbrook and Hirschman 1982). The following year, in an article titled "Gift Giving in Anthropological Perspective," anthropologist (by training) John Sherry (1983) developed a rather complicated four-stage model of the gift exchange process that described the myriad consumer behaviors of donors and recipients. Dennis Rook (1985), who happened to have been Sid Levy's student at Northwestern, investigated another cultural side of consumption in "The Ritual Dimension of Consumer Behavior." Rook examined the phenomenon's constructs, typologies, and significance in detail and presented results from two empirical studies of young adult personal grooming rituals, the artifacts involved, and their psychosocial contents.

Russell Belk shared the concerns and research interests of those who refused to see consumers as more or less rational information processors. On January 9, 1985 he wrote a letter to nine colleagues proposing a remedy:

> In a nutshell, the idea is for a small group of us to travel from coast to coast one summer in order to qualitatively document various buyer and consumer behaviors via videotaped in-situ consumer interviews, largely unobtrusive still photos, and impressionistic journals. The goal would be to approach people shopping, buying, and consuming products and services, in a largely unstructured way without a priori hypotheses or quantitative/structured measures....
>
> (Belk 1991, 1)

In the summer of 1986, with the help of seed grants from the Marketing Science Institute and Needham Harper Advertising, Belk's dream was realized when a rented van transported rotating groups of consumer researchers across the country from Los Angeles to Boston (Figure 2.6). Over the course of this "Consumer Behavior Odyssey" teams interviewed, photographed, audiotaped and video recorded a wide range of consumers as they "went to swap meets, antique sales, art shows, fast food outlets, into people's homes to souvenir shops, hotels, grocery stores, parades, riverboat cruises, hospitals, county fairs, shelters for the homeless, and to nursing homes" (Belk 1991, 8–9). More thorough accounts can be found in the edited book, *Highways and Buyways: Naturalistic Research from the Consumer Behavior Odyssey* (Belk 1991) and in the retrospective article "The Labors of the Odysseans and the Legacy of the Odyssey" (Belk 2014). The Consumer Odyssey had its zany side, and even inspired John Schouten (1991) to

Figure 2.6 The Consumer Behavior Odyssey, 1986. Photo shows the rental van in Wyoming and, from left, Russ Belk, Melanie Wallendorf, Rick Pollay, and Joe Cote.

Source: Photo courtesy of Russell W. Belk.

write a poem, "Life Among the Winnebago," but ultimately this project helped transform the discipline of consumer research by popularizing interest in what later became known as consumer culture theory.

Nineteen years after the Odyssey, Eric Arnould and Craig Thompson (2005) published an invited thematic review article, "Consumer Culture Theory (CCT): Twenty Years of Research." The literature they considered, mostly articles appearing in the *Journal of Consumer Research*, constituted just a part of the broader body of research, as the authors readily conceded. Yet their account did help to identify many kinds of knowledge relevant to a potential CCT discipline. Arnould and Thompson further maintained that CCT research embraced methodological pluralism, but admitted that qualitative data and associated analytical techniques predominated. This appears to remain the case to the present day. Institutionally, a Consumer Culture Theory Conference has been held annually since first meeting at the University of Notre Dame in August 2006. This confab typically has drawn several hundred participants. Judging from conference attendance, among other indicators, female academics and researchers from outside the U.S. show great interest in the CCT project. The Sidney J. Levy Award for the best CCT article to come out of a doctoral dissertation has been bestowed annually since 2008. Thought leaders organized and formally incorporated a Consumer Culture Theory Consortium in 2011. The CCT network has been further extended through doctoral consortiums and other special events around the world (Arnould and Thompson 2015). Although no dedicated journal has been established, the editors of the annual volume, *Research in Consumer Behavior* have invited conference papers for publication. Thus, as of this writing, CCT is well on the way to becoming a full-fledged academic discipline.

Meaning

Meaning, a word with a great many connotations, can be defined as something that is intended, indicated, or conveyed, especially by language, but also through behavior (Merriam-Webster 2017a). In the context of consumption, goods and services carry and express meaning, as do the attendant activities of purchasing, using, recycling, and disposing. My understanding of meaning for the purposes of this book has been shaped by the work of five authors – Grant McCracken, Russell Belk, Marsha Richins, Don Slater, and Ashlee Humphreys – whose contributions will be briefly reviewed in chronological order. Obviously, many additional writers in consumer research and other fields also have considered meaning, but the present chapter and its sections intend to be just a primer on the subject and not an exhaustive literature review.

In his seminal *Journal of Consumer Research* article, "Culture and Consumption: A Theoretical Account of the Structure and Movement of the Cultural Meaning of Consumer Goods," Grant McCracken (1986) theorized cultural meaning as something mobile, something constantly in transit from the culturally constituted world to consumer goods to individual consumers. The culturally constituted world consists of everyday experiences and how they are shaped and constituted by cultural beliefs and assumptions. This, in short, is meaning, characterized in terms of cultural categories (e.g., age, gender, status) and cultural principles (e.g., being "modern" or "traditional"). Meaning is transferred to goods through advertising and also by way of product design through the fashion system. Once embedded into material objects, it can then move to the consumer through exchange rituals (birthday and Christmas gifts), possession rituals (cleaning, arranging, and otherwise doting on objects), grooming rituals (dressing up, polishing shoes), and divestment rituals (repainting a newly purchased house). McCracken, a historically oriented anthropologist and student of American consumer culture, elaborated upon these ideas in his 1988 book, *Culture and Consumption*, and next applied them to the process of celebrity endorsement (McCracken 1989b). In a nutshell, celebrities epitomize cultural meanings regarding gender, age, lifestyle, and personality type. Companies hire them so that these star-studded qualities can be shifted to their products.

Possessions and their meanings both contribute to and reflect consumer identities. In his influential 1988 article, "Possessions and the Extended Self," Russell Belk presented ample evidence in support of this proposition. For example, self-perception research demonstrated that feelings of greater control over possessions correlated with their relevance to sense of self. Social psychological studies of the loss of possessions through misfortune (e.g., theft, natural disaster) or from being institutionalized (e.g., joining the military, being incarcerated) showed diminished sense of self. Anthropologists saw possessions as symbols of self when they examined grave goods that had been buried with the dead. Belk (1988) further examined the functions of the extended self that possession help create. Among many examples given, one with historical relevance is how possessions inform the individual's sense of the past. Belk (1988, 148) said it best:

> Possessions are a convenient means of storing the memories and feelings that attach our sense of past. A souvenir may make tangible some otherwise intangible travel experience. An heirloom may record and recall family heritage just as a historic monument may help to create a sense of a nation's past.

Of particular interest to me is the special case of collecting whereby an assemblage of objects has distinctive meaning that goes beyond that of an isolated item. In addition to manufactured goods, money, pets, other people, and even individual body parts can all be central to a person's conception of self. Quoting Belk (1988, 160) once more: "It seems an inescapable fact of modern life that we learn, define, and remind ourselves of who we are by our possessions." As we shall see, a great deal of historical research, not the least of which being Belk's (1992) expert analysis of documents from the Mormon migration to Utah in the mid-nineteenth century, strongly suggests that this "inescapable fact" about possessions also applied to consumers in earlier time periods. "Possessions and the Extended Self" initially received some flak from a few skeptical consumer researchers, but it has gone on to garner more citations than any other article ever published in the *Journal of Consumer Research* (Ladik, Carrillat, and Tadajewski 2015).

In a pair of articles, "Valuing Things: The Public and Private Meanings of Possessions" and "Special Possessions and the Expression of Material Values," Marsha Richins (1994a, 1994b) reported empirical findings from several surveys whose data were subjected to content analyses and multidimensional scaling. She found that the meanings assigned to objects by society at large does not always coincide with the personal meanings held by their owners and based upon direct experience. Status, for example, carried more weight among the public, whereas appearance had more private importance. Her subjects communicated their material values through the socially constructed stereotypes possessions had accrued, but also through their personal relationship with things. Compared to low-materialism respondents, who emphasized the interpersonal/symbolic value and the hedonic potential of possessions, those high in materialism seemingly stressed more utilitarian, appearance, and status concerns. Such distinctions may have existed in the past and thus are something historians should try to investigate provided their primary sources reveal the inner feelings of consumers.

Don Slater's (1997) incisive book, *Consumer Culture and Modernity*, devoted an entire chapter to the meaning of things. Slater, who is a sociologist of economic life, contended that all consumption is cultural and always involves meaning because consumer needs and the actions taken to fulfill them derive from making sense of situations, objects, and available resources. Consumers share these meanings and even the apparently individual, utilitarian calculations theorized by economists and psychologists existed within a larger cultural matrix. Furthermore, Slater (1997, 138) argued,

> all forms of consumption are culturally specific. They are articulated within, or in relation to, specific meaningful ways of life ... it is through culturally specific forms of consumption that we produce and reproduce cultures, social relations, and indeed society.

Through specific forms of consumption the meanings embedded in objects participated in cultural reproduction (Slater 1997).

Additional constructs have been applied to the meaning of things. For example, critics of modern consumer culture sometimes have identified "basic needs" and "basic objects" and have purported to show how modern advertising and marketing practices have attached extraneous meanings to them so as to manipulate demand. Basic needs should be distinguished from superficial luxuries and basic objects should be purely functional. Such thinking has required the separation of culture and consumption when, historically, cultures have always constituted consumption according to Slater (1997). What has been considered "basic" or "functional" has depended upon the specific cultural frame of reference. The past and the present differ in their cultural systems for organizing and reproducing meaning. Before the advertising and fashion systems became the primary agents of conveyance (McCracken 1986), direct observation, language (word of mouth, story telling), and myth making transferred meaning.

Ashlee Humphreys (2010) drew from institutional theory and semiotics to examine how one consumption practice, casino gambling, became legitimate during the period 1980 to 2007. The legitimacy of consumption practices, according to institutional theory, occurs at regulatory, normative, and cultural-cognitive levels.

> Regulative legitimacy is the degree to which a practice conforms to rules and regulations set forth by a superseding organization, usually the government. Normative legitimacy is the degree to which the practice is perceived to be congruent with dominant norms and values, irrespective of legal status. Cognitive legitimacy is the degree to which the practice is "taken for granted," the ease with which it can be categorized and understood according to existing cognitive schemas and cultural frameworks.
>
> (Humprheys 2010, 492)

Consumption practices are legitimated or delegitimated through changes in meaning. To document shifts in discourse over time, Humphreys (2010) studied the semiotics of newspaper articles pertaining to casino gambling. Using a procedure similar to Belk (1992), she created a dictionary of binary meanings including purity and filth, wealth and poverty, tax cycling and corruption. Each category consisted of frequently used words such as ethical, ordinance, commissioner, law, legal, Bible, and religion for the meaning of purity. The word frequencies of the binaries changed over time and thus helped determine the cultural and normative legitimacy of casino gambling.

Humphreys' research thus added newspaper journalism to the advertising and fashion systems (McCracken 1986) as a third conduit for transferring meaning from the culturally constituted world to a product, in this case gaming services rather than a tangible good. The legitimization of meaning was shaped by selection, valuation, and realization. Journalists chose some information sources rather than competing ones (selection). Through choice of language (valuation) they portrayed a consumption practice as either compatible or incompatible with cultural norms and values. And by discussing a practice in the first place (realization), they validated its legitimacy. These theoretical insights are very germane to the re-legitimation of alcohol and cannabis consumption in America to be discussed in Chapters 6, 8, and 9.

Gender

The noun "gender" refers to the grammatical categorization of words prevalent in many languages, but above all it describes biological sex, male or female, along with a variety of psychological, behavioral, and cultural traits usually associated with one sex or the other (Merriam-Webster 2017b). The adjective "gendered" reflects the experience, prejudices, or orientations of one sex more than the other and also involves gender differences or stereotypical gender roles. The word "gender" in English has been used since the fourteenth century, whereas "gendered" dates only to 1972. Gender concepts have an historical dimension. As Steven Lubar (1998, 8–9) put it: "Gender is an ideological and cultural construction, the complex of cultural ideals and ideas tied to the words *male* and *female*. Masculinity and femininity are socially constructed and historically contingent." Lubar's second sentence deserves particular notice because it implies the high likelihood of cultural change in how consumption is gendered. Granted, social definitions of what constitutes being masculine and feminine have shown long continuities during American history, but some qualities have faded in importance and new ones have emerged. Unlike their forebears in the eighteenth century, American men in the new millennium no longer have been expected to be proficient at hunting and fishing, and American women do not have show competence at spinning, weaving, and sewing.

Historians tell us that gender has mattered greatly in consumption history. It has shaped the physical ambience of sites of consumption, such as department stores and shopping centers (Benson 1986; Cohen 2003; Leach 1984), has guided much new product development (Clarke 1999; Cowan 1983; Lavin 1995; Shrum 2012; Stole 2003), and has "informed marketing strategies and assumptions (often fallacious) of male designers and the stubborn preferences of female consumers" (Horowitz and Mohun 1998, 2). Gender has defined decision-making influence within families and the allocation of household purchasing roles (Perkins 1991; Witkowski 1999, 2004), has been the focus of the cult of domesticity and related discourses (Lewis 1987), and has been foregrounded in the persistent needling of female materialism and sometimes in the belittling of male domestic competence, among other topics and practices. Multiple threads of gender run through American consumption history. However, as Victoria de Grazia (1996) cautioned, "When consumption has been taken as a central axis of analysis, the conspicuousness of the female figure, in contrast to her real powerlessness, has resulted in a kind of overtheorization" (19). From the point of view of some feminists, women's freedom to purchase has been more apparent than real. Placed in a subordinate social and economic position, women have been exploited by the fashion and advertising systems of the commercial culture.

The fields of marketing and consumer research have had a long-standing interest in the relative influence of husbands and wives on purchasing decisions for different product categories. The reason, of course, has been the hope that this knowledge could benefit the sales and advertising strategies of companies. Robert Ferber (1955) questioned the reliability of data collected from different family members, and thus its value for managerial purposes, but other researchers (e.g., Wolgast 1958) disagreed and numerous studies of the topic were conducted. Research in the 1950s through the 1970s typically entailed quantitative analyses of survey data collected from panels or large cross-sectional samples (Ferber and Lee 1974; Green and Cunningham 1975; Munsinger, Weber, and Hansen 1975; Sharp and Mott 1956). Over time, increasingly rarefied methodological issues and theory building, rather than actionable descriptive statistics, became focal concerns (see, e.g., Davis 1970, 1971). This research stream drew primarily from the disciplines of social psychology and family sociology. It was not particularly cultural and none of the articles cited above actually used the term gender. Chapter 8 will treat some of these studies as historical documents and incorporate their findings into the period narrative.

More culturally oriented inquiries into gender and consumption arrived in the 1980s and scholars have continued to mine this vein up to the present day. Figure 2.7 depicts the results from a search for the word "gender" in the Association for Consumer Research North America Conference Proceedings from 1974 until 2015. Rarely mentioned in the first ten volumes, an uptick in usage occurred in Volume 11 (1984) and an even steeper rise commenced with Volume 31 (2004). The preponderance of CCT research on gender has leaned toward women's issues, but the gendered roles of male consumers have also been examined. The range of topics extends far beyond purchasing influence and much CCT research has employed qualitative methodologies and interview data rather than the quantitative surveys. The area started to become a subfield in its own right in 1991 when consumer researchers sponsored the first of many biennial gender and consumer behavior conferences, which have disseminated interest in the area. The following are a few exemplars of CCT research on gender and American consumption.

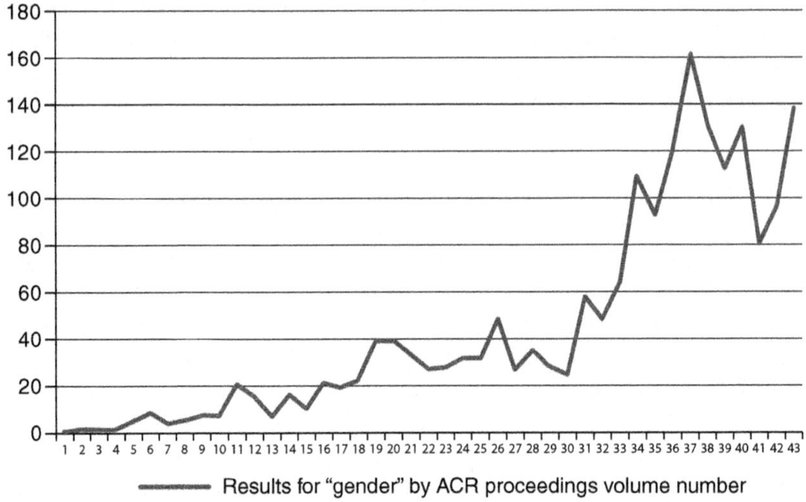

Figure 2.7 Results of Search for Word "Gender" in ACR North American Proceedings by Volume Number Where 1 = 1974 and 43 = 2015.

Source: Association for Consumer Research Website.

Eileen Fischer and Stephen Arnold (1990) examined gender roles and Christmas gift shopping through a field study of 299 men and women using structured questionnaires during in-home personal interviews. Collecting both quantitative and qualitative data to test their hypotheses, the authors measured gender role attitudes, gender identity, and a variety of Christmas shopping behaviors. Having a more feminine gender identity and being a more communally oriented male predicted somewhat more involvement with shopping for gifts. Not surprisingly, even stronger evidence showed that Christmas shopping was by and large women's work. A few years later in a forceful theoretical paper, Julia Bristor and Eileen Fischer (1993) outlined three different feminist perspectives – liberal feminism, women's voice/experience feminism, and poststructuralist feminism – and then used them to critically assess various aspects of consumer research. Held to feminist scrutiny were the ideal of scientific objectivity, research problematics (what aspects of the world need explaining), available theories, and methods of data collection and analysis. According to the authors, critically applying these feminist perspectives uncovered many unwarranted assumptions and androcentric (i.e., male) biases in the practice of consumer research at the time.

Much CCT research has interpreted qualitative interview data collected from small convenience samples of consumers. In the gender literature, Craig Thompson's (1996) "Caring Consumers: Gendered Consumption Meanings and the Juggling Lifestyle" has been frequently cited. This article reported a study of working mothers who needed to balance career with traditional household responsibilities. A key question was what meanings they assigned to their consumption experiences.

From a small empirical sample of just seven informants and a data set consisting of verbatim transcripts from qualitative interviews, Thompson extracted a number of consumption meanings grouped under the metaphors of staying on schedule, negotiating compromises, envisioned ideals/practical concessions, and holding it together/falling apart. Theoretically rich, this type of research can be criticized for its lack of external validity, that is, its questionable representativeness of the overall population of American women.

In "Man-of-Action Heroes: The Pursuit of Heroic Masculinity in Everyday Consumption," Douglas Holt and Craig Thompson (2004) investigated what they called the "compensatory consumption thesis," the proposition that American men in the late twentieth and early twenty-first centuries have turned to their consumption activities to counteract their economic and social emasculation. They conducted interviews with 15 white, married men from both working- and middle-class backgrounds in smaller Midwestern and eastern American cities, but presented interpretive findings from just two of the informants. Based on this evidence, Holt and Thompson (2004, 426) concluded, "the compensatory consumption thesis fails to capture some of the most powerful masculine identifications that men forge through their consumption." Instead, they postulated the "man-of-action hero," an identity pursued through a variety of consumption practices that vary according to social class. For the consumption historian, this account suffered from having a very limited sample and sketchy descriptive findings, and perhaps from indulging in a bit too much longwinded theorizing, but it raised a highly provocative thesis about men and masculinity to be explored further in the gender sections of Chapters 5, 8, and 9.

Through long interviews with 23 male informants, Risto Moisio, Eric Arnould, and James Gentry (2013) investigated the gendering of what CCT researchers call "productive consumption." Also known as "prosumption," "craft consumption," or "co-construction," the concept refers to how "some forms of consumption enlist consumer labor that creates rather than depletes value" (Moisio, Arnould, and Gentry 2013, 300). Of course, for centuries American consumers, especially women, toiled awfully hard at their domestic consumption routines (e.g., cooking, cleaning, washing, ironing, and sewing). The need for such work diminished as the market provided labor saving alternatives and standards of living rose. Thus, productive consumption, which implies having a choice, became an option. Moisio and his colleagues found that differences in men's social class (or higher v. lower cultural capital, as the authors tactfully put it) were a key explanatory variable for do-it-yourself (DIY) home improvement endeavors. For the former, higher cultural capital group, DIY activities constituted a form of "therapeutic class tourism" that separated them from workplace tensions, whereas for the latter group, who often experienced inability to fulfill their male breadwinner roles, DIY enacted an identity ideal of the family handyman. Because of a lack of primary source documents, consumption historians often find it difficult to identify such inner motivations.

CCT researchers have intertwined threads of gender with those of meaning as exemplified in the article "Is Meat Male? A Quantitative Multimethod Framework to Establish Metaphoric Relationships" by Paul Rozin, Julia Hormes, Myles Faith, and Brian Wansink (2012). The authors argued that insights developed from ethnographic or qualitative studies, however insightful, might not convince skeptics from outside the field. Thus, to explore six hypothesized relationships between meat and masculinity, the authors devised one linguistic, one demographic, and four psychological studies using large samples of mainly undergraduates attending American universities. Their research produced consistent and convergent quantitative evidence that

> mammal muscle meat stands in some positive relation to maleness, although maleness is likely not one of the most salient properties of meat. The male–meat link is supported by data on meat preferences and vegetarianism incidence, attributions of maleness based on meat preference, implicit associations, and gendering of meat-relevant words and most clearly by direct maleness and femaleness ratings of foods.
>
> (Rozin *et al.* 2012, 640)

The authors also raised the possibility of increased meat eating being an instance of compensatory consumption when masculine self-identity was threatened. In Chapter 8, the discussion of the barbecue culture in the 1950s will revisit this topic.

Finally, from a different analytical perspective Jonathan Schroeder and his co-authors have applied art criticism and visual theory to questions of gender and consumption. He and Janet Borgerson (1998) explained consumer representation in art and advertising, discussed descriptive and interpretive tools for visual analysis, and showed how art historical referents (the nude, the captured woman) were present in contemporary advertising images. They also described techniques for objectifying the female form, such as focusing on just part of a woman's body, presenting women as sexual objects, and sometimes depicting them as objects of male violence. Schroeder and Detlev Zwick (2004) applied the methods of art history to male representations in advertising images. Of particular historical interest, they discussed the genealogical influences of three genres – portrait photography, nineteenth-century *cartes de visite* (photos on card stock traded among friends and visitors), and the male pin-up as hunky eye candy – on advertising portrayals of men. To illustrate their approach, they analyzed in much detail three print ads that represented the male body and masculine lifestyles in interesting ways for the purpose of attracting consumer gaze. The term "genealogy" as used in CCT writing comes from the work of French philosopher and intellectual historian Michel Foucault (1926–1984). Broadly speaking, it refers to the history of thought or discourse.

Resistance

In the CCT literature, much of the research probing consumer resistance has concentrated on topical critiques of unbridled consumerism and materialism, dominant social paradigms, and corporations and commercial marketing. When put into practice, such anti-consumption rhetoric has taken the forms of environmentally virtuous consumer behavior, politically motivated boycotts of offending products and companies, and hostility toward governmental policies of austerity and control. Generally speaking, these have been the concerns, across a number of disciplines, of left-leaning scholars in the late twentieth and early twenty-first centuries. I have met many CCT researchers, some of whom are my opinionated Facebook friends, but cannot recall any of them being politically conservative in the American mold.

For example, Robert Kozinets (2002) reported ethnographic findings from the 1999 Burning Man festival. At this weeklong art and culture event, held yearly in a Nevada desert, participants have attempted to distance themselves from the market and profit-seeking corporations through rhetoric that supports communitarian ideals and disparages vending and brand names. Festivalgoers have engaged in practices of alternative exchange such as sharing and gift exchange, and through re-positioning consumption as self-expressive art. In another study, Kozinets and Jay Handelman (2004) interviewed respondents from three different groups of consumer activists. One group attacked advertising for encouraging forms of consumerism having a deleterious effect upon ecosystems; another was organized in opposition to the Nike brand; and the third objected to genetically modified food, industrial agriculture, and globalization. The authors saw an historical connection: "We conceptualize our consumer activists as a type of modern day Puritan who seeks changes in consumption culture through seeking to reform the wrongs of the unenlightened" (Kozinets and Handelman 2004, 701–702).

Craig Thompson and Gocken Coskuner-Balli (2007) discussed how the organic food movement that emerged as part of the larger 1960s' counterculture, later became coopted by the organic-industrial complex of large-scale agriculture and corporate controlled branding and distribution. This in turn led to countervailing producer and consumer opposition in the form of community-supported agricultural systems where, in exchange for produce, participants either buy shares in a particular farm or agree to supply labor for the endeavor. Here, price was less important for consumers than a shared ideology of resistance, relationships, and decommodification. Resistance to corporate directed marketing systems can encourage alternative forms of exchange and consumption that resemble those prevalent in earlier times.

In their theoretical article, Jennifer Sandlin and Jamie Callahan (2009, 79) argued that understanding consumer resistance movements requires taking "into account the role of emotion in fighting against consumerist ideologies and global corporate control." Of particular interest was the practice of "culture jamming," where protestors have confronted consumers with symbols and activities intended to cause emotional dissonance and questioning of consumerist memes and rhetoric. For example, "subvertisements" have reversed the meanings of stock advertising images, slogans, and body copy. In many ways, culture jammers have attempted to create within audiences a sense of "détournement" or "authentic emotions to help consumers shake themselves free of inauthentic, emotionally scripted lives" (Sandlin and Callahan 2009, 107). Sometimes, however, these efforts have fallen flat and actually have angered some people who perceive elitist and patronizing attitudes. Chapter 7 will show how jamming was embraced by *Ballyhoo* magazine in the 1930s, and Chapter 9 will discuss the present-day antics of *Adbusters* magazine and the daffy performance art of "Reverend Billy" and his "Church of Stop Shopping" gospel choir.

Still another type of resistance has been the history of opposition to controls over and the banning of certain products and forms of consumption. Individually and collectively, and especially among subaltern groups, American consumers repeatedly have chosen to advance their freedoms in the marketplace in the face of imposed orthodoxy and taboos. Examples to be discussed in subsequent chapters include the willful flouting by ordinary men and women of seventeenth-century sumptuary laws in New England, the conspicuous consumption of urban black families in the South after Reconstruction, the scorning of Prohibition and the Volstead Act by thirsty drinkers in the 1920s and early 1930s, the organized protesting of Jim Crow laws (statutes enforcing segregation) by African Americans and their white allies during the Civil Rights movement of the 1950s and 1960s, and, since the 1960s, the widespread smoking and celebration of marijuana despite harsh federal and state restrictions. In other words, resistance can be both anti- and pro-consumption. These nonstandard acts of consumption have been termed "rebel consumerism" (Glickman 2009). They share some features, yet are not quite the same as consumer "buycott" campaigns where activists encourage purchasing from what they consider to be virtuous companies (Friedman 1999). The threads of American consumer resistance have been multilayered.

Threading the Narrative Loom

The next seven chapters follow these three groups of cultural threads as they weave through the history of American consumption. The word "thread" has several connotations. In one sense it represents the three themes of meaning, gender, and resistance viewed over time. An irresistible metaphor visualizes these bundles of threads as longitudinal cultural warps in the fabric of American consumption. The transverse wefts (woofs) can be imagined as people or events that evoke the themes at different times and places. In another sense, the image of threads suggests continuity, that both the symbolic and performative aspects of consumption and consumer culture are connected ideologically and through practice over time. Take, for example, refinement in consumption as an important social value. As a thread of meaning it has existed in America for 300 years. Some of its expression in 1750, such as an emphasis on good manners, was not so different from what it became in 1950. Yet historical continuity in meaning is often accompanied by change. The good penmanship that became a hallmark of colonial refinement seems to have little relevance to Americans living in the new millennium who communicate with the tools of a much different material culture. In a third sense, the thread metaphor has a strong gender connotation in that textiles and clothing have often been at the very heart of female consumption and, before the twenty-first century, of much female production at home and in factories. The story of American consumption told in this book emphasizes the roles women have played, not just as household and independent purchasing agents and consumers, but also as gatekeepers of consumption meaning, and as frequent instigators of consumer resistance. This book is thus a yarn about the female consumer, so to speak, but the male gender will not be ignored. Aspects of men's consumption will be explored in Chapters 5 and 6 and the topic of threats to masculinity and male coping through consumption will be featured in Chapters 8 and 9. The visual pun in Figure 2.8 shows me threading this narrative loom.

Figure 2.8 The Author Threading His Narrative Loom, February 16, 2017.

Source: Taken at California State University, Long Beach by Professor Diedrick Brackens, Fiber Program Head.

Most chapters begin with a brief overview section, "material life and the market," that summarizes some macro-economic, political, social, and marketing developments during the period under discussion, and then will proceed to the separate sections on meaning, gender, and resistance. Although this book has a reasonably strong cultural slant, I also have drawn from economic history and the consumption data economists have marshaled and analyzed. The meaning, gender, and resistance section titles are varied from chapter to chapter to avoid repetition and also to attempt to capture the essence of the historical discussion. Chapter 7 on the Great Depression and World War II is an exception to this structure. Because the era it covers is relatively short yet quite distinctive, it commingles the macro context and three theoretical threads more or less chronologically. A brief summary recaps the major points of the chapters.

The historical narrative is regularly augmented with visual data that in a few instances, such as nineteenth century genre paintings and World War II poster campaigns, will be interrogated at greater length. A photograph in Chapter 1 illuminating material culture methods of inquiry and three in Chapter 4 illustrating the meaning of patriotic symbols, heroes, and national pride in the early nineteenth century are of antiques and art from our family collection (okay, mostly my obsession). Including them allows me to share with readers some of my personal collecting enthusiasms that stimulate my scholarly work. While writing this book I could not resist purchasing some Depression-era ephemera on eBay that will appear in Chapter 7. (I only spent $43.89 with shipping and so got off cheaply this time.) The brief concluding chapter will revisit this history in terms of continuities and change, additional threads deserving of further research, and some lessons for consumer culture theory.

Summary

The history of American consumption presented in this book is positioned within the research tradition of consumer culture theory. CCT is not a unified theory or overarching model. It is a diverse school of research interests concerned less with the psychology of consumer decision-making and individual buyer behavior than with the cultural dimensions of consumption including symbolism, ideology, aesthetics, rituals, identity projects, and marketplace customs. The number of CCT studies burgeoned after the mid-1980s although a few earlier examples can be found as far back as the 1930s. The CCT literature largely emerged from the field of consumer research as it had developed within marketing departments in business schools. Marketing academics had acknowledged the importance of studying consumer behavior as early as the 1920s, but serious interest did not commence until about the 1950s when cognitive psychology became popular. Consumer research also has lineages within the field of home economics and through social surveys on living standards that go back to the late nineteenth century. When writing this chapter, I did not intend at first to write so much about the intellectual history of consumer research, but the more I learned about the topic, the more compelling it became. The disciplinary history of consumer research still awaits a comprehensive treatment.

3 Colonial Consumption from 1607 to 1790

This chapter begins with a brief review of the material life of early Americans and how it related to both a local and global market economy. Next will follow discussions of the changing meanings colonial consumers assigned to their goods, the gendered allocation of household purchasing roles, and finally the religious and ideological resistance to consumerism and the political opposition to British imports and trade policies. Given the difficult conditions European settlers experienced over much of the seventeenth century, their consumption was limited. The earliest arrivals worked mightily to survive in the face of deprivation, conflict with the Indians, and high death rates. Pioneers on the colonial frontier continued to struggle well into the eighteenth century, but in more established rural areas, villages, and small cities, living standards gradually improved and a culture of consumption began to emerge. Thus, most of the discussion focuses on the new consumer society developing in the second half of the eighteenth century.

Material Life and the Market

The population of the American colonies numbered about 250,000 by 1700 and reached approximately 2.5 million by 1776 (U.S. Bureau of the Census 1976). People of English descent constituted the majority, but there were also significant numbers of Africans (21 percent), Scots and Scots-Irish (10 percent), Germans (8.6 percent), south Irish (3.7 percent), Dutch (3 percent), and French Huguenots (2.3 percent) (Randel 1973). Nearly two-thirds of all Americans at this time were immigrants or the children of immigrants and perhaps one-quarter were legally bound to others as indentured servants or slaves. Some 95 percent of the colonists lived in rural areas. The estimated populations of the major port cities – Philadelphia (24,000), New York (22,000), Boston (16,000), Charleston (14,000), and Newport (9000) – paled in comparison to London and its 700,000 inhabitants (Baugher and Venables 1987). People generally married early and raised large families, six to eight pregnancies being typical (Scholten 1977). Infant mortality and overall death rates, quite high by twenty-first century standards, compared favorably with other eighteenth-century societies. Generally abundant harvests, lower population densities, and plentiful wood supplies for home heating improved health and imparted resistance to infectious diseases. Stature was an indicator of nutrition. The average heights of native-born soldiers recruited to fight in the Seven Years War (1756–1763) and the War for Independence (1775–1781) were taller than those of contemporary Europeans and close to the twentieth-century figure of 5′9″ (175 cm) (Perkins 1988; Steckel 1999). Available data sources apply mostly to men, however, and the pervasive exceptions to gender equality to be discussed below suggest exercising interpretive caution regarding colonial nutrition in general.

Public elementary schools were uncommon outside of New England. Most children received their basic education from family members or private tutors, male and female. Secondary schools, called academies or grammar schools, were few in number and usually private. "Latin" schools prepared boys for college, while "English" schools specialized in a more practical curriculum. Few colonials could afford these schools, especially if they lived on the frontier and had to board their children away from home. Colleges were even more expensive. Main (1965) estimates that only one in ten Americans had the resources to send a son off to college. Those priced out of the educational system learned what they could from available books and newspapers.

The colonial economy grew over time, immigration and the foreign sector being major drivers, but it did experience periods of expansion followed by contraction (McCusker 1999). According to Jones (1980), per capita annual income in 1774 ranged from £10.7 to £12.5, or $1530 to $1790 in 2014 dollars (Officer and Williamson 2017). Meager by later U.S. standards – $57,300 per capita in 2016 based on purchasing power parity (CIA 2017) – colonial incomes were among the highest in the world, exceeded only by those of Great Britain. Lower taxes and greater access to land, wild game, and firewood afforded colonial families a higher standard of living than was usual in England. The rich in colonial America did not control an overwhelming amount of wealth compared to either their fellow citizens or to the English aristocracy (Henretta 1984). For all 13 colonies in 1774, the richest 10 percent of the total population (including slaves) owned 56 percent of the total physical wealth. Comparing the wealthy in colonial America with their counterparts in England, Jones (1980, 265) stated that "the percentage of wealth owned by the top 1 percent in England in the latter part of the eighteenth century was probably considerably greater than our figure of 13 percent for total physical wealth of free wealth-holders." Still, wealth tended to become more concentrated in the upper classes as the century progressed. The urban lower classes saw their share of community assets deteriorate and, in the 1760s, experienced an absolute decline in their standard of living (Nash 1979).

The Europeans who colonized North America in the seventeenth and eighteenth centuries undoubtedly produced more of their goods and services within their households and local communities, and depended far less on impersonal markets than did Americans in later periods. Still, complete self-sufficiency was not an option for most people. Often lacking tools, simple machines, some materials, and practical know-how, the earliest settlers in the 1600s required provisions from England (Breen 1986; Main 1994). As the years passed, households acquired equipment and became more productive, but still performed just a step or two in a production process and relied upon neighbors or local craftsmen for the remainder. Take the spinning and weaving of cloth from wool, flax, and cotton. Probate inventories indicate that only 49 percent of households surveyed in Massachusetts in 1774 owned spinning wheels, and this percentage may have been inflated by the patriotic spinning fad brought on by the nonimportation movement (Shammas 1982a, 1982b). Looms for weaving were less common. According to probate data analyzed by Ulrich (1998), mention of looms ranged from 10 to a bit over 30 percent in three Massachusetts counties. Southern plantations, because of their larger scale and pool of slave labor, were more self-sufficient than Northern farms. Nevertheless, households everywhere in the colonies needed to obtain some things from other parties through barter, credit arrangements, and various forms of specie (coin money).

Locally produced items accounted for the majority of market purchases, but 27.5 percent of expenditures in the 1760s were for items produced in other British colonies, especially the Caribbean, or in England (Shammas 1982a). Foodstuffs, primarily wine, rum, salt, tea, and molasses, as well as woolen, linen, and cotton cloth and garments, were the most important categories of imported merchandise. Colonial consumers also purchased imported household items, including looking glasses, brass candlesticks, glassware and ceramics, and personal items such as silver and brass buttons and buckles. Firearms have been a noteworthy consumer good throughout American history. In the colonial period, most guns were brought from England or assembled locally from new and reused parts made abroad. An analysis of several sets of probate records from different colonies recorded between 1638 and 1790, showed that 50–73 percent of male estates, and 6–38 percent of female estates included firearms (Lindgren and Heather 2002). One of the authors' databases (from 1774) had more estates containing guns (54 percent), than Bibles (25 percent). Interestingly, Native Americans found the lure of firearms irresistible and "by the mid-eighteenth century, the gun played a far larger role in Indian than in white culture" (Bellesiles 2000, 136).

Retail institutions emerged gradually and by the 1760s consisted of itinerant peddlers, rural general stores, more specialized city shops, and auction sales of new and estate goods. Itinerant peddling was one of the earliest forms of distribution in America, and the so-called Yankee peddler probably originated in Boston in the 1600s (Dolan 1964). At first, young men would buy small quantities of manufactured items, such as needles, pins, buttons, combs, and spools of thread, from sailors or at dockside auctions and carry them about town. By the 1700s, with supplies of dry goods (fabrics and sewing accessories) furnished by urban merchants, they had taken to the road and were fanning out into New England, the mid-Atlantic colonies, and the South. In the coastal cities of Boston, New York, Philadelphia, Baltimore, and Charleston, merchants advertised via newspapers and handbills the arrival of new shipments of goods and, when augmented through word of mouth, this market information undoubtedly became widely known among the relatively small urban populations. Storekeepers first appeared in the port cities and by the 1740s had begun moving into the rural interior. According to historian Gloria L. Main (1994, 62–63), "Proportionately, there were nearly as many retailers in Massachusetts in 1771 as there were in the United States in 1929." As they did for itinerant peddlers, merchants advanced their wares on credit to aspiring fixed location retailers.

With an abundance of land for the taking and ample natural resources to exploit, colonial living standards were among the highest in the world outside of Great Britain. True, most people of the times lived in cramped, poorly heated, and insufficiently lighted quarters without indoor plumbing, but by the 1700s a typical middle-class family

> owned earthenware, bed and table linen, knives, forks, and a Bible. A family with income above the median might possess a few fancy clothes, a watch, china plates, fine furniture, some silver items, and other small amenities. The wealthy might possess fine clothes and furniture, exquisite china and silverware, nonreligious books, a man's wig, artwork, a carriage, and a large volume of luxury goods.
>
> (Perkins 1988, 228)

Slaves, indentured servants, and poor whites had very few possessions aside from the tattered clothing on their backs, a few eating utensils, and perhaps a bed, table, and a couple of chairs. Yet, even the wealthier merchants in the North, along with successful planters in the South, maintained a rather plain style of living well into the 1700s (Witkowski 1989).

A Revolution in the Meaning of Things

From their arrival in the seventeenth century, Puritan and Quaker settlers promoted a "Christianity writ plain" that set an enduring standard for American consumption (Shi 1985). People were supposed to be thrifty and frugal. Recreation was acceptable, but only in order to rest for more work, and not as an end in itself. Up until the middle of the eighteenth century, these traditional values of discipline and self-restraint, along with the harsh challenges of early colonial life, kept most consumption to basic necessities. Some of the more successful Puritans and Quakers, as well as a number of Southern planters, amassed substantial fortunes, but they still maintained a rather plain style of living. Based on her study of Maryland probate inventories recorded between 1650 and 1720, historian Gloria L. Main (1982) found consumption differences between poor and more affluent planters were largely of degree, not kind. Although the upper third had the wherewithal to consume with some panache, they instead chose to live in a relatively plain and simple manner. Probate records indicated "few planters, even among the rich and powerful, cared to introduce any decorative note to the interior furnishings of their homes" (Main 1982, 166). Similarly, Lois Green Carr and Lorena S. Walsh (1980) in their study of probate records from St.

Mary's County, Maryland, 1658–1777, found relatively few nonessentials appearing until after 1715, and especially not until after 1754.

Yet, by the middle of the eighteenth century a consumer revolution was afoot and new meaning poured into more valuable possessions (Clemens 2005; Haulman 2005; Martin 1993). As colonial society became richer and more established, a desire for gentility emerged among the gentry and percolated down to the middle classes. Surviving material artifacts and written records document this development. Colonists began building larger and more stylish homes and gardens, purchasing better crafted furniture, using higher quality tableware, improving their penmanship, reading courtesy books to cultivate good manners, and, in general, becoming more refined (Breen 1986, 2004; Bushman 1992). Americans of all classes drank prodigious amounts of tea and those with genteel aspirations purchased fine Chinese export teapots, silver spoons and tea caddies, mahogany tea tables, and other accoutrements. More affluent colonists may have consulted books such as *The Art of Dancing Explained by Reading and Figures*, printed in London in 1735 for the author, Kellom Tomlinson, to advance their refinement (Figure 3.1). On a sadder note, it became de rigueur for wealthy families in New England to distribute dozens, even hundreds of pairs of leather, satin, and silk gloves to those in attendance at funerals (Bullock and McIntyre 2012).

Meanwhile, the allure of European fashions intensified. Some upper-class men adopted a ruffled, heavily powdered, "macaroni" style and women of means displayed elaborate hairstyles consisting of high rolls (Haulman 2005). In 1772, for example, Charles Willson Peale (1741–1827) painted the impressive portrait of John and Elizabeth Lloyd Cadwalader and their daughter Anne shown in Figure 3.2. John and Elizabeth, respectively a Philadelphia merchant and well-to-do Maryland heiress, wore elaborately ruffled attire and fashionable hair, while little Anne sat on an exquisite mahogany tea table. Both 30 years old when painted, Elizabeth died in 1776 and John just ten years later in 1786. The elaborate suite of Chippendale style furniture they commissioned from local cabinet-makers now resides in several major museums. Their distinguished neighbors, Samuel and Elizabeth Powel, redecorated their impressive home in 1769–1770 in a Palladian architectural style with Rococo embellishments (see Figure 3.3). The Cadwalader home was demolished in 1816, but the Powel house still survives. However, later owners sold architectural woodwork from the second floor rear parlor to the Metropolitan Museum of Art in 1918. The Philadelphia Museum of Art acquired the plaster ceiling and woodwork from the second floor ballroom in 1925. Both museums converted their purchases into sumptuous period rooms, eye candy consumed by visitors.

Macro-economic data lend credence to this transformation in consumption meaning. Imports of luxury goods from the mother country increased considerably in the mid-eighteenth century. Before 1750, the American colonies received sufficient returns from exports and shipping charges to pay for their imports. By 1760, in contrast, net indebtedness with England totaled about two million pounds. In the five years 1768 to 1772, imports exceeded exports by £2 million, and in 1772 total indebtedness stood at £4 million (Henretta 1973). This deteriorating balance of

Figure 3.1 Page from *The Art of Dancing Explained by Reading and Figures*, 1735.
Source: The Library Company of Philadelphia.

payments occurred despite high commodity prices and booming Southern exports of tobacco and rice and middle colony exports of wheat. Some individual planters who could pledge future harvests as collateral began to amass large debts with English middlemen.

The demand for many English consumer goods was partly a matter of their increasing availability, affordable prices, and relatively quick transport from

Figure 3.2 Portrait of John and Elizabeth Lloyd Cadwalader and Their Daughter Anne, 1772. Painted by Charles Willson Peale, 50½ × 41¼ inches (128.3 × 104.8 cm).

Source: Philadelphia Museum of Art.

major ports. Artisans in Britain, among the best and most efficient craftsmen in the world, had the advantage of production economies made possible by incipient industrialization and budding mass markets at home (McCusker and Menard 1985). American potters made utilitarian items, but could not match the low prices of the fine earthenware from Staffordshire (Cushion 1976). Furthermore,

Figure 3.3 Samuel Powel House Rear Parlor, Philadelphia, 1769–1770.
Source: Metropolitan Museum of Art.

English export firms extended very generous credit terms, sometimes circumventing wholesale merchants to deal directly with small retailers (Breen 1988). Port cities like Philadelphia were frequently awash with imported consumer goods (Doerflinger 1986). The American merchants who received these goods had larger operations and more political influence than struggling local artisans (Olton 1975).

Yet, even in those trades that favored American craftsmen, some consumers still preferred English goods. A good example was furniture making. American joiners and turners had the cost advantages of abundant local wood supplies and, being closer to consumers, much lower shipping costs. They possessed high levels of woodworking skills and, to many twenty-first century eyes, produced superior designs. Nevertheless, select English items were imported throughout the eighteenth century, especially in the South (Heckscher 1985), but in New England as well (Jobe and Kaye 1984). American silversmiths also produced a fine quality product, but consumers still insisted on buying some of their sterling from London makers, either through overseas agents or from local smiths like Joseph Richardson of Philadelphia, who augmented their incomes by reselling imported merchandise (Fales 1974). The examples from the furniture and silver trades suggest that the demand for English imports was partly a matter of prevailing cultural tastes, and not entirely a rational preference determined by availability, quality, and price. The majority of Americans descended from British stock and, until the 1770s, most considered themselves to be the King's loyal subjects. Presumably, they desired to live as well and as fashionably as other Englishmen of their class, who themselves were participating in a rising consumer society (McKendrick *et al.* 1982; Robinson 1987).

The upper classes were among the first to adopt these newer values and behaviors, with demand for imported luxury goods particularly strong in the South where the plantation lifestyle, championed by an elite circle of old families, engendered emulation of the English aristocracy. For some, burgeoning material appetites became ever more ruinous financially. As Emory G. Evans (1962, 518–519) noted,

> The gentry's increase in wealth and its assumption of political and social leadership had been accompanied by a desire for the refinements of the more cultivated existence enjoyed by it counterpart in Britain. Trouble came when this desire outran income. By the 1750s and 1760s few commentators failed to mention the extravagant, luxurious, and even ostentatious tastes and habits of the large Virginia planters.

Both the size of each Southern householder's debt and the number of those indebted grew rapidly in the decades before the Revolution, despite increased revenues from higher tobacco prices. Compared to Northern colonists, Southerners of means owned greater amounts of capital against which they could borrow, and they did not have quite the restraining ideology of simple consumption commingled with their religion.

Although large planters were the most heavily obligated, small planters and family farmers also amassed new debts, indicating social comparison processes in action. Throughout the colonies, people of more middling circumstances began to acquire small luxuries such as silver spoons. Carr and Walsh (1980) interpreted this as a signal change in consumer behavior where the lower orders incorporate some aspects of the lifestyles of their betters into their own consumption. Historian Timothy Breen (2004) contended the desire to obtain imported English goods promoted an "industrious revolution" where entire families labored to obtain additional disposable income, in effect, trading leisure time for material things. Thus, the second half of the eighteenth century marks the birth of true consumerist desire and a culture of consumption in America.

The Gender of Household Purchasing Roles

Early American society conferred on its men a great many rights and privileges. They usually received better educations than did women, and only men attended the few nascent universities established in the colonies. Very few women acquired more than basic reading and writing skills. As late as the end of the colonial period, only 40 to 45 percent of all New England females could sign their names, compared to about 80 percent of all males who could do so (Lockridge 1974). Female literacy did not become nearly universal until the 1840s (Cott 1977). Craft apprenticeships were reserved for boys and young men, and virtually no women, aside from the wives and daughters of printers (Tunis 1965), ever learned male-dominated trades. Millinery and midwifery were among the most highly skilled female occupations. Males could choose their lines of work, except when race and economic status limited their options. If they owned enough property, men could vote for political candidates, hold government office, and serve as ministers, elders, justices, and jurors. Men had more freedom to travel independently outside their neighborhoods and developed better skills of horsemanship. Some women could ride well, but powerful conventions of posture (riding sidesaddle) and clothing (restrictive corsets) limited their ability to control horses (Larkin 1988).

"For eighteenth-century women, there was little illusion of choice; they could either marry or remain single" (Karlsen and Crumpacker 1984, 10). Virtually every free white woman who reached the age of maturity in colonial America married, and nuptial rates for women remained high well into the 1800s. Spinsters were held in very low esteem (Norton 1980; Spruill 1938/1972). Social institutions dictated that married women were secondary to and dependent on their spouses. Husbands were supreme in affairs outside the home. Wives were expected to be cheerfully obedient. A patriarchal religion accompanied the first New England colonists during the early seventeenth century, and its dogmas were widely enforced. Patriarchal ideals also came with the Chesapeake settlers but were not applied consistently until the early 1700s (Kulikoff 1986). The surplus of immigrant men, a shortage of labor, and a high mortality rate that necessitated frequent remarriage gave women additional bargaining power that lasted until the more settled conditions of the eighteenth century.

Under English common law, a married woman (*feme covert*) could not own real or personal property, and whatever she brought into the marriage became her husband's. He could spend her money, sell her livestock, and even appropriate her clothing and jewelry. He could not sell real property without her consent, but he could manage it as he pleased. Wives could not make legally binding contracts. Only widows and spinsters (*femes sole*) were legal individuals. When a man died intestate, his wife was entitled to a minimum share of his estate, called her dower right, but statutes otherwise favored the eldest son (Norton 1984). Husbands' legal authority remained unchallenged until the 1830s (Cott 1977). Yet, unless a marriage turned bad, the seemingly harsh doctrine of coverture meant relatively little. Joan Gunderson and Gwen Victor Gampel (1982) examined hundreds of eighteenth-century wills and did not find a single instance in which a man tried to bequeath his wife's personal property to another individual. Furthermore, married women could and did participate in the legal system. Husbands and wives sometimes filed joint suits and executed joint wills. Equity law, administered by courts of chancery, enabled a couple to sign a contract known as a marriage settlement that gave the woman far more control over her own property. However, prenuptial agreements seem to have been uncommon except among widows about to remarry (Salmon 1982; Watson 1981).

Early American society expected a husband to take his wife's opinions and interests into consideration, and if he were prevented from fulfilling his role, then his wife could and did stand in his place as a deputy husband. Some Puritan ministers preached spiritual equality and recognized that marriage meant a partnership of near equals. In 1726, Samuel Willard wrote in his *Complete Body of Divinity*, "Of all the Orders which are unequals, these do come nearest an Equality, and in several respects they stand upon even ground. These do make a Pair, which infers so far a Parity" (cited in Ulrich 1976, 30). The sermons of Cotton Mather spoke very highly of women's traditional roles and even promoted increased intellectual activity for women. These clergymen might have been responding to the growing proportions of women in their congregations. Indeed, religion was one area in which women could establish a separate, albeit strictly spiritual, authority.

Despite these public ideals, the real balance of power between the sexes shifted from one sphere of life to another. In New England, women had primary responsibility for the policing of sexual conduct (Ulrich 1982) and this prerogative was enhanced by the intimacy of early American towns and villages wherein people became familiar with each other's personal affairs. Throughout the colonies, women controlled midwifery and made childbirth a communal event that excluded men until male physicians eventually claimed it for themselves in the late eighteenth century (Scholten 1977; Ulrich 1982, 1990). The web of horizontal relationships between housewives and their female neighbors and family members presented a barrier to the exercise of male authority. Men might control "official" sources of power such as the law, but female communication networks gave women access to much important information. Finally, because petty thievery often was a problem, valuables and household provisions were stored in boxes, chests, closets, and rooms fitted with a variety of locks. Housewives carried the keys in baskets, in their pockets, or dangling from chatelaines. Keys were a symbol of control and were carefully counted and polished (Garrett 1990).

Popular literature discussed the topic of domestic authority. A content analysis of 15 American magazines published between 1741 and 1794 (Lantz *et al.* 1968) coded discussions of power as being exerted overtly by the male, overtly by the female, subtly by the female, or cooperatively by both. The researchers found 136 discussions of male power (all overt), 147 discussions of female power (42 overt, 105 subtle), and 38 discussions of mutual cooperation. In the area of finances, the authors recorded six discussions of male power, 14 discussions of overt female power, one discussion of subtle female power, and two discussions of mutual cooperation. Although published in New England and written for the middle and upper classes of both genders, these texts suggested that at least some Americans recognized a good deal of female power in daily life.

Near the close of the colonial period, husband-dominated marriages became less popular, first among colonial elites and then among the prosperous middle classes (Woloch 1984). Before the Revolution, as Marylynn Salmon (1982, 669) observed, wives

> deferred to their husbands on most questions and relied on men to manage family finances. By the end of the [eighteenth] century, however, this deferential relationship was changing. Marriages became more egalitarian as wives abandoned passivity to participate in broader decisions concerning family affairs.

The famous letters exchanged by John and Abigail Adams reveal one such relationship. Revolutionary ideology declared "patriarchal domination the chief obstacle to happy and virtuous marriage" (Lewis 1987, 693). Ironically, the introduction of the "republican-mother" ideal, the notion that women had a special responsibility in setting moral standards for the new nation, facilitated the development of more clearly delineated male and female roles (Norton 1984) and, therefore, pointed toward the Victorian "cult of domesticity" in which women's consumption choices reflected on their families' social standing (Witkowski 2004).

Historians still do not agree on the true status of early American women, but given the available documentation, it seems reasonable to believe that they had fewer employment opportunities and lower public standing than did the men of their time, and had far less of each than did females in the twenty-first century. Less clear is how this affected the household balance of power. Carol Karlsen and Laurie Crumpacker (1984) indicated that deference to male authority was so ingrained that women, even when writing to each other, frequently cloaked in irony any deprecating comments about the opposite sex. However, this literary evidence also can be interpreted as resulting from upper-class norms of gentility and refinement (Bushman 1992). Thus, the data do not preclude strong female influence within the domains of consumer decision-making influences and private household consumption activities. The formal structure of marital authority was complemented by an informal structure of married power. Whatever the prevailing social norms, the relative influence of husbands and wives must have varied from one household to the next. Some husbands might have been more amenable than others in deferring to their wives' opinions and expertise. Some intelligent, voluble, and strong-willed women conceivably might have gained an equal or upper hand in their marriages. Conjugal life and love surely overrode public ideology in many homes. There was no simple continuum between patriarchy, on one hand, and gender equality in consumption, on the other.

According to Jean Gordon and Jan McArthur (1985), the ideology of male supremacy in early America had profound implications for family decision-making:

> During the first two and a quarter centuries of our history, most consumption decisions were made by men.... Unless a woman was acting as an agent for her husband or as a widow, most of her consumption choices were confined to her personal clothing.
>
> (36)

Gordon and McArthur provided no evidence to support their sweeping statement other than citing a few instances in which a husband or father provided a young wife with a completely furnished house. By contrast, John Demos (1970, 181) found much more egalitarianism. Writing about family life in the Plymouth colony during the period from 1620 to 1690, he contended, "In certain most important areas of family life – the sale of real property or the disposition of children – the couple would make decisions together." As will be seen, there are numerous accounts of joint decision making during the late eighteenth and early nineteenth centuries.

Husbands held ultimate legal authority within the family, but, in a number of areas, wives were the ones who wielded the real power. Females probably had strong influence regarding consumer goods because, as a domestic matter, these decisions were nominally within the sphere of women's competence. Moreover, traditional rules and norms did not anticipate the onset of a consumer society with its profusion of new products for the household. Women may have developed the ability to imagine and want new things more quickly than did men (Campbell 1987). In her pioneering history of Southern women, Julia Cherry Spruill (1938/1972) argued that advertisements "dangled before feminine imaginations" irresistible finery that "must have sorely tempted colonial ladies" (282). The challenge for consumption historians is finding documentation for these internal family processes. Because the dead cannot be interviewed, the best one can do is to make inferences based on indirect evidence such as court testimonies, letters, newspaper items, and probate records.

Probate inventories (Main 1982) consistently showed that beds and beddings were the most valuable household furnishings during the eighteenth century, usually costing more than horses. This indicates strong female influence if one assumes that wives were more concerned with having these most intimate of comforts than were their husbands. The acquisition of other domestic amenities such as forks and table linens increased during the middle 1700s (Carr and Walsh 1980; Ulrich 1982). Taken alone, probate inventories might not paint an entirely accurate picture (Witkowski 1994), but early correspondence repeatedly discloses that husbands sought their wives' advice in the selection of textiles, carpets, and wallpapers (Garrett 1990). On the other hand, the well-known lives of men such as Benjamin Franklin (1705–1790) provide numerous examples of male concern and responsibility for household purchases (Cott 1977). Moreover, Campbell's (1987) thesis of consumerist imagination, an individualist hedonism of anticipatory pleasure, might not necessarily coincide with the persistence of strong family and class obligations that could override personal preferences (de Grazia 1996). Until more data are uncovered, the relative influence of men and women on decision-making remains undecided. However, little evidence has suggested habitual female deference in consumer decision-making.

Household shopping and purchasing activities were much better documented than were decision-making influences. Numerous surviving account and letter books show that upper-class males and some females requested, on behalf of their families, that their London agents buy household items. In 1767, for example, the very rich Bostonian and future Massachusetts Governor, John Hancock (1737–1793), ordered a mahogany cabinet from London. Four years earlier, he had instructed his agent "When any Article is wrote for Family use.... Send it of the best kind, Cost what it will" (cited in Jobe and Kaye 1984, 378). In the summer of 1769, Virginia planter and future U.S. President, George Washington (1732–1799), commissioned a new 250-piece table service of "ye most fash^{n} kind of Queen's ware" (cited in Detweiler 1982, 53). The emphasis on fashion suggests that the Washington household made appearances a priority concern. Generally speaking, requisitions such as these were not very specific about product attributes. Even orders for wearing apparel frequently omitted exact sizes and left the choice of color, size, and style to the discretion of the agent or, in some cases, the agent's wife (Spruill 1938/1972). Bear in mind, however, that only the colonial elite were in a position to obtain goods through an English agent. Most Americans purchased or bartered what they needed locally or through provincial channels of distribution.

The chronic shortage of specie in the early American economy made establishing a good credit relationship with local shopkeepers essential to the viability of the household. To avoid becoming too dependent on one store, people frequently spread their debts among a variety of local traders (Ulrich 1990), as well as among their neighbors, given that people frequently bartered and borrowed things from each other. Because it took place outside the household, arranging credit at stores was one activity that generally devolved on husbands (Ulrich 1982). However, the diary of the industrious midwife, Martha Ballard (1735–1812), indicates that female spouses sometimes had individual shop accounts (Ulrich 1990), as did single, widowed, and divorced women (Perkins 1991).

In the event of separation or divorce, husbands frequently placed notices in newspapers informing creditors that they no longer would honor debts contracted by their wives. The *Connecticut Gazette and Universal Intelligencer* printed the following example on October 18, 1782:

> Whereas Submit, the wife of me the subscriber, hath eloped from my bed and board and refuseth to dwell with me, and therefore I take this method to warn all persons not to credit her on my account, for I will not pay any debt she shall contract after the date hereof.
>
> Lebanon, 23d September, 1782
> JAMES NEWCOMB

The phrase "my bed and board" suggests that Newcomb considered himself the sole owner of their material possessions, which might have been true under the law. Nevertheless, as indicated by the following ad from the *South Carolina and American General Gazette* (March 27–April 3, 1776), there could be other points of view:

> John Cantwell has the Impudence to advertise me in the Papers, cautioning all Persons against crediting me; he never had any Credit till he married me; as for his Bed and Board he mentioned, he had neither Bed nor Board when he married me; I never eloped, I went away before his Face when he beat me.
>
> SARAH CANTWELL

When husbands and wives separated by mutual consent, they sometimes published the terms of their postnuptial settlements. On February 10, 1774, two witnesses to an agreement between Coleman and Elizabeth Theeds placed an advertisement in the *Virginia Gazette* that said, in part, "This Notice is given to the *Gazette* that no Person, after this Date, may credit the Wife on the Husband's Account, or the Husband upon that of the Wife's." The text implied that Elizabeth had her own line of credit.

Diaries record that some couples engaged in joint shopping expeditions. For example, Elizabeth Drinker of Philadelphia noted that on a trip to New York in 1769, she and her husband spent many mornings in what might be called comparison shopping (Bridenbaugh 1955). Unfortunately, such references are infrequent and tersely worded. The diary of Esther Burr, for example, provides only scant information about her buying excursions. In October 1754, she "rode out … to speak for Winter Tirneps, Apples, and syder, and butter," and two months later, she was "out erly in the Morn on business, got Me a long Scarlet Cloth Cloke and some things for famaly use" (cited in Karlsen and Crumpacker 1984, 51, 74). In 1756, she wrote to a friend in Boston and asked her to procure several small items including pencils, gum arabic, and shortcake pans. Nancy Shippen's journal, written between 1777 and 1800, mentioned shopping just four times, with the most detailed entry stating, "I pass'd almost all this morn'g in shopping & made several pretty purchases" (cited in Armes 1935/1968, 219).

Store ledgers further documented women's purchasing, but they also indicated that men were by far the most frequent store customers during the eighteenth century. Women accounted for only 8 percent of all purchases at the Simpson-Baird store in Prince George's County, Maryland, in 1769 (Kulikoff 1986). At the Simpson-Baird store, "Widows who held store accounts sent their sons or unrelated men to the store to gather their goods three times as frequently as they ventured there themselves" (Kulikoff 1986, 225).

Breen (1986) has argued that making choices in the marketplace provided colonial women a liberating experience: "Shopping must have heightened their sense of self-importance. It was an arena in which they could ask questions, express individuality, and make demands" (489). Breen's statement seems plausible except that the written record left in diaries and letters so rarely mentioned purchasing behavior. Furthermore, it seems equally reasonable to speculate that the emerging consumer society of the second half of the eighteenth century afforded men similar satisfactions. As late as 1820, however, "few Americans, male or female, had the wealth, opportunity, or inclination to while away their time examining imported luxuries in fashionable shops" (Ryan 1975, 97). Thus, the psychological impact on average citizens of expanding product availability and choice probably accrued very slowly.

The gendering of household consumption in the colonial era varied over time, by place, and across social strata. The relative influence of men versus women in consumer decision processes is difficult to determine. Some wives bartered independently with neighboring females and storekeepers, trading the eggs, butter, and spun linen they produced, and cooking, washing, and midwife services they offered (Ulrich 1990). Being legally part of their husbands' household, however, women's influence ultimately rested on their persuasive abilities. Surviving letters and diaries show that married couples engaged in comparison shopping, but at all social levels, husbands usually established credit accounts with local shopkeepers. Men took shopping trips by themselves or with their wives; infrequently did women venture out on their own.

Anti-Consumption, Resistance, and Revolt

The growing allure of consumerism did not go unchallenged. Colonial Americans voiced anti-consumption rhetoric and organized significant consumer resistance. Drawing from a Western Judeo-Christian tradition skeptical of excess in acquisition, Puritans and Quakers favored productive work for the benefit of society and frowned upon consuming more than necessity required (Shi 1985). Noted colonial historian Edmund Morgan (1967, 5) phrased it this way:

> A man was but the steward of the possessions he accumulated. If he indulged himself in luxurious living, he would have that much less with which to support church and society. If he needlessly consumed his substance, either from carelessness or from sensuality, he failed to honor the God who furnished him with it.

But whereas Quaker critiques stressed utilitarian ideals and did not attack on consumption per se, Puritans were driven by a spiritual principle asserting that the love of consuming itself was an evil (Dröge *et al.* 1993; Schudson 1991). To forestall impious materialism, the Massachusetts Bay and Pennsylvania colonies enacted sumptuary laws in the seventeenth century (Hollander 1984), and New England ministers preached jeremiads against worldliness well into the eighteenth century. The Great Awakening, a widespread religious revival of the 1730s, stressed the virtues of simple living, and a generation later, "Americans of the Revolutionary period in every colony and state paid tribute to the Puritan Ethic and repeated its injunctions" (Morgan 1967, 7). Between 1732 and 1757 in his *Poor Richard's Almanack*, the very secular Benjamin Franklin preached frugality as a moral virtue with sayings like "Beware of little expenses; a small leak will sink a great ship" (Witkowski 2010a, 239).

Yet, stern admonitions and legal restrictions met their match in the pleasures consumption afforded. The Massachusetts Bay Colony passed sumptuary laws in 1634, 1639, and 1651, the last specifying a ten shilling penalty for either men or women with a net worth under £200 who wore gold or silver buttons or lace, bone lace above two shillings a yard, and silk hoods or scarves. Enforcement was sporadic, but not uncommon. For example, the authorities charged Hannah Westcarr with the crime of wearing silk in 1673 and again in 1675 and 1677. In 1676, a year in the midst of King Philip's War, a deadly conflict with New England's remaining Indians, 38 maids and wives and 30 young men were accused of wearing silk, flaunting manners, and displaying other extravagances. One insolent 16-year-old girl even wore her offending silk to the proceedings (Ulrich 2001, 125). Colonial ministers and moralizers were not always effective when it came to combating the relatively low-level consumerism of their day. Droll stories were told about one itinerant preacher, the Reverend James Davenport, who in 1743 convinced true believers in New London, Connecticut, to consign their English import fineries and "Gay Cloaths" to a large bonfire of the vanities. At the very last moment before the flame was lit, the semi-nude sinners had second thoughts about this path to salvation and rescued their transgressing garments for use in the here and now (Breen 2004).

Sumptuary laws eventually faded away, but another strain of resistance arose when American consumption practices and the meanings assigned to possessions became highly politicized in the decade before the Revolutionary War. Three times in the 1760s and 1770s, colonists organized mass boycotts of English goods in order to inflict economic hardships on English merchants and manufacturers who, they believed, would then pressure Parliament in London into rescinding the objectionable taxes. Known in later times as the "nonimportation movement," this outbreak of serious consumer resistance stressed frugality along with the manufacture and purchase of products made in America. Thus, nonimportation became the first organized consumer revolt in America, and perhaps in the entire world.

In terms of the intensity of its political and economic actions, the nonimportation movement unfolded in three waves. The first wave of protest, from 1765 to 1766, came in response to the British Stamp Act of 1765. Desperately in need of additional revenues to offset increased expenses in North America stemming from the French and Indian War (1754–1763), Parliament imposed taxes on books, playing cards, and various documents, and required newspapers to use only paper stamped "duty-paid." It also levied a two-shilling levy on each advertisement (Presbrey 1929). Up and down the Atlantic seaboard an outpouring of political opposition, including nonimportation initiatives, brought about repeal of the Stamp Act in 1766 (Bunker 2014). The teapot in Figure 3.4, made *c.*1766–1770, possibly by the Cockpit Hill Factory from the Derby, England, carried the bright, bold message "No Stamp Act/America Liberty Restored." If it

Figure 3.4 Teapot Proclaiming "No Stamp Act/America. Liberty Restored," *c.*1766–1770. Lead-glazed and hand painted earthenware. Possibly made by the Cockpit Hill Factory, Derby, England.

Source: The National Museum of American History, Kenneth E. Behring Center.

were intended for the colonial market, this object documents both the potter's agility in turning current events into a sales opportunity and the desire by Americans to express themselves politically through the purchase of goods. As later chapters will show, such partisan consumption has continued up to the present day.

The second wave, from 1767 to 1770, followed the imposition of new duties on glass, paint leads, paper, and tea. They were provisions of the 1767 Townshend Act. Parliament imposed these taxes in order to pay the salaries of governors and judges, which previously had been the responsibility of the colonial assemblies, to enforce trade provisions, and to set a precedent for the future. Widespread and well-organized political and economic protests broke out, especially in Boston where troops sent to quell the unrest faced a mob of protestors and killed five men in the "Boston Massacre" of March 5, 1770. Ironically, on the very same day the new Prime Minister, Lord North, introduced a motion in the House of Commons calling for a partial repeal of the Townshend Act. After a month of debate, all duties were rescinded save the tax on tea, retained as a symbol of British authority. Emotions cooled, the boycotts collapsed, and people like John and Elizabeth Cadwalader could again splurge on personal consumption without facing much reproach from fellow colonists.

However, the growing financial difficulties of the East India Company (EIC) led to the passage of the Tea Act in May 1773. This legislation allowed the EIC to ship tea directly to the colonies without having to pay additional import taxes and middlemen markups in London. With only the Townshend duty remaining, EIC tea would become more price competitive with the vast amount of Dutch tea being smuggled into the colonies. Parliament expected colonial acquiescence, but instead met with great anger from colonial merchants, who were cut out of the deal, and from any number of anti-British firebrands. Thus, when seven ships filled with EIC tea arrived in North America, outraged colonists turned them away in Philadelphia and New York, while in Charlestown, South Carolina customs officers confiscated and stored the offensive cargo (Norton 2016). Three tea ships were able to dock in Boston, but then on December 16, 1773, patriots dressed up like Indians dumped the EIC tea into the harbor, an act of protest that later became known as the "Boston Tea Party" (Figure 3.5). A deeply offended

Figure 3.5 Americans Throwing the Cargoes of the Tea Ships into the River, at Boston, 1789. Engraving by W.D. Cooper in *The History of North America*, London: E. Newbury.

Source: Rare Book and Special Collections Division, Library of Congress.

Parliament retaliated the following year by passing the Coercive Acts (called the Intolerable Acts by Americans) that among other punitive provisions shut down the city's port. With patriot fever high and rising, the First Continental Congress launched the third and final nonimportation surge in 1774 and 1775 with a pledge to boycott an assortment of English goods starting December 1, 1774. This became something of a moot subject by April 1775 when the start of armed hostilities at Lexington and Concord Massachusetts focused attention upon military matters.

Interest in nonimportation was widespread. Movement activities were concentrated in the port cities of Boston, New York, and Philadelphia, but Americans living in small towns and rural areas also took part. The most important movement ritual was the public signing of agreements to cease the importation and consumption of English merchandise. In the New England and middle colonies, groups of merchants, later joined by artisans and other citizens, did the signing. In the plantation colonies, which lacked a preeminent commercial class, broader based bodies endorsed the agreements (Maier 1973). The dates and durations of these agreements varied from place to place and from one wave of the movement to another. For example, the agreements formulated in response to the Townshend duties were not signed until April 1768 in New York, October 1768 in Boston, March 1769 in Philadelphia, and May 1769 in Virginia. Similarly, the terms of the agreements ranged from a total ban of all English merchandise, to partial bans of luxuries, to boycotts of just a few items subject to disputed taxation. Agreements formulated in the South tended to emphasize nonconsumption more than nonimportation (Maier 1973). Figure 3.6 shows the first page of a nonimportation agreement dated October 28, 1767. The document listed dozens of items to be excluded (imported funeral gloves were the last one mentioned) and was signed by 650 Bostonians including some women and a young silversmith, engraver, and patriot named Paul Revere (1735–1818) who on April 18, 1775 would literally ride into history warning his fellow patriots about an impending attack on Lexington and Concord. Artisans eventually played a very influential role in the movement. They constituted a sizeable proportion, about 30 percent or more, of all urban property owners in the mid-eighteenth century and clearly had much to gain from reduced foreign competition (Bridenbaugh 1955; Olton 1975). Persuaded by exhortation, secondary boycotts, and the threat of mob violence, American merchants generally complied with the agreements.

Trade statistics demonstrated how seriously economic sanctions disrupted Atlantic commerce, at least temporarily. By the summer of 1765, the colonists had slashed their orders for English goods by £600,000 (Nettels 1963). The value of sterling silver products exported from England to colonial America, exceeding £4700 in both 1760 and 1761, dropped to £949 in 1766 (Fales 1974). During the second wave of the movement, Boston's import trade was cut in half, while Philadelphia's declined from £441,000 in 1768 to £134,800 in 1770. In the third wave, exports from Britain to New York fell dramatically, from £437,000 in 1774 to a mere £1228 in 1775 (Nettels 1963).

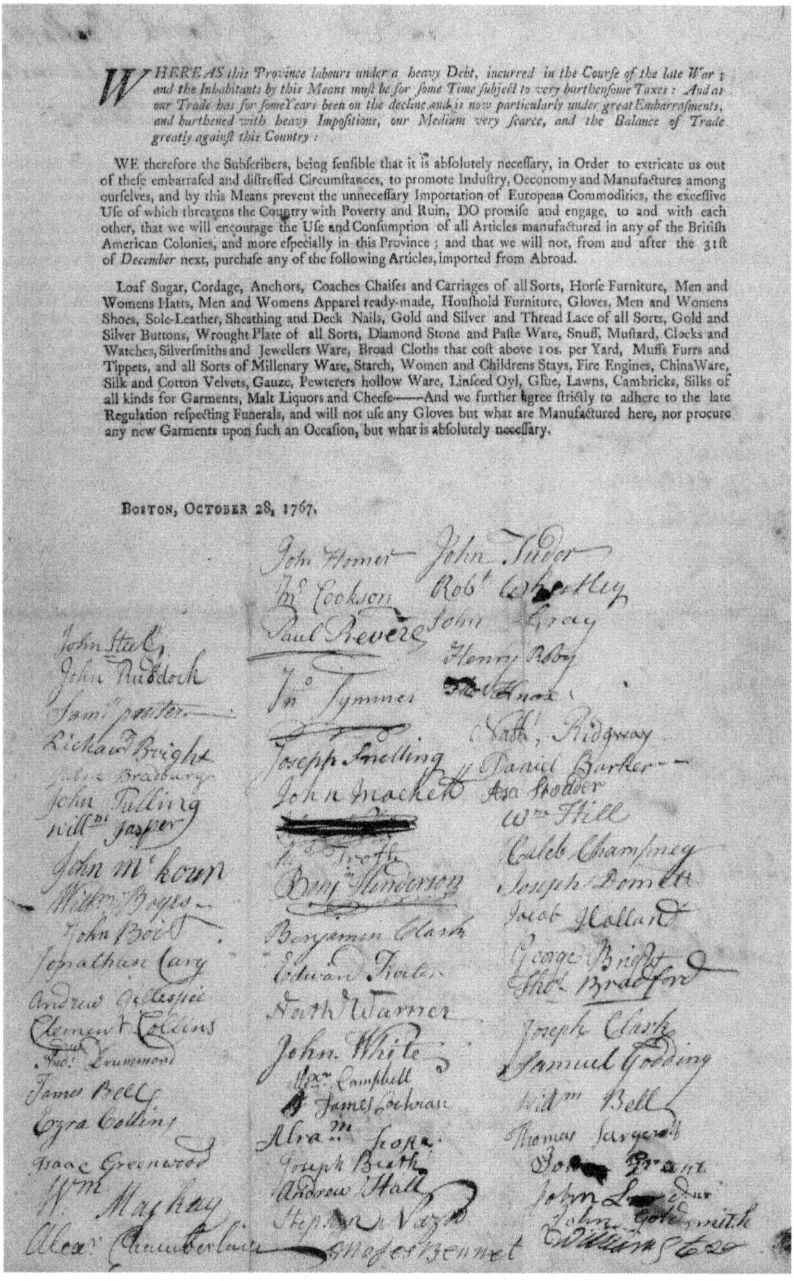

WHEREAS this Province labours under a heavy Debt, incurred in the Courſe of the late War; and the Inhabitants by this Means muſt be for ſome Time ſubject to very burthenſome Taxes: And as our Trade has for ſome Years been on the decline and is now particularly under great Embarraſments, and burthened with heavy Impoſitions, our Medium very ſcarce, and the Balance of Trade greatly againſt this Country:

WE therefore the Subſcribers, being ſenſible that it is abſolutely neceſſary, in Order to extricate us out of theſe embarraſed and diſtreſſed Circumſtances, to promote Induſtry, Oeconomy and Manufactures among ourſelves, and by this Means prevent the unneceſſary Importation of European Commodities, the exceſſive Uſe of which threatens the Country with Poverty and Ruin, DO promiſe and engage, to and with each other, that we will encourage the Uſe and Conſumption of all Articles manufactured in any of the Britiſh American Colonies, and more eſpecially in this Province; and that we will not, from and after the 31ſt of December next, purchaſe any of the following Articles, imported from Abroad.

Loaf Sugar, Cordage, Anchors, Coaches Chaiſes and Carriages of all Sorts, Horſe Furniture, Men and Womens Hatts, Men and Womens Apparel ready-made, Houſhold Furniture, Gloves, Men and Womens Shoes, Sole-Leather, Sheathing and Deck Nails, Gold and Silver and Thread Lace of all Sorts, Gold and Silver Buttons, Wrought Plate of all Sorts, Diamond Stone and Paſte Ware, Snuff, Muſtard, Clocks and Watches, Silverſmiths and Jewellers Ware, Broad Cloths that coſt above 10s. per Yard, Muffs Furrs and Tippets, and all Sorts of Millenary Ware, Starch, Women and Childrens Stays, Fire Engines, China Ware, Silk and Cotton Velvets, Gauze, Pewterers hollow Ware, Linſeed Oyl, Glue, Lawns, Cambricks, Silks of all kinds for Garments, Malt Liquors and Cheeſe——And we further agree ſtrictly to adhere to the late Regulation reſpecting Funerals, and will not uſe any Gloves but what are Manufactured here, nor procure any new Garments upon ſuch an Occaſion, but what is abſolutely neceſſary.

BOSTON, OCTOBER 28, 1767.

Figure 3.6 A Nonimportation Agreement, Boston, October 28, 1767. Paul Revere's signature is in the second column, third from top.

Source: Houghton Library, Harvard University.

Other movement activities attempted to stimulate local production. Associations were formed in New York, Philadelphia, and Boston to establish cloth-manufacturing enterprises using the poor as employees (Nash 1979). The New York Society for the Promotion of Arts, Agriculture and Oeconomy conducted a fortnightly market for the sale of New York manufactures, and in Philadelphia, a similar market offered Pennsylvania wares for sale (Schlesinger 1917/1957). All over New England, spinning and weaving parties became centers of social activities. Towns competed with each other over the number of skeins spun and yards produced. Massachusetts awarded premiums for the best piece of cloth – serge, sagathy, and shalloon (lightweight wool fabric) – woven in the colony (Andrews 1918/1968). Home spinning "probably reached a high point on the eve of the Revolution when owning a spinning wheel, whether it received much use or not, demonstrated a love for one's native soil" (Shammas 1982a, 256).

The nonimportation movement produced a number of positive economic outcomes. Halts in the import trade allowed merchants to dispose of surplus, slow-moving inventories at higher prices. Also, many colonial artisans benefited from the embargos, especially metal and textile workers; furniture, coach, and instrument makers; and cordwainers, saddlers, hatters, and glovers who worked for the gentry (Nash 1979). According to Carl Bridenbaugh (1950, 98), "the rate of development of already established manufactures quickened, as by forced draught, and in 1770 industries were much further advanced than they would have been under ordinary conditions." For brief periods, the movement helped the colonies reduce indebtedness to the mother country and, in so doing, renewed self-respect among the people.

On the other hand, the movement caused hardships for many and ultimately disappointed its more enthusiastic proponents. Merchants, as well as the petty retailers who purchased from them, felt the pinch as soon as their inventories began to disappear. Some artisans could not function well without the glass, glue, metals, and other component parts they imported. Building craftsmen, shipwrights, and a few types of woodworkers, such as coopers and turners, frequently were hurt by nonimportation (Nash 1979). The textile factories established in New York and Philadelphia during the first wave of protest in 1765–1766 failed as soon as the boycotts lapsed and English imports flooded the market with better quality goods. Efforts to establish new crafts in the rural South also made little headway in this economically undiversified region. Finally, it was difficult for political leaders to restrain demand for imported luxuries and to induce lasting preferences for American-made products.

Testifying before the House of Commons in 1766, Benjamin Franklin (quoted in McCusker and Menard 1985, 278–279) warned how the nonimportation movement threatened Britain's export trade:

> The goods they (the colonists) take from Britain are either necessities, mere conveniences, or superfluities. The first, as cloth &c. with a little industry they can make at home; the second they can do without, till they are able to provide them among themselves; and the last, which are much the greatest

> part, they will strike off immediately. They are mere articles of fashion, purchased and consumed, because the fashion in a respected country, but will now be detested and rejected.

In Franklin's opinion, perhaps exaggerated for political effect, the colonies could easily live without any imports, especially those "superfluities" that were "mere articles of fashion." Yet, little evidence indicates that the nonimportation movement altered American consumer preferences and consumption patterns in the long run.

Clearly, a vigorous and extensive persuasive effort called upon Americans to refuse English merchandise and switch to locally produced products. Leaders like John Adams condemned the "vicious, luxurious and effeminate Appetites, Passions, and Habits" created by the growing consumption of "foreign trifles" and "Baubles of Britain." As one writer put it: "SAVE YOUR MONEY AND YOU WILL SAVE YOUR COUNTRY" (Morgan 1967, 10). These views were aired at town meetings and disseminated via letters reprinted in colonial newspapers. In the meantime, published reports described the increase and perfection of local manufactures. The *South Carolina Gazette* in 1769 "urged local workmen to purchase their breeches and gloves from Peter Girard, stocking-maker, because his goods were all of American or South Carolina make" (Bridenbaugh 1950, 72). In 1768, the *Newport Mercury* inserted all advertisements for Rhode Island textiles free of charge (Schlesinger 1971/1957).

The nonimportation campaign also began to infiltrate the advertising columns of colonial newspapers. Traditionally, local artisans had played upon any English, and particularly London, connections. Their ads frequently boasted that they had recently emigrated "from London" and claimed workmanship "as neat as in England" (Dow 1927/1967; Gottesman 1938/1970). These appeals continued during the nonimportation movement (a telling indicator of the persistence of fashion and, possibly, Tory sympathies), but were increasingly challenged by advertisements with contradictory messages. Some colonial craftsmen, for example, raised questions about the quality of imported products. A Philadelphia cutler, Stephen Paschall, complained about imported sickles deceptively stamped, "S. Pachall" in imitation of his mark "S. Paschall." A Philadelphia anchor maker, Daniel Offley, pointed out the inferior quality of imported anchors, publicly refused to repair them, and even threatened to stop making his own unless Philadelphians ceased purchasing the cheaper imports (Olton 1975). Other artisans also claimed superior craftsmanship, lauded the special virtues of locally produced items, and promised additional services not available to those who purchased foreign imports. "John Fromberger, furrier, advertised free fur storage to those who bought his furs in preference to imported; Nathanael Cope, smith, offered to clean the smoke and roasting jacks he made for local customers" (Olton 1975, 23).

Encouraged by a barrage of propaganda, colonial consumers changed their consumption patterns, dress behavior in particular. According to the distinguished Yale historian Charles Mclean Andrews (1918/1968, 35):

> To practice abstention and so to decrease the demand for European goods was within the range even of the humblest, and to lay off ribbons, laces, velvets, silks, and other forms of expensive dress became the first object of the new movement. To wear colonial-made clothing, native homespun, was the inevitable corollary.

In August 1764, a group of 50 Boston merchants pledged to curtail expenditures on imported mourning apparel, a practice that within a few years spread as far south as Charleston. In 1768, members of the Massachusetts Council and House of Representatives, as well as many clergymen, promised to wear cloth and shoes of American manufacture, and the senior classes of Harvard, Yale, and the College of Rhode Island (now Brown University) appeared in homespun clothes at their graduation ceremony (Andrews 1918/1968). The tailors of Newport promised to work four pence cheaper on American-manufactured cloth, and artisans agreed to wear only work aprons made of American leather. To help increase the supply of wool, fire companies and various individuals pledged not to eat mutton and lamb. Soon, "the wearing of homespun clothes became a sign of patriotism while the display of imported finery was condemned as an attack on economic self-sufficiency" (Henretta 1973, 144). In 1770, newspapers up and down the Atlantic Seaboard proudly reported the trip of one Henry Lloyd from Boston to the Southern colonies, and one such report is quoted in Bridenbaugh (1955, 282): "And it was observed that the Gentleman's whole Apparel and Horse Furniture were of American Manufacture. His Clothes, Linnen, Shoes, Stockings, Boots, Gloves, Hatt, Wigg, and even Wigg Call, were all manufactured and made-up in New England."

Two further examples illustrate the range of nonimportation and home-consumption activities. Yale undergraduates demonstrated their patriotism in November 1764 by voting unanimously to abstain from foreign liquors (apparently their domestic supply was sufficient), and in 1768, Harvard students resolved not to drink imported tea. Eventually, people throughout the colonies made similar resolutions. In Boston alone, 1500 families vowed to abandon tea (Schlesinger 1917/1957). An English print from 1775 satirized American women from Edenton, North Carolina, who responded to the Continental Congress resolution of 1774 to boycott English goods. They dumped tea from their caddies and signed a pledge to forego further purchases (Figure 3.7). Since tea was so widely consumed by the second half of the eighteenth century (Norton 2016), these were important symbolic gestures.

In its repudiation of the perceived dissipation and corruption of England, nonimportation and nonconsumption reaffirmed the old Puritan and Quaker ethics. As stated by Thomas M. Doerflinger (1986, 184),

> The boycotts played an important ideological role as well, for by rejecting the debilitating vices and luxuries of the Old World they translated into action the moral component of a republican ideology. Nonimportation thus provided a means of atoning for the sins of avarice and materialism in an increasingly secular age.

Figure 3.7 A Society of Patriotic Ladies at Edenton in North Carolina. Printed by Robert Sayer and John Bennett, London, March 1775.

Source: Library of Congress, Prints & Photographs Division, Washington, D.C.

Moral rhetoric appealed in particular to the disadvantaged members of colonial society. Servants, ordinary seamen, common laborers, and struggling artisans supported patriotic simplicity more vigorously than the upper classes (Shi 1985), and women showed more enthusiasm than men (Andrews 1918/1968). These groups may have sensed an opportunity for improving their own status by criticizing the consumption of others. Since clothing was one area where women had the right to make their own choices (Gordon and McArthur 1985), they may have affected simple attire partly to express their sexual liberation.

Nonimportation also expressed a desire for cultural independence. Boycotts of English objects meant more than just the refusal of the things themselves and the pleasures they brought. These acts were a rejection of the cultural meanings embedded within the imports. The rituals and equipage associated with tea drinking subtly reminded some Americans of the hegemony of English tastes. Renouncing tea was a way of escaping this domination. These decisions about consumer goods linked like-minded individuals throughout the colonies and helped to forge a separate American culture. Still, not everyone was motivated by such cultural considerations. Many people engaged in nonconsumption because of political principles or because their families, friends, and neighbors compelled them to do so (Breen 1988).

In the final analysis, the nonimportation movement faced an uphill battle in its attempt to re-instill the old values of consumer restraint and create new preferences for domestic manufactures. The true extent of nonconsumption is difficult to determine. Contemporary accounts, when available, cannot always be trusted since writers frequently had a political axe to grind. Staunch Tories, perhaps one-third of the population, obviously were not enthusiastic at all. Trade statistics showed that once the immediate crisis had passed, Americans resumed their free-spending ways. In the years 1771–1774, roughly the period between the second and third waves of the movement, the value of imported commodities was 47 percent greater than it had been ten years earlier (Henretta 1973). During the Revolutionary War, luxury items from France, Spain, and Holland quickly replaced those from Great Britain and "by 1777 colonial newspapers were again filled with advertisements announcing new shipments of European finery" (Shi 1985, 68). Once hostilities ceased in 1780s, British vessels delivered large quantities of consumer goods and British merchants offered easy credit. Even leading patriots could not resist the temptation to buy English merchandise for personal use as long as such purchases were not banned specifically by an existing nonimportation agreement. As mentioned previously, John Hancock ordered furniture from London in 1767 and George Washington requested a Queens Ware dinner service in 1769. The forward thinking potter and marketer, Josiah Wedgwood, had coined the term "Queen's Ware" for promotional purposes just two years earlier, proving how quickly knowledge about the latest branded goods crossed the Atlantic. Washington's emphasis on "the most fashionable kind" suggests that he, like other men of his class, definitely was concerned with appearances.

After the Revolution, support for consumer restraint and frugality would remain a strong force in American culture and politics. John Adams believed that government, in conjunction with the family, schools, community, and religion, could counterbalance excessive materialism. His great colleague, intermittent friend, and political rival, Thomas Jefferson (1743–1826), encouraged for others – Jefferson himself loved his luxuries – a modest, agrarian lifestyle (Shi 1985). Both men expressed dismay with former patriots who discarded "republican simplicity" in favor of renewed acquisitiveness and indebtedness to foreign merchants. Consumerism was simply wrong when it substituted for productive work and distracted citizens from their civic duties (Dröge *et al.* 1993; Schudson 1991).

American women participated actively in the nonimportation movement and thus became associated with virtuous consumption. Indeed, by the 1790s, in the early federal (i.e., national) period, a "republican-mother" ideal gained traction. Proponents believed that female virtue could be harnessed to build the new, democratic nation (Evans 1989; Norton 1980). On the other hand, some commentators held more critical views about women and consumption. A letter from 1787, published in a Philadelphia magazine called *American Museum*, described how female influence could override a farmer's better judgment:

> When his second daughter prepared her trousseau, his wife insisted that the girl be furnished with store-bought goods – a calico gown, stoneware tea cups, pewter spoons, and so forth. Although the farmer protested that homespun was good enough, he gave his wife the money. Upon the marriage of the next daughter, his wife again demanded money and this time she bought silk and china. From that point on, no money could be saved because all of the profits went for market luxuries.
>
> (Cited in Shammas 1982a, 248)

Intended as both social and gender criticism, this letter suggested that some women placed a higher priority on household luxuries than did their menfolk, and were notably earlier adopters of the more prestigious, store-bought items. They were, in other words, developing a propensity to consume characteristic of modern consumerist culture (Slater 1997; Witkowski 1999). Chastising women for frivolous spending continued to be a standard part of a male critical repertoire into the late twentieth century (Stearns 2001) and, among some angry men's rights activists, continued on into the twenty-first (Kimmel 2013). Thus, the thread of consumer resistance intermingled with strands of gender and meaning.

Summary

Consumption in colonial American began at subsistence levels in the seventeenth century, but had achieved comparative prosperity by the revolutionary period. "Comparative" is the operative word here because eighteenth century living standards for almost everyone were far below what they would become in the twentieth century and new millennium. The basic consumer infrastructure of home heating, lighting, and indoor plumbing, the range of available products to buy, and the small-scale of distributive institutions would seem primitive to later generations of Americans. Throughout the colonial period households produced much of what they consumed or procured things locally, but manufactured items from Britain, Europe, and China reached America from the outset. After the middle of the eighteenth century, imports flooded the market and sometimes were carried by peddlers to frontier settlements.

Rudimentary advertising and fashion systems, operating largely through word-of-mouth and personal observation, but increasingly enhanced by visual depictions in books, popular prints, and posh oil paintings, transferred new meanings of refinement and social distinction to possessions. The gender of colonial consumption tilted toward men when it came to procuring more expensive items and making credit arrangements. Traditional social norms, legal doctrines, and Christian theology favored American males in many ways, but female influence on consumer decision-making was always present and grew stronger over time. Colonial women maintained their own networks for trading foodstuffs, homespun textiles, and services such as midwifery and sewing. Puritans and Quakers preached against materialism and sometimes helped enact sumptuary legislation mandating consumption according to social class. Yet, as early as the seventeenth century, consumers defied these restrictions. In the 1760s and 1770s, resistance became highly political and consumers and merchants organized up and down the Atlantic seaboard to resist British taxation through boycotts and home production.

4 Consumption in a New Nation, 1790 to 1865

This chapter covers the early federal or national era from 1790 to 1815, continues through the antebellum years of 1815 to 1861, and closes in 1865 with the end of the Civil War. The first section will briefly review the economic and social context of the period's consumption. Then several threads of meaning will be followed, with particular emphasis on the patriotic symbols and budding nationalism embedded in consumer goods. The third section on the threads of gender will describe a gradual shift toward greater female agency in domestic consumption. It will illustrate this process by analyzing some of my favorite genre paintings from the 1850s. The threads of resistance section will revisit long-standing religious and moral interrogations of consumption, but also introduce new consumer entanglements with the increasingly bitter sectional conflict over the institution of slavery. We will see how Northern abolitionists in the 1820s started a "free produce" movement encouraging consumers to buy products made by free labor, while Southerners began advocating "nonintercourse," or the boycott of goods originating with abolitionist hotbeds and supporters in the North.

Material Life and the Market

Between 1790 and 1860, the United States (generally used as a plural or collective noun before the Civil War) more than doubled their size geographically. They added vast new territory west of the Mississippi with the Louisiana Purchase in 1803, acquired Florida by treaty with Spain in 1819, annexed Texas in 1845, gained the Oregon Territory in 1846, took lands ceded by Mexico in 1848, and made the Gadsden Purchase from Mexico (now the southern part of Arizona and New Mexico) in 1853. The population increased from 3,929,214 in 1790 to 31,443,321 in 1860 of which 3,953,761 or 12.6 percent were slaves. In 1860 the five largest cities were New York (813,669), Philadelphia (565,529), Brooklyn (266,661), Baltimore (212,418), and Boston (177,840) (U.S. Bureau of the Census 2016a).

Various sources have compiled estimates of national Gross Domestic Product (GDP) – the measure of goods and services produced and exchanged in the market – from 1790 until the present (see, e.g., Johnston and Williamson 2017). GDP per capita provides an approximation of living standards and, when adjusted by price indexes, allows constant dollar comparisons over time. These metrics have shortcomings. In his very well-researched and provocative economic history, *The Rise and Fall of American Growth,* Robert J. Gordon (2016) contended that until recently GDP figures have on many dimensions understated improvements in living standards, such as the lessening of the drudgery of home consumption, and that price indexes have overstated price increases by missing the welfare benefits conveyed by innovative new products. Moreover, growth in average GDP per capita may be misleading when the top tier of people has benefited far more than those at the bottom, as has been the case in America since the recession of 2008–2009.

With these caveats in mind, the nominal GDP of the United States, which was $189 million ($4351 million in 2009 dollars) in 1790, rose to $9977 million ($113,725 million) in 1865. Similarly, nominal per capita GDP of $48 ($1107 in 2009 dollars) in 1790 increased to $284 ($3232) in 1865 (Johnston and Williamson 2017). Economic growth was not smooth. The Embargo Act of 1807, which banned exports to Britain and France as punishment for their harassment of U.S. shipping, caused economic hardship that lasted until 1814. The financial crisis, known as the Panic of 1837, created a major recession that persisted until about 1844. Subsequently, the advent of steam power, the telegraph, railroads, and domestic manufacturing, augmented by immigrant labor and the demands of the Civil War, spearheaded fairly continuous growth in the Northern states until the end of this period.

Material conditions gradually improved for many, but far from all Americans. The nation continued to be predominantly rural and the majority of its people had relatively limited purchasing opportunities. Consumer goods were usually made and consumed locally. As physical distribution systems evolved with the completion of the Erie Canal in 1825, which connected Lake Erie to the Hudson River, and then with the railroads after 1830, these largely generic products traveled longer distances to market (Porter and Livesay 1971). Americans also imported good quality ceramics and other luxury goods from Britain, France, and China. Newly arrived immigrants and pioneers moving west usually owned relatively few possessions, and African Americans, most of whom were enslaved, had even fewer goods. But some men amassed great fortunes, and urban centers, above all New York City, became sites for the most fashionable consumption of the era (Milbank 2000; Peck 2000).

Although distribution was still spotty and advertising remained unsophisticated, a few bold retailers, above all Alexander Turney Stewart (1803–1876), experimented in the 1840s with more opulent and larger-scale merchandising formats that would eventually evolve into full-fledged department stores (Benson 1986; Blaszczyk 2009; Resseguie 1964). Born in northern Ireland, Stewart relocated to America and opened his first dry goods store in New York City in 1823. Dry goods lines include fabrics, notions, and other items related to sewing. The term "dry goods" dates from the colonial era when small import merchants in coastal cities sold both "wet" rums and "dry" calicoes (Blaszczyk 2009, 74). From 1846 to 1848 Stewart opened and then enlarged his "marble palace" dry goods emporium on Broadway near City Hall (see Figure 4.1) and in 1862

(a)

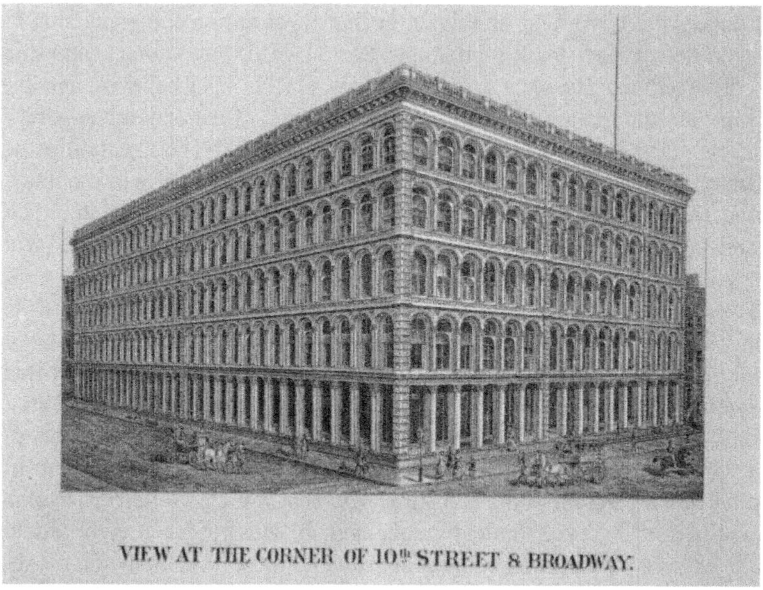

(b)

Figure 4.1 (a) Alexander T. Stewart, *c.*1860, and (b) his "Marble Palace," 1869.

Source: The Miriam and Ira D. Wallach Division of Art, Prints and Photographs: Print Collection, New York Public Library.

opened an even more elaborate location on Broadway at 10th Street that was known as the "cast iron palace." These buildings became major attractions and made traditional shops appear paltry by comparison. Stewart became one of the richest men in America and his marble palace, later known as the Sun Building, still exists with later additions. Other retailers joined the fray, such as Rowland Hussey Macy (1822–1877), who moved to New York City in 1858 and opened his own impressive dry goods store. These businesses could price low because they bought their merchandise directly from manufacturers and sold for cash only, thus avoiding the mark-ups of wholesalers and the costs of credit arrangements. They featured broad product lines, eliminated haggling by selling at fixed prices, and stressed customer satisfaction through money-back guarantees.

In the 1830s, the Penny Press (the name given to the less expensive newspapers aimed at a broad audience in urban centers) distributed news about current consumption and provided a medium for retail advertising. Limited circulation magazines had existed in the colonial era, but in the nineteenth century national news magazines attained substantial popularity. *Harper's Weekly*, launched in 1857, became a top selling publication by the end of the Civil War. Much of its appeal came from its detailed illustrations and striking political cartoons and commentaries. In 1865, the editors wrote: "the circulation of the Weekly has steadily increased from the first. The average circulation for the past year has been largely over 100,000 copies per week. On some occasions over 200,000 copies have been sold of a single issue" (cited in Henning and Witkowski 2013, 423–424). Other numbers suggest a circulation of at least 300,000 during the Civil War and again at that level during the paper's 1871 campaign to defeat New York's infamous Boss Tweed. Pass-along readership undoubtedly extended *Harper's* reach. Presbrey (1929, 454) believed that the *Weekly* was "an important influence for the upbuilding of national advertising." In our article, "The Advertising of E. Remington & Sons: The Creation of an Iconic Brand, 1854–1888," Robert Henning and I showed how gun manufacturers used *Harper's* as the vehicle for targeting the civilian market for their pistols and revolvers before, during, and immediately after the Civil War (Henning and Witkowski 2013).

On Tuesday, November 6, 1860, Americans elected Illinois politician Abraham Lincoln (1809–1865) to the office of President of the United States. His Republican Party platform opposed the expansion of slavery and so within a few months 11 states, unwilling to abide any restrictions on their "peculiar institution," chose to secede from the Union to form the Confederate States of America. On April 12, 1861, the Civil War began with the bombardment of Fort Sumter in Charleston, South Carolina. The War inflicted a horrific human cost on the nation, but, economically speaking, it boosted the already industrializing Northern states. For Southern consumers, the Union blockade gradually choked off all export and import trade, thus ruining their economy, creating shortages of manufactured and luxury goods, and forcing product substitutions, such as homespun cloth for European fabrics and chicory for coffee. By the spring of 1863 food shortages and price inflation had become serious enough to instigate mass protests by working-class women in Richmond (Levine 2013, 200–202).

Proliferation of Meaning

In the last decade of the eighteenth and into the nineteenth century goods and their consumption continued to acquire various associations with gentility and status differentiation. This was especially true for homes and their furnishings. The very affluent constructed grand houses on both urban and rural sites throughout much of the country, while the new homes of ordinary people increasingly incorporated formal halls and parlors for welcoming visitors, sitting rooms for routine family life, and other elements of refinement, such as separate libraries, open staircases, and carpeting. Many people refurbished their existing houses along these lines, while also improving their lots with fenced yards and plantings. Builders and architects published numerous books that spread these ideas of refinement. Books and reading, by oneself or to others, were status markers "invariably associated with that most powerful of nineteenth-century ideas, improvement" (Bushman 1992, 285). Bookcases and even humble bookshelves symbolized sophistication.

Habits of personal cleanliness also attracted new adherents, starting first with the wealthy and then spreading among the middle classes. In the early years of the nineteenth century, an era when indoor plumbing and running water were very rare home amenities, a few people started buying portable, tin-lined bathtubs, and more and more of them owned washstands (commodes), basins, and pitchers. An analysis of probate inventories from Chester County, Pennsylvania by Bushman and Bushman (1988, 1227) showed that for 1800–1809 only one out of 763 estates had a washstand. The numbers grew as follows: 1810–1819 (13 washstands/1049 inventories), 1820–1829 (71/1565), 1830–1839 (145/1294), and 1840–1849 (278/1444). Being easily movable property that heirs may have scooped up before probate audits, the incidence of washstand ownership was probably undercounted. In the early 1800s, soap was not commonly used for washing skin, but rather for doing laundry or cleaning floors. Most was homemade. Eventually, however, manufactured French and American toilet soaps, a branch of the perfume industry, became more common and by the Civil War the idea of using common hand soaps for bathing had taken hold. Cleanliness became an important marker for distinguishing between the genteel and vulgar.

Possessions could acquire many additional meanings. In his computer-assisted analysis of diaries, letters, and other documents from the 1847–1869 Mormon migration to the Utah territory, Russell Belk (1992) identified five major types of symbolism – sacred, material, personal, familial, and communal – that the pioneers associated with their durable goods. Among the sacred meanings was the purifying act of sacrifice where small luxuries would be left behind to facilitate the move West. Material meanings were expressed when migrants retained possessions for survival and sometimes picked up items other Mormons had left behind. Many objects, such as guns and woodworking tools for men and sewing machines for women, embodied the personal meanings of competence, transformation, and domesticity. Familial meanings were articulated through the preservation and transportation of heirlooms and wedding dresses. Caring for others through sharing possessions expressed communal meanings. Belk (1992, 357) found that although men created more of the surviving documents than women,

> the greatest number of deep possession attachments and meanings are found among women.... This has been interpreted here in terms of women's desires for attachment and continuity and men's views of the journey as a challenge and a separation.

We do not know the extent to which these religiously motivated migrants differed from other settlers on the frontier, or from Americans in general, in their identifications with possessions. Based on his findings, along with additional research, Belk speculated that the Mormons and other long-distance movers might have had much in common. He also sagely advised using gender as an analytical category for exploring meaning in possessions.

Americans in the nineteenth century undoubtedly bestowed many additional meanings onto their consumer goods. Of particular interest to later collectors and curators of Americana were the many expressions of national pride via the consumption of patriotic symbols, folk heroes, and images of buildings, places, and people. Symbols of America included the bald eagle, the U.S. flag, the female icons of Columbia and Liberty, and Brother Jonathan and Uncle Sam (Horwitz 1976). The eagle became part of the Great Seal of the United States in 1782 and before long carved, etched, appliqued, painted, and printed versions appeared on building signage, ship mastheads, and innumerable consumer goods and folk art (see Figure 4.2). The American flag – variously nicknamed Old Glory, the Stars and Stripes, the Red, White, and Blue, and the Star-Spangled Banner – originated during the Revolutionary War when, in 1777, the Second Continental Congress specified its design. It too became embedded in folk art, printed on imported pottery, and etched on sword blades and other military accoutrements. Columbia was the heroic female personification of America in the eighteenth century and later of the new United States. Among many cultural references, she was popularized in the 1843 patriotic song "Columbia, Gem of the Ocean." The image of Liberty, who was derived from Libertas, the Roman goddess of freedom, appeared on the first coins produced in 1793 by the U.S. Mint in Philadelphia and eventually grew more popular than Columbia. The Brother Jonathan character, something of a hayseed whose character stood for New Englanders, dates to the seventeenth century. During the Revolution, British soldiers applied the term to the rebels. Uncle Sam, a personification of the U.S. government, came into use during the War of 1812 and, by the end of the Civil War in 1865, had supplanted Brother Jonathan. Both appeared repeatedly in folk art and trade signs.

No folk hero during this period was considered more illustrious than George Washington, the eminent Virginian, devoted husband, slave-owning planter,

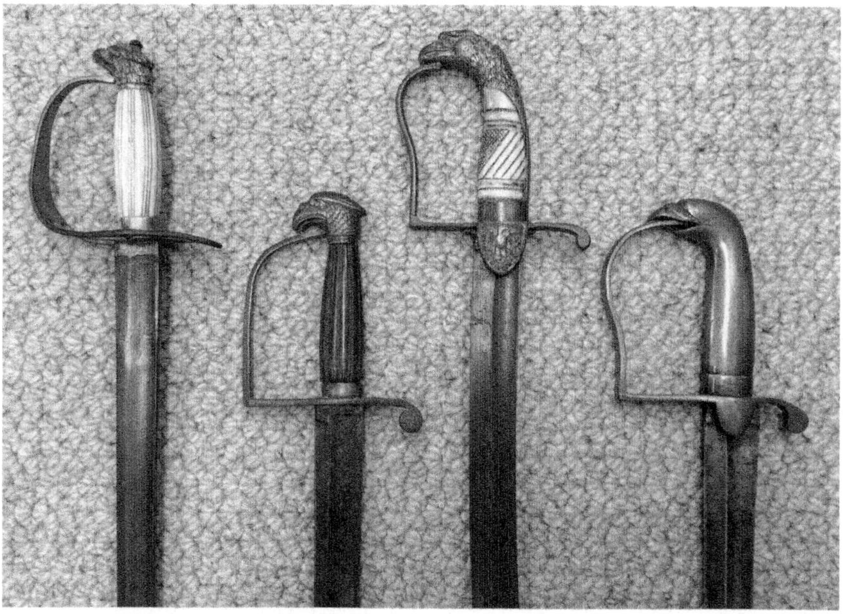

Figure 4.2 Eagle Pommel Swords for the American Market, *c.*1795–1850. From left: England, *c.*1795, England, *c.*1805, A. Berger, Paris, *c.*1825; W.H. Horstmann, Philadelphia, *c.*1850.

Source: Author's collection.

Revolutionary War general, political leader, and first President of the United States. His majestic stature contributed to his political success. As John Adams once joked, Washington was usually the tallest person in the room when the group in session chose its leader (Ellis 2004, 68). After his death on December 14, 1799, Congress commissioned a former officer and close friend, Virginia's Henry "Light Horse Harry" Lee (1756–1818), to write a eulogy. Lee's immortal words accurately captured the national feeling: "First in war, first in peace, and first in the hearts of his countrymen." Washington's image appeared over and over again in and on oil paintings, folk art, popular prints, ceramic and glass objects, and many other items throughout the nineteenth century, and into the future (Horwitz 1976; Hyland 2005; McKearin and Wilson 1978; Snyder 1995; Teitelman, Halfpenny, and Fuchs 2010). English manufacturers supplied the American market with some textiles and a variety of plates and jugs decorated with his portrait, and sold figurines such as the Staffordshire George Washington in Figure 4.3. Images of somewhat lesser folk heroes, such as Benjamin Franklin and Thomas Jefferson, also appeared on export wares. Ironically, these three founding fathers were crucial in stripping the colonies from Britain, but business was business and English manufacturers and merchants had a keen sense of prevailing American tastes they were very willing to exploit.

Figure 4.3 Staffordshire George Washington, *c.*1800–1830.

Source: Metropolitan Museum of Art.

In the second half of the eighteenth century, potters in Staffordshire and Liverpool mastered "transfer printing," a technique for decorating different types of ceramics, especially creamware and pearlware, and sometimes porcelains (Nelson 1980; Teitelman, Halfpenny, and Fuchs 2010). This process entailed transferring a decal, which often was copied from an existing print, from an etched copper plate to the unfired clay at a cost far less than painting by hand when manufacturing in quantity. In the years 1816 to 1824, known as the "Era of Good Feelings" because political disputes had subsided and national pride burgeoned, American consumers selected goods that expressed their patriotic feelings. British manufacturers responded with great quantities of ceramic exports that later collectors have dubbed "Historical Staffordshire." Plates, bowls, teapots, tureens, and other items featured images of American heroes, ships, trains, scenery, historical events, cities, towns, and buildings. John and William Ridgway (in partnership 1814–1830) flattered their American market by naming their building series "Beauties of America." Through the 1820s, dark blue patterns predominated, but then as underglaze techniques advanced, more transfers appeared in red, brown, green, purple, and other shades. After about 1845, demand for these images among American middle-class consumers began to decline. The British Copyright Act of 1842 prohibited copying of registered original designs for three years and thus forced potters to turn to more formulaic scenes (Snyder 1995).

Figure 4.4 shows four examples from my own collection. The blue and white plates depict the Nahant Hotel in Massachusetts *c.*1825 and the Landing of Lafayette at Castle Garden, New York in 1824. Nahant is a small island in Massachusetts Bay connected to the mainland by a narrow spit. Its first hotel, built in 1802, catered to visitors from nearby Boston. Tourism was just beginning in the early nineteenth century and the plate shows people at leisure strolling, fishing, and, this being America, discharging a firearm. The return of the Marquis de Lafayette, who had fought heroically for the Continental Army during the Revolutionary War, became a major event and this plate illustrates a celebratory flotilla of boats and ships in the harbor. The *c.*1835 plate in green features an image of New York City Hall, which finally opened in 1812 after years of construction delays. The pink plate, titled "Columbia Star" and dated October 28, 1840, has a view of a man plowing in front of a log cabin. It commemorates the humble birthplace and presidential campaign of William Henry Harrison who had the misfortune of dying from pneumonia one month after assuming office in 1841. Much Historical Staffordshire on the collectors' market today shows only minor signs of wear. These surviving examples probably represent just a fraction of original production, most pieces having disappeared from the ravages of use and time. However, their good condition suggests that in some households these ceramics may have served more decorative than utilitarian functions. During a period when consumers had limited opportunities to acquire pictorial art, these items for table and cupboard helped serve the aesthetic aspirations of middle-class American consumers.

By the 1830s advances in lithographic printing gave Americans a new and exciting visual medium for expressing and consuming their national identity and

Figure 4.4 Staffordshire Plates for the American Market, *c.*1825–1840. Clockwise from top left: Nahant Hotel by Ralph Stevenson, *c.*1830 (9 inches/22.9 cm); Landing of Lafayette by James and Ralph Clews, *c.*1825 (10 inches/25.4 cm); Columbia Star by John Ridgway *c.*1840 (8¾ inches/22.2 cm); New York City Hall by Job and John Jackson, *c.*1833 (10¼ inches/26 cm).

Source: Author's collection.

contemporary values. Printmakers fed this demand with thousands of different scenes featuring people going places and doing things – the action of everyday life in America. Carefully drawn with crayons on stone and printed in black ink, the lithographs were then hand-colored by teams of young women. Nathaniel Currier opened his eponymous firm in New York City in 1835 and was later, in 1852, joined by James Merritt Ives, who made full partner in 1857. Currier and Ives sold their prints locally from their retail shop near City Hall and engaged pushcart peddlers to take them around town. They also hired sales agents outside New York, sold through dealers in major U.S. cities, had an office in London, and took on additional agents in Europe (Le Beau 2007). Smaller prints (from 8 × 12 inches to 11½ × 15¾ inches) retailed from 15 to 25 cents. Larger sizes distributed through harness shops, general stores, and barrooms sold from $1.50 to $3.00. Twenty-five cents in 1850 was worth $7.20 in 2016 dollars and $3.00 equaled $86.36 (Minneapolis Fed 2017). Images depicted American historical events and presidential portraits, ships and ship disasters, fires and firemen, Civil War battles, bucolic country and farm scenes, railroads and Mississippi steam boats, views of New York and its busy streets, adventures on the western frontier, hunters and fishermen, horse racing and other sports, sentimental portraits of children and animals, and much, much more (Baragwanath 1978; Deák 1976; Peters 1942; Rawls 1979). Figure 4.5 depicts a nostalgic view of George Washington at his Mount Vernon estate and a newsy picture of the clipper ship, Golden Light, which was struck by lightning the evening of February 12, 1853 and set completely on fire while en route to San Francisco from Boston.

Save for a few simple woodcuts, newspaper advertising in this period was largely composed of text in various font sizes (Presbrey 1929). However, some printed promotional media were highly visual (Jay 1987) and they too carried meanings celebrating American life. Joanna Cohen (2014) found that pictorial ephemera in the form of invoices, trade cards, catalogs, and lithographed prints began in the 1840s and 1850s to replace traditional images emphasizing production and trade with depictions of consumers engaged in purchasing activities. Trade cards of the 1810s and 1820s, which in landscape layout would be roughly 4 × 6 inches, typically portrayed assortments of finished products (e.g., glassware) or an image of the manufacturing process (e.g., a printing press). Some trade cards featured allegorical or patriotic figures (Indians, Columbia, the American eagle) and still others sported images of commerce (sailing ships, wharfs, warehouses).

In the mid-1840s styles changed and commercial artists became fascinated with images of storefronts, signage, glass windows, proprietors, clerks, and, above all, male and female customers. Their art depicted consumers strolling down streets, looking at merchandise on display, physically examining goods, and interacting with salespeople indoors. Cohen (2014, 176) termed this new pictorial style a "retailscape":

> The retailscape encompassed both shop interiors and exteriors and lavished particular artistic attention on the goods that a store had to offer. Despite variations in size and detail, all retailscapes depicted shop and shopper in an attractive and elegant configuration. Among the many other kinds of urban scenes that were on sale in the mid-nineteenth century, the retailscape represented a particular vision of the antebellum city's shopping districts and the Americans who frequented those sidewalks and stores.

This new graphic style reflected changes in political economy. Ideas of free trade now championed the consumer interest; urban shopping districts and streets, such as Broadway and environs in New York City, started to emerge, and

(a)

(b)

Figure 4.5 Currier and Ives America, (a) *Washington at Mount Vernon, 1797* (1852) and (b) *Burning of the Clipper Ship "Golden Light"* (1853).

Source: Author's collection.

merchandising through more open and ornate store designs became more visual. Above all, these retailscapes conveyed the meaning of consumption as one of pleasure: "They depicted consumption as leisure, refinement, sociability, visual delight, and sensual gratification. Consumers who saw these images would have found it hard to resist the idea that shopping constituted one of the great enjoyments of urban life" (Cohen 2014, 186). This contrasted with long-standing moral concerns about debt and excessive luxury. Thus, along the lines theorized by McCracken (1986, 1988), advertising art was transferring new meaning to goods and to the act of shopping.

Cohen's thesis is reasonable, but some evidence undercuts her conclusions. In his book on American trade cards, Robert Jay (1987) reproduces a *c.*1785 card from Edward Pole, Fishing Tackle Maker, Philadelphia, and a *c.*1790 engraving from Ebenezer Larkin, Bookseller and Stationer, Boston. The former includes an illustration of an angler (and target customer) and companion landing a fish, while the engraving shows an interior store scene of a clerk attending to two elegantly dressed patrons. Thus, the portrayal of consumers engaged in buying and using goods dates to the eighteenth century in American advertising. Like much historical writing, Cohen's article does not describe the data sources she consulted nor whether the author actually counted frequencies within a sampling frame.

A Pivot toward Female Consumption Agency

As discussed in the previous chapter, men generally dominated family purchasing decisions in the colonial period. This pattern persisted in the new nation. An analysis of the John W. Hunt Daybook in Lexington, Kentucky (July–September 1796), indicated that women made just 15 percent of all visits (Perkins 1991). Some husbands did all the shopping, whereas others allowed their wives and daughters to make purchases. Wives did all or nearly all of the shopping for three families, and John Fowler's wife made shopping trips almost weekly (Perkins 1991). Each family had its own dynamics and consumer historians need to be cautious about overgeneralizing. Still, as with public taverns, men more than women appear to have patronized these early general stores. This activity might have been due to their greater mobility (command of the family horse) as much as to role prescriptions. Given their frequent pregnancies and large families, women in the early republic simply might have found it very difficult to get away from their homes.

As they did in the colonial era, men and women of more affluent means, especially those living in or near cities, continued to shop together. Garrett (1990, 267–268) gives the following examples:

> During the summer of 1800, Elizabeth Bleecker McDonald frequently met her husband at his Manhattan office and they went together "to look at some Chairs," "to look for Carpeting," "to look for Paper," or "to see about a Picture." In rural areas, young couples might have to travel farther afield,

> but they, too, often selected their "outfitting" together. In November 1796 Thankful Phelps married Charles Hitchcock of Northampton, Massachusetts, and several months later they "set out for Springfield to get furniture"; and five months after Mary Guion was wed to Samuel Brown in Westchester, they went to New York City to buy theirs.

Other diaries from the late eighteenth and early nineteenth centuries document women spending hours "going to the shops" alone or with female companions (Ryan 1975). The detail from the *c.*1816 watercolor *The Shop and Warehouse of Duncan Phyfe* shown in Figure 4.6 illustrates women in New York City getting out and about.

Figure 4.6 Detail from *The Shop and Warehouse of Duncan Phyfe*, New York City, *c.*1816. Watercolor on paper.

Source: Metropolitan Museum of Art.

In the middle of the nineteenth century socioeconomic trends gradually began to favor greater female agency. Income could be earned in the market economy. In addition to the traditional patterns of home production and local exchange discussed in the previous chapter (Main 1994; Ulrich 1998), some middle-class single women supported themselves teaching, while their working-class counterparts found jobs in New England textile mills or as servants. By 1850, 15–30 percent of urban American households supported at least one live-in domestic (O'Leary 1996). Married women generated income by taking in boarders or laundry (Bose 1987). Further, as the nineteenth century progressed, more and more American women (primarily native-born whites) became literate, an important skill for reading ads and otherwise negotiating the marketplace (Cott 1977). Women also had a gradually increasing presence in public spaces. Close inspection of nineteenth-century drawings, prints, and photographs of city scenes reveals much evidence of women on the streets alone, in pairs, or with children (see, e.g., images in Black 1973; Deák 1976; Milbank 2000; Peck 2000). An engraving in *Gleason's Pictorial* (December 1854), titled "Interior View of John P. Jewett & Co.'s New and Spacious Bookstore," showed well-dressed, presumably educated women out shopping for books (Burke 2001, fig. 48). Thus, by the 1850s a shift toward greater female agency in shopping, buying, and consumption was entering the cultural milieu. Middle-class women were becoming increasingly active as their households' purchasing agents and mavens of domesticity (Witkowski 1999, 2004). Still more visual evidence has been found in several oil paintings depicting vigorous female characters in domestic genre scenes. These images of women showing initiative as consumers were consistent with their gaining access to public places, forming associations, and collectively demanding their political rights (Witkowski 2004).

Lilly Martin Spencer (1822–1902) both exemplified and documented female agency. Lilly Martin was born in England of French parentage and came with her family to America in 1830, living first in New York City and then in Marietta, Ohio, where her father farmed and taught French at a nearby seminary. Her mother was a woman's rights activist and her father a utopian socialist (Masten 2004). In 1839, she exhibited for the first time and soon caught the attention of Nicholas Longworth, a wealthy attorney, who helped finance her move to Cincinnati in 1841, where she obtained formal art instruction. She married Benjamin Rush Spencer, a tailor, in 1844. The Spencers relocated to New York City in 1848 where Lilly could find a better market for her artistic talents. Working in a largely male profession, Spencer was sometimes treated with condescension. Art critics, for example, rarely failed to describe her as a "female artist." The National Academy of Design only would let her study its drawings in the evenings and, in 1850, made her an honorary, but not a full member (Johns 1991). Nevertheless, she became one of the most popular artists of her day, painting and selling portraits, pictures of children, and numerous scenes of family life, some of which reaching a wider audience through print reproductions. She gave an insider's view of the domestic sphere with herself, husband, children, and servants as models.

Spencer's work had fallen out of favor by the end of her long career, but was "rediscovered" by art historians in the early 1970s (Bolton-Smith and Truettner 1973). For modern audiences, she has become a feminist exemplar since she supported her family financially while giving birth to 13 children, seven of whom survived to maturity. Her husband even became her business agent and studio assistant. Although Spencer's art may appear cloying and socially conservative today, in the mid-nineteenth century her sentimental, sometimes offbeat renderings subverted the traditional authority of the male. Her art "was an act of female instrumentality and agency, of antebellum women taking hold of the most effective weapon at their disposal, culture, and using it on their own behalf" (Lubin 1993, 143).

Influenced by Dutch genre art Spencer had seen in Cincinnati and New York, her works typically dealt with private, family life (O'Leary 1996). A few images are particularly noteworthy sources for the history of female agency in household consumption. *Shake Hands?*, an oil on canvas from 1854, depicts an animated woman standing in a well-stocked kitchen who is interrupted in the process of mixing bread dough or stuffing. With a loopy grin, she extends her hand to the viewer. Now owned by the Ohio Historical Society in Columbus, the image received critical acclaim and established the artist's reputation through exhibitions in several cities and two editions of popular prints (Bolton-Smith and Truettner 1973; Masten 2004). The observer's eye-to-eye perspective and the woman's good-natured, but forthright gesture signaled equality. Since etiquette books of the period advised that only superior persons should initiate a handshake, the cook had been granted the "upper hand" (O'Leary 1996). There is no question that in this kitchen, replete with foodstuffs and a glowing cast-iron stove, a woman ran the operation and a man might feel discomfort if he strays into her workplace. This painting, like much of Spencer's work, took on a subversive quality. It transgressed the time-honored convention that women in genre pictures should be demure – no grins, giggles, or laughs – and be the recipients of male action (Johns 1991; Lubin 1993). Spencer's cook posed for *Shake Hands?* Ironically, in letters to her mother, Spencer indicated she needed servants in the household so she could find time to paint (O'Leary 1996).

The Young Husband: First Marketing (Figure 4.7) was one of a pair of paintings also completed in 1854 that poked fun at newly wedded life. Its mate, *The Young Wife: First Stew*, has been lost, but we know of it because Spencer also executed a preliminary study (now in the collection of the Ohio Historical Society), while an unknown artist created another version in the form of a small, cast bas-relief plaque. The scene showed the frustrations of an inexperienced cook, thus undermining the prevailing concept that women were inherently suited for domestic labor (O'Leary 1996). In *The Young Husband* period viewers saw a well-dressed city man having difficulties managing the produce, eggs, and plucked chickens in his market basket while walking home in rainy weather. Another man laughs derisively at his predicament. His gaze is downcast as the viewer takes in his embarrassment. According to Johns (1991), critics disliked this painting both on aesthetic grounds – the head is oversized and the bodily

Figure 4.7 *The Young Husband, First Marketing*, Lilly Martin Spencer, 1854. Oil on canvas, 29½ × 24¾ inches (74.9 × 62.9 cm).

Source: Metropolitan Museum of Art.

positions awkward – and for reasons of gender politics. Probably intended to amuse female viewers, this depiction of ineptitude and humiliation challenged commonly held notions of men's confident and capable self-image.

Spencer was probably familiar with the popular 1832 commentary *Domestic Manners of the Americans*, by Frances Trollope, who observed Cincinnati gentlemen sallying forth to market six mornings a week. An engraving of an elegant young man returning with a basket over his arm accompanied Trollope's description (Bolton-Smith and Truettner 1973). It is not known if New York men in the 1850s typically shopped for food, but given the "autobiographical" nature of Spencer's paintings – the frequent use of household members as artist models – one suspects that she may actually have witnessed such a scene. Perhaps it was even her good-natured spouse doing the bumbling since another of her paintings, *The Artist and Her Family at a Fourth of July Picnic* (*c.* 1864), shows him breaking a wooden swing and falling on his rump. Neither *The Young Husband* nor its companion painting, *The Young Wife*, found a buyer during their exhibition at the National Academy of Design.

In 1856 *Kiss Me and You'll Kiss the 'Lasses* (Figure 4.8) was commissioned and marketed by the Cosmopolitan Art Association, an organization explicitly devoted to women's taste. The composition directed the viewer's gaze toward the young woman's bare arms and figure. Spencer depicted her as shapelier, better dressed, and more elaborately coiffed than the subject in *Shake Hands?*, and ladling molasses was a more refined activity than stuffing poultry. She represented the new affluence of the people who bought Spencer's paintings (Masten 2004). Yet, both women were friendly and feminine, outgoing and attractive, and through their bearing and gestures indicated that they were not to be trifled with. Spencer's device of painting her females to look out directly toward the viewer signaled social and gender equality with the audience, male and female, and through the character's interpellation or hailing, an invitation to accept this cultural value.

The scene in *Kiss Me* gushed with domestic abundance. Baskets and bowls overflowed with fruits and vegetables, while fine glass and pottery pitchers flank the woman. The 'Lasses in the title perhaps referred to the molasses which she threatens to fling at the presumably male viewer who might be tempted to steal a kiss. "Lasses" also could have signified young women in general or a common expression of the time "lips as sweet as 'lasses." Here Spencer transformed the woman into an object of desire associated with other objects of abundance and, looking through the open doorway to the well-appointed parlor, with Victorian ideals of domesticity. Now it was the woman who was to be consumed. Ironically, the Spencer family suffered financial setbacks the year this pert image was created. Few paintings sold, the maid had to be let go, and the children received no Christmas presents. The Panic of 1857 made matters worse, forcing the Spencers to relocate to less expensive Newark, New Jersey the following year (O'Leary 1996).

A New York contemporary of Lilly Martin Spencer, Francis W. Edmonds (1806–1863), also explored female agency through his painting. Born in Hudson, New York, the seventh child of a military officer father and a Quaker mother, Edmonds was a banker by profession. He began his career in 1823 as an "under-clerk" at Tradesman's Bank in New York City. Rising through a series of positions at other banks, he eventually became quite prominent in New York financial circles. Among his lasting contributions, Edmonds played an important role in the founding of the New York Clearing House in 1853. Following a

Figure 4.8 *Kiss Me and You'll Kiss the 'Lasses*, Lilly Martin Spencer, 1856. Oil on canvas, 29¹⁵⁄₁₆ × 24¹⁵⁄₁₆ inches (76 × 63.3 cm).

Source: Brooklyn Museum of Art.

controversy in 1855 regarding his role in an alleged misappropriation of bank funds, he voluntarily resigned his positions in the world of finance and moved permanently to his country house in Bronxville, New York. He also formed a new company with two partners to engrave bank notes.

The engraving business was an apt choice, for Edmonds was also a very talented painter who showed artistic promise as a boy, but had no formal training until age 20 when he began night classes at the newly established National Academy of Design (Witkowski 2004). Edmonds was greatly influenced by early Dutch genre scenes from the 1600s. He first saw this art reproduced in books and later in person during an extended trip to Europe in 1841 following his first wife's death and his own nervous breakdown. Taking inspiration from the Dutch masters, his paintings probed human relationships within a broader social context (Clark 1988). Edmonds' lifetime artistic output was relatively small, but highly regarded, and his contemporaries commented very favorably on his accomplishments in the disparate fields of art and finance (Clark 1988; Mann 1977). He befriended other important artists and was quite active in cultural and art organizations including the National Academy of Design, the Sketch Club, the Apollo Association, and the American Art-Union.

Edmonds touched upon the theme of female consumers in several of his works, one of which will be discussed in the next section, but for now let us focus on *Bargaining (The Christmas Turkey)*, an oil on canvas painted in 1858 (Figure 4.9). This picture illustrated a wary older woman peering over her spectacles to closely examine a fowl held by a somewhat younger seller. The protagonists are indoors, sitting down, and similarly dressed. Since genre artists sometimes made older women the butt of jokes (Hills 1974), the portrayal of a knowing, strong woman was especially commendable. Unlike the playful scenes

Figure 4.9 Bargaining (The Christmas Turkey), Francis W. Edmonds, 1858. Oil on canvas, 16½ × 23⅜ inches (41.9 × 59.4 cm).

Source: Collection of the New York Historical Society.

Lilly Martin Spencer created, Edmond's image was more subdued and serious. The overall impression created by this fine painting is one of visual intensity, and of equality.

> The concentration of the figures on their given tasks – the woman to assess the bird and the salesman to assess the woman's reaction – generates dramatic tension and signifies the expertise that each brings to their assignments. One generation is played off against the other, and while neither seems to have an advantage, Edmonds eloquently states his sympathetic reading of the elderly.
>
> (Clark 1988, 129)

Note how the woman clutched her purse, indicating both her interest in the transaction and the fact that she had ready cash. Perhaps the shortages of specie that had plagued early America were ending by 1858.

The Morality of Consumption

Several forms of rhetoric challenged expanding consumerism in the nineteenth century. On the religious front of the 1820s and 1830s, Lyman Beecher (1775–1863) advocated a conservative, moralistic, even Puritan "Christian simplicity." Reverend Beecher, who gained fame from his sermons castigating dueling and alcoholic intemperance, worried about materialism undermining the established social order (Shi 1985). He and other ministers repeated the old accusation that "the parade of luxury" undermined the "more durable riches than those this world can offer" (Stearns 2001, 52). This was the period of the Second Great Awakening, a Protestant religious revival movement that lasted from about 1790 to 1840. Beecher was a leader of the Sabbatarians who advocated boycotting businesses open on Sunday and thus, in their eyes, in violation of God's Fourth Commandment. He founded its most important organization, the General Union for Promoting the Observance of the Christian Sabbath. In 1826, a group of Presbyterians urged ministers and church members to patronize livery establishments, steamboats, canal boats, and other public conveyances that did not violate the Sabbath. In Rochester, New York, wealthy evangelicals established just such a freight company naming it the Pioneer Line (Glickman 2009).

During the middle 1800s, criticism of consumerism began shifting from a moralistic disapproval of the upper classes buying luxuries to a concern about working-class consumers unable to restrain themselves from purchasing the increasingly alluring array of goods presented in stores (Harris 1981). Mid-century genre artists, who depicted the nation's ordinary people and the vicissitudes of their everyday lives, also began commenting on the morality of buying and selling (Witkowski 1996). Even the farmyard could be a place for serious marketing exchange, as portrayed in a very striking oil on canvas painted by William Sidney Mount (1807–1868) in 1835. *Farmers Bargaining* (Mount's title) or *Bargaining for a Horse* (the title of an 1839 engraving after this work) showed two farmers, one older and one younger, both standing while whittling away as they cautiously negotiate the sale of a sleek saddle horse. They avoided looking each other in the eye and smile as though to suggest that this deal is not a serious matter. Far in the background the farmer's wife stood by the house, apparently straining to follow the transaction. This detail suggested that the sale was indeed of considerable importance to the family, but that horse-trading in the barnyard was entirely the husband's domain. Set on Mount's own farm in Stony Brook on Long Island, this popular image received critical acclaim (Johns 1991) and was twice published as an engraving (Stebbins, Troyen, and Fairbrother 1983). Printmaking enabled artists to reach a wider audience and, in so doing, to cultivate a democratic demand for art.

Francis W. Edmonds explored the morality of sellers and consumers in several of his paintings, most notably in *The Image Pedlar* (*c.*1844), where an itinerant peddler of plaster casts with wife and babies in tow engages an entire family with his wares, in *The Speculator* (1852), where a nattily-dressed, but possibly shady character tries to sell a skeptical rural couple a lot near a new railroad line, and in the above mentioned *Bargaining: The Christmas Turkey* (1858) where the protagonists are evenly matched (Clark 1988; Witkowski 1996). However, his painting most relevant to the morality of creeping consumerism was *The New Bonnet* (Figure 4.10), completed in 1858, and donated to a benefit auction for the widow and children of fellow painter, William Ranney. One of Edmonds' most visually striking works, it attracted curiously little attention when first exhibited, although later it received favorable reviews in two journals (Clark 1988).

The New Bonnet told a story of consumption with sharply defined characters on a carefully arranged stage. A young woman keenly admires her just-delivered acquisition, while her parents, having been presented the bill of sale, give a horrified reaction to their daughter's "extravagance." Edmonds played down the broad humor in the situation in favor of carefully weighing the morality of luxury. He contrasted the relatively simple dwelling and plain dress of the older couple with their daughter's more stylish, albeit still somewhat provincial, appearance. The juxtaposition of the forlorn little delivery girl and the expensive new garment perhaps raised the issue of consumption inequality. Nevertheless, the bonnet was the title and focal point of the picture and the young woman, enthralled by her new hat, was oblivious to the activities around her. This painting echoed timeworn concerns about unbridled female purchasing, but clearly showed some admiration for the object in hand with its pretty blue ribbons and lacy blue and white trim. Foreign visitors commented upon the stylish dress of New Yorkers, both male and female, and headwear like bonnets were highly visible garments. In 1850, novelist Charles Dickens described what he saw during a visit to New York:

> Heaven save the ladies, how they dress! We have seen more colours in these ten minutes, than we should have seen elsewhere, in as many days. What various parasols! What rainbow silks and satins! What pinking of thin

Figure 4.10 *The New Bonnet*, Francis W. Edmonds, 1858. Oil on canvas, 25 × 30⅛ inches (63.5 × 76.5 cm).

Source: Metropolitan Museum of Art.

> stockings, and pinching of thin shoes, and fluttering of ribbons and silk tassels, and display of rich cloaks with gaudy hoods and linings!
>
> (Cited in Milbank 2000, 244)

In *The New Bonnet*, Edmonds delicately positioned frugality with things as a moral opposite to consumerism. Yet, the art does not appear judgmental and seems to have asked viewers to draw their own conclusions about the morality of consumption.

Edmond's powerful visual image placed consumerism within the confines of private, bourgeois domesticity (Slater 1997; Witkowski 2004). This resonated with a different resistance discourse of the period: the stress on frugal domesticity. For example, Andrew Jackson Downing (1842/1981, 1850/1968), in his essays, books, and architecture, advocated the building of utilitarian cottages and farmhouses for the people and unostentatious, moderate homes for country gentlemen. Magazines, such as *Godey's Lady's Book* (founded in 1837), instructed middle-class women on how to tastefully furnish and manage their houses

(Shi 1985). Lydia Marie Child's popular manual for homemakers, *The American Frugal Housewife*, first published in 1828, and with 12 editions by 1833, was "dedicated to those who are not ashamed of economy" (Child 1833). Along with her advice for frugally performing the various domestic arts, Mrs. Child railed against new forms of consumerism and popular entertainment:

> There is one kind of extravagance rapidly increasing in this country, which, in its effects on our purses and our habits, is one of the worst kinds of extravagance; I mean the rage for traveling, and for public amusements. The good old home habits of our ancestors are breaking up – it will be well if our virtue and our freedom do not follow them! … A republic without industry, economy, and integrity, is Samson shorn of his locks. A luxurious and idle republic! Look at the phrase! – The words were never made to be married together; every body sees that it would be death to one of them.
>
> (Child 1833, 99)

Catharine E. Beecher (1800–1878), an educator and prominent daughter of preacher Lyman Beecher, echoed some of these sentiments in her books, *A Treatise on Domestic Economy* (1841) and *The Domestic Receipt Book* (1846). She was the sister of the even more famous Harriet Beecher Stowe (1811–1896), who authored the abolitionist clarion call, *Uncle Tom's Cabin* (1852), and sold 300,000 copies within a year after publication (Goodwin 2005, 161).

In their lectures and writings, philosophers Ralph Waldo Emerson and Henry David Thoreau endorsed consumer restraint in the form of a more spontaneous, liberating, and romantic "transcendental simplicity" (Shi 1985). Emerson, who himself lived comfortably and genteelly, saw frugality as a means to a higher end: "Economy is a high, humane office, a sacrament, when its aim is grand; when it is the prudence of simple tastes, when it is practiced for freedom, or love, or devotion" (cited in Shi 1985, 133). Thoreau's sojourn at Walden Pond in 1845–1847 taught him to value self-sufficiency in raising food, making clothes, and building shelter and furniture. High thinking was preferable to high living:

> Most of the luxuries, and many of the so called comforts of life, are not only not indispensable, but positive hindrances to the elevation of mankind. With respect to luxuries and comforts, the wisest have ever lived a more simple and meager life than the poor.
>
> (Thoreau 1971, 14)

Thoreau particularly disliked the enervating and corrupting influence of salesmanship and the excessive consumption it encouraged (Friedman 2004; Horowitz 1985). Yet, the audience for this supposedly uplifting philosophy may have been limited. Thoreau was not a very popular public lecturer and it took him eight years to sell the 2000 copies of *Walden* that were printed in 1854.

Starting in the 1820s, anti-consumption moralists increasingly questioned a widespread American pastime: imbibing alcohol. Colonial society had condoned drinking, in moderation, of beer, hard cider, wine, and distilled spirits as long as the tippler was white and not an Indian or African American. Annual consumption of spirits, mostly rum, reached 3.7 gallons per capita in 1770. In the period between 1790 and 1830, however, heavy drinking became quite commonplace and consumption, now mostly whiskey, increased to five gallons per capita in 1830. That year the total annual intake of pure alcohol (ethanol) from all sources peaked at four gallons per capita (Rorabaugh 1979). The young nation clearly had developed a drinking problem. In response to such intemperance, a new movement started to organize and "by 1831 the American Temperance Society had 170 local societies with a reported membership of 170,000" (Gusfield 1963, 48). Not yet coercive in its approach, the Temperance movement advocated abstinence as a pathway toward self-improvement and becoming a better husband, worker, credit risk, and citizen as Nathaniel Currier vividly illustrated in a print from 1848 (Figure 4.11). Temperance had a strong nativist component – it was spearheaded by a northeastern Federalist class in social decline – and was opposed by Irish and German immigrants and their communities (Gusfield 1963). This and parallel anti-consumption threads will be followed further in subsequent chapters.

Figure 4.11 *The Fruits of Temperance*, 1848. Lithograph by Nathaniel Currier published by J. B. Allen, New York. The caption reads: "Behold the son of Temperance, with buoyant heart and step, returning to his home, the partner of his bosom looks up and smiles his welcome, his children fly to meet him, their little arms embrace him, and with lip and heart they bless him."

Source: Library of Congress, Prints & Photographs Division, Washington, D.C.

As was true before the Revolutionary War, some nineteenth-century resistance to consumption in America went beyond abstention and frugality. Often overlooked by consumption historians was an expression of opposition to slavery known as the "free produce" movement led by Quakers and free black abolitionists (Glickman 2004, 2009). Inspired by the anti-slavery sugar boycotts in 1790s' Britain, proponents wanted to undermine the economics of slavery by encouraging consumers to avoid slave-produced merchandise and instead to purchase goods made by "free labor." So that consumers could have an alternative to slave-produced merchandise, supporters began to open free produce stores starting with one in Baltimore in 1826. Eventually, activists including a number of women as proprietors established some 50 such stores, many of which were in Philadelphia, but also spread across eight other states. They carried mostly clothing and dry goods, but also shoes, soaps, ice cream, and candy. Most were short-lived. Finding "free labor" cotton and sugar was a challenge and the quality of many items failed to meet consumer expectations. The last one closed in 1867. This was two years after the Thirteenth Amendment had abolished slavery.

Glickman (2004, 2009) does not report any evidence pertaining to individual or aggregate store sales, but indicates the free produce effort did not achieve much success in practice. However, the movement made an ideological contribution to the extent it firmly implanted the notion of consumer sovereignty. Unlike the colonial nonimportation movement, which focused more on curtailing merchant activities, now consumer demand was seen as the lynchpin. When consumers purchased slave goods, they directly supported the slave system. In no uncertain terms, an undated pamphlet declaimed:

> The northern merchant who purchases the cotton, sugar and rice of the southern planter … the auctioneer who cries his human wares in the market, and sells those helpless victims of cupidity … yea, even the heartless, murderous slave-trader, are each and all of them, only so many AGENTS, employed by and for the CONSUMER in extracting and transferring the products of the unrequited toil, of the poor down trodden suffering slave.
>
> (Cited in Glickman 2004, 895)

If consumers made ethical decisions, markets could be harnessed for moral purposes. The point was not nonconsumption for its own sake, but rather more of virtuous "buycott" of ethical products (Friedman 1999). Activists feared that a strident message of self-denial would not be very popular. Yet, celebrating the power of consumers did not sit well with all abolitionists, many of whom questioned the market, deemed free produce impractical and inconvenient, and leaned more toward abstention and denigration of fashion (Glickman 2004, 2009).

Some early proponents of free produce eventually became disenchanted with the program. William Lloyd Garrison, the famous abolitionist editor of *The Liberator* newspaper, "among others, criticized the movement he had once supported for self-righteous holier-than-thou posturing" (Glickman 2009, 73). These critics saw the institution of slavery as so pervasive in American life, the crops slavery produced so commonly traded, and the wealth slavery created so often spent on Northern manufactured goods, that opting out through consumption was simply not possible and, in fact, distracted participants from the escalating political fight. Analogous to the modern fair trade movement, which asks consumers to pay higher prices for certain goods in order to benefit their developing country producers beyond what they receive from normal trade, not every shopper may have liked the product assortment and quality in free produce stores. Thus, abolitionists developed a different strategy. Starting in 1834, antislavery fairs became popular venues for raising funds for abolitionist organizations in New England and Pennsylvania. Usually held in mid to late December, they championed consumerism and originated the customs of Christmas trees and holiday shopping in America. The fairs included free produce items, as well as some of the first ethically labeled goods, but were less concerned about the moral provenance of what was on offer.

Ironically, another antebellum outbreak of consumer resistance served the diametrically opposed cause. In a deliberate replay of the colonial nonimportation movement, Southern white firebrands advocated nonintercourse with Northern producers who they saw as imposing a form of economic colonialism on the South. The Northern states, especially in the northeast, played the role of England in their minds, while the Southern states were the downtrodden colonial subalterns. As a further parallel, they castigated the North as overly consumerist, while also encouraging Southern homespun manufacturing. This point required some rather convoluted reasoning for its justification since wealthy Southern slave owners spent lavishly on Northern and European merchandise in pursuit of their enviable consumer lifestyles. The third parallel with the colonial nonimportation entailed advocacy for generating and patronizing more Southern manufactures including homespun goods. The nonintercourse movement aimed to protect the Southern way of life, which meant supporting the institution of slavery by lashing out at Northern abolitionist groups (Glickman 2009).

The nonintercourse movement first emerged about the time of the protectionist national Tariffs of 1828, known as the Tariff of Abominations, which favored northern and western agricultural interests, but raised the cost of living in the South. Nonintercourse gained further momentum with the sectional tensions of the 1850s and then peaked on the politically heated eve of the Civil War. Not surprisingly, South Carolina was a movement hotbed. No quantitative data appear to have surfaced as yet to assess the economic impact of this movement. It appears to have been mostly rhetorical, and played out in newspapers, than an implemented program. Advocates did not have a consistent action plan and proposed, variously, boycotts against firms owned by abolitionists, the city of Boston, the states of Massachusetts and Vermont, and Yankee peddlers based in the South. Similarly, no consensus existed about the extensive black list of goods.

> Among those they enumerated were farm animals, booksellers (and the books they sold; they often singled out *Uncle Tom's Cabin* as a book that

> should not be bought or sold in the South), candles, food ... nutmeg, popular culture and theater, preachers, medical schools, printers, schoolteachers, universities, resorts, and vehicles.
>
> (Glickman 2009, 103–104)

Not unlike the skeptical critics of the free produce movement, some Southerners found the whole idea of nonintercourse to be nonsensical within a complex national economic system. In any event, nonintercourse became a mounting reality during the Civil War as the Union blockade of Southern ports became tighter and tighter. Even then some trade between the warring union and confederate states continued on the side.

These nineteenth-century examples of consumer resistance in thought and in practice have left a legacy for later movements. The religiously based opposition to consumerism would be replayed in blue laws and other controls that continued to exist into the twenty-first century. The free produce movement and anti-slavery fairs made use of available advertising media and sometimes benefited from celebrity endorsers. Outbreaks of internal dissension among movement theorists seem to have been par for the course. Above all, the concept of ethical consumption – where long supply chains should be monitored and the welfare of distant producers should be of real concern when purchasing – has remained a vital issue.

Summary

Over the 75-year period from 1790 to 1865 the American economy expanded greatly due to population increases, territorial expansion and land development, and nascent industrialization. Living standards improved slowly for many, but not all Americans, and sometimes progress was interrupted by political events (e.g., Embargo Act of 1807, War of 1812) and financial implosions (e.g., the Panic of 1837). Most people still lived in small towns and rural areas where change came more slowly than it did in the cities. American consumer lifestyles in 1865 probably had much more in common with those of 1790 than they would with those in 1940. Marketing institutions, particularly dry-goods stores and printed media, especially newspapers, also evolved with help from new infrastructure in the form of canals, telegraph lines, and the railroads.

Threads of meaning from the eighteenth century pertaining to refinement and self-improvement continued to influence consumption choices. These were accompanied, as shown by evidence from the Mormon migration, by bundles of sacred, material, personal, familial, and communal meanings given to possessions. Especially noteworthy, Americans eagerly consumed national identity in the form of patriotic symbols, heroic figures, and scenes of progress embedded in signage and folk art, popular prints, and imported ceramics, among other goods. By midcentury the gendering of consumption showed an increasingly female inflection that would continue into the twentieth century. With regards to resistance, protestant ministers, transcendentalists, temperance advocates, and perceptive genre painters questioned the morality of consumption and preached frugality and abstinence. Resistance also became embroiled in both sides of the slavery issue, with abolitionists promoting free produce stores and anti-slavery fairs and Southern defenders of their "peculiar institution" advocating nonintercourse with Northern opponents.

5 The Gilded Age, 1865 to 1900

Mark Twain – the pen name of Samuel Langhorne Clemens (1835–1910) – was still known mostly for his humorous travel books when, in 1873, he and his Hartford, Connecticut neighbor, the writer and editor Charles Dudley Warner (1829–1900), co-authored a novel they dubbed *The Gilded Age: A Tale of Today*. Their social satire of greed, land speculation, and corruption within government and among the newly rich gave the post-Civil War decades their lasting soubriquet – the Gilded Age. Like Shakespeare's King John, who is advised "To gild refined gold, to paint the lily,/ … Is wasteful and ridiculous excess," the extravagance of the very wealthy and powerful was a signal issue of the day (Cashman 1993). Indeed, extreme income inequality did characterize this period. Industrialists and financiers accumulated unprecedented wealth through deftly exploiting the prevailing system of laissez-faire capitalism. This did not go unnoticed among their numerous and often hostile critics who in 1882 coined the term "robber barons," another soubriquet that would become part of the American lexicon (Tipple 1959). The expanding working classes, augmented by waves of new immigrants, found jobs in the factories and on the railroads, but lived under harsh conditions, toiled long hours at low pay, and suffered from very high rates of industrial accidents (Gordon 2016). Workers joined labor unions and, among other actions, organized massive railway strikes in 1877, 1886, and 1894 that inevitably resulted in deaths and violence.

This chapter begins with an overview of the material and market context of Gilded Age consumption. In addition to reviewing key macro demographic and economic highlights, this section will briefly trace institutional developments in consumer marketing – department stores, five-and-ten cent stores, direct mail catalogs and distribution, chromolithographic printing, national magazines, and modern packaging – that affected many aspects of consumption. The next section on meaning follows the long-standing cultural threads of refinement and patriotism expressed through consumption, and then introduces the important topic of consumer brands and branding. The gender section first reviews female agency through new shopping environments (e.g., the department store) and new products (e.g., the bicycle), and then strings a new thread – men's consumption and how it may have been shaped in part as compensation to real and perceived threats to male social status and masculinity. The threads of resistance will recount some of the critiques of leisure class excess and will introduce and explicate an important new term: to boycott. Conceptual distinctions pertaining to boycotting will be delineated along with a recap of some boycott actions taken in the 1880s and 1890s.

Material Life and the Market

The 1860 census population of 31,443,321 more than doubled to 76,212,168 by 1900 (U.S. Bureau of the Census 2016a). America acquired the vast Alaska territory from Russia in 1867 for a mere $7.2 million or $123.4 million in 2016 dollars (Minneapolis Fed 2017) and, during and after the ethnic cleansing of the Indians, proceeded to rapidly settle the prairie states and points farther West. In an 1893 paper, a young Wisconsin historian named Frederick Jackson Turner (1861–1932) argued from data collected by the 1890 Census that the American "frontier" had finally closed. Turner contended that the ability to acquire land on the frontier had shaped American character, its individualism and egalitarianism, and hence its democracy for nearly three centuries. This thesis became highly influential and sometimes controversial among historians (Potter 1954). Perhaps given public nostalgia for adventurous times now passed along with a craving for heroic myths to resolve growing cultural tensions, the thesis resonated within the larger popular culture (Murdoch 2001; Slotkin 1992).

The nominal 1865 GDP of $9977 million ($113,725 million in 2009 dollars) jumped to $20,766 million ($456,861 million) in 1900. Interestingly, GDP per capita declined in nominal terms from $284 to $272, but because of price deflation it more than doubled when standardized to 2009 dollars, from $2815 to $6004 (Johnston and Williamson 2017). The destruction of the once wealthy Southern economy (Levine 2013) was a relatively insignificant factor in the overall national economy. However, severe, multi-year economic recessions began in 1873 and again in 1893. Contemporaries aptly named these economic shocks "panics" since they were triggered, among other reasons, by speculative railroad investments and subsequent bank failures.

In the post-Civil War decades, urbanization, industrialization, and technological and managerial innovations greatly transformed the country (Chandler 1977; Gordon 2016; Porter and Livesay 1971; Walker 1971). In much of the U.S. living standards rose as incomes grew and the world of goods expanded through product innovation, mass production, and new forms of distribution such as department stores and direct mail marketing (Boorstin 1973; Gordon 2016; Leach 1984). Some areas of the defeated South languished and grinding poverty faced many of the new arrivals from Europe, Asia, and Latin America who took hard jobs in coal mines, steel mills, and garment factories. Freed African Americans fared the worst, both in employment and in their consumption opportunities. The Thirteenth Amendment to the U.S. Constitution abolished slavery in 1865, while the Fourteenth (1866) and Fifteenth (1869) Amendments granted blacks citizenship and the right to vote. During Reconstruction, the era from 1863 to 1877 when federal troops occupied the former Confederate states,

African Americans made some initial headway toward full and free participation in American life and its consumer culture. By 1900, however, these gains had largely evaporated and blacks were being brutally subjugated under rampant efforts in the region to institutionalize white supremacy (Hale 1998). New state laws in the South implemented voting requirements that excluded African Americans and, in 1896, the Supreme Court in *Plessy* v. *Ferguson* endorsed the constitutionality of "separate but equal" facilities. These Jim Crow laws limited black Americans' access to consumption settings throughout much of the twentieth century, and their legacy has continued into the twenty-first.

Large-scale dry goods stores, such as A.T. Stewart's emporiums in New York, were doing business before the Civil War, but the true department store format really started hitting its stride during the Gilded Age. The term "department store" entered the American lexicon in 1887 (Blaszczyk 2009, 76) and referred to enterprises carrying far more diversified product lines than did dry goods stores. The largest was in Philadelphia, the nation's second largest city until Chicago surpassed it in 1890. John Wanamaker (1838–1922) purchased an abandoned Pennsylvania Railroad station in 1876 and converted it into his eponymous establishment in time for the American Centennial Exposition (see Figure 5.1). He refurbished the interior and added new lines (1877), pioneered an in-store restaurant (1876), the January white sale (1878), electrical lighting (1878), and electric elevators (1889). A devout Christian, Wanamaker refused to advertise on Sundays, but did invent the price tag so customers equal before God would also be equal before price (PBS Online 2004). Fixed- and one-price policies homogenized and democratized the American marketplace (Boorstin 1973).

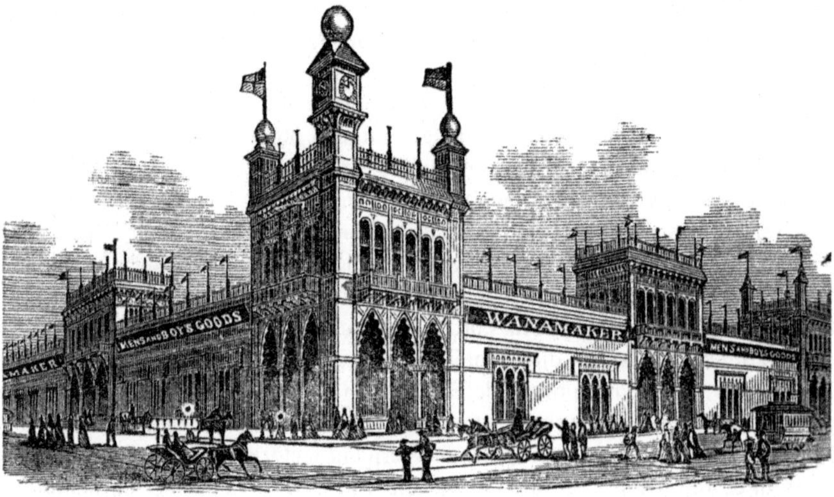

Figure 5.1 John Wanamaker's Clothing House on Market St. Philadelphia, 1876. This building was originally a railroad station.

Source: From James D. McCabe (1876, 288) *The Illustrated History of the Centennial Exposition.*

Wanamaker positioned his store as luxury retailing and, in 1880, established a Paris Bureau so his buyers could better keep up with European fashion trends whose cachet would then be shared with American consumers (Blaszczyk 2009, 78). Department stores thus became arbiters of taste and middle-class standing and offered buyers hope of upward social mobility through the right possessions (Abelson 1989, 51–53).

In Chicago, Potter Palmer (1826–1902) opened a dry goods store in 1852, renamed Field, Palmer, Leiter & Company in 1865, and officially becoming Marshall Field & Company in 1881. The wholesale division, which sold in bulk to smaller merchants throughout the central and western states, provided most revenue, but the retail division was growing rapidly. Marshall Field (1834–1906) took a customer orientation with the assistance of a young Harry Gordon Selfridge (1858–1947) who happened to be in his employ. Selfridge started as a stock boy and during his 25 years at Field's blossomed into a retail-merchandising prodigy who helped transform the business into a prototype modern department store where "the customer is always right." Selfridge amassed a fortune, married into a prominent Chicago family, and eventually decamped for London to found his own famously eponymous emporium in 1909. More will be said about department stores in the section on gender.

American towns and cities grew impressively during the late 1800s, accommodating many working-class immigrants and other consumers of modest means. A new retail institution, the five-and-ten cent store, served this market with a wide variety of humble items priced at a dime or less. Five-and-tens adopted the innovations of dry goods and department stores – buying factory direct, encouraging self-service, selling for cash, and turning over stock several times a year – and borrowed the chain store concept from the Great Atlantic & Pacific Tea Company, or A&P for short. The most successful entrepreneur in the five-and-ten category, Frank Winfield Woolworth (1852–1919), opened his first dime store in Lancaster, Pennsylvania in 1879 and his chain grew to 59 stores by 1900 including a few in the really big cities (Blaszczyk 2009, 80). Through organic growth and mergers, Woolworth's numbered over 600 branches in 1913, expanding to 1581 in 1927 (Leach 1994, 274). Woolworth made so much money that he essentially paid cash for his namesake skyscraper at 233 Broadway in New York City, the world's tallest building from its completion in 1913 until the Chrysler Building took the honor in 1930.

In the mid-1800s some retailers and manufacturers used mail order to sell to small merchants (Blaszczyk 2009, 84–85), but marketing to consumers this way did not start achieving popularity until the 1870s and 1880s when Aaron Montgomery Ward (1844–1913) and Richard Warren Sears (1863–1914) established their famous companies in Chicago, the nation's railway hub. Their catalogs brought an enormous assortment of goods to rural and small town Americans who did not have easy access to city department and specialty stores, but who could accept packages, especially after the advent, in 1896, of postal service Rural Free Delivery (RFD). Before RFD, remote farm families had to travel to distant post offices for their mail or pay private carriers for home delivery. Ward sent out his first, single page price sheet in 1872. It grew to a 240-page catalog in 1884 (Boorstin 1973) and over 630 pages in 1895 (Montgomery Ward 1895). Sears started selling watches to station agents in 1886, moved to Chicago in 1887, and, in 1893 formed Sears, Roebuck and Company with his first employee, Alvah Curtis Roebuck (1864–1948). The Sears catalogs exceeded 500 pages by 1894 and had a circulation of 318,000 in 1897 and more than one million by 1904 (Boorstin 1973). The 1897 catalog had 708 pages of product illustrations and dense descriptive text (Sears Roebuck and Company 1897). Due in part to RFD, Sears' sales skyrocketed from $746,000 in 1895 to $10 million in 1900 to $41 million in 1908 (Blaszczyk 2009, 87). The catalog companies competed fiercely with local stores and doomed the itinerant peddlers who had supplied isolated families since colonial times (see Figure 5.2).

Chromolithography, which enabled efficient and inexpensive printing in color, reached an advanced state of development during the last quarter of the nineteenth century. It was applied to trade and business cards, cigar and tobacco box labels, city directory advertisements, promotional calendars, sheet music covers, and large illustrated posters (Last 2005). As mentioned in the previous chapter, trade cards had been in use since the eighteenth century, but after the Civil War they reached their full maturity as an advertising medium. By 1880 most trade cards were printed on both sides (Jay 1987). One side featured the visual imagery while the reverse consisted of text in black and white explaining

Figure 5.2 The Peddler's Wagon, Harper's Weekly, June 20, 1868. Wood engraving drawn by Charles Green Bush (1842–1909).

Source: Library of Congress, Prints & Photographs Division, Washington, D.C.

the product and often imprinted with the dealer's name. Drummers, salesmen who represented wholesalers, distributed trade cards to local merchants who, in turn, gave them to their customers. Trade cards were also sent to consumers via mail (Last 2005). Collecting trade cards became common among aficionados who would paste them into ornate albums. The medium began to decline in the 1890s because of increasing visual competition from newspapers and national magazines. Manufacturers in important new industries, such as bicycles, typewriters, and electrical goods, used the print media exclusively (Jay 1987). The introduction of simple and even less expensive halftone photolithography in the 1890s enabled magazines to start featuring color images.

Magazines expanded in size and circulation during the Gilded Age. America's growing population was becoming more literate and willing to pay for news, information, and entertainment in print. In the 1890s, general interest monthly magazines, such as *Century* and *Harper's Monthly*, were carrying 150 or more pages of advertising (Jay 1987). Six major titles – *Ladies' Home Journal, Woman's Home Companion, Good Housekeeping, Delineator, McCall's*, and *Pictorial Review* – and countless smaller publications served just the woman's segment (Blaszczyk 2009, 118). Men had their own magazines. The number and circulation of daily and weekly newspapers expanded rapidly supported by advertising from local retailers and service providers. The growth of the print media also benefited from an important institutional innovation – the formation of advertising agencies such as N.W. Ayer and Sons founded in 1869 and J. Walter Thompson, established in 1878. They placed ads for clients and eventually developed the ability to create content and manage campaigns. Advertising of the time embodied a happy optimism infused with flamboyance (Laird 1998; Lears 1994), while satellite promotional schemes became increasingly aggressive. In the 1870s, chain stores like the Great Atlantic & Pacific Tea Company began giving away premiums such as ceramics, glassware, cutlery, and kitchen gadgets (Blaszczyk 2000). Additional threads of meaning transferred by advertising and brands will be discussed in the next section.

The last two decades of the nineteenth century witnessed the birth of modern consumer packaging (Twede 2012). Paperboard "set-up" boxes had been used for hats since the early 1800s and folding cartons had been around since the 1850s, but the technology advanced quickly during the 1870s when the Robert Gair Company found ways to mechanize the process. At the very end of the Gilded Age in 1899 this firm introduced the revolutionary Uneeda Biscuit carton for crackers. It included a moisture barrier and was arguably the first truly modern consumer package (Twede 1997). Putting heat-processed foods into tin-plated iron cans for storage and distribution dated to *c.*1810 and by the Civil War soldiers were eating fruits, vegetables, and condensed milk from these containers (Hine 1995; Schmidt 2009). Making tin cans was a tedious process until 1883 when Norton Brothers in Chicago invented machinery for mass-producing this form of packaging. Canned goods had a long shelf life and cans provided a good surface for lithographed color labels as illustrated by examples in Last (2005) for fruits, vegetables, and fish (see also Strasser 1989, 39–42). Glassmaking in

America dated to the colonial period and by the 1860s reusable glass bottles were commonly used to sell beer, soft drinks, patent medicines, and many other products. Bottles were blown manually in batches until the process was fully automated during the 1890s (Twede 2012). All of these packaging innovations meant that manufacturers could reach a national market of consumers more directly with a greater variety of branded and shelf-stable foods. In effect, packages with their increasingly bright and cheery graphics and product information became the true salesmen to end consumers and thus helped to increase the power of manufacturers at the expense of wholesalers and retailers.

Meanings and Brands

The threads of meaning Americans had attached to their possessions during the colonial, federal, and antebellum periods proceeded after the Civil War, albeit sometimes in new ways. In the pursuit of refinement, one development worth noting was the establishment of serious new institutions for uplifting public consumption. The Metropolitan Museum of Art (chartered in 1870), the Philadelphia Museum of Art (1876), the Museum of Fine Arts, Boston (1876), and the Art Institute of Chicago (1879) all endeavored to edify the American people through the sharing of their rapidly growing collections. The Met's original 1870 mission statement emphasized "encouraging and developing the study of the fine arts, and the application of arts to manufacture and practical life, of advancing the general knowledge of kindred subjects, and, to that end, of furnishing popular instruction" (The Met 2016). Supported largely by the upper classes, these museums undoubtedly conveyed an elitist vision of refinement that frequently valorized European cultural artifacts over those produced in America. Still, these institutions were far more culturally enriching than P.T. Barnum's popular American Museum in New York (1841–1865) and its commercial imitators, which featured truly eclectic assemblages meant to entertain, in part, through the display of curiosities, freaks and oddities. So-called "high culture" pushed aside popular amusements and their lower class patrons (Belk 1996, 107). Phineas Taylor Barnum (1810–1891) was not so pretentious. An extraordinary showman, at age 60 he entered the circus business and went on to form the renowned Barnum & Bailey Circus in 1888.

Consumers assembled an identity kit of possessions – a single-family home, an appropriate assemblage of furniture, and fashionable clothing – to symbolize their middle-class status. House plans featured long entry halls typically furnished with impressive hallstands, elaborate hall chairs, and cast metal card receivers. The hallstand consisted of a small table, a looking glass, hooks and pegs for hats and coats, and a receptacle for umbrellas. In his influential article, "Meaning in Artifacts: Hall Furnishings in Victorian America," material culture scholar Kenneth Ames (1978) observed how the prominent placement, detailed ornamentation, and sheer size of hallstands exceeded their utilitarian functions and, along with card receivers and calling (visiting) rituals, conveyed notions of status and conspicuous leisure. Less expensive furniture made from oak combined hallstands and chairs. Catalogs for Montgomery Ward (1895) and Sears, Roebuck (1897) referred to these items as "hall trees" and "hall racks" (see Figure 5.3) and priced them from \$6.75 to \$17.90, or \$194.32 to \$515.31 in 2016 dollars (Minneapolis Fed 2017). These Victorian furniture forms were in decline by 1900 and had mostly disappeared by 1920 (Ames 1978).

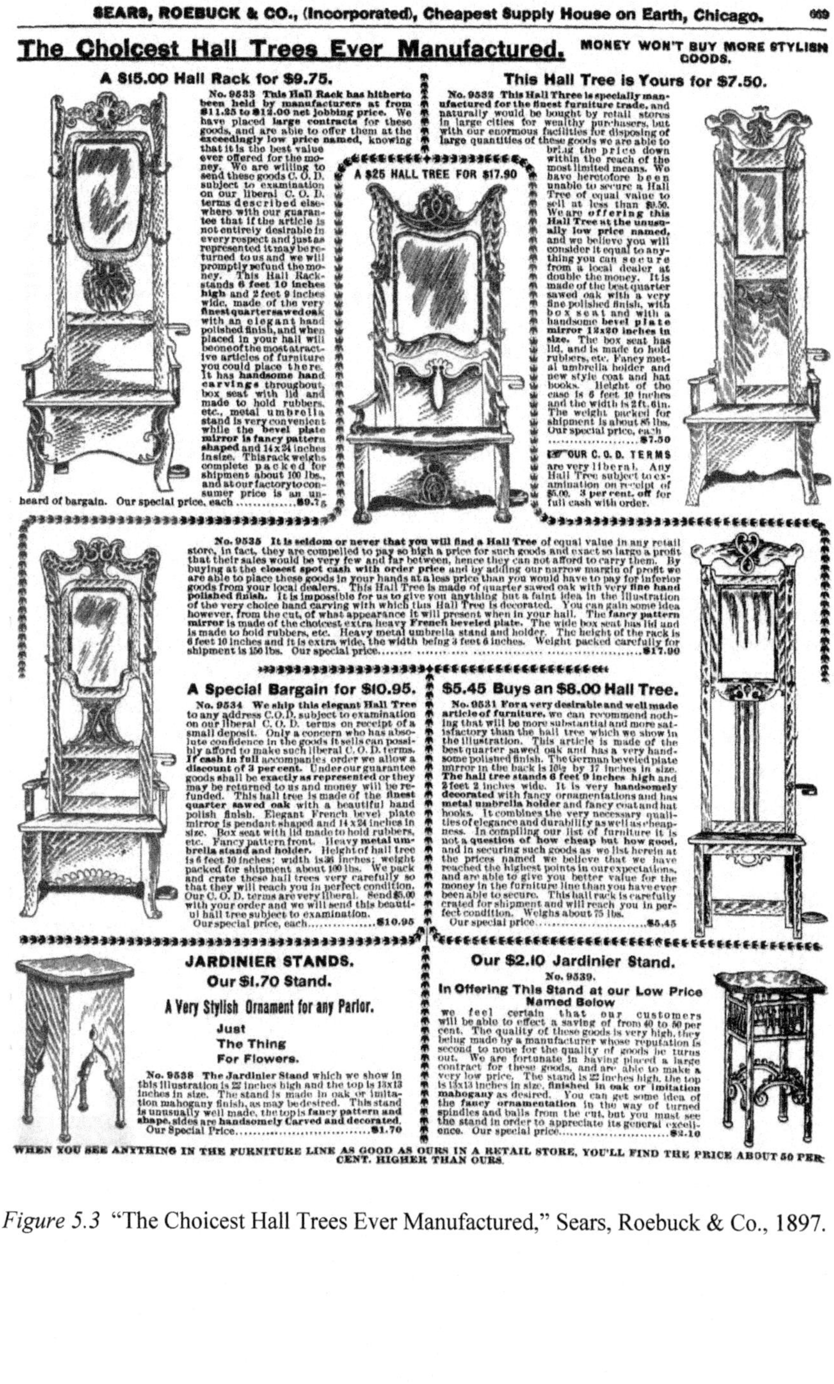

Figure 5.3 "The Choicest Hall Trees Ever Manufactured," Sears, Roebuck & Co., 1897.

Adjacent to the hall was the parlor, the home's most important public space. As stated by Regina Lee Blaszczyk (2009, 38–39),

> To Victorians, the parlor represented the pinnacle of the family's achievement and taste. Families used this room for entertaining visitors and marking rites of passage, such as birthdays, weddings, and funerals. The parlor presented the family's best face to world through the careful display of prized possessions. The precious atmosphere was intentional. This was a ritualistic, aesthetic space that made a house into a home and a statement.

Parlors, with their mix of fabrics, furniture, and personal possessions can seem busy to present day eyes, but at the time their eclecticism conveyed sophistication. The meaning of things depended in part upon department stores, which had become arbiters of taste and the definition of social class. These retailers held out hopes for social mobility through furniture and décor (Abelson 1989), while also emphasizing change and identifying it with modernity. By 1900, less cluttered aesthetics, embodied in bungalow homes with more open floor plans and multipurpose living rooms and conveyed in the plain lines of craftsman and mission style furniture, became fashionable for middle- and working-class families (Blaszczyk 2009).

Familiar patriotic symbols – the bald eagle, the American flag, Columbia, Lady Liberty, and Uncle Sam – appeared again and again in folk art, on products, and in various advertising media. George Washington remained the most popular founding father and, in commemoration of the 1876 Centennial and the Philadelphia Centennial Exposition, his image appeared on souvenir plaques, bookmarks, handkerchiefs, textiles of all kinds, flatiron trivets, belt buckles, and bitters bottles. More Washington kitsch was produced to celebrate the one hundredth anniversary of his first inauguration on April 30, 1789 (Marling 1988). Americans also memorialized new folk heroes, Abraham Lincoln above all others, and sometimes repurposed their likenesses for commercial purposes (Horwitz 1976). In 1877, for example, Quaker Oats registered a trademark featuring a man in Quaker garb who looked suspiciously like William Penn, the founder of the Pennsylvania colony.

Based on his analysis of trade cards in institutional collections, Jay (1987) identified five major thematic categories in the late nineteenth century: patriotism, urban versus rural life, racial stereotypes, womanhood and the home, and children. These themes embodied meanings drawn from the culturally constituted world of the Gilded Age. Trade card images transferred them to consumer goods and a variety of cultural rituals subsequently moved these meanings to consumers (McCracken 1986, 1988). For example, Figure 5.4 depicts a *c.* 1880 trade card for America Baking Powder. In the center stands a female Liberty figure holding a sword in her right hand and a shield festooned with stars and stripes in her left. She wears a Phrygian cap, an ancient symbol of freedom, and behind her crouches a bald eagle. When consumers used this product, theory predicts, they could indulge a bit of patriotism. However, this baking powder may

Figure 5.4 America Baking Powder Trade Card, *c.* 1880. Lithograph, 4½ × 2¾ inches.
Source: Warshaw Collection of Business Americana, Smithsonian Institution.

have been sold in bulk without colorful paperboard packaging to reinforce the ritual transfer at time of use.

Trade cards frequently conveyed pride in the urban landscape by showing images of stores, factories, and monumental structures like the newly built Brooklyn Bridge. Rural scenes tended to be more idyllic and nostalgic. Caricatures of blacks appeared frequently, especially in trade cards for tobacco, and frequently showed African American adults mimicking whites. Agonizingly racist and grotesque by later standards, these depictions treated blacks with derision: "The black was usually represented as a simple and good-natured soul, always lazy, often ridiculous, but never malicious or dangerous. The poor rural black of the South was the predominant stereotype ..." (Jay 1987, 70). These images often had no connection with the product being advertised. They drew attention, entertained, and "addressed white fears of upwardly mobile blacks by insisting that African Americans could never integrate into middle-class society" (Hale 1998, 157). Trade cards portrayed American Indians with greater dignity, which was interesting given long-standing race hatreds and the de facto ethnic cleansing policies of the U.S. government. Trade cards also portrayed Chinese, usually as more sinister characters, whereas images of the Japanese stressed an exotic and refined culture. In 1885, W.S. Gilbert and Arthur Sullivan's comic opera, *The Mikado*, became a smash hit in New York and one of its characters, Yum Yum, endorsed Allen B. Wrisley's White Borax Soap in an 1886 trade card (Jay 1987). Young, well-dressed white women appeared on trade cards for home goods, corsets, and a wide variety of patent medicines some of which addressed ill-defined "female complaints." The portrayal of children appeared more frequently than any other thematic category, perhaps reflecting the "cult status of childhood among the middle class in late nineteenth-century America" (Jay 1987, 90).

The many new products introduced into the American market after the Civil War more or less began as blank slates from the consumer's perspective, but soon accrued meanings through advertising, direct selling, word-of-mouth, and personal familiarity. Equally noteworthy was the growing presence and cultural impact of brands and their markers in the form of brand names, visual symbols, and other identifiers. Incipient brands and branding can be traced back to the seventh century BCE Mesopotamia (Wengrow 2008), as well as to ancient Greece, Rome, India, and China (Moore and Reid 2008; Eckhardt and Bengtsson 2010). By the late eighteenth century Josiah Wedgwood was creating innovative brand names to market his distinctive lines of pottery (Koehn 2001; McKendrick, Brewer, and Plumb 1982). In the United States, a number of consumer brands – American Express, Borden, Brooks Brothers, Colt, and Tiffany – had become well established by the time of the Civil War (Schmidt 2009). However, strong national brands supported by imaginative advertising, aggressive promotions, and organized sales forces truly started to emerge in the United States in the 1870s (Koehn 2001; Low and Fullerton 1994; Strasser 1989). Brands had received some legal protection earlier in the nineteenth century through tort cases brought before state courts involving the false passing off of one product for another. At the federal level, legislation in 1842 authorized registration of unique product or package design patents. Additional federal statutes were enacted in 1870 and 1881, but U.S. Supreme Court declared the former unconstitutional in 1879 and the latter applied only to trademarks used in foreign commerce and business with Indian tribes. Nevertheless, 8000 trademarks had been registered by 1879 and 22,000 by 1893 (Petty 2011, 2012).

Brand names and trademarks became convenient mental vessels into which consumers could pour a profusion of meaning starting with beliefs about product safety, quality, and reliability, but also including perceptions of psychological and social benefits. How company advertising and promotion shaped the transmission of brand meaning during this period can be documented through primary source material, such as articles in trade journals and other reporting, newspaper and magazine ads, posters and trade cards, and much additional ephemera. Harder to support through surviving evidence, but quite likely to have occurred, was the communication of brand meaning by word-of-mouth from traveling salespeople, local retailers, and consumers among themselves (Friedman 2004; Spellman 2016). Some brands took on mythic qualities in association with historic episodes and eras (Witkowski 2016a). Both the Colt single action army revolver (aka "the Peacemaker") and Winchester lever action rifles and carbines became emblems of the "winning of the West" as some have put it. By the end of the nineteenth century, the multiple threads of brand meaning were embedded in the fabric of American consumption.

Gender in Shopping, Cycling, and Shooting

After the Civil War, cultural threads of gender continued to lead toward greater female agency in matters related to domestic consumption. A supportive ideological discourse – the idea of separate spheres for men (work outside the home) and women (within the home) – could be found within books aiming to instruct an audience of middle-class American women on how to manage and decorate their homes. Among the most influential of the genre was the *American Woman's Home* written by Catherine Beecher and Harriet Beecher Stowe and published in 1869 (see Figure 5.5). The formidable Beecher sisters covered a number of topics ranging from healthy cooking and cleaning to child and elder care to economically decorating the all-important parlor with lithographic prints. They happened to favor the work of Louis Prang from Boston, but Currier and Ives prints were still readily available and their catalog contained several hundred religiously themed examples along with many more sentimental prints featuring the home, children, and moral virtues (Le Beau 2007). From these instructional guides and other print media, such as the flourishing *Ladies' Home Journal* magazine and women's columns in newspapers, American woman gained expertise as household consumption mavens. The knowledge accrued empowered them over the long run and eventually became a foundation of the home economics movement discussed in Chapter 2.

However, the somewhat nostalgic image of domesticity suggested above was far from the whole story of female consumption. For most American women in the Gilded Age, running a household still entailed relentless drudgery. Women washed clothes using laundry soaps and washboards or hand cranked washing machines that required hauling many gallons of fresh and dirty water to and fro. Irons were heavy objects that needed to be heated and reheated on top of a cast iron stove or in a fireplace. Cooking required toting wood or coal for fuel and then removing the ashes from hearths or stoves (Strasser 1982). Beyond these routine chores, women tended to their family's clothing. Unless they were

Figure 5.5 *The American Woman's Home*, 1869. Catherine E. Beecher and Harriet Beecher Stowe (New York: J. G. Ford, 1869).

Source: Library of Congress, Washington, D.C.

affluent and could hire seamstresses and patronize retail shops, wives in the Gilded Age purchased fabrics and sewed their own clothes, many of their children's garments, and some of their husband's attire. Farm and working-class wives made simple dresses, but their middle-class counterparts faced social pressures to construct better-tailored outfits (Gordon 2016, 85). Improvements in sewing machine technology helped. In 1846 Elias Howe Jr. (1819–1867) had patented the first modern sewing machine, but while searching for investors willing to finance production, other entrepreneurs, including Isaac Merritt Singer (1811–1875), entered the industry with copycat models. After a long patent fight, Howe eventually received royalties. Singer introduced smaller models for home use and, along with similar machines made by E. Remington and Sons and several other companies, offered a most useful tool to families who could afford it. Montgomery Ward sold Singer models in addition to its own house brand, while Sears marketed its sewing machines under names such as "Success," "Iowa," "Minnesota," "New Queen," and "Acme" (Montgomery Ward 1895; Sears, Roebuck and Company 1897). By 1900, affordable, ready-made clothing sold in stores and through mail order catalogs was replacing home sewn garments. Cutting and sewing clothing was technically demanding and very time consuming and few women could match the quality of manufactured wearables.

In the latter part of the nineteenth century retailers gendered shopping as a female activity. They transformed crockery emporiums, tea stores, and five-and-tens into appropriate public spaces for women and girls. F.W. Woolworth, for example, urged its suppliers to create goods with "lady lure" (Blaszczak 2000, 275). Big city department stores deliberately feminized their ambiences for the enjoyment of women shoppers and by the 1890s relatively few men frequented them (Benson 1986). Department stores made great use of the visual merchandizing. Interior architecture, decorations, and sophisticated displays, often presented against exotic "oriental" backgrounds, dazzled the eye (Laermans 1993). In addition, they gave away ice cream and soda water, hosted cooking lectures, and operated on-premise restaurants and decorous tearooms. At the turn of the century the "woman orchestra" in the New York branch of Siegal-Cooper attracted huge crowds (Abelson 1989, 48). This Chicago-based emporium came to New York City in 1896 and opened its "Big Store," a Beaux-Arts masterpiece, in the "Ladies Mile" shopping district, a stretch of Broadway from about 9th to 23rd Streets and near the mansions then lining posh 5th Avenue.

In Theodore Dreiser's novel, *Sister Carrie* (1900), the year was 1889 and protagonist Caroline Meeber had come to Chicago looking for employment as a store clerk. She walked into the fictional "The Fair," modeled after Marshall Field's, and could not take her eyes off the merchandise. Dreiser wrote:

> They were handsome, bustling, successful affairs, with a host of clerks and a swarm of patrons. Carrie passed along the busy aisles, much affected by the remarkable displays of trinkets, dress goods, stationery, and jewelry. Each separate counter was a show place of dazzling interest and attraction. She could not help feeling the claim of each trinket and valuable upon her personally, and yet she did not stop. There was nothing there which she could not have used – nothing which she did not long to own. The dainty slippers and stockings, the delicately frilled skirts and petticoats, the laces, ribbons, hair-combs, purses, all touched her with individual desire, and she

> felt keenly the fact that not any of these things were in the range of her purchase.
>
> (Dreiser 1900, 17)

Carrie also noticed the fashionably upscale lady patrons, but was even more intrigued by the shop girls, how pretty they were, and how they carried themselves with an air of independence and indifference. As Susan Porter Benson (1986) recounted in *Counter Cultures: Saleswomen, Managers, and Customers in American Department Stores, 1890–1940*, the "clerking sisterhood" developed its own shop floor culture.

From the street, the promotional and myth-making powers of storefront visualizations were greatly enhanced by the introduction of plate glass. Pioneered by France's Bon Marché in 1877 and quickly adopted by counterparts in the U.S. and elsewhere, plate glass windows became vital to the success of big city department stores and to many smaller retail concerns including corner grocery stores (Spellman 2016, 31). Plate glass presented a clear visual expanse to draw in passers-by, male and female, to do some "window shopping." They also were easier to clean than traditional divided-light windows composed of multiple panes of glass. Combined with new electrical lighting, window displays could dazzle at all hours and stores started to compete to create the most elaborate tableaux (Mosher 2012). Store windows became part of the urban scene known for their "resplendent temptations" (Abelson 1989, 70). Trade publications, such as the *Dry Goods Economist* in New York and the *Dry Goods Reporter* in Chicago, recognized the power of these windows. An article aptly titled "Windows and Temptations" observed:

> Window space all over the city is given over to the goods that are rich, showy and expensive, with the result that there were never before seen such crowds of eager and envious-eyed women lined up along the store fronts … the gay colors added to the shimmer and sheen of gold and spangles make a combination that the average woman finds almost impossible to resist.
>
> (*Dry Goods Economist*, October 10, 1900, cited in Abelson 1989, 72–73)

Store windows later became a popular subject for early twentieth century photographers and through this medium their mythic properties were enhanced (see Rose 2012, 20–23).

Department store visual merchandizing and incessant promotional hoopla excited impulse purchasing and overbuying. Such aggressive retailing had an even darker side to the extent it incited some women to steal, as Elaine Abelson (1989) recounted in her fascinating book, *When Ladies Go A-Thieving: Middle-Class Shoplifters in the Victorian Department Store*. Shoplifting had a long history and the use of term "kleptomania" to describe a particular form of uncontrollable and irrational stealing dated to 1816 (Fullerton and Punj 2004). But such theft became more pronounced with the growth of impersonal big cities, the spread of retail stores openly displaying merchandise, and the rise of department stores as urban cathedrals of commerce selling vast arrays of manufactured goods. Period commentators noted how frequently American women could be seen on the streets and in increasingly crowded stores purchasing for themselves and on behalf of their families. They also engaged in idle shopping as a form of recreation and temporary escape from the considerable demands of keeping house. Thus, they found more opportunity to shoplift as a form of consumer misbehavior. By the 1890s the female "klepto" had become part of American popular culture as an archetypical character in songs, drama, vaudeville skits, novels, and newspaper articles (Abelson 1989, 8). The stereotype of the "department store kleptomaniac" had become associated with social class and privilege:

> These unfortunates were perceived to be socially respectable middle- and upper-class women who because of their neurological disability could not control themselves in department stores. Those further down the social scale, however, were, when caught shoplifting, perceived of and treated as low-life criminals who had acted of their own free will; they could not be kleptomaniacs.
>
> (Fullerton and Punj 2004, 11)

Women caught shoplifting, some of whom could well afford the items they swiped, tried to shift blame to the stores for creating temptations too great to resist and defended their misconduct by explaining "everyone stole from the shops" (Abelson 1989, 62). They also pled innocence due to their condition of kleptomania.

Department stores tried to mitigate the shoplifting problem in several ways. Management alerted staff to be on their guard and hired more and more house detectives to patrol the floors. These private police forces included some females who, unlike their male counterparts, did not stand out while mingling with customers. Stores hung mirrors that, while indulging ladies who wanted to see themselves, also allowed clerks added angles of visibility for surveillance. Just as important, stores introduced better interior lighting and placed their more expensive merchandise within glass counters and showcases where goods could be seen, but not easily pilfered. These installations changed the look of sales floors and, naturally, stimulated the growth of the store fixture industry.

Yet, social class biases hindered efforts to stop shoplifting. In December 1870, Macy's in New York City had four women arrested for thievery, one of whom being Mrs. Elizabeth B. Phelps, a prominent philanthropist and suffragist. Because of the women's perceived respectability, charges were dismissed. To make matters worse for the merchant, their cases became a cause célèbre: "Macy and his employees were denounced in the strongest possible terms in newspaper articles and in letters to the editor by a public unwilling to believe that any of the arrested women could be guilty of theft" (Abelson 1989, 120). Instead, people castigated Macy's working-class saleswomen and referred to them contemptuously as "waiter-girls." By the turn of the century, however, attitudes toward social class had evolved. *The Kleptomaniac* (1905), an early silent movie by film pioneer Edwin S. Porter (1870–1941), contrasted the fate of a wealthy shoplifter caught in the act but later acquitted in court, with that of a poor woman with hungry children who stole an unattended loaf of bread, was arrested, and then sentenced to a jail term. In the final tableau, a blindfolded Lady Justice holds scales containing a loaf of bread in one pan and a bag of money in the other. One of her eyes peeked through the blindfold and her scales tipped toward the money.

After the Civil War many new products targeted female consumers. They ranged from new soaps to improve hygiene to patent medicines addressing a variety of female ailments. In Lynn, Massachusetts, Lydia E. Pinkham (1819–1883) commercialized a home remedy she had concocted, an herbal-alcoholic "women's tonic" to relieve menstrual and menopausal pains. Branded as Lydia E. Pinkham's Vegetable Compound, it became one of the most successful packaged goods of its day. Lydia's face appeared on the label and her advertising featured testimonials from satisfied customers. An April 1882 ad in *Frank Leslie's Popular Monthly Magazine* claimed the Compound cured a number of problems including inflammation, ulceration, spinal weakness, faintness, flatulency, bloating, headaches, nervous prostration, general debility, sleeplessness, depression, indigestion, and kidney complaints. The copy was not shy about mentioning the ovaries and uterus by name (Figure 5.6). Extensive national advertising helped sell this product, as did the fact that it contained 20.6 percent pure alcohol, a not uncommon attribute among patent medicines, but rather incongruous for this brand given that its namesake was a temperance worker (Okrent 2010, 194). Pinkham's children carried on with the company after her death and retained control until the 1930s.

The bicycle had considerable impact upon the gendering of female dress and consumption activities. Bicycle technology developed slowly during the nineteenth century. Two wheeled walking machines or velocipedes along the lines of the ones built by Karl von Drais, a German Baron, came to America *c.*1819. Riders straddled a bar connecting the wheels and moved the wooden contraption by walking or running. With enough momentum they could lift their legs and glide for a few seconds or more when cruising downhill. Velocipedes attracted a very limited following in and around eastern cities. A half century later around 1869, models with improved steering and pedals were introduced, but they too found few buyers. Paved roads and streets were uncommon in the United States. The high wheel or "Ordinary" bicycle became fairly popular from 1875 to 1885, but its design endangered riders almost all of who were adventurous males. Inventors had kept their eye on the female market, however, and they created numerous versions of these different bicycle forms – along with adult tricycles – for the ladies. Apparently, very few were sold (Aronson 1952; Herlihy 2004; Petty 1995, 1997).

Then, the invention of the safety bicycle in 1885, followed by pneumatic tires in 1890, changed everything. With its diamond frame and driven by a sprocket and chain propelled by pedals beneath the saddle, the safety bicycle would be instantly recognizable today. By the mid-1890s cycling had become a national

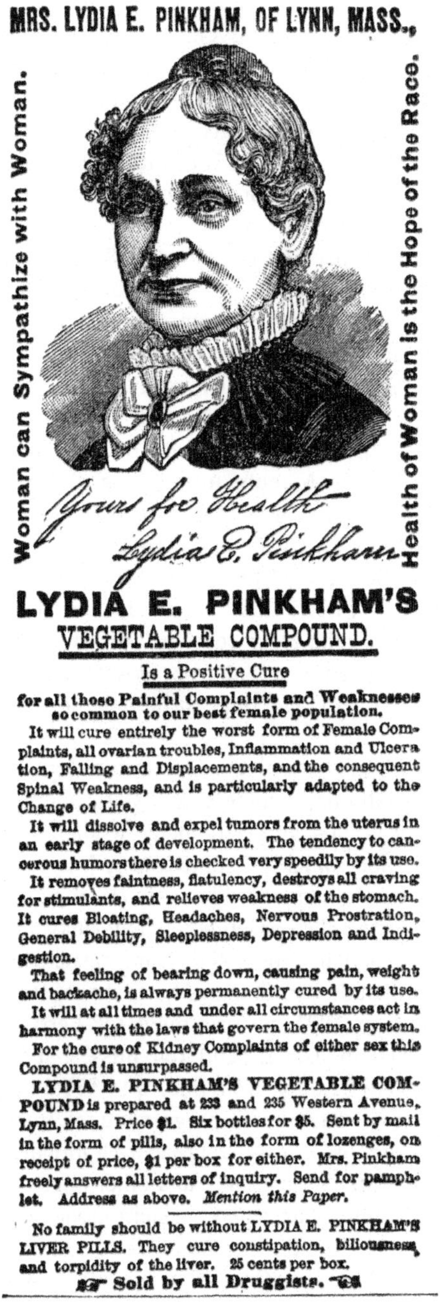

Figure 5.6 "Lydia E. Pinkham's Vegetable Compound," *Frank Leslie's Popular Monthly Magazine*, April 1882.

mania, at least among more affluent consumers who could afford the high prices. The bicycle industry not only contributed to advances in the mass production technologies that would soon be applied to motorcycles and automobiles, but also it was on the forefront of mass marketing strategies and tactics in market segmentation and research, annual model changes, and promotion via trade shows, sponsorship, and celebrity endorsements (Petty 1995). In his survey of collections of American trade cards, Robert Jay (1987, 60) found bicycles to be a relatively rare category, indicating that their manufacturers had moved on to more modern advertising media.

Women adopted cycling enthusiastically and by the mid-1890s constituted about a third of the overall market (Herlihy 2004, 266). The industry responded to this demand with inventiveness and market outreach. In 1887 W.E. Smith made the first woman's bicycle and in 1889 the Starley Brothers mass-produced the curiously named "Psycho Ladies' Bicycle." Soon thereafter another model, the "Ladies Rover," eliminated the top bar in the diamond, while reinforcing the one in front, to allow bicycling in a full skirt. The industry promoted cycling by women. The Pope Manufacturing Company produced a booklet, "Cycling for Ladies," and *Cycle Age* magazine devoted itself to "Wheelman and Women" (Petty 1997). Two women edited another magazine entitled *Wheelwoman*, published between 1895 and 1902. Mainstream woman's magazines, which frequently carried ads for bicycles, published fictional stories of the socially proper, middle-class courtship of young couples that met while cycling. Bicycle advertisements and color posters addressed a reasonably broad cross-section of woman and thus furthered the appeal of female cycling (Petty 1997).

Victorian dress codes of the 1890s dictated that women wear long-sleeved blouses, tightly laced corsets, and usually dark, ankle-length skirts supported by petticoats. The bicycle craze of the 1890s attracted many women who, for reasons of safety, audacity, and fashion, quickly adopted new, less restrictive attire. Skirts became shorter and some women wore bloomers (long pantaloons) as illustrated in Figure 5.7. Shocking to prudish observers, female ankles became exposed and some controversy, and perhaps some fetishism, ensued. Bicycle clothing lines quickly expanded to include coordinating hats, shoes, stockings, and even corsets. Figure 5.8 shows an 1897 advertisement for Ferris' Good Sense Corset Waist for Bicycle Wear with sizes for children, misses, and ladies. The ladies line was priced from $1.00 to $2.00 or from $28.79 to $57.58 in 2016 dollars (Minneapolis Fed 2017). First wave feminists, progressive reformers, and even temperance advocates had been organizing a broader "rational dress" movement that opposed voluminous skirts, tight lacing, and other ungainly Victorian fashion impositions, such as crinoline cages and the stern mounted bustle, which potentially afflicted women's health and restricted their social liberation. According to Sidney Aronson (1952, 308) "The effect of the bicycle on women's clothing was truly revolutionary – within a period of two or three years the bicycle gave the American woman the liberty of dress which reformers had been seeking for generations."

Figure 5.7 "The Start" (Woman Standing with Bicycle), 1897. Copyright by R.Y. Young, American Stereoscopic Company.

Source: Library of Congress, Prints & Photographs Division, Washington, D.C.

Figure 5.8 Ferris' Good Sense Corset Waist for Bicycle Wear, 1897.

Source: Smithsonian National Museum of American History, Kenneth E. Behring Center.

The, um, body copy in the Ferris corset ad also states how the product was suitable for "the tennis court or gymnasium," indicating that women were engaging in a variety of strenuous athletic pursuits. At the time, some physicians opposed women's cycling because they thought it would lead to maladies such as "cyclist stoop" and "bicycle face" along with hernias, varicose veins, and weak hearts to name a few, but the industry countered with its own doctors touting a list of health benefits (Aronson 1952; Petty 1997). The bicycle thus contributed to a broader acceptance of women's outdoor athletics. Moreover, bicycles and cycling came to be associated with feminism and woman's suffrage. As Herlihy (2004, 266) succinctly put it: "To feminists, the bicycle affirmed nothing less than the dignity and equality of women." While some killjoys worried about women roaming about without a chaperone, female cycling received testimonials from social reformer Susan B. Anthony (1820–1906) and from educator Frances Willard (1839–1898), the president of the Women's Christian Temperance Union. In the July 20, 1895 issue of the *Literary Digest*, leading feminist Elizabeth Cady Stanton (1815–1902) wrote "Many a woman is riding to the suffrage on a bicycle" (cited in Aronson 1952, 308).

A touching poem entitled "Wheels and Wheels" by Madeline Bridges (1893, 460) and published in *Outing* magazine suggested the liberation bicycles conveyed by contrasting the spinning wheel of the past with the bicycle wheel of the present:

> The maiden with her wheel of old
> Sat by the fire to spin,
> While lightly through her careful hold
> The flax slid out and in.
> To-day, her distaff, rock and reel
> Far out of sight are hurled,
> And now the maiden with her wheel
> Goes spinning round the world.

The well-illustrated book, *Riding High: The Story of the Bicycle* by Arthur Judson Palmer (1956, 101), reproduced a bicycle catalog cover with a "Then" image of a woman in a long print dress working a spinning wheel in front of a fireplace and a "Now" image of a woman wearing a jaunty hat and knickers and riding her bicycle out of doors. Having examined numerous photographs from the 1890s of women and their bicycles, I am impressed by how happy the subjects looked, at least in comparison to the more serious facial expressions in portrait photos from the era. Victorian etiquette codes and beauty standards dictated facial control and small mouths and these norms did not change until about the World War I era when Kodak and other advertisers started promoting consumer happiness and open smiles (Kotchemidova 2005; Schroeder 1998).

Although working-class males retained control over their meager family expenditures, middle- and upper class American men of the Gilded Age ceded a large share of domestic consumption activities to their wives, daughters, mothers, and sisters. These men retained preeminence over home library and smoking rooms, as well as within their out-of-home offices, but parlors, dining rooms, kitchens, and bedchambers became ever more decidedly female spheres. While women filled their homes with china cabinets and whatnot shelves jammed with pottery and glassware, men with the necessary wherewithal focused on buying upmarket cut glass and crystal "tobacco jars, whiskey and brandy flasks, decanters, and punch bowls encased in silver, ornamented with horn, and engraved with figures of yachts, dogs, or horses" (Blaszczyk 2000, 32). Women had their etiquette books, but men could emulate the decorative practices prescribed for them in business magazines. They could, that is, if they had the means and social standing. Many working-class, immigrant, and black American males did not.

Sociologist Mark Swiencicki (1998) has argued that American male consumption during the late nineteenth and early twentieth centuries has been understudied and insufficiently theorized. Historians and sociologists have focused on the buying of retail goods for the home and have neglected masculine personal consumption and spending on services. Based on data from the 1890 census, Swiencicki analyzed expenditures on 18 different types of personal and recreational goods. Products entirely or mostly consumed by men included their clothing, alcohol, tobacco, billiard tables, and sporting goods. Those entirely or mostly consumed by women included their dresses, millinery, corsets, perfumery and cosmetics, jewelry, and pocket books. Swiencicki assumed that men and women consumed other product categories – boots and shoes, hosiery and knit goods, hats, caps, gloves and mittens, furs, umbrellas and canes, and watches – in about equal proportions. He calculated the total value of male consumption ($1130 million) was more than double that of female consumption ($551.5 million). The clothing category ($446.2 million for men vs. $182.5 million for women) may be biased since men were buying off the rack whereas women were still making their own, but even when subtracting clothing, the ratio was still 65 percent male to 35 percent female (Swiencicki 1998, 780). Hard data on service-oriented expenditures are not available, but American men in the late Victorian period joined numerous clubs and fraternal organizations that required purchase of paraphernalia. They also spent heavily on male-only entertainment in the form of concert saloons, cheap variety theaters, gambling halls, peep shows, and brothels.

Men also engaged in outdoor sports such as horse and harness racing and target shooting. Currier and Ives created a substantial number of prints in the 1860s and 1870s with men and horses for subject matter (Baragwanath 1978; Peters 1942; Rawls 1979). The proliferation of these vibrant images indicated the acceptance of manly equestrian sports within the wider culture. Informal target shooting, which had been a popular male pastime in the nineteenth century, became something of a national mania. In 1871 attorney and New York National Guard Captain George Wood Wingate, along with William Church, editor of the *Army and Navy Journal*, launched a serious shooting organization:

the National Rifle Association (NRA). Wingate and Church were dismayed by what they considered a steep decline in manly American shooting skills and wanted to promote marksmanship among the general public. Wingate introduced a British system of rifle training and, after receiving grants from the State of New York, Brooklyn, and New York City totaling $35,000, the NRA purchased land on Long Island and started building the fine Creedmoor rifle range, which opened in 1873.

That year a team of Irish marksman trounced their competition at Britain's Wimbledon match and so became putative world champions. Looking for further victories, but unaware of the newly formed NRA, on November 22, 1873 the Irish publicly challenged the Americans to a shooting contest in an open letter printed in the pages of the *New York Herald* (Rose 2008). The Americans accepted and were quickly supported by E. Remington and Sons and the Sharps Rifle Manufacturing Company who offered their countrymen expensive target rifles and put up a $500 stake, $10,200 in 2016 prices (Gilmore 1999; Williamson 2016). The competition was scheduled for September 26, 1874 and on that day thousands of people arrived at Creedmoor to observe the shoot off. To everyone's surprise, the underdog American team bested the highly rated Irish on the very last shot (Gilmore 1999; Henning and Witkowski 2013; Rose 2008; Whittaker 1876). This caused a sensation and the outpouring of patriotism and shooting fervor was widely covered in the America press (see, e.g., *Harper's Weekly* 1874). An ad for E. Remington and Sons showed the positions of famous marksmen (Figure 5.9) and enthusiasts established new shooting clubs in cities and at universities across the U.S.

The mania for target shooting reached a crescendo in the 1880s when it inspired popular tunes including:

> "The Gallant Rifles Parade," (a jaunty quickstep), "Maguire's Rifle Corps," the "International Rifle-Match" (a waltz sportingly dedicated to the English team), the "National Rifle Quickstep," the "American Rifle Team March," and, of course, the "American Rifle Team Polka."
>
> (Rose 2008, 201)

By the end of the decade, however, shooting fever started to subside and assume a lower profile in American life compared with other spectator sports, such as men's baseball, boxing, college football, and lawn tennis, which began drawing bigger and bigger crowds (Witkowski 2016b).

Despite the accomplished manliness implicit in the sport, women also participated in shooting clubs and as sharpshooting entertainers. The most famous deadeye in American life was the unassuming, five foot tall Annie Oakley (1860–1926) who became the star attraction at Buffalo Bill's Wild West Shows from 1885 to 1901 (Figure 5.10). Her husband, Irish immigrant Francis E. Butler (1847–1926), was also a crack shot and the two performed together, but recognizing her celebrity power, Butler wisely accepted playing second fiddle to his wife and became her manager and publicist. Their marriage lasted 50 years.

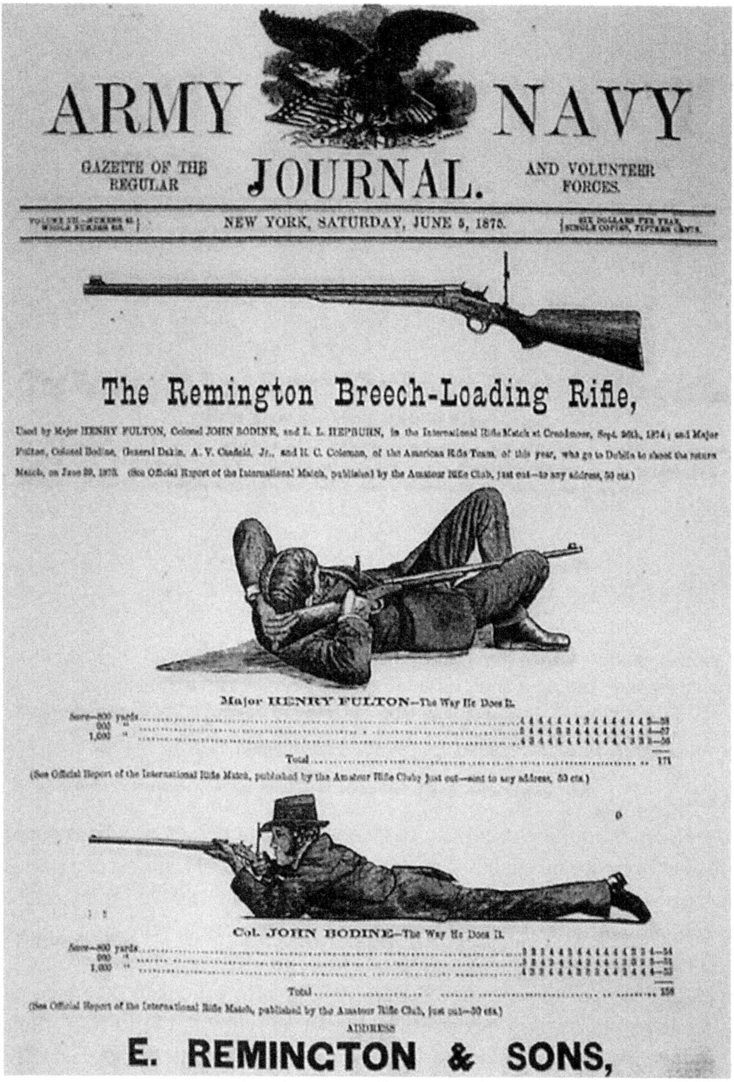

Figure 5.9 "The Remington Breech-Loading Rifle," E. Remington & Sons, *Army and Navy Journal*, June 5, 1875.

Born Phoebe Ann Mosey and nicknamed "Little Sure Shot," Oakley suffered from injuries she sustained in a 1901 train accident and in a 1922 auto mishap, making the photo of the smiling older Oakley in Figure 5.10 particularly evocative. With the assistance of her husband, she demonstrated her shooting prowess in a very early (November 1, 1894), 20-second film made at the Black Maria studio of the Thomas Edison Company. Edison and his team intended this

Figure 5.10 Annie Oakley, 1899 (left) and 1922 (right). She is adorned with shooting medals and holding a shotgun in 1899 and posing with a Winchester rifle in 1922. William F. "Buffalo Bill" Cody (1846–1917) gave her the rifle.

Source: Library of Congress Prints & Photographs Division, Washington, D.C.

short film to be seen via a kinetoscope, a device where one person at a time could peep at the moving picture through a viewer on its top. The first kinetoscope parlor had two rows of machines and opened in New York City in 1894. Similar establishments quickly materialized from Chicago to San Francisco. The first public screening of a film via projection did not occur until 1901 (Musser 1990).

Near the end of the century, women began pouring into offices to take jobs as secretaries, stenographers, and accounting clerks (Figure 5.11). From their employers' perspective, these mostly young and single females were usually docile, did not expect advancement, and could be paid half of what men earned (Gordon 2016), but now some workspaces could no longer remain as assertively masculine as they once had been. Spittoons disappeared, décor began to resemble home parlors, and language became more genteel. Even more troubling for men, the increasingly bureaucratic nature of office work, situated in ever larger and more impersonal cities, presented difficulties for middle-class males in finding the occupational and social distinction they craved. With the introduction and adoption of the cash register in the 1880s, young, single female cashiers began replacing trained male bookkeepers. This transition in business technology, in the words of historian Susan Spellman (2016, 70), "limited male clerks'

Figure 5.11 Women Working in Office Jobs, 1906. Photo taken by Byron Company of the accounting or records department at the Siegal Cooper Company department store at 6th Avenue and 18th Street.

Source: Museum of the City of New York.

opportunities to rise through the ranks and become partners or proprietors, narrowing the pathway to independence through business ownership." Historians have posited that by century's end men were compensating for threats to their masculinity by an increasingly feminized American culture through male gendered consumption behavior (Kimmel 1994; Swiencicki 1998). As E. Anthony Rotundo (1993, 251) put it

> when changes in the workspace caused men to feel uncertain of their manhood, their primary response was to seek new forms of reassurance about it. Strenuous recreation, spectator sports, adventure novels and a growing cult of the wilderness all served this need.

Theodore Roosevelt, soon to become President, epitomized this bold manly spirit. He reveled in guns, hunting, and the great outdoors. Men flocked to gyms and athletic fields to build their manly physiques and read Wild West adventure fiction to fantasize about masculine exploits (Kimmel 1996).

In addition to workplace encroachment, many women went further and began to lambast popular male pastimes, such as gambling, attending boxing matches, and, above all, hanging around saloons drinking beer. Beer consumption in the United States had jumped from 36 million gallons in 1850 to 855 million gallons in 1890, while the number of saloons climbed from 100,000 in 1870 to nearly 300,000 by 1900 (Okrent 2010, 25–27). American men may have been justified in seeking some release from workplace drudgery, but too many wasted scarce family resources on alcohol, left work undone, lost their jobs, and engaged in domestic violence. A string of fiercely dedicated women emerged to fight against alcohol, among them educator Frances Willard (1839–1898) who founded the Woman's Christian Temperance Union (WCTU) in 1874. Along with women's suffrage, prison reform, and free kindergartens, eliminating the scourge of alcohol to protect the home and family became a chief concern of the WCTU. With some 250,000 members and the hyperactive Willard as its president, the WCTU was "the nation's most effective political action group in the last decades of the nineteenth century" (Okrent 2010, 16). The Temperance Movement and its great political triumph, Prohibition, will be discussed in the next chapter and the question of how men have dealt with threats to their masculine identity via compensatory consumption will be revisited in Chapters 8 and 9.

The Leisure Class, its Critics, and Boycotts

Although the buyer behavior of the middle and lower classes continued to come under scrutiny (Horowitz 1985), leading intellectuals, such as William Dean Howells, editor of the *Atlantic Monthly*, E.L. Godkin, editor of *The Nation*, Charles Eliot Norton, editor of the *North American Review*, and the philosopher William James, declared much more disgust with the crass materialism of the newly rich (Cashman 1993; Shi 1985). Of course, somewhat older money also could be showered on luxury consumption. Figure 5.12 depicts "The Breakers," the massive Newport, Rhode Island summer home of Cornelius Vanderbilt II designed by Ogden Codman and completed in 1895. Cornelius II was the lucky grandson of Cornelius "Commodore" Vanderbilt who had built the family fortune through regional and ocean-going steamship lines and later the New York Central Railroad. Overlooking the Atlantic Ocean, The Breakers boasted 70 rooms in an opulent Italian Renaissance style. It is now a National Historic Landmark and the most popular attraction in Rhode Island. Less than a mile away, William Vanderbilt, a younger brother of Cornelius II, already had built a 50-room mansion called "Marble House" between 1888 and 1892. An early example of the Beaux-Arts style designed by the prominent New York architect Richard Morris Hunt, it too is a National Historic Landmark. George Washington Vanderbilt II, the youngest brother, topped them both with his "Biltmore House" in Asheville, North Carolina. Designed in the Châteauesque style by Richard Morris Hunt and constructed between 1889 and 1895, Biltmore remains the largest private residence ever constructed in America, a National Historic Landmark, and a major tourist attraction. What were once sites of intense private

Figure 5.12 "The Breakers," Newport, Rhode Island, 1895. Matt H. Wade photographed this iconic Gilded Age mansion in 2009.

Source: Wikimedia Commons.

consumption later became venues for popular public consumption. Americans in the twenty-first century have indulged a penchant for vicariously consuming the lifestyles of the rich and famous, whether British aristocrats, such as those portrayed on the hit PBS series, *Downton Abbey* (2010–2015), or their own homegrown variety.

Gilded Age writers published best-selling manuals for achieving a "simplified life." In *The Decoration of Houses*, authors Edith Wharton and Ogden Codman, Jr. (1897) argued for a simple aesthetic and less cluttered domestic space. Wharton (1862–1937), who herself came from old money, was a keen observer of the social ambitions of heirs and parvenus in late nineteenth-century New York society, as revealed in her later novels, *The House of Mirth* (1905) and the Pulitzer Prize-winning *The Age of Innocence* (1921). Codman (1863–1951), who was the architect for The Breakers, also helped Wharton remodel her "cottage" in Newport, which she called "Land's End." For the very rich, resisting consumption meant consuming tastefully, to convey one's class and elegant breeding, not as a denial of material things for religious reasons, nor as a refusal to buy to achieve larger political ends.

At the very end of the nineteenth century, Thorstein Veblen (1857–1929) became American plutocracy's greatest critic. In his pioneering *Theory of the Leisure Class*, Veblen (1899/1953) wrote a scholarly, but highly influential, frugality sermon combining wry social criticism with new insights from economics and cultural anthropology. He contended that consumption had become so grossly conspicuous in order to create invidious distinctions and to mark status. Part of this process entailed the historical transformation of women from domestic laborers to household consumers. Those men who could afford the show paraded their finely attired females in public as gaudy signs of their commercial or professional success. The more visible idleness these wives and daughters enjoyed, the greater their symbolic value. Veblen (1899/1953, 121) implicated the corset in such conspicuous waste: "The corset is, in economic theory, substantially a mutilation, undergone for the purpose of lowering the subject's vitality and rendering her permanently and obviously unfit for work." Images of very well dressed, somewhat bored looking women at leisure appeared in a number of works by American painters around the turn of the century. For example, in 1888 artist Julian Alden Weir (1852–1919) painted a large, oil on canvas he aptly titled *Idle Hours* (Figure 5.13). This impressionistic work depicted his wife and four year old daughter lolling on their sumptuous sofa. Social pose of this sort irritated Veblen who had a high regard for productive work.

Americans of more humble station adopted a new term, "to boycott," and proceeded to deploy the tactic against merchants perceived to be unfair to workers. The expression had Irish roots. Charles Cunningham Boycott, a retired British officer, served as the land agent in Ireland for an absentee landlord. In 1880,

Figure 5.13 Idle Hours, Julian Alden Weir, 1888. Oil on canvas, 51¼ × 71⅛ inches (130.2 × 180.7 cm).

Source: Metropolitan Museum of Art.

after he evicted tenants following a dispute over the wages they earned for harvesting crops, the local community ostracized him and his family. In America the following year, a Scottish immigrant, journalist, and radical abolitionist named James Redpath (1833–1891) transformed the surname to a verb and descriptive noun. This new usage quickly caught on, eventually denoting a socially organized protest to reject an idea, person, or activity (Friedman 1999; Glickman 2009).

In his comprehensive history, *Consumer Boycotts: Effecting Change Through the Marketplace and the Media*, Monroe Friedman (1999) provided a number of helpful conceptual distinctions pertaining to boycotts. For example, boycotts have varied in terms of geographic scope (local v. national), time duration (weeks to years), and targets (stores, companies, brands, industries, and destinations). Boycott sponsors have been ad hoc groups and voices, such as those behind the already mentioned colonial nonimportation and antebellum nonintercourse movements, but also more established bodies. In the Gilded Age labor unions became involved in these protests and, as will be seen in subsequent chapters, women, racial and ethnic minorities, religious, environmental, and gay rights groups, and many additional interests have staged boycotts. Boycotts have been instrumental with practical ends in mind or have been more value-expressive, a therapeutic venting of frustrations. Some boycotts, such as actions on behalf of labor, have directly benefitted the participants themselves, while others, such as the environmental and animal rights protests of the late twentieth century, have helped non-human constituencies. Finally, while many boycotts have been implemented, others have never progressed beyond the threat stage. Media coverage in and of itself has been a powerful shaming tool that has sometimes diminished the reputation of targets in the marketplace, while potentially prompting new political initiatives.

In the 1880s and 1890s thousands of small boycotts broke out, with 1352 between 1885 and 1892 alone (Glickman 2009, 340). Often under the auspices the Knights of Labor, a powerful labor union in the 1880s, these collective acts of resistance supported workers being mistreated by local establishments ranging from bakeries and breweries to theaters and newspapers. To gain wider public sympathy, boycott organizers distributed posters and broadsides in area neighborhoods and some paraded about wearing "sandwich boards" displaying the protest's message (Friedman 1999). Tactics included secondary boycotts, concerted acts of resistance taken against other businesses that continued to support the primary targets. In the mid-1880s three different newspapers in New York, Chicago, and Topeka, Kansas adopted the name, the *Boycotter*. Boycotters were often working-class Irish and German immigrants, but many other lower status groups also participated. Sadly, in retrospect, labor interests also deployed boycott tactics against Chinese shop owners in California and in a few other American cities (Glickman 2009). In 1882 Congress passed and President Chester A. Arthur (1829–1886) signed the racist Chinese Exclusion Act that severely restricted further immigration from China. When the Act was extended in 1902, Chinese retaliated in Asia by boycotting imports from the U.S.

Unsurprisingly, a variety of business and status quo interests, supported by a number of big city daily newspapers, pushed back against labor directed boycotts and questioned their morality, legality, and threat to free enterprise. *Puck*, a very successful humor magazine published from 1871 until 1918, printed chromolithographed cartoons poking fun at boycotts. One example, "The Absurdities of the Boycott," appeared on the front page of the December 30, 1885 issue (Figure 5.14). In it a laborer read a notice stating, "You are hereby ordered to

Figure 5.14 "The Absurdities of the Boycott," *Puck*, December 30, 1885. Chromolithograph by Frederick Burr Opper (1857–1937).

Source: Library of Congress, Prints & Photographs Division, Washington, D.C.

boycott as follows. Fifth Avenue Hotel, New York Tribune, Straiton & Storms' Cigars, Thalia Theatre, All Fashionable Clothing Stores, All Turkish Baths, All Champagnes, by order of the Labor Union." Except for the newspaper, all of the items listed – and also illustrated by a circle of little sketches – were probably beyond the financial means of this man who mused, at the bottom of the page, "I guess the Labor Union is trying to make a fool of me!" *Puck* crusaded for good government, with New York City's Tammany Hall political machine a favorite target, but also lashed out at the Irish and the Catholic Church. In its May 8, 1886 issue, *Harper's Weekly* presented a more sinister image of the boycotter in a woodcut titled "The Root of the Problem" where a big, presumably Irish man holding a whip threatened an American blacksmith (Figure 5.15). In the caption

Figure 5.15 "The Root of the Problem," *Harper's Weekly*, May 8, 1886.
Source: Hathi Trust Digital Library.

beneath the picture the boycotter said, "You must stop work, because *I* have a grievance against your employer, no matter whether you have any, or whether your family suffers meanwhile. *I must show my power.*" On the wall a poster proclaimed, "Obey Orders or you Die."

In April of 1886, a minor boycott of widow Esther Gray's small, nonunion bakery in New York City garnered a great deal of negative attention in newspapers across the country and led to a counter- or anti-boycott where local consumers patronized her business in a show of support (Glickman 2009, 140). After Chicago's Haymarket Affair of May 4, 1886 – a dreadful incident where someone threw a bomb that killed seven policemen in the process of dispersing a peaceful labor demonstration for an eight-hour workday – anti-union sentiment greatly intensified across the country. By 1890, the Knights of Labor had declined precipitously, but eventually other unions were formed. As subsequent chapters will show, the boycott as an act of consumer resistance would endure throughout the twentieth and into the twenty-first century.

Summary

In many ways the Gilded Age marked an intermediate period in American consumption history, a time bridge between the largely agrarian, pre-industrial past and the increasingly urbanized, materially abundant lifestyles of the future. Transformative new technologies including electric power and lighting, internal combustion engines, the telephone and phonograph, and very rudimentary motion pictures were being invented and tested, but were not sufficiently refined to reach a broad market until after 1900. The consumer marketing infrastructure saw the development of department and five-and-ten cent stores, mail order selling and distribution, magazine publishing and color printing, and new types of consumer packaging. Yet, these innovations also would not fully permeate society until the twentieth century. Per capita incomes increased after the Civil War, but aggregate statistics masked rising inequality based on race, ethnicity, and occupational status.

Traditional threads of refinement found new modes of expression in public art collections and through the privately furnished spaces of Victorian parlors and hallways. Inspired by the 1876 Centennial celebrations, goods continued to carry patriotic associations, while brand names and promotional ephemera, especially trade cards, became repositories for a wide assortment of meanings including some that played upon racist stereotypes. The gendering of household consumption activities and products became more pronounced with women increasingly assuming domestic primacy. Retailers clearly understood this trend and increasingly focused on their female clientele. Yet, by the end of the century, the separate sphere of men's consumption was becoming problematic especially in regards to the drinking of alcohol. The ostentation and materialism of the very rich received a well-deserved share of criticism, while common people adopted the consumer boycott as a tactic in their collective struggles with unbridled and powerful capitalism. Overall, however, resistance to consumption norms was rather muted in the Gilded Age. That would change in the twentieth century.

6 Consumption Progress, 1900 to 1930

The year 1900 is a nice round number and thus a convenient choice for separating periods, but events around this year also have relevance to the history of American consumption. In 1898, the U.S. defeated Spain in a ten-week war and thus extended its economic reach into the Caribbean and over the Pacific to the Philippines. Also in 1898, following years of political skullduggery, it annexed the Hawaiian Islands. In September 1901, an assassin took the life of President William McKinley six months into his second term. He was succeeded by his Vice President, Theodore Roosevelt (1858–1919), who battled predatory corporations, protected consumers by signing the Pure Food and Drug Act of 1906, and championed public consumption through the founding of new national parks, forests, and monuments. He was a leader in what became known as the Progressive Era, from the 1890s to the 1920s, when reformers sought to remedy the social and economic ills that had accumulated during the Gilded Age. A number of progressives supported Prohibition and even more backed women's suffrage. Both causes succeeded when they became, respectively, the Eighteenth and Nineteenth Amendments to the U.S. Constitution. The former had an immediate effect upon drinking behavior and the latter had longer-term implications for women's agency. Finally, the Ford Motor Company was incorporated on June 16, 1903. Automobiles and light trucks were enormously transformative consumer goods during this period. So 1900 can be justified as a reasonable dividing line in American consumption history.

After a quick survey of the American economy, social changes, and a few of the most important product and marketing system developments from 1900 to 1930, the chapter will investigate threads of meaning. Particular emphasis will be given to the expanding advertising system and how it became an increasingly powerful transmitter and amplifier of cultural ideas. In addition, colonial revivals in architecture and decorative arts will be examined as a consumer driven movement of meaning that reinvented the past in order to reinforce the cultural dominance of certain native born groups. Threads of gender will lead to cultural assumptions about the increasingly powerful female consumer in the domestic sphere. Women asserted themselves through new fashions and were cultivated as consumers by a number of industries including greeting cards, tobacco, and home appliances. In time-honored tradition, female consumption also received flak from misogynist tropes and sniping. The threads of resistance to be considered are especially diverse. They will range from meat boycotts to critiques of overconsumption and a crusade for thrift to Prohibition and the counter resistance it engendered to the conspicuous display of elite African Americans and, finally, to black boycotts of streetcars in the South as protest against the enactment of degrading Jim Crow laws.

Material Life and the Market

Despite frequent, albeit relatively mild, recessions during the first three decades of the twentieth century, the U.S. economy generally trended upward. Nominal GDP of $20,766 million ($456,861 million in 2009 dollars) in 1900 rose impressively to $104,600 ($1,056,600) in 1929. On a per capita basis, GDP increased over the same years from $273 ($6004) to $858 ($8669) (Johnston and Williamson 2017). Population grew from 76,212,168 in 1900 to 123,201,624 in 1930. By 1920 slightly more Americans (51.2 v. 48.8 percent) lived in urban than in rural areas (U.S. Bureau of the Census 2016b). Immigration surged in the first two decades of the twentieth century with 1,285,349 arriving in the peak year of 1907 and more than one million a year in 1905, 1906, 1910, 1913, and 1914 (Homeland Security 2013). My own Polish Catholic grandparents arrived in Chicago *c.* 1902 to 1907. A politically potent backlash to this wave of immigration eventually developed. The federal Quota Acts of 1921 and 1924 targeted Eastern and Southern Europeans (Slavs, Jews, Italians, Greeks, and others) that the majority Protestant culture deemed ethnically and religiously undesirable. The inflow of new arrivals quickly abated. The Chinese Exclusion Act of 1882, the informal Gentlemen's Agreement with Japan in 1907, and the Immigration Act of 1917 already had blocked most new arrivals from Asia. As they had for three centuries, immigrants added new products (e.g., ethnic foods) and consumption practices to American culture, but also as we shall see provoked new efforts to assimilate them along nativist lines.

The period spanning the 1890s into the 1920s came to be known as the Progressive Era. A response to the severe social consequences of industrial capitalism and other excesses of the Gilded Age, Progressivism attacked political corruption and business overreach, championed woman's suffrage and the prohibition of alcohol, and promoted modernization, science, and technology. Congress passed antitrust laws, such as the Sherman Antitrust Act (1890) and the Clayton Antitrust Act (1914), intended to regulate business activities harmful to competition including the formation of cartels and monopolies, price discrimination, and tying and exclusive dealing arrangements. The Federal Trade Commission Act (1914) also addressed unfair and deceptive practices that injured competition. Preserving competition benefited American consumers through lower prices and product innovation, or at least that is what economic theory has told us. Major regulatory initiatives, such as the Pure Food and Drug Act (1906), also served the consumer interest in enforcing product safety and transparency. Among other provisions, the FDA Act required the labeling of over-the-counter pharmaceuticals containing alcohol, cocaine, opiates, and cannabis. These had often been the active, but too often understated ingredients of popular patent medicines.

A generation of outstanding editors and reporters advanced Progressive and consumer interests during a time when print media could wield great influence. Led by the brilliant Samuel S. McClure (1857–1949), and often publishing their fine investigative pieces in the popular *McClure's Magazine* (1893–1929), these "muckrakers" included Ida Tarbell (1857–1944), Lincoln Steffens (1866–1936), William Allen White (1868–1944), and Ray Stannard Baker (1870–1946). In 1904 Upton Sinclair (1878–1968) spent seven weeks working incognito in the meatpacking plants at the Chicago stockyards. Based on this experience, this outspoken socialist wrote a novel, *The Jungle*, which shined a brilliant light on the revolting factory conditions and mistreatment of immigrant workers. Serialized in a small socialist newspaper in 1905, five book publishers rejected Sinclair's manuscript until Doubleday accepted and published its edition in February 1906. An instant bestseller, the book caused a sensation and even caught the attention of Theodore Roosevelt. He ordered an investigation, and, after federal officials confirmed Sinclair's account, helped hasten the passage of the Pure Food and Drug Act within just a couple of months. Implementing this groundbreaking legislation was another matter. The food processing industry resisted and cities and states needed to pass their own rules for inspections (Goodwin 2013; Gordon 2016).

Standards of living rose dramatically as Americans increasingly connected their homes to fast expanding electricity, water, sewage, and telephone systems. In 1900 penetration rates for these utilities were low to almost nonexistent, but by 1930, 68 percent of U.S. households had electricity, 60 percent had running water, 50 percent had indoor flush toilets, and 45 percent had telephones (Gordon 2016). Electric light bulbs provided far more light than candles and kerosene and did not gutter, smoke, smell, and cause fires. Not only was indoor running water convenient and labor saving, but also its provision reduced the incidence of water-borne diseases and encouraged more bathing and better hygiene. Indoor toilets gave more privacy and comfort than outdoor privies, and sewage systems positively affected public health. According to Harvard's David Cutler and Grant Miller (2005), clean water technologies – filtration and chlorination – had a tremendous impact on reducing infant, child, and total mortality rates in the major cities they studied. Telephones obviously facilitated instantaneous communications that strengthened personal bonds within increasingly impersonal urban areas. More affluent householders enjoyed the benefits of these networks before the middle class and the poor and their diffusion occurred faster in urban than in rural areas and in the northern and western states than in the South.

With the possible exception of electric utility service, the automobile was the most revolutionary consumer product of the early twentieth century (Blaszczyk 2009). Despite many initial mechanical shortcomings, motor vehicles were still much faster than horses and carriages, had greater range, and did not dump tons of manure and urine on city streets. Americans bought cars as soon as they could afford them and were helped along by an expansion of installment selling and consumer credit. Rare before 1900, and still uncommon in 1910, by 1930 autos could be found in 60 percent of American households. When adjusted for major improvements in quality, such as making standard windshields, horns, headlights, electric starters, speedometers, and closed tops, auto prices actually declined over this period (Gordon 2016). Unlike the utilities described above, which took additional decades to reach rural areas, farm families purchased automobiles at about the same rate as their urban counterparts. Driving sturdy Model T Ford cars, motor trucks, and even tractors greatly reduced rural isolation and enabled families to get to larger towns for shopping, recreation, and amusements. Automobility greatly aided the spread of roadside restaurants – in 1921 Kirby's Pig Stand in Dallas opened the first drive-in (Witzel 1993) – and the eventual dominance of supermarkets. Being able to bring home several bags of food in their cars all in one trip meant that consumers might prefer to shop weekly at just one store rather than make daily visits to butchers, bakers, and produce stands to buy smaller quantities.

An outpouring of increasingly affordable and technically more sophisticated devices entertained American consumers. Phonographs were uncommon in 1901, the year the Victor Talking Machine Company was organized in Camden, New Jersey, and also acquired the rights to the famous trademark showing the fox terrier, Nipper, listening to a gramophone. By 1930 about half of all U.S. households owned a phonograph (Gordon 2016, 190). Victor perfected flat-disc recording technology, but its early machines with their external cranks and trumpet-shaped horns were unsightly. In 1906 the company introduced the Victrola, which hid its components within a fine cabinet built from solid mahogany, thus making the device a suitable addition to living-room furniture. The advertisement shown in Figure 6.1 depicts seven different Victrola models sold by the Lyon & Healy music company in Chicago. The ad dates from *c.*1916, the year they moved to their new retail and headquarters location at Jackson Boulevard and Wabash Avenue. According to *The Music Trade Review* (1916), the first floor was devoted to Victrolas, sheet music, and music books and the second floor displayed Victor records, retail and wholesale. Victor also produced content through its Red Seal and Black Seal record labels. The former appealed to more classical tastes, but also leveraged celebrity power with recordings by famous conductor and military march composer John Philip Souza (1854–1932) and the star Italian operatic tenor, Enrico Caruso (1873–1921) as shown on the extreme left and right in Figure 6.1. Black Seal featured popular music and arguably launched the Jazz Age by recording the African American Original Dixieland Jazz Band. In 1921 the industry sold 106 million records (Blaszczyk 2009, 144). However, a new sound distribution medium – radio – was soon to displace the primacy of phonographs. Radio diffused very rapidly from just a few hobbyists in 1920 to half of all households in 1930 and 80 percent by 1940 (Gordon 2016). This exciting new broadcast medium, its culturally transformative content, and its highly successful business model will be discussed further in subsequent chapters.

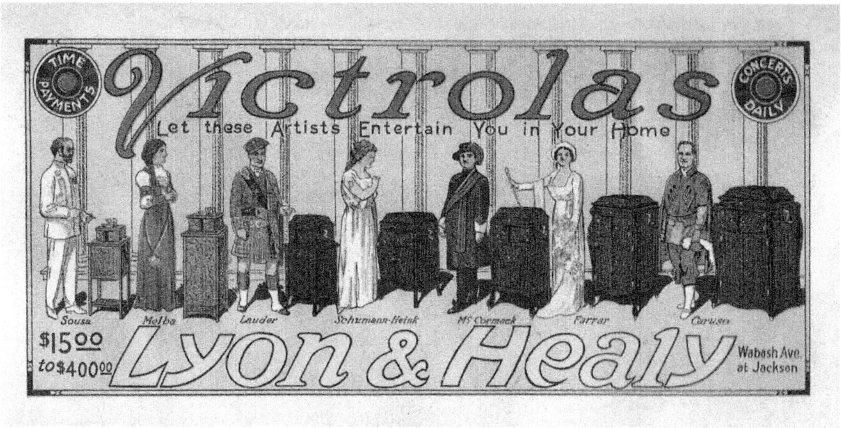

Figure 6.1 "Victrolas," *The Music Trade Review*, July 19, 1916. Founded in Chicago in 1864 by George Washburn Lyon and Patrick J. Healy, the firm is still in business.

Source: Reprinted by Mechanical Music Registration Project.

In 1900, the Eastman Kodak Company of Rochester, New York introduced its first "Brownie" camera, priced at just one dollar and initially targeted toward youngsters. Unlike previous models using the "Kodak System," where consumers had to ship everything back to Rochester to have their film processed and cameras reloaded, they could now load, unload, and re-load these simple devices all by themselves. Supported by heavy advertising expenditures, Kodak sold millions of Brownies over subsequent decades in a great variety of models and along with kits for home developing and printing. Kodak formed the Brownie Camera Club of America and, as indicated by the 1900 ad from *Youth's Companion* magazine, the company envisioned schoolboys and girls as primary users (see Figure 6.2). This model line, along with others, such as the Hawkeye cameras and the 1928 Vanity Kodak for females, firmly established both amateur photography and the dominance of the Eastman Kodak Company for nearly a century (Baker 2016; Kotchemidova 2005; Spira 2001; Strasser 1989, 102–106).

The marketing of processed foods and beverages, personal hygiene products, and cigarettes and tobacco also matured quickly. Coca-Cola's marketing was brilliant. First developed and sold at an Atlanta soda fountain in 1886, the drink could be found at nearly every fountain in America by 1920. Bottling began in Chattanooga, Tennessee in 1899 and within ten years 379 bottling plants were operating across the country supplying grocery stores and saloons. Coke started using modern bottle caps around the turn of the century and patented its iconic contour bottle in 1915. Cardboard six-pack carrier packages, introduced in 1923, encouraged multiple purchases (Pendergrast 2000). Coke advertised heavily in newspapers, magazines, and on the sides of buildings. The company produced

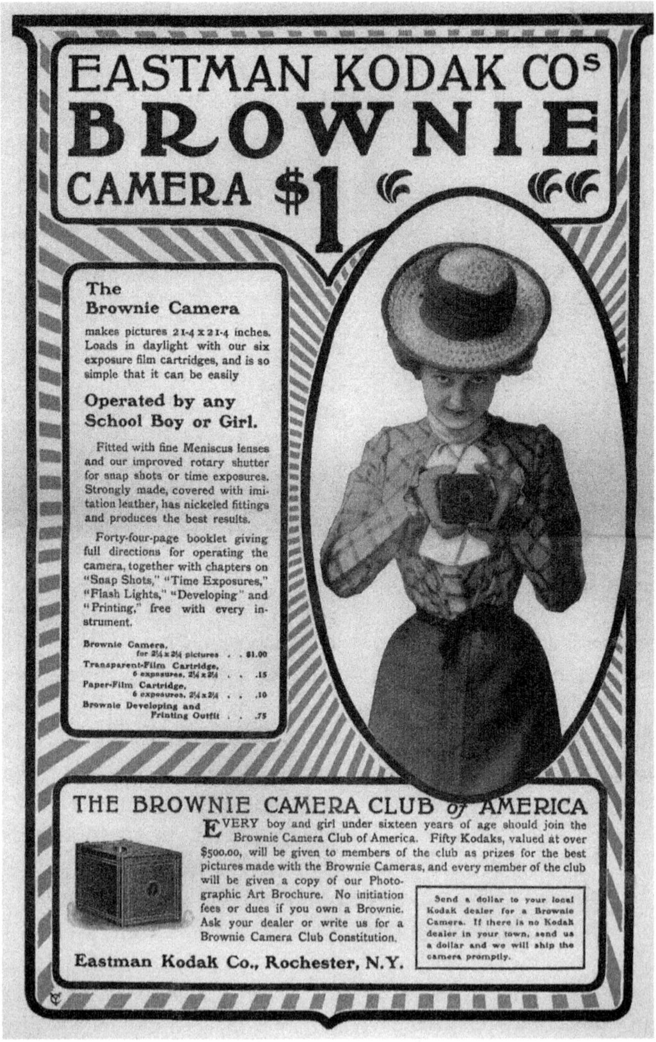

Figure 6.2 "Eastman Kodak Co^s Brownie Camera $1," *Youth's Companion*, 1900.

Source: Duke University Libraries Digital Collections.

an enormous quantity of beautifully illustrated promotional material during this period including a variety of tin, cardboard, porcelain, and glass store signs, door bars and pulls, wall calendars, wooden thermometers, posters, trolley car signs, change trays, and much more. Surviving examples of early Coke bottles and ephemera are avidly collected in the twenty-first century.

The weight of advertising and promotion, along with direct personal use experience, meant that consumers were learning brand names. In a pioneer study of consumer recall published in the third issue of the *Journal of Applied Psychology*, L.R. Geissler (1917) found that his 300 subjects, a sample of college men from schools in seven different states, "could name 812 different brands of 20 articles, or on an average about 41 brands per article" (280). The most common reason for thinking of a brand name was personal ownership or previous use with the second most frequent reason being advertising. The author used the phrase "community of ideas" to describe these results, which he attributed to national advertising. The effect was stronger for articles of necessity (soaps, toothpaste, shirts and shirt collars, shoes, garter belts, and hats) than for luxury or only occasionally used goods (tobacco, soft drinks, cameras, magazines, baseballs, candy, penknives, and notepaper).

The pace of change in U.S. consumer culture seemed to accelerate in the 1920s as "modernization" became equated with consumerism. "This is the age of real estate, consumer credits and cars: modern appliances, bought by modern methods, placed in a modern household" (Slater 1997, 13). Being modern also meant that consumers needed to learn to serve themselves. In the early 1900s cafeterias and clothing retailers started adopting self-service formats (Spellman 2016) and, in 1916, a visionary named Clarence Saunders (1881–1953) founded Piggly Wiggly, the first self-service grocery store, in Memphis, Tennessee. Consumers entered and exited through turnstiles and needed to pay in cash rather than on credit. Credit arrangements were then very commonplace among independent grocers and small retailers, but the cost of the service required higher prices (Strasser 1989, 67–71). Other grocery stores and chains quickly adapted Saunders' self-service, cash and carry model, forcing consumers to pay greater attention to brands and advertising. Home delivery service also declined. Interestingly, this practice had been attacked during World War I as a wasteful use of manpower (Spellman 2016).

The decline in buying groceries on credit was more than offset by a massive increase in loans for consumer durables and mortgages for home purchases. Installment buying of furniture, pianos, and sewing machines by higher income families dated to the 1850s, but the practice became much more widespread after 1900 and especially during the 1920s. For example, the upper left corner bullet of the *c.*1916 Victrola ad by Lyon & Healy in Figure 6.1 offered "time payments" as a purchasing option. Total retail installment credit jumped from \$1 billion in 1910 to \$7 billion in 1929 (Blaszczyk 2009, 174). The establishment of General Motors Acceptance Corporation (GMAC) in 1919 led to large-scale automobile financing and ten years later consumers purchased 61 percent of new cars and 65 percent of used cars on installment (Gordon 2016). In the late 1920s Columbia University economist Edwin Seligman estimated that consumer credit financed "80–90 percent of furniture, 75 percent of washing machines, 65 percent of vacuum cleaners, 18–25 percent of jewelry, 75 percent of radio sets, and 80 percent of phonographs" (cited in Gordon 2016, 299). Outstanding consumer credit balances, between 3 and 4 percent of GDP in 1900, jumped to over 7 percent in 1930. The value of outstanding real estate mortgages also zoomed upward from under 4 percent of GDP in 1920 to about 9 percent in 1930, before then declining precipitously during the Great Depression. It has been argued that the growth of installment credit during the 1920s greatly facilitated American consumerism. However, while credit for consumer durables doubled between 1900 and 1930, the ratio of real expenditures on consumer durables to GDP stayed relatively constant, fluctuating around 6 percent (Gordon 2016). Thus, other components of GDP, such as spending on consumer nondurables and services, grew at a similar rate as durables.

Meaning Transfer by Advertising and Consumers

American advertising became a much larger and increasingly more sophisticated business during the first three decades of the twentieth century (Cruikshank and Schultz 2010; Fox 1984; Laird 1998; Pope 1983; Strasser 1989). By the 1920s, campaigns executed via full-page, four-color ads in magazines had become powerful tools for transmitting copious meaning to all sorts of consumer goods. Instead of extolling the virtues of the product with detached "reason-why" appeals, more and more ad campaigns conveyed product benefits to consumers, often by invoking emotionally charged rhetoric and frequently deploying stunning visual images. For example, the immortal Woodbury's Soap slogan, "The Skin You Love to Touch," broke new ground when it first appeared in 1911. It was about being alluring and having sex appeal, not just boasting about a brand of soap. Figure 6.3 shows an example from 1916 published in the *Ladies' Home Journal*. The color illustration was gorgeous, but the black and white body copy and the picture of John H. Woodbury on a soap bar still harkened back to nineteenth century practice. Helen Lansdowne (1886–1964), who worked as a copywriter for J. Walter Thompson, created this popular campaign. She married Thompson executive Stanley B. Resor (1879–1962) in 1917 and for many years the pair remained highly influential in the agency and among their ad industry peers. Lansdowne would become the first woman inducted (posthumously, alas, in 1967) into the Advertising Hall of Fame. She was also active in the woman's suffrage movement and supported the philosophy of "planned parenthood" (Fox 1984, 94).

In his important history of the interwar years, *Advertising the American Dream: Making Way for Modernity, 1920–1940*, historian Roland Marchand (1985) provided an exceptionally thorough account of these meaning creation processes. He showed how ads in the late 1920s and into the early 1930s frequently told stories through stock social tableaux explained by copious amounts of elegantly written body copy. Brands of toothpaste, shaving creams, and razors starred in the "parable of the first impression" where they facilitated the crucially important outward appearances of consumers. Other parables included "the democracy of goods" where everyone could enjoy the pleasure, convenience, and benefits of consumption, "civilization redeemed" where brands ensured healthy living, and "the captivated child" where products played an instructive role in child guidance (Marchand 1985). Presumably, this plethora of advertiser driven meaning-creation resonated with consumers.

Figure 6.3 "A Skin You Love to Touch," Woodbury's Facial Soap, *Ladies' Home Journal*, September 1916.

The advertising and fashion systems during this era developed still more new meanings for goods and services by associating them with concepts of youth and with a youth market. Advertisers began to realize the potential of young people as buyers themselves and as consumer mavens who could spread awareness of their national brands and thus influence family purchasing decisions. A number of periodicals in the early twentieth century catered to young readers. Titles included *The American Boy*, *The American Girl*, *St. Nicholas*, *The Youth's Companion*, and from the Boy Scouts of America, *Boys' Life*, which had the tag line "An Out-of-Doors Adventure Magazine for Boys" (Figure 6.4). By 1928,

Figure 6.4 *Boys' Life*, September 1919. Illustration by Henry Botkin (1896–1983).

J. Walter Thompson was telling its clients that each year magazine advertising reached two million kids aged ten to 20 (Blaszczyk 2009, 129). The young were more malleable and receptive to consumerist messaging, advertisers believed, and should be targeted directly to overcome parental conservatism in the marketplace (Ewen 1976).

As Stanley C. Hollander and Richard Germain (1992) discussed in their charming little book, *Was There a Pepsi Generation before Pepsi Discovered It? An Historical Approach to Youth-Based Age Segmentation*, the definition of youth can be tricky. Historians have debated whether a phenomenon of socially recognized "youth" even existed before very modern times and marketers have not always agreed about where to set chronological age limits. Further, as McCracken (1986, 72) observed, cultural categories like age may have unique characteristics in North America:

> First, they possess an indeterminacy that is not normally evident in other ethnographic circumstances. For instance, cultural categories of person are marked by a persistent and striking lack of clarity, as are cultural categories of age. Second, they possess an apparent "elective" quality. Devoted as it is to the freedom of the individual, contemporary North American society permits its members to declare at their own discretion the cultural categories they presently occupy. Exercising this freedom, teenagers declare themselves adults, members of the working class declare themselves middle class, the old declare themselves young, and so on.

Cultural categories were more strictly specified and policed in more traditional societies, which would have included the U.S. before the twentieth century. There may also have been more rigidity in the early 1900s than when McCracken wrote many decades later or, for that matter, in the twenty-first century when even biological sex and cultural gender have become transmutable.

The perception of a youth market may have been shaped by rising educational attainments. In 1900, less than 9 percent of American teenagers received a high school diploma. In 1930, about 30 percent finished their secondary education (Gordon 2016, 284–285). College enrollments also grew much faster than the overall population and these mostly privileged youths, in turn, influenced high school students. Gathered together in schools, as opposed to being dispersed in workplaces under more direct adult supervision, young people could form their own brand and consumption communities. By the 1920s courtship practices were switching from formal visits in the home to dating in public, while the automobile gave young swains increased mobility and freedom from parental control.

With youth having a growing presence in the cultural milieu, advertising agencies built youth-based campaigns for Coca-Cola, for Woodbury's Soap (see Figure 6.3) and, starting in 1928, for Jantzen swimwear whose logo featured a graceful young female diver. Youth infused many goods and services, particularly cosmetics, women's hosiery, men's shirts, athletics and sporting goods, some automobiles and travel destinations, cigarettes, dancehalls, jazz music, and motion pictures. Hollander and Germain (1992) interpreted these phenomena as manifestations of the therapeutic ethos of consumption described by T.J. Jackson Lears (1983). Already in the late nineteenth century, and definitely by the early twentieth, American culture stressed how consumers had a duty to be fit, attractive, healthy, and youthful. Youthfulness and the therapeutic ethos remained powerful consumption meanings throughout the twentieth into the twenty-first century.

Other product meanings emerged relatively less from product advertising campaigns and more from collectivities of grassroots consumers, what researchers today variously have described as consumption communities, subcultures, and tribes (Canniford 2011; Schouten and McAlexander 1995). The colonial revival movement constituted one such community. Its advocates reinterpreted history through the collecting of early American artifacts, the making and selling of reproduction furniture and décor, and the building of colonial style homes and other structures. The roots of this movement extended back to recreations of New England kitchens first assembled at Civil War charity bazaars called Sanitary Fairs, then at the 1876 Centennial Exhibition in Philadelphia, and again at the 1893 Chicago World's Columbian Exposition (Hosmer 1985; Roth 1964; Schoelwer 1985). These displays may not have been entirely accurate in their depictions of colonial interiors, but they did stimulate a widespread interest in early American life. By the 1870s and 1880s, affluent antiquarians were collecting American furniture, silver, and other objects made in the colonial and federal eras (Stillinger 1980). Meanwhile, patriotic associations in New England and the Middle Atlantic States were preserving and restoring memorials to the Revolutionary War (Hosmer 1965). Between 1890 and 1910, middle-class readers made best sellers out of historical novels set in the colonial period (Seaton 1985). In the visual arts, Eastman Johnson, Frank Benson, Childe Hassam, and other talented American artists painted quiet colonial or New England interiors as backdrops for their pensive, *fin de siecle* female characters (Betsky 1985) and even Thomas Eakins (1844–1916), the acclaimed realist painter, produced several variations of a colonial spinner at her wheel (Monkhouse 1983).

However, enthusiasm for early America really hit its full stride during the first few decades of the twentieth century when entrepreneurs seized upon the colonial meme. Wallace Nutting (1861–1941), a former Congregational minister, began a thriving business in 1904 selling hand-colored photographs, many of which illustrated New England scenes and colonial interiors (Barendsen 1983). Figure 6.5 depicts a photo he staged on May 31, 1913. In this sentimental composition two young women wearing period attire balled yarn in front of a large fireplace with pewter plates on a shelf above the mantle. Nutting put together an encyclopedic collection of antique furniture and, in 1917, established a furniture and ironware workshop that reproduced them for sale to the general public. He produced illustrated catalogs and distributed his merchandise through gift, furniture, and department stores. In the realm of tableware, Tiffany and Gorham started copying early American silver about 1912, while the silversmith George

Figure 6.5 Wallace Nutting, "Colonial Houses – Three Chums," May 31, 1913.
Source: Library of Congress, Prints & Photographs Division, Washington, D.C.

Gebelein of Boston embraced both eighteenth-century styles and traditional handcrafted procedures in the making of expensive tea and coffee services in the 1920s and 1930s (Carpenter 1985). Naturally, all these colonial goods deserved a house with a period look. In 1918, Aladdin Homes targeted the middle-class with a largish two-story model, "The Colonial," for a then midrange price of \$2518.45 or a quite low \$40,100.19 in 2016 dollars (Minneapolis Fed 2017; Rhoads 1977). From 1908 to 1940, Sears, Roebuck and Company catalogs successfully marketed more than a dozen different types of prefabricated colonial house kits delivered by train and assembled by carpenters on site (Stevenson and Jandl 1986).

Consumption of colonial antiques, reproductions, adaptations, and other trappings conveyed a variety of meanings. Native-born WASPs (White Anglo-Saxon Protestants) purchased and displayed period antiques for status presentation and ethnic identification. They appropriated early American life in order to assert their social standing and cultural hegemony and to set themselves apart psychologically (Stillinger 1980). Ethnic identification – a social process through which groups define themselves and form boundaries with other groups (Barth 1969; Roosens 1995) – tends to accelerate following increased contact with outsiders. In the late nineteenth and early twentieths centuries native-born Protestant Americans encountered a great influx of Catholic and Jewish immigrants from Ireland,

Germany, and southern and eastern Europe. Perhaps sensing these social tensions, in 1900 the Berkey and Gay Furniture Company of Grand Rapids, Michigan titled its catalog "The Old Feeling, or the Past Revived." Illustrations and elaborate copy showed how its traditional pieces recaptured the past *and* built moral fiber, as in the following description of a colonial toilet table:

> Who could be brought in daily association with such unassumed, impressive elegance, without being somewhat fashioned after it? As well say that the rays of a 4th of July sun could not warm your body as to say that such furniture can have no bearing on the development of refinement in character.
>
> (Cited in Lindquist and Warren 1993, 39)

At this time, the colonial revival was about heritage as much as actual history. The latter term refers to attempts to reconstruct and understand the past, including its ugly side, through evidence, its interpretation, debate, and revision in light of new evidence. Heritage, in contrast, mythologizes the past, strips it of the bad parts, and plays upon emotion (Conn 2015).

Early American décor also conveyed nostalgia for handcrafted authenticity, became a form of tradition making, and suggested at least a partial rejection of modernity. Proponents of neocolonialism had a specific domestic vision: "Colonial meant cozy – a cozy home with a big kitchen, a broad chimneypiece, and ancestral relics strewn about in quaint profusion" (Marling 1988, 34). In the 1920s and 1930s, photographs of colonial interiors depicting authentically costumed women socializing or doing household chores, such as the one in Figure 6.5, were extremely popular as wedding gifts (Witkowski 1998). Tableaux, such as the pensive woman drinking tea from a dainty cup and the energetic mistress spinning thread by her glowing kitchen hearth, became *the* images of an imagined colonial past (Monkhouse 1983). Finally, the taste for colonial revival objects and designs bespoke a strain of aesthetic conservatism among American consumers. Not everyone was as enchanted with modernity and its meanings as Marchand (1985), Slater (1997), and other historians might have us believe.

America's Purchasing Agent

For the middle and upper classes, household spending and consumption increasingly and perhaps even decidedly became a female domain in the first three decades of the twentieth century (Blaszczyk 2009; Deutsch 2010; Witkowski 2004). On the national level, women finally won the right to vote in 1920 with the ratification of the Nineteenth Amendment to the U.S. Constitution. In their campaigns, suffragists promoted the cause through adept use of advertising, buttons, pageants, and souvenirs (Deutsch 2010), and now women could "vote" with their family's dollars as well. At least that is what "free market" apologists thought when they equated purchasing choices with citizenship (Schwarzkopf 2011). Companies and the media worked together to target increasingly empowered female consumers. For example, the high profile brands of fast moving packaged goods including Palmolive and Ivory soaps, Listerine mouthwash, and Fleischmann's Yeast placed full-page ads in major national magazines (Atwan, McQuade, and Wright 1979; Marchand 1985). Brand advertising made women less and less reliant on the say so of male storeowners and clerks. In the meantime, chain grocery stores in urban areas reached female customers through ads run in the evening newspapers. Morning editions tended to target males on their way to work (Deutsch 2010).

Other industries that focused on female consumers included greeting cards, cigarettes, and home appliances. The greeting card industry traced its roots to the 1830s when commercial valentine cards started to become common in the United States. By the 1880s, the Boston-based chromolithographer, Louis Prang and Co., had developed cards for Christmas, New Year's, and Easter. After 1900, even more types of cards with more emphasis on printed sentiments became available. The National Association of Greeting Cards Manufacturers was organized in 1914 and, four years later, launched national advertising campaigns with slogans like "Scatter Sunshine with GREETING CARDS: There is one for EVERY occasion." Promotional cutouts and banners were given to retailers and books with titles such as *Greeting Cards: When and How to Use Them* educated consumers on greeting card etiquette. Between 1913 and 1928 industry sales surged from \$10 million to \$60 million annually (Schmidt 1991). In 1910, a young Nebraska man, Joyce C. Hall (1891–1982), started selling cards in Kansas City and by 1923 Hall Bros. (later Hallmark) had 120 employees. In the 1920s, greeting cards companies were advertising in the women's service magazines, such as *Ladies' Home Journal* and *Good Housekeeping*. Greeting cards constituted a form of social media by way of stationery, handwriting, and postage stamps. As with Facebook and Pinterest in the twenty-first century, women were avid consumers, probably more so than men.

Tobacco companies aggressively worked to enlarge the female segment of cigarette smokers with new brands and appeals, the most notorious being the "Reach for a Lucky Instead of a Sweet" campaign of the late 1920s (Beard and Klyueva 2010; Witkowski 1991). Controversies over young females who smoked flared repeatedly during the 1920s and moral activists reprimanded cigarette advertising for tempting women and young people (Page 1929). However, these criticisms accomplished little except perhaps to further associate cigarettes with youth, urban sophistication, and cool naughtiness, trends propelled further by the blatant resistance to Prohibition discussed in the next section. Indeed, women used cigarettes, a social symbol of considerable power in the 1920s, to establish new identities that separated them from women in the past (Schudson 1984). American culture, having helped endow cigarettes with a new, positive image, now witnessed a movement of meaning from the product to the smoker. Following McCracken's (1986) theory, smoking rituals – lighting up, inhaling, exhaling, and discarding ashes – allowed consumers to claim the symbolic attributes of cigarettes for themselves. Through smoking, therefore, women could project a much-admired modern image.

The latest household network technologies discussed above (electricity, running water, and indoor plumbing), along with new appliances (electric irons, gas stoves, mechanical refrigerators, vacuum cleaners, and wringer washers), clearly lessened the sheer drudgery of many chores. The Western Electric ad from October 1916 in Figure 6.6 stressed this point by dressing a woman

Figure 6.6 "The New Enlightenment," Western Electric Company, *Good Housekeeping*, October 1916.

vacuuming as Lady Liberty. Ironically, the overall amount of time women spent on housework did not diminish appreciably. As noted by Ruth Schwartz Cowan (1983) in her classic book, *More Work for Mother*, acceptable housekeeping standards also rose in the late nineteenth and early twentieth centuries (see also Lupton 1993). A new cultural construction of cleanliness was championed by magazine articles, advice manuals, social reformers, home economists, nutritionists, and, above all, advertising copy for soaps and other products that reiterated the importance of sanitation and hygiene in combatting disease. As Joel Mokyr (2000, 21) put it: "Homemakers spent more time cleaning, nursing, laundering, cooking, and looking after their children because they had become convinced that the health of the members of their household was under their control and part of their responsibility."

A 1929 advertisement for General Electric's "National Mazda" brand light bulbs (Figure 6.7) featured an attractively fashionable young woman speaking these words:

> Let Me SEE Your Wares
> *I am the purchasing agent of America. I buy four-fifths of all things that are bought in stores.*
> *I buy little which I do not see. Seeing arouses my desire. Seeing satisfies my caution. I must see or I won't buy.*
> (National Mazda Lamps, 1929)

Smartly dressed, gazing ahead purposefully, reaching into her open purse while striding through the urban canyons of a big city, her body language, like her dialogue, was perfectly clear: American women were sophisticated, vigorous consumers, purchasing for themselves and for their households. What they bought depended upon the arousal of their desires, wants that could be visually stimulated, according to General Electric, but wants ultimately governed by rational caution. Perhaps not everyone at the time would have accepted this frank image and its implications, but by the late 1920s, at the crest of a wave of mass consumption, it had become mainstream (see Frederick 1929). America's purchasing agent was now a woman.

However, some interpretive caution is in order. First, the assumption that shopping and domestic consumption were largely women's work may have resulted as much from active campaigning by advertisers, magazine editors, and writers for industry publications (e.g., *The Dry Goods Economist*, *Printer's Ink*), as they were an accurate reflection of social reality. Swiencicki (1998, 795) put it this way:

> In order to attract clients and business, marketers of the goods that women often bought (i.e. clothing, foodstuffs, detergents, makeup, etc.) began running articles and advertisements in trade journals and general interest magazines which claimed that the best way to sell goods was by marketing them directly to women.

Figure 6.7 "Let Me SEE Your Wares," General Electric National Mazda Lamps, *Saturday Evening Post*, May 11, 1929.

Source: Courtesy of Museum of Innovation and Science, Schenectady, NY.

Edward William Bok (1863–1930), who edited the ultraconservative *Ladies' Home Journal* from 1889 to 1919, was particularly keen on gendering consumption as female and, for good measure, professionalizing housework (Blaszczyk 2009; Scanlon 1995). The ideology of female-dominant consumption became so pervasive that later historians, such as Roland Marchand (1985), may have relied too heavily on advertisements from women's magazines at the expense of publications targeting males (Swiencicki 1998, 792–793). Men's magazines, such as *Outing*, *Forest & Stream*, and *Field & Stream*, carried numerous ads for hunting, fishing, and camping equipment, beer and tobacco, and other products for the male market. The July 4, 1925 issue of the general interest magazine, *Saturday Evening Post*, targeted 39 percent of its ads toward men, 16 percent to women, and 42 percent to either sex (Swiencicki 1998, 794).

Second, a parallel discourse expressed by curmudgeonly male pundits, such as the humorist H.L. Mencken (1880–1956), twitted women with a litany of their consumption shortcomings ranging from inferior taste to prudishness to outright man hating. A long tradition of criticizing female spending on fashion and luxury goods went back to back to the colonial era, as discussed previously in Chapter 3. *Esquire* magazine, which debuted in 1933, took it to a new level. When it was not visually depicting women as sexy pinups, airheads, and gold diggers, this publication's nonfiction writers regularly excoriated female cooking, eating habits, home decoration proclivities, gardening decisions, and much more (Breazeale 1994). Thus, *Esquire* contested the femininity of domestic consumption and the dominance of women in the cultural marketplace.

American men in the early twentieth century retained their predominance in a number of product categories and sites of consumption. For example, they attended to the purchase, care, and feeding of the family automobile and, if they owned one, their personal motorcycle. Until the advent of the electric starter, cranking a Model T required male strength, and shifting gears and steering on unpaved roads was demanding. Men became the target market for new packaged goods such as the disposable razor sold by King Gillette and his company (Strasser 1989, 97–102). Men bought most of the tickets for spectator sports, especially baseball and boxing, now being played in ever larger and more elaborate stadiums and indoor arenas, such as Madison Square Garden in New York City (Seifried and de Wilde 2014). Working-class men patronized saloons in great numbers until Prohibition ruined these overwhelmingly male establishments. Ironically, this created a new group of public drinkers: "Women's new willingness to drink in public – or at least in the semipublic atmosphere of the speakeasy – owed much to Prohibition's achievement, the death of the saloon, whose masculine culture no longer governed norms of public drinking" (Blocker 2006, 238). The tantalizing topic of women breaking taboos during Prohibition will be discussed further in the next section.

During and after World War I, American women impinged upon the male domain through fashion choices hinting at androgyny. Women's fashions underwent an enormous change in the mid-1920s that bent, blended, and made ambiguous traditionally gendered notions of appropriate male and female dress. Following the example of celebrities like the charismatic and trendsetting dancer, Irene Castle (1893–1969), hemlines rose to just below the knees, silhouettes became tubular, breasts were flattened, and hair was bobbed (cut short around the head at about jaw-level). Women, like the Mazda lamp maven illustrated in

Figure 6.7, finally abandoned their corsets and instead wore brassieres and simplified undergarments. This attire was less restrictive, more comfortable, and in the guise of the "flapper" suggested youthful rebellion.

Fashion can be seen as the pursuit of change and novelty for their own sake. Fashion in clothing has had a long history (see, e.g., Breward 2015). In colonial America, upper class men duded it up with wigs, waistcoats, and breeches in imitation of their British counterparts, but by the middle of the nineteenth century male attire became rather drab and standardized, whereas female clothing and its excesses took pride of place and women became the primary domestic mavens in the realm of clothing. The American fashion system as an institution started to become a potent force in the mid-nineteenth century when illustrations in print media, such as the plates in the popular *Godey's Ladies' Book*, supplemented traditional person-to-person observation on the street and at public events. In the early twentieth century, periodicals and catalogs continued to disseminate fashion trends, but by 1930 had become increasingly augmented by the potent combination of motion pictures, fan magazines, and celebrity culture that extolled the lifestyles of the rich and glamorous (Blaszczyk 2009, 104–107). Although women still made some of their own garments, they increasingly purchased ready-to-wear clothing for themselves from department stores, specialty shops, and mail order catalogs.

Explaining past changes in fashion preferences is complicated, especially in regards to androgyny. American women had a long history of adopting elements of men's clothing, such as the tall stiff collar and narrow necktie shown in a 1907 ad for Arrow shirt collars (Figure 6.8). Perhaps one reason women in the "Roaring Twenties" chose to dress somewhat male was to appropriate part of the higher value American society attributed to masculinity. In the 1930s after the Great Depression had eroded male status by putting numerous men out of work and reducing the incomes of many others, women's fashions returned to a more feminine profile. Other theories of fashion – trickle down, across, and up – also explain the spread of a particular look (Simmel 1904/1957; Veblen 1899/1953),

Figure 6.8 Arrow Collar Androgyny, 1907. Illustration by Joseph Christian Leyendecker (1874–1951).

Source: Wikimedia Commons.

and certainly pertain to the gender of consumption, but space limitations prevent a fuller treatment of this fascinating topic and cultural thread.

Boycotts, Thrift, Prohibition, and More Resistance

Women also became prominent in different forms of resistance to consumption. In 1899, women from the Progressive movement followed the example of Consumers League of New York (founded in 1891) and chartered the National Consumers League (NCL). Led by Florence Kelly (1859–1932), a well-educated and energetic socialist and advocate for African-American civil rights among other causes, the NCL aimed to educate uninformed female shoppers on efficient and ethical consumption and, equally important, to direct their purchasing toward the benefit of female workers. Consumers needed to know the industrial provenance, such as sweatshop labor, of the goods they purchased. Unlike often short-lived and local consumer boycotts, its organizers intended the NCL to be an umbrella group that provided expertise and was meant to last, which it still does to this day. During the early twentieth century the "consumer" finally became recognized as a class of people, "a distinct group with their own interests, rights, and responsibilities, one which required a lobby to protect its interests" (Glickman 2009, 159). By the late 1920s the term "consumer movement" had become familiar in the American lexicon.

Women participated vigorously in two significant meat boycotts of 1902. At the national level consumers organized boycotts of meat whose prices had been rapidly increasing, participants believed, because of the nefarious doings of the "Beef Trust," the pooling arrangement begun in 1885 by Armour, Swift, Nelson Morris, and other firms in the meat-packing industry (Piott 1981). Such trusts had become commonplace in the late nineteenth century when companies in the steel, oil, railroad, tobacco, and many additional industries joined forces to dampen competition and to create monopoly or near monopoly power. Congress passed the Sherman Antitrust Act in 1890 to address the problem, but implementation lagged and the public became increasingly wary of trusts and their excuses for raising prices. People simply did not accept the corporate argument that their combinations and centralizations represented a modernizing process. After hearings at the Missouri Supreme Court in 1902 "not only confirmed that the trust artificially increased meat prices, but it also forced consumers to purchase an inferior product" (Piott 1981, 47), workers and consumers organized beef boycotts in cities across the country. Consumption declined and beef prices stabilized, but many small meat shops had to close. As with other boycotts, the direct consequences of resistance to meat consumption were difficult to assess (Friedman 1999), but they did buttress the political will to initiate further antitrust actions at the state and, during Theodore Roosevelt's Administration, federal levels.

While the national meat boycott took its course, in New York City Jewish women resisted price increases at kosher markets (Hyman 1980). On May 15, 1902 a riot broke out on the Lower East Side when protesters entered butcher shops, flung meat into the streets, and intimidated customers. The police arrested and charged with disorderly conduct about 70 women and 15 men the first day and 100 more people the next. More boycotters established pickets in front of shops, went from house to house asking for support, and, on Saturday, May 17, interrupted Torah readings at synagogues. On May 22 the Retail Butchers' Association reluctantly joined the boycott. On June 5 the strike concluded after prices rolled back 9 cents a pound at wholesale and 14 cents a pound at retail. Middle-aged housewives with children led this movement. While a few Rabbis with ties to the meat packing industry opposed the boycott, most of the larger immigrant Jewish community, including the socialist newspaper *Forward* and the Orthodox *Yiddishe Tageblat*, supported the women. Kosher meat prices began rising again not long after the three-week boycott, so its success was qualified. Still, a precedent of neighborhood consumer resistance had been set and direct action would appear again with local rent strikes in 1904 and 1907–1908 (Hyman 1980), and additional meat boycotts in 1910 (Figure 6.9).

Figure 6.9 East Side Women Discussing Meat Prices during Boycott, April 1910.
Source: Library of Congress, Prints & Photographs Division Washington, D.C.

In addition to direct action through boycotts, the thread of criticism directed at over-consumption remained popular. The English translation (from French) of Charles Wagner's *The Simple Life* (1904) made the author a celebrity in America. He reprimanded readers for their ostentation, modernity, and abandonment of family tradition. He neither believed in an atavistic renunciation of worldly goods nor in a socialistic redistribution of wealth, but rather that people in all stations needed to make an individual and personal commitment to their authentic and spiritual selves. Wagner's ideas were popularized by the *Ladies' Home Journal* (Scanlon 1995) and found a particularly receptive audience among "middle-class urban Americans of liberal evangelical background. Many of these people, who felt morally uncertain or guilty about their increased wealth and comfort, found simple-life philosophy appealing" (Leach 1994, 203). Ironically, Philadelphia's John Wanamaker, who had become one of America's richest men and was a major financial backer of mainstream, Protestant institutions, became a disciple of Wagner. Wanamaker preached simplicity while at the same time turning luxuries into commodities and necessities for sale in his ornate department stores (Leach 1994; Vanderbilt 1996).

During World War I popular writer Stuart Chase (1888–1985) picked up these threads of consumer resistance through simplicity when he became convinced that reducing luxuries was "not only a personal necessity but a patriotic duty to eliminate waste and extravagance" (cited in Horowitz 1985, 112). Chase went on to write *The Tragedy of Waste* (1925) and, with F.J. Schlink (1891–1995), *Your Money's Worth* (1927). These books promoted restrained and informed buying rather than renouncing or resisting consumption altogether. Chase and Schlink also founded the product testing and advocacy group, Consumer's Research in 1929, which was the precursor organization to Consumer's Union and its publication, *Consumer's Report*. The history and ideology of Consumer's Research and its relationship with more activist resistance will be continued in the next chapter. Samuel Strauss (1870–1953) was a lesser-known consumption critic of the time. A newspaper publisher and contributor to periodicals such as *The Atlantic Monthly*, Strauss coined the term "consumptionism" in 1924. He contended that America's modern marketing systems were changing democracy by replacing the role of citizen with that of the consumer (Renouard 2007).

A slightly different thread of anti-consumption advocacy, in the tradition of Benjamin Franklin, received new impetus with the founding of the National Thrift Movement in 1916. Its crusading leaders wrote popular books and magazine articles, gave talks to civic and youth groups, formed local Thrift Committees across the country, published *National Thrift News*, sponsored a National Thrift Week, and organized public service ad campaigns. The American Federation of Labor passed a resolution at its 1919 convention in support of the Thrift Movement (Wolfe 1920). In January 1920, the entire contents of the *Annals of the American Academy of Political and Social Sciences* were devoted to "the new American thrift." In his article, "The Relation of Thrift to Nation Building," T.N. Carver of Harvard University concluded, "Remember that thrift consists in buying, but in buying wisely. Urge everyone, if you please, to buy and buy now, but URGE HIM TO BUY THINGS THAT WILL GIVE HIM MORE BUYING POWER NEXT YEAR AND EVERY YEAR" (Carver 1920, 8). Like other American critical discourses of the time, this one did not reject consumption outright, but instead instructed (in capital letters no less) on what Roy G. Blakey (1920) termed the "proper use" of goods.

American anti-consumption took a draconian turn on January 16, 1920 when the Eighteenth Amendment to the U.S. Constitution went into effect exactly one year after it was ratified by three-quarters of the then 48 states. As interpreted, the Amendment banned most production, importation, transportation, and sale (but not possession or consumption) of intoxicating beverages. Enforced by the Volstead Act, Prohibition was in part an expression of Progressivism's desire to reduce the negative effects of mostly male alcohol consumption on their families and themselves. Prohibition also became allied with another Progressive cause, women's suffrage, because women would be more inclined than men to vote dry (i.e., anti-alcohol) at the ballot box. The dominant ideology motivating Prohibition, however, was a straight-laced, religious, and frequently nativist breed of anti-consumption sentiment long apparent in American history. Local "blue laws," around since the seventeenth century, prohibited alcohol sales and other commercial activities on Sundays, the Christian Sabbath. These laws privileged the stern theology and, hence, political dominance of conservative Protestants over more tolerant Catholics, Jews, and even more liberal Protestants. On the nativist front, Prohibition aimed to stifle the drinking of the Irish, the Germans, and more recent immigrant groups from eastern and southern Europe now heavily concentrated in the rapidly growing cities. The resurgent Ku Klux Klan vociferously attacked Catholics and Jews at the time – persecuting African Americans only later topped its hateful agenda – and banning alcohol became a powerful weapon against these perceived others (Okrent 2010). During World War I, public opinion turned quite hostile toward Germany and Germans and, with family names like Blatz, Busch, Miller, Pabst, Piels, and Schlitz, brewers and their brands became easy targets for nativist jingoism. As sociologists have long known, drug laws (and alcohol is a drug) are as much about afflicting and controlling the types of people perceived to be users as they are about the substances themselves (Gusfield 1967).

The Woman's Christian Temperance Union (WCTU) remained influential in the movement to ban alcohol, but expended its energy on multiple causes. In contrast, the Anti-Saloon League (ASL), founded in 1893, focused chiefly on the politics of changing liquor laws at the state and federal levels and, above all, on amending the U.S. Constitution. With an overwhelmingly Methodist and Baptist leadership, the ASL soon became the preeminent political organization in the movement to ban alcohol. Like the National Rifle Association in the latter twentieth and early twenty-first centuries, the ASL was exceptionally successful in mobilizing voters to support sympathetic candidates, but unlike the more partisan gun group, the League worked on behalf of both dry Republicans and dry Democrats in political contests. The ASL printed vast quantities of propaganda – over 100 million leaflets and pamphlets from 1909 to 1923 (Sinclair 1962, 113)

– distributed through thousands of churches. Its de facto leader and head lobbyist, mild-mannered Wayne Bidwell Wheeler (1869–1927), campaigned brilliantly for the cause through astute political intimidation and coalition building (Okrent 2010).

Anti-alcohol sentiments eventually pervaded the mass media. In *Prohibition: The Era of Excess*, Andrew Sinclair (1962, 310) cited a study showing that in 1915 articles in middle-class magazines supporting Prohibition outnumbered those opposed by 20 to 1. Popular fiction, theater, and the new medium of motion pictures usually portrayed drinkers and drinking in negative terms and more and more newspapers and magazines would not accept liquor ads (Blocker 2006; Okrent 2010). Dry propagandists even rewrote the lyrics of evangelical hymns, the most popular song being "The Saloon Must Go" (Sinclair 1962, 113). Because of the growing weight of anti-drinking opinion and the spreading enactment of state-level restrictions, alcohol consumption declined in the early twentieth century. After Prohibition went into effect, drinking then fell to about 30 percent of its immediate pre-Prohibition level. Within a few years, however, alcohol consumption returned to 60–70 percent of the pre-Prohibition level and continued to grow a bit more until Repeal in 1933 (Miron and Zweibel 1991).

Prohibition was state sanctioned resistance to alcohol consumption, but perhaps its most notable feature was the widespread counter resistance it engendered. Across the country, millions of drinkers flouted the law, while sympathetic local authorities often looked the other way especially when bribed by traffickers, as they usually were. From the beginning, many Americans simply felt Prohibition to be an illegitimate infringement upon their right to consume beverages of their choice. Even some supporters of dryness, who may have themselves been moderate drinkers, were surprised by the scope of government intrusion on private behavior. Rebellious college students turned against Prohibition and some wets (as drinkers were called) became even more indignant when they learned how the KKK had championed the ban (Blocker 2006). Demand for alcohol was vast and, given an entire year between ratification and implementation, numerous distribution channels to provision it were established from the get-go. Booze was smuggled from Canada, the Bahamas, and other places and ports of origin. Ships loaded with alcoholic cargo floated outside the three-mile territorial limit (extended to 12 miles in 1924) in what was termed "Rum Row" and did not have to wait long before being visited by flotillas of speedy smaller craft that took the liquid to shore. Meanwhile, California growers legally transported huge quantities of grapes back east for home wine making, while the brewers in the Midwest sold malt syrup for productive consumption through home fermentation. Also legal were markets for sacramental wine and industrial alcohol that could be diluted and flavored to approximate the taste of distilled spirits. Farmers were allowed to ferment apple cider and doctors wrote countless prescriptions for medicinal liquor in the states that permitted the practice. The federal government, states, and municipalities allocated paltry amounts for upholding the Volstead Act and, despite some well-publicized busts, alcohol traffickers usually overpowered enforcement efforts.

In the 1920s, drinking acquired deeper cultural meaning:

> Being able to drink was a mark of conspicuous consumption and rebellion; it meant a person had the cash necessary to indulge a habit not sanctioned by the government. It appealed to that old American streak of individuality, the chance to thumb one's nose at authority.
>
> (Young and Young 2002, 113–114)

Unlike in the old days before Prohibition, when females rarely drank in public and saloons were a male preserve, women now flocked to speakeasies and other venues where the thirsty gathered. Figure 6.10, dated February 13, 1922, depicts a cheerful young woman seated at a soda fountain table ostensibly pouring alcohol into a cup from a cane flask, rather than the more common hip flask. The large Coca-Cola advertisement behind her carried some irony in that company founder Asa Candler (1851–1929) was a teetotaler. Coke's sales tripled during Prohibition and, when used for a mixer, the soda helped disguise the poor taste of much bootleg booze (Okrent 2010, 215). Speakeasies ranged in quality, as did the alcohol they served, but the clubs took on a glamorous sheen popularized in silent films such as "After Midnight" (1927) starring Norma Shearer and "Our Dancing Daughters" (1928) featuring Joan Crawford. The fiction of alcoholic writer F. Scott Fitzgerald (1896–1940), such as *The Beautiful and the Damned* (1922) and *The Great Gatsby* (1925), celebrated drinking and alcohol also featured prominently in *The Sun Also Rises* (1926) written by heavy drinking author Ernest Hemingway (1899–1961). According to some who were there, speakeasy culture pressured patrons to drink more than they would have liked, or would have consumed in a legal bar (Okrent 2010, 374).

The November 1928 election resulted in large and vengeful dry majorities in the U.S. Senate and House of Representatives who then passed the harsh Jones-Stalker Act in 1929. This legislation, which turned Volstead violations from misdemeanors into severely punished felonies, went too far for most people. It caused public opinion to tilt decidedly against Prohibition and prompted much of the American press to become openly wet. Newspapers, such as the *Chicago Tribune* and the 28 dailies in the Hearst syndicate, reported extensively on misguided enforcement activities and, with barely disguised glee, on the hypocrisy of politicians who voted dry, but were apprehended with booze in their possession (Okrent 2010, 323–326). Calls for changing the Volstead Act and even repealing Prohibition multiplied. Then, the onset of the Great Depression led to massive gains for wet forces in Congress in both the 1930 and 1932 elections. Undoubtedly, the very bad economy, along with the need to replace tax revenues that had dried up, made bold change possible. On December 5, 1933, the Eighteenth Amendment was repealed by the ratification of the Twenty-first Amendment, the only time in American history when a constitutional amendment has been reversed.

A second demonstration of early twentieth-century consumer resistance to social norms came from elite African Americans who, in defiance of white

Figure 6.10 Resisting Prohibition, February 13, 1922. Seated at a soda fountain table, she is ostensibly pouring alcohol into a cup from a cane flask.

Source: Library of Congress, Prints & Photographs Division, Washington, D.C.

expectations, consumed rather conspicuously. The number of elites was small, perhaps 250,000 in 1910, about 2.5 percent of the overall black population (Branchik and Davis 2009). Some were professionals, many ran small service businesses, and like blacks of all social classes they tended to keep to themselves. They bought nice homes when and where permitted by dominant whites, drove good automobiles, wore high quality and fashionable attire, established exclusive clubs that hosted lavish parties, and on college campuses formed seven black Greek-letter fraternities and sororities between 1906 and 1920. Elites even patronized black vacation enclaves, such as Idlewild in western Michigan, known as the "Black Eden." Materialistic tendencies and a drive for status differentiation undoubtedly motivated some of this behavior, but in the face of escalating racial hostility and segregation after 1900, black consumerism also "was a form of social protest – a means of seeking respect and demonstrating equality" (Branchik and Davis 2009, 48).

This marketplace activism was not without risk and whites frequently attacked unlucky African Americans who displayed their wealth in the wrong place at the wrong time. Given these persistent racist threats, the elites, like other blacks, were not shy about buying, keeping, and bearing firearms. Beginning in the 1890s, outspoken black journalist Ida B. Wells had called on her people to purchase Winchester repeating rifles for armed defense. During the so-called "Gay Nineties," white terrorists in the South lynched an average of two blacks a week (Johnson 2014). Lynching continued to be a serious and too frequent problem throughout the first three decades of the 1900s, into the 1930s, and, sadly, right up to the Civil Rights movement of the 1960s. After the 1906 Atlanta race riot, W.E.B. Du Bois (1868–1963), a professor of economics and history at Atlanta University, and a preeminent black intellectual, raged: "I bought a Winchester double-barreled shotgun and two dozen rounds of shells filled with buckshot. If a white mob had stepped on the campus where I lived I would without hesitation have sprayed their guts over the grass" (cited in Johnson 2014, 151). Firearms brought another layer of meaning to the idea of consumer resistance in America.

For most poor and struggling African Americans in the early 1900s, gaining social respect and equality through conspicuous consumption was almost unimaginable. Nevertheless, many had the courage to battle white oppression through organized consumer boycotts. Starting about 1900, cities and states in the South began passing laws that segregated streetcars by requiring blacks to use a separate compartment in the rear. The trolley companies resisted at first, not wanting the hassle of complying and fearing blowback from black customers, but given the overwhelming potency of white racism, they eventually fell into line with Jim Crow. The new laws were particularly humiliating and galling for blacks who remembered the heyday of Reconstruction when restrictions on public consumption had been less frequent and the races had lived more or less harmoniously, albeit paternalistically. Thus, part of the reason for resistance was to preserve the status quo. Furthermore, municipal statutes in effect gave police power to conductors and motormen who generally came from the lower rungs of white society and had gained a bad reputation among the black community. When these bills were being considered, blacks petitioned the cities and states, but they were contemptuously ignored.

Based largely on articles from local newspapers, August Meir and Elliot Rudwick (1969, 1973) identified black boycotts in 27 cities and all of the states of the former Confederacy between 1900 and 1907. This may be an undercount since white-owned newspapers, not wanting to encourage the resisters, had reason to de-emphasize or ignore their protests. The boycotts lasted from a few weeks to several years. Led by African-American businessmen and professionals, this consumer resistance caused a great deal of economic harm to the trolley companies. Black-owned transportation alternatives were established, but pressure from the authorities put them out of business. Unlike previous episodes of consumer resistance, which had generally targeted merchants, the black boycotts challenged governments and the companies they had chartered (Glickman 2009, 184).

In spite of everything, the laws were not changed and, eventually, most blacks returned to the segregated streetcars. The following stanza from a poem published on April 30 by O.M. Steward (1904) in the black newspaper, the *Richmond Planet* provided an apt summary:

> Of all the towns beneath the stars,
> Old Richmond beats for Jim Crow cars,
> They thread her streets and all around
> Her suburbs Jim Crow cars abound.
> And some are fast and some are slow,
> But in the rear all serve Jim Crow.

The Richmond Planet was a weekly newspaper published from 1882 until 1938 when it merged with the Baltimore *Afro-American.* The *Planet* focused on segregation, voting rights, the Ku Klux Klan, and lynching, but also included national and international news, poetry, and much more. Many of its copies, which include ads for black-owned restaurants, food marts, furniture stores, banks, dentists, undertakers, and hair tonics, are now available online for inspection by consumption historians (see link in Steward 1904). Organized black resistance to the legal and normative limits imposed upon their consumption would resume in force in the 1930s and continue into the 1960s.

Summary

Over the first three decades of the twentieth century, American consumption made great strides, perhaps changing more during this time frame than in any prior or subsequent periods. Standards of living rose for broad segments of the population who benefited from the new technologies of electrification, water and sewage systems, motor vehicles, and sound reproduction and dissemination through telephones, phonographs, and later radios. Grocery stores grew in size, formed chains, and introduced concepts of self-service and cash and carry, while manufacturers of consumer durables expanded opportunities for buying on credit. Individual companies, such as Coca-Cola, Hallmark, and Kodak, achieved great success with their mass-market consumer goods. Of course, tobacco companies also were quite accomplished in spreading the smoking habit, which eventually would have serious consequences for the nation's health.

An increasingly robust advertising system moved various meanings (e.g., modernity, youth, sex appeal) into products and on to ultimate consumers, but as documented by the popularity of the colonial revival, consumers themselves could imbue a decorative style with the meanings (e.g., elitism, nativism, heritage) they championed. American women appear to have achieved parity if not primacy in household consumption, but evidence suggests that the assessment of later historians may have been influenced by the concerted campaigns of the publishing industry to promote females as purchasing mavens. Threads of resistance in the form of thrift sermons and boycott activities by marginalized consumers carried forward from earlier periods and were joined by something new, the marketplace activism of more affluent blacks. The imposition of Prohibition and its subsequent flaunting not only entailed highly organized cultural and political resistance to alcohol consumption, but also widespread counter resistance to enforcement attempts. Consumer resistance to anti-consumption policies would reappear later in the century among cannabis aficionados, a topic to be covered in Chapters 8 and 9.

7 The Great Depression and World War II

Following the initial stock market crash of October 1929, the American economy quickly spiraled downward into the Great Depression. Nominal GDP declined 45.3 percent between 1929 and 1933 (about 26.3 percent adjusted for deflation). Per capita GDP, which had reached a high of $858 ($8669 in 2009 dollars) in 1929, did not return to an equivalent level until 1939 when it hit $714 ($8881 in 2009 dollars adjusting for deflation) (Johnston and Williamson 2017). This economic catastrophe so disrupted American consumption – and was so quickly followed by an equally disrupting major war – that the two events are here treated together. These 15 years constitute the shortest period of this book. Unlike in other chapters, threads of meaning, gender, and resistance will be intermingled chronologically rather than examined in separate sections. This chapter also includes an extended discussion of a favorite visual topic of mine: World War II era government sponsored poster campaigns designed to encourage frugal consumption on the home front (Witkowski 2003).

Consumption in Crisis

The 1930s posed a serious challenge to previously established consumption patterns and consumerist mindsets (Ewen 1976; Marchand 1985). With wages down and unemployment rates averaging 17.9 percent between 1930 and 1940, many people were forced to greatly lower their material expectations and to scrimp wherever they could (Hill, Hirschman, and Bauman 1997). People who lost their jobs too often became homeless and some were forced to live in tents and makeshift huts constructed from crates, cartons, and assorted scrap materials and furnished with some bedding and a stove. These shantytowns came to be known as "Hoovervilles," named after President Herbert Hoover (1874–1964) in whose first and only term the Depression had befallen the nation and whose policies for recovery proved ineffectual, if not counterproductive. By 1932 consumers were staging hunger marches in a number of American cities and small food riots had begun to occur. Charitable organizations ran soup kitchens and surviving photos of long breadlines attest to great deprivation. The photograph in Figure 7.1, taken in February 1931, shows unemployed men queued in front of a soup kitchen opened in Chicago by mobster Al Capone (1899–1947). Few if any

Figure 7.1 Unemployed Men Queued in Front of Chicago Soup Kitchen, 1931.

Source: National Archives and Records Administration, Washington, D.C.

Americans starved to death, but many suffered from hunger and malnutrition. Although the 1930s saw increases in the percentage of U.S. households with inside flush toilets and electric lighting and appliances, many families lacked a modern consumer infrastructure. In 1940, with the economy finally on the mend, 33 percent of all Americans still cooked with wood or coal and another 33 percent had no inside running water. Moreover, 67 percent lacked central heat, 47 percent did without indoor bathing equipment, and 48 percent had no refrigerator (Green 1992, 7–8). Because telephones were rented rather than purchased, many households quickly economized and the percentage of those with phone service plummeted from 45 percent in 1929 to 33 percent in 1933 (Gordon 2016, 189).

Prominent documentary photographers like Dorothea Lange (1895–1965), Walker Evans (1903–1975), and Margaret Bourke-White (1904–1971) took thousands of haunting pictures of poor and distressed Americans some of which directly contrasted with boastful commercial slogans. A famous February 1937 image by Bourke-White showed a line of African Americans displaced by a flood in Louisville standing in front of a billboard depicting a smiling white family in their automobile. Sponsored by the National Association of Manufacturers (NAM) as part of a multi-media public relations campaign begun in 1933 to improve the tarnished image of business (Schwarzkopf 2011; Stole 2006, 99), the billboard boldly crowed "World's Highest Standard of Living: There's no way like the American Way." This photo raised the issue of racial disparities and how the Depression particularly afflicted blacks. Another ideologically charged billboard from NAM was titled "It's the American Way" and touted "Freedom of Religion – Speech," "Opportunity," "Representative Democracy," and, unsurprisingly, "Private Enterprise." A photograph taken in Dubuque, Iowa in 1940 by John Vachon (1914–1975), who then worked for the U.S. Farm Security Administration, shows a migrant man with his back to the camera taking in one of these billboards (Figure 7.2). These images utilized the rhetorical strategy of incongruity to convey an alternative perspective on reality to viewers who would then question the claims made by capitalism's apologists (Cooper 2014).

Standards of living did not decrease across the board and over the entire period of the Great Depression. For example, motor vehicle registrations dipped at first, but eventually returned to the levels of the late 1920s (Gordon 2016, 115, 162). People drove more and gasoline sales rose 16 percent from 1929 to 1935 (Cross 2000, 69). The many miles of new and better (resurfaced) roads constructed by two New Deal work relief programs, the Civilian Conservation Corps (1933–1942) and the Works Progress Administration (1935–1943),

Figure 7.2 "It's the American Way," April 1940. Migrant man looking at billboard, Dubuque, Iowa. Photograph by John Vachon.

Source: Library of Congress, Prints & Photographs Division, Washington, D.C.

encouraged auto mobility. By 1942, 58 percent of all U.S. families owned at least one automobile (55 percent urban v. 69 percent farm), a percentage about the same as in 1930 (60 percent) and still more than double the 1920 figure of 26 percent (Lebergott 1993). Along with light trucks and tractors, cars helped rural denizens to overcome their isolation. Farmers and their families could motor about searching for better prices for the products they sold and for the goods they purchased, and likewise engage in recreation and amusements they could not reach by horse and buggy. These vehicles also enabled thousands of destitute rural families to flee the Dust Bowl in Oklahoma for better prospects in California as documented by the photos of Dorothea Lange, the folk songs of Woody Guthrie (1912–1967), and the Pulitzer Prize winning novel *The Grapes of Wrath* (1939) by John Steinbeck (1902–1968) who later won the 1962 Nobel Prize for Literature.

Consumption of entertainment varied across media and types of events. The percentage of households owning radios soared from 35 percent in 1929 to 82 percent in 1940 (Gordon 2016, 189). The number of broadcasting stations and the types of content they aired expanded quickly and thus added value to the medium. Moreover, once a consumer purchased a radio set, further use was essentially free save minor charges for electricity. Weekly motion picture attendance dropped by a third in the early 1930s, but returned to near record levels by the end of the decade (Gordon 2016, 201). The crowds attending professional baseball games decreased during the decade and did not recover until after 1945 (Young and Young 2002, 133). Slickly promoted film and professional sports stars were lionized by the mass media (Green 1992). Many forms of gambling attracted consumers to myriad sites ranging from slot and pinball machines in hotels and stores to pari-mutuel betting at racetracks to casino gaming in Las Vegas, which was legalized in 1931. With unemployment high, many people had additional time on their hands and a wide selection of inexpensive home leisure activities – from playing solitaire to assembling jigsaw puzzles to building model kits – became quite popular. Considering the meaning of hobby consumption, William H. and Nancy K. Young (2002, 133) observed:

> Their most important contribution during the Depression years was a capacity to impart a sense of self-worth to the hobbyist. Jobs might be scarce, but working hard at a hobby fulfilled the need for self-esteem – that what a person was doing had value – and the hobby itself took attention away from the economic difficulties of the day.

After his inauguration on March 4, 1933, President Franklin Delano Roosevelt (1882–1945) issued executive orders and worked with Congress to implement programs collectively referred to as the "New Deal." These initiatives were meant to address the immediate economic concerns, such as the banking crisis, but also to improve the longer-term well being of workers, the elderly, and other groups. The Roosevelt administration also began to envision the consumer as an important social category and so part of the aim of the National Industrial

Recovery Act (NIRA) passed in June 1933 was to support employee wages while keeping a floor under and a lid over prices. This greater spending power would precipitate a virtuous cycle of business recovery. The National Recovery Administration, one of the agencies that implemented the NIRA, began prodding some 19,000 different industries into settling upon specific codes for minimum prices and work hours. Given the time-consuming enormity of such an endeavor, Roosevelt announced stopgap "blanket codes" to take effect in August 1933. As soon as companies complied with the blanket code standards for the minimum wage, maximum workweek, and right to bargain collectively, they could display the NRA Blue Eagle emblem. The emblem was meant to signify patriotism and, therefore, provide companies on board with a competitive advantage (Cohen 2003; Deutsch 2010; Stole 2006; Taylor 2007).

Figure 7.3 shows some examples of the Blue Eagle. The eagle's right talon held a wheel symbolizing industry, while its left grasped lightning bolts symbolizing power. The day after the program was announced, 10,000 businesses sent telegrams pledging support and requesting NRA paraphernalia. When these ran out, the government allowed private firms to print Blue Eagle ephemera. Retailers got together and sponsored newspaper ads announcing their compliance. Consumers could also express support by going to their post offices and signing "Statements of Cooperation" in which they pledged to purchase only from stores that cooperated with the NRA (Taylor 2007). Some stores, like Sampeck Clothes in New York City, bought and distributed buttons with the word "consumer" printed in red across the Blue Eagle. Whatever effects all this hoopla may have had at first, it quickly seemed to peter out, according to economist Jason Taylor (2007) who found across three different newspapers a rapid decline in advertisements with the Blue Eagle emblem during the Fall of 1933. Consumers may have ended up paying more because an underlying rationale of the NIRA was to inhibit cutthroat price competition that was hurting companies. These controls became so broad and burdensome that support from an increasingly skeptical business community drained away until, in May 1935, a conservative Supreme Court ruled the mandatory codes section of the NIRA to be unconstitutional.

Other major New Deal legislation with implications for consumption survived legal challenges. The Social Security Act of 1935, which created the American social welfare system, provided income for retired people and assistance for the unemployed. Amendments have expanded benefits over the years, but one of its important impacts was to reduce poverty rates among the elderly, many of whom previously had to work until they dropped or otherwise depend upon support from kin, neighbors, and charity. The Fair Labor Standards Act of 1938 institutionalized the 40-hour workweek, set a national minimum wage, mandated time and a half for overtime in certain occupations, and banned child labor except in agriculture. In the late nineteenth century factory workers typically toiled for 60 hours over six days, but after World War II the standard settled at 40 hours over five days (Gordon 2016). This gave ordinary laborers more time to engage in consumption activities ranging from shopping and entertainment to the many do-it-yourself or "productive consumption" endeavors at home, to be discussed in

Figure 7.3 (a), (b), (c) and (d) NRA Poster, Postage Stamp, and Sampeck Clothes Consumer Button, *c.*1933–1935. The stamp depicts a farm worker, a businessman, an industrial worker, and a female consumer “In a common determination.” Button, about ¾ inch (20 mm) in diameter, is from author’s collection.

the next chapter. Reducing child labor encouraged longer school attendance and indirectly contributed to the rising youth culture also covered in Chapter 8.

Private sector marketing and distribution came under great scrutiny during the Great Depression. For example, chain stores, especially in the food and pharmacy fields, were an increasingly disruptive institutional force that benefited consumers in terms of lower prices and wider assortments, but sometimes brought abuses and naturally created many enemies among hard-pressed small businesses. During the 1930s chains experienced severe political blowback as rival interests attempted to hobble their competitiveness (Deutsch 2010; Hollander and Omura

1989; Spellman 2016). About half the states, mostly in the South and West, passed anti-chain tax legislation. Thanks to the lobbying of retail druggists, many states also instituted resale price controls – known at the time as "fair trade" – that put floors under prices (Hollander and Omura 1989; Palamountain 1955). Consumers appeared supportive of bashing chain stores. In the *Journal of Retailing* Louis Bader (1939) reported a survey of 3600 consumers in New York City and its suburbs conducted in the winter of 1939. Nearly half (45.5 percent) of city respondents and 36.0 percent of suburban respondents favored new taxes on chain stores and 56.6 percent of the former and 46.3 percent of the latter favored discouraging further chain store growth.

Advertising campaigns in the 1930s began to echo and play upon public concerns about economizing, job security, and day-to-day survival. More and more ads in national magazines stated prices, giving them the look of newspaper advertisements. In opposition to conventional industry wisdom, some ads invited comparisons with their competitors' products. Trade magazine editors and writers dismissed advertising from the late 1920s as too pretty and effete and called for a more hardboiled advertising, "Advertising in Overalls," that would better resonate with hard times. Layouts became more cluttered with small "news" photos and graphs until some ads looked like a page out of a tabloid newspaper. Still other ads introduced speech balloons, cartoons, and even comic strip layouts. Clenched faces and clenched fists, a visual cliché of many advertising tableaux, mirrored consumer anxieties as well as a mythic determination to somehow prevail over adversity (Marchand 1985).

A 1934 article in *Parents Magazine* written by sociologists Robert and Helen Lynd warned against instilling children with false optimism about the downturn soon ending (Horowitz 2004, 22). On a similarly pessimistic note, advertising industry pundits discussed the threat posed by consumer frugality in trade publications, where they complained about hoarders, a "buyer's strike," and "consumer constipation." The gloomiest prophets worried about an impending collapse in the consumption ethic:

> Columbia professor Walter B. Pitkin warned in 1933 and 1934 of a potential "return to the primitive, a back-to-the-soil type of living" that would disdain progress and "the finer things." "Millions of rising consumers" might well relinquish "what we now consider the American standard of living," he declared. [...] Hart, Schaffner and Marx tried to re-stimulate the buying instincts of men who were becoming accustomed to "skimping" on themselves, and American Telephone and Telegraph worried that people who gave up on their phones during the depression years might lose the "telephone habit." Not only had it become the fashion to be thrifty, complained advertising writer, Robert Updegraff, but people were beginning to get "vain, virtuous, and vulgar about it in public." Advertising was going to have to work hard to combat this "degenerate type of social prestige," warned Professor Pitkin.
>
> (Marchand 1985, 300–301)

And so it did. Contests attractive to the wishful thinking of struggling consumers appeared more frequently in magazine advertising of the 1930s than in any other decade between 1900 and 1980 (Pollay 1985). In 1932, the Salem (Ohio) China Company came up with one of the cheesier schemes when it promoted "dish nights" at movie theaters where tableware giveaways encouraged midweek attendance (Blaszczak 2000). On the burgeoning new medium of radio, inventive product premium schemes were woven into soap opera plots (Lavin 1995).

Gary Cross (2000) has argued that these fears of consumerism's collapse were overblown. Yes, lack of income frustrated many immediate buying plans, but people still clung to their old habits and dreams as long as they could. Moviegoers flocked to see musicals with opulent production numbers by Busby Berkeley and seemed fixated on lifestyles where gorgeous gowns, top hats, white ties, and tails seemed to be everyday attire. Writing about the 1935 movie *Top Hat*, starring Fred Astaire and Ginger Rogers with songs by Irving Berlin, film critic Roger Ebert eloquently identified the powerful attraction of this entertainment

> Because we are human, because we are bound by gravity and the limitations of our bodies, because we live in a world where the news is often bad and the prospects disturbing, there is a need for another world somewhere, a world where Fred Astaire and Ginger Rogers live. Where everyone is a millionaire and hotel suites are the size of ballrooms and everything is creased, combed, brushed, shined, polished, powdered and expensive. Where you seem to find the happiness you seek, when you're out together dancing cheek to cheek.
>
> (Ebert 2005)

Depression audiences consumed the film and the fantasy consumption it portrayed. More than 80 years after *Top Hat*'s release, its extraordinary artistry, music, and art deco sets still enchant viewers who continue to live in an often troubled world.

Consumption Criticism and Activism

At the outset of the Depression poor economic conditions engendered a critical sentiment that condemned 1920s greed and ostentation, excessive consumer credit, waste in manufacturing, and, for good measure, the alleged immorality in the movies (Cross 2000). Unlike previous discourses on frugality, which tended to be somber reflections disseminated by elite thinkers, Depression-era critiques had a more populist flavor and conveyed its message through comic texts and images. For example, the 1934 Walt Disney cartoon "The Grasshopper and the Ants" promoted an ethic of industry, saving, and deferred consumption (Lears 1994, 237). In the same theaters that screened the upper class kissing musicals mentioned previously, the popular films of the Marx Brothers and the Three Stooges, among other comedians, loved to twit and humiliate the pompous rich who, like the wealthy widows played by Margaret Dumont in seven different Marx Brothers movies, seemed blithely unaffected by the Depression. This was the rhetoric of scapegoating where ordinary American consumers could shift blame for economic troubles away from themselves and instead place it on a convenient target.

In August 1931 Dell Publishing Company in New York City, a fount of pulp fiction and movie fan magazines, launched a humor monthly, *Ballyhoo*, that skewered advertising and high-pressure salesmanship, consumer culture in general, inanely rich society women, and culpable politicians and business leaders (Cooper 2014; McFadden 2003). Edited by Norman Hume Anthony (1889–1968), a veteran writer and comic artist, *Ballyhoo* was instantly successful and ran until 1939 reaching a peak circulation of more than 1.9 million. The magazine did not accept advertising (at least at first) and, given its racy cover art, cartoons, and other content, such as attacks on increasingly unpopular Prohibition, appeared to primarily target urban males. Several competing titles soon appeared including *Hullabaloo*, *Tickle-Me-Too*, and *Hooey* (*Time* 1931).

Ballyhoo fiercely attacked the fraudulent nature of mass marketing through parodies of brands, ad campaigns, and the mainstream media in which they appeared. It reworded trade names and slogans (e.g., "Scramel" cigarettes and "Balmolive" soap to "Keep that Foolgirl Complexion"), puffed fake products (e.g., "Lady Pipperel Bedsheet De Luxe"), concocted fake spokespersons (e.g., "Mrs. Poopdyke Manners") to deliver bogus testimonials, mocked magazine titles (e.g., "Unpopular Mechanics"), and encouraged readers to "Become a Toucher Upper!" and go out with paint to mess up outdoor posters (Klein 1999; Marchand 1985; McFadden 2003; Rorty 1934). The inside front cover of *Ballyhoo's* June 1932 issue contained a biting parody of Lucky Strike advertising and its repeated use of celebrity endorsers. Speaking on behalf of "Ducky Wucky Cigarettes," fictional opera singer Sophia Zilch said:

> "I always duck Duckies"
> "I can't afford to take chances with my voice. That's why
> I duck Duckies. In fact, I don't smoke at all, but what the
> hell, a lady must live!"

These incongruities appropriated and then reversed the meanings conveyed by standard advertising (Cooper 2014, 126–127). By turning the rhetorical tables, *Ballyhoo* tapped into the public's anger at the economic mess and disillusionment with marketing and capitalistic systems that had promised so much just a few years earlier.

During the 1930s the nascent consumer movement experienced an ideological schism between the technocratic, usually male-dominated product testing interests and the more grassroots, often female-led activists dedicated to using buying power for social purposes. Consumer Research (CR), the testing organization headed by F.J. Schlink, epitomized the former. Its aim was to provide individual consumers with the information they would need to make rational consumer decisions. In August 1935 a majority of CR workers, who were usually college-educated, went out on strike in protest of low wages and the summary dismissal of three colleagues for organizing a chapter of the American Federation of Labor's Technical, Editorial, and Office Assistants Union. The dramatic strike featured picketing, strikebreakers, private detectives, some violence, and a few arrests. This turmoil delighted business critics of the consumer movement. In 1936 the National Labor Relations Board found CR had engaged in unfair labor practices and ordered that the fired workers be reinstated and given back pay (Glickman 2009; Stole 2006).

Great damage had been done, however, and a group of workers led by CR board secretary Arthur Kallet and Amherst College Economics Professor Colston Warne formed a rival testing organization, Consumers Union (CU), which, starting in May 1936, published the magazine *Consumers Union Reports*, today known as *Consumer Reports*. CU membership soon dwarfed that of CR. In 1933 Kallet and Schlink had co-authored the bestselling book, *100,000,000 Guinea Pigs: Dangers in Everyday Foods, Drugs, and Cosmetics*. Many of the concerns Kallet and Schlink identified – regulatory capture of U.S. government agencies, pesticides and herbicides in food production, and misleading advertising by the pharmaceutical industry – remain highly charged issues in the twenty-first century. Schlink's other co-author, Stuart Chase, also abandoned him and CR for CU. Schlink himself rejected the New Deal and became a staunch anticommunist (Glickman 2009; Stole 2006).

While these middle-class whites squabbled, African Americans in the 1930s resisted with renewed vigor the limits imposed on their consumption activities. As described in the previous chapter, Southern blacks during the first decade of the twentieth century had battled the institutionalization of segregation through boycotts of streetcars. On an individual level, blacks in the South refused to patronize stores that treated them poorly if they could find a less discriminatory alternative (Branchik and Davis 2009). In the urban North, stores that served a largely black clientele, but did not hire sales people of color became an explosive issue. Since World War I African Americans had been migrating in large numbers from the South to cities in the North in search of economic opportunity and voting rights, and to escape white oppression. The Great Depression hit them especially hard with unemployment rates exceeding 50 percent in the Northern cities. The moderate and middle-class National Association for the Advancement of Colored People (NAACP) urged white employers in black neighborhoods to hire black workers, but this effort went nowhere (Friedman 1999). American racism and Jim Crowism were not just Southern phenomena. Yet, their numbers and concentration in Northern urban areas gave black consumers new economic and political leverage.

The resistance movement began in the fall of 1929 in Chicago's "Black Belt" of neighborhoods then considered to be the economic capital of African America. Picketing activity and consumer boycotts confronted Woolworth's and a grocery chain. Under pressure, both companies started employing blacks and soon Sears, Roebuck, A&P food stores, Walgreen Drugs, and other retailers followed with their own hiring initiatives. Similar black protests quickly blazed across cities in the North and even in Richmond, Virginia with campaign taglines such as "Don't Buy Where You Can't Work" and "Spend Your Money Where You Can Work" (Cohen 2003, 44). In the spring of 1934, the movement reached Harlem and the largest department store in its 125th Street shopping district, L.M. Blumstein, whose owners refused to hire black clerks and cashiers even though people of color accounted for 75 percent of its sales. After weeks of picketing and boycotts the store relented and much jubilation and an impromptu parade ensued. The campaign then turned its attention to other stores, but near the end of 1934 local courts ruled picketing illegal in the absence of a labor dispute. Three years later, however, the U.S. Supreme Court affirmed the legality of demonstrations and boycotts. By then, Harlem consumers had engaged in rent strikes against white landlords, shut off their power one day a week to protest Consolidated Edison hiring policies, and, in a rider redux of the streetcar crusade 30 years earlier, boycotted the Fifth Avenue Bus Company (Cohen 2003). This activity did not question consumption or capitalism. It was about securing rights in the marketplace.

International developments led to boycotts among other groups of Americans. Soon after Hitler's rise to power in March 1933, Jewish defense groups in America, Britain, and several other countries began a movement to boycott Nazi goods and services (Friedman 1999; Gottlieb 1973; Orbach 1982). On March 8 and 9 Storm Troopers in several German cities had picketed Jewish stores and aggressively hailed passers-by to bully them into boycotting these establishments. Many American Jews clearly perceived the ominousness of these threats and several of their groups organized and received support from some labor and Christian groups. The Jewish community itself was hardly unified on the topic of the boycott. Some Jews did not believe it was within their traditional way of doing things, while others feared it would stir up anti-Semitism at home, endanger Jews in Germany, and fail to meet its objectives. Other Jews, in the spirit of the Zionist movement, argued that traditional passivity no longer served the Jewish people and something had to be done (Orbach 1982). Boycott tactics included writing letters to merchants asking that they stop selling German goods and, when this produced negligible results, picketing of stores ensued. By the late 1930s a majority of Americans supported the boycott (Friedman 1999, 137). However, the overall economic impact on Germany was slight and the historical die had been cast. Thus, like many other boycotts in American history, the anti-Nazi protests were more successful in realizing the value-expressive needs of its proponents than in meeting instrumental goals and changing behavior.

Women spearheaded a new demonstration of politically motivated consumer resistance from 1937 to 1940 when they orchestrated boycotts of both silk and manufactured goods imported from Japan (Glickman 2005, 2009). Many Americans had been horrified by the catastrophe that befell China following the full-scale Japanese invasion in July 1937. Since Japan depended heavily upon trade, a boycott appeared to be a powerful lever, just as nonimportation of English goods had pressured Parliament to rescind taxes on Americans in the 1760s and

1770s. In January 1938, the League of Women Shoppers (LWS) in Washington D.C. put on a pageant titled, "Life Without Silk: From Morning to Midnight in Cotton and Rayon," where socialites modeled non-silk fashions and sensational tap dancer Eleanor Powell (1912–1982) appeared with her famously shapely legs sheathed in cotton stockings. Formed in 1935, the LWS sought to educate consumers to make connections between their choices as consumers with the rights of laborers. Activists staged hundreds of silk boycott events throughout 1938 and 1939, some of which featured discreet silk stripteases by women of their stockings and undergarments and by men of their silk neckties.

The American Federation of Labor (AFL) and the Congress of Industrial Organizations (CIO) endorsed the boycotts of Japanese manufactured goods, but opposed actions against silk since the boycotts threatened jobs in the apparel industry. Indeed, one union, the American Federation of Hosiery Workers (AFHW), protested the anti-silk campaign while simultaneously claiming to represent the right of American women to dress fashionably. Like their opponents in the LWS, these women also showed off their legs and encouraged other American women to do so as well. The uncovering and ogling of female limbs had been something of a national pastime since the early 1920s. According to historian Lawrence Glickman (2005), both sides of the silk boycott viewed consumption as a moral and political act. They did not degrade fashion and pleasure and valorize sacrifice. "Instead, they demonstrated that consumers could be activists not just when they refused goods and eschewed pleasure but also when they consumed goods and enjoyed them" (577). The silk boycott became a moot point in early 1942 when all Japanese goods were embargoed.

The cover of the May 1938 issue of *Ballyhoo* added a darkly satirical take on the silk boycott (Figure 7.4). It portrayed a woman from the waist down wearing a red dress, black stockings, and black heels. She had hiked up her dress to expose the label "cotton" at the top of her hose. Next to her left leg, printed in a faux Japanese script, was the quip "Boycott Meets Girl!" The cover's yellow background color alluded to Japanese skin tone and to reinforce the racial overtones the issue was dubbed, again in ersatz font, "The Jap Number." Inside, the magazine devoted nearly all of its 80 pages to highly inflammatory and racist parodies of Japan, Japanese society, and Japanese culture and language. The theme was "The United States of Japan! How Life Will Be When the Japs Take Us Over" (*Ballyhoo* 1938, 9). I bought a copy from an eBay seller in September 2016 and, as I leafed through the pages, was shocked by the coarse vitriol (even by 2016 Presidential campaign standards). *Ballyhoo* may not have been representative of American opinion toward Japan, but race hostility was definitely in the air and thus heralded the brutality of the upcoming War in the Pacific and the eventual atomic bombing of Hiroshima and Nagasaki in 1945. On their part, ultranationalist Japanese nursed blatant contempt for all foreign races and the atrocities they committed in China had motivated the silk boycott movement in the first place (Dower 1986).

Figure 7.4 Cover of *Ballyhoo* Magazine, May 1938.

Frugal Consumption on the Home Front

Better business conditions in 1941, helped along by a rapid increase in military spending, were once again creating a buoyant economy that put money in workers' pockets. Then, the bombing of Pearl Harbor on December 7 and the subsequent waging of total war initiated a new period of substantial change for most Americans. After years of grueling economic depression, consumers suddenly found themselves with greater spending power. Gross Domestic Product leaped from $93.5 billion in 1939 ($1163.6 billion in 2009 dollars) to $228.2 billion ($2217.8) in 1945 (Johnston and Williamson 2017), and the economy created 17 million new jobs (Blum 1976). The effects of this rising economic tide were widely distributed. Family incomes grew even faster for African Americans and households at lower economic levels than for the population as a whole. Moreover, millions of women found jobs and, by 1943, had an additional $8 billion in pocket money (Blum 1976). Consumers indulged themselves with many of the necessities and some of the comforts they had forgone in the 1930s. Even taking into account a 25 percent inflation rate during 1940–1943, total purchases of all goods and services were approximately 10 percent higher in the first quarter of 1943 than in the first quarter of 1940. John Morton Blum (1976) contended that the new prosperity and surge in buying created a mood of buoyancy and excitement among consumers, as well as dreams of even more when the war ended.

However, the exigencies of the war effort frustrated much consumer spending. The War Production Board allocated scarce materials and stopped or limited the production of civilian goods, causing the sale of durable goods at retail to drop 33 percent from 1941 to 1942 and an additional 50 percent from 1942 to 1943 (Williams 1943/1972). Crucial shortages developed in the areas of housing and medical services, while the Office of Price Administration (OPA) froze many consumer prices and rationed common items such as gasoline, coffee, butter, shoes, sugar, and meat. Adding to these market distortions, wartime scarcity necessitated changes in product and packaging materials, forms, and colors (Hine 1995; Sitikoff 1994; Ward 1994a). To economize on fabric, for example, women's hats became smaller, skirts shorter, and many items of clothing simpler and more informal (Blaszczk 2009; Williams 1943/1972). Rayon replaced silk and nylon in hosiery until it too became scarce. Because tin was in short supply, companies switched from metal cans to glass jars and paperboard lids.

Intent on controlling consumer spending and mobilizing society for a sustained global conflict, the U.S. government advocated an ideology of frugal consumption and provided instruction for its day-to-day practice. The message was unambiguous. Consumers must economize on goods and services, recycle waste and scrap, plant Victory Gardens and can the vegetables, comply with price controls and rationing laws, and put discretionary income into war bonds (Bredhoff 1994; Crawford 1979; Nelson 1991; Ward 1994a). "Produce and Conserve, Share and Play Square" exhorted one War Food Administration slogan. Thus, the old threads of consumer resistance to spending and a commitment to patriotic frugality in product use received official sanction during World War II.

Several different agencies of the U.S. government – with the help of the mass media, libraries, schools, and volunteer groups – organized propaganda campaigns to rally the home front and achieve compliance with various program mandates. The Office of War Information (OWI), established on June 13, 1942 by Executive Order 9182, coordinated this massive effort to mold public opinion and consumption behavior. The OWI conveyed its messages to different audiences through the press, radio, motion pictures, and other media. For example, the photo in Figure 7.5, which shows the lovely black singer and actor Lena Horne (1917–2010) demonstrating how to save fuel, was intended for African Americans. Poster campaigns were the responsibility of the OWI Bureau of Graphics, which reviewed campaign proposals submitted by other federal

Figure 7.5 Lena Horne Demonstrating How to Save Fuel (Gas), *c.* 1942–1945.
Source: Office of War Information.

agencies, supervised the creation of graphic materials, gave advice on how to solve printing and distribution problems, and distributed posters for the OWI and other agencies (NARA 1994). Some firms, such as Texaco and the Douglas Aircraft Company, also commissioned posters. The OWI made available sheets of stock logos and clip art, such as the war bond minuteman, for inclusion in commercial advertising (Witkowski 2003).

The three posters in Figure 7.6 illustrate variations on the conservation theme of being thrifty with consumer goods and services. "Use It Up–Wear It Out–Make It Do!" depicted time-honored and gendered household roles in which the wife brandished a sewing needle and thread, while her husband sharpened the blade of his lawn mower. Women sewing and men using edge tools had characterized the division of labor in American households since colonial times (Larkin 1988; Strasser 1982; Ulrich 2001). These skills came in handy during the War. Repairmen became scarce, and according to a 1943 survey conducted by the American Home Economics Association, 55 percent of the respondents complained about deteriorating quality in their shoes and clothing (Campbell 1984). In the 1930s, most American housewives had practiced frugal consumption to a greater or lesser extent. To save money, they relearned traditional domestic arts and how to make do with what they had (Hill, Hirschman, and Bauman 1997), but "when the nation went to war, the rhetoric changed. Concern for family was replaced with a call to enlist in a great national effort" (McFeely 1994, 106). The second poster, "Food Is a Weapon, Don't Waste It!", showed how food, like so much else in American life, had become charged with a new, patriotic meaning: a weapon of war. The nutrition reference in the bottom subheading was the topic of numerous war posters that encouraged Americans to take steps to maintain their health. I own a copy of this poster. It reminds me of how my mother always insisted that I finish the food on my plate. The third poster, "SERVE our fighting men abroad, CONSERVE these services at home," was a two-color sheet sponsored by the War Production Board. It reminded consumers that they must be frugal with electrical, water, telephone, and transportation services, as well as with tangible goods. It was also evidence of just how networked Americans had become in the twentieth century.

In Figure 7.7, two posters illustrate an important component of the conservation message: why and how drivers should save on gasoline and automobile tires. During World War II, the United States was able to supply its petroleum needs through domestic production, so gasoline shortages were not too serious a threat, but it was necessary to save wear and tear on automobiles, trucks, and especially their tires. Rubber and replacement parts, not gasoline, were in short supply (Blum 1976). "I'll carry mine too!" juxtaposed soldiers marching in full battle gear with a woman walking home carrying packages in one arm and a bag of groceries in the other. The other poster took a more psychological turn. A haggard GI directly addressed the viewer: "Have You Really Tried to Save Gas by Getting Into a Car Club?" This question headline combined guilt with a specific behavioral initiative (ride-sharing) that commuters could adopt. As the War progressed, the portrayal of American soldiers in poster art became increasingly realistic and more apt to show suffering and death. Given the widespread ownership of and dependence upon motor vehicles, most consumers disliked gasoline rationing.

Three examples of recycling-themed posters compose Figure 7.8. "Save Your Cans: Help Pass the Ammunition," by McClelland Barclay USNR, featured a compelling illustration that imagined tin cans leaving a woman's outstretched arm to become an ammunition belt feeding into a machine gun. In the lower left corner were printed the steps consumers should take to "prepare your tin cans

(a)

(b)

(c)

Figure 7.6 Posters for Conserving Goods and Services, 1943.

Sources: (a) Office of War Information, 1943 (b) Office of War Information, 1943 (c) War Production Board, 1943.

(a)

(b)

Figure 7.7 Posters for Conserving Gasoline and Tires, 1943–1944.

Sources: (a) Office of Defense Transportation, 1943 (b) Harold Von Schmidt for Office of Price Administration, 1944.

for war." Henry Koerner's "Save Waste Fats for Explosives" made another stunning visual connection between the kitchen, represented by a well-manicured female hand pouring a stream of fat from a frying pan, and actual hostilities, epitomized by a veritable explosion of bullets, bombs, and shells. At the bottom of the poster, consumers were commanded to "take them to your meat dealer." Neighborhood butchers and grocery stores handled much of the recycling of waste fats. This responsibility added to their close, often onerous contact with federal agencies that were deluging them with requests to promote the most plentiful food commodities, educate their customers about changing rules, and administer price ceilings and ration coupon redemption (Marchand 1994). In "Wanted for Victory" a photograph showed a mother, father, and son all doing their part in recycling. America's children, organized through schools and youth groups, contributed greatly to the recycling effort. They picked their neighborhoods clean of paper, scrap metal, and old tires (Bailey 1977).

Additional campaigns encouraged frugality through growing and preserving food at home. Outside the densely populated urban centers of the East Coast and upper Midwest, most Americans still lived on farms, in small towns, or in sparsely populated cities where it was possible to have a garden. In my little oral history study with Ellen Hogan of surviving World War II consumers in Southern California, several respondents mentioned raising chickens (Witkowski and Hogan 1999). Examples of the canning/rationing theme in Figure 7.9 include

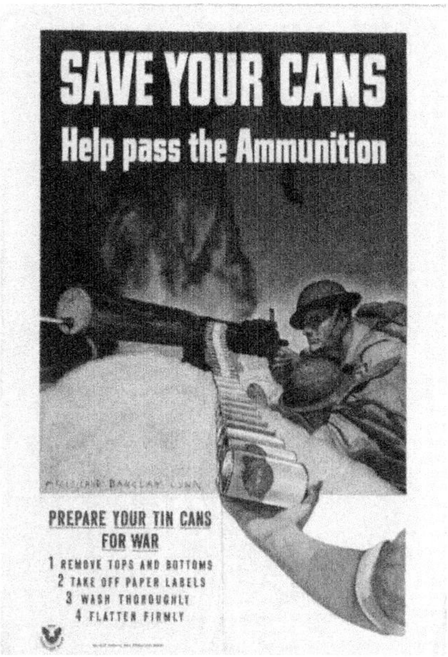

(a)

(b)

(c)

Figure 7.8 Posters for Recycling, 1941–1943.

Sources: (a) McClelland Barclay for War Production Board, Salvage Division, 1941–1942 (b) Henry Koerner for Office of War Information, 1943 (c) Office of Production Management, 1942.

(a)

(c)

(b)

Figure 7.9 Posters for Home Production and Canning, 1943–1945.

Sources: (a) Office of War Information, 1943 (b) War Food Program, 1944 (c) Hubert Morley for War Food Administration, 1945.

"Can All You Can: It's a Real War Job," "Grow More ... Can More ... in '44," and "Your Victory Garden Counts More Than Ever!" These posters all contained a contradiction, in that their messages about the need for tending gardens and home canning were somewhat undercut by images of abundance in the form of giant-sized vegetables. Victory Gardens may have been more important psychologically than substantively since they gave Americans a sense of participation. In a November 1941 press release, the U.S. Department of Agriculture actually warned against planting "emergency" or "defense" gardens because farmers were producing plenty of food more efficiently, and citizens could better devote their labor to other war jobs (Nelson 1991). However, as gardens proliferated, the government saw their symbolic propaganda value and began to commission new posters. The reference to canning supplies in "Grow More ... Can More ... in '44" belied the fact that pressure cookers and other canning supplies, especially sugar, were in short supply. Thus, women across the nation organized community canning centers to share equipment and learn techniques (McFeely 1994).

The OPA was particularly keen on controlling prices by getting consumers to obey rationing dictates. An extremely complex and far-reaching endeavor, rationing required the concerted efforts of the OPA in Washington, its 93 district offices, a multitude of volunteer boards, public school systems, local newspapers and radio stations, and, above all, countless retail grocers. Figure 7.10 depicts Miss Elizabeth Law teaching an adult homemaking class in Washington D.C. and a customer using her ration book in a grocery store. Four different rationing programs were created. Certificate rationing, which began in January 1942, permitted, on the basis of need, the purchase of single items such as automobiles and tires. Differential Coupon Rationing allowed some people, like physicians, to have more commodities, such as fuel oil and gasoline. Uniform Coupon Rationing, used for shoes, sugar, coffee, and other items, applied the principle that everyone should share alike. Point Rationing, the final program, which began in February 1943, was based on the British model and gave every person his or her own individual coupon book. Consumers could then choose food according to individual preferences (Ward 1994b). Three billion ration stamps changed hands each month (Bailey 1977).

Figure 7.11 illustrates three posters that explained these limits on consumption behavior: "Keep the Home Front Pledge" by Fred G. Cooper, "Rationing Means a Fair Share for All of Us" by Herbert Roese, and "Rationing Safeguards Your Share." They utilized three visual techniques: illustration, cartoon, and photomontage, as well as four- and two-color printing. The image of the housewife taking a pledge had been deployed early in the War when the OPA's Consumer Division produced a small, mail-in card, "The Consumer's Victory Pledge" that people were supposed to sign and return (Nelson 1991). Roese's cartoon employed the often-lampooned stereotype of the buxom, greedy matron. Finally, the photos of the woman holding a market basket while surveying the contents of a well-stocked grocery store indicated the still small scale and personal nature of much American grocery shopping. According to Marchand

(a)

(b)

Figure 7.10 Rationing Instructions and Practice, 1943. Preparing for point rationing (a) and "How many points will it take?" (b). Photographs by Alfred T. Palmer.

Source: Library of Congress, Prints & Photographs Division, Washington, D.C.

(a)

(b)

(c)

Figure 7.11 Posters for Controlling Prices Through Rationing, 1942–1944.

Sources: (a) Fred G. Cooper for Office of Price Administration, 1944 (b) Herbert Roese for Office of Price Administration, 1943 (c) Office of Price Administration, 1942.

(1994), the War gave independent food retailers a temporary competitive edge in their battles with national and regional chains and emerging supermarkets. Gasoline rationing tended to keep shoppers within their own neighborhoods and the gradual breakdown of refrigerators, due to the lack of parts and new replacements, necessitated more frequent trips to the local store.

The U.S. Department of the Treasury sponsored perhaps the single largest group of posters. Based on the precedent of the five Liberty Loans of World War I, the federal government initiated seven different bond drives during the World War II period. The first was launched in May 1941, even before war had been declared, and the last ran into 1946. These campaigns asked Americans to forgo their immediate consumption and, instead, to buy bonds and defense stamps to finance the War effort. In Figure 7.12, "Don't Let That Shadow Touch Them," artist Lawrence B. Smith portrayed innocent children and an exaggerated physical proximity of the enemy to arouse fears and thus encourage war bond purchases. "Wanted – *Fighting Dollars*" by an artist named Wilkinsons was more cheerful, with its red, white, and blue color scheme and image of a smiling workingman wearing a denim cap and overalls. "This Is My Fight Too!" glamorized the contribution of female factory workers. The photograph's staging and pretty model, her arm daintily smudged with grime for the camera, imparted the feel of a Hollywood publicity still.

Posters targeted Americans in all walks of life but were often directed at the women who managed the nation's home front consumption (Campbell 1984; McFeely 1994). Women needed to understand rationing programs and cope with their restrictions; shop different stores in search of scarce supplies; prepare meals in the face of meat, sugar, and butter shortages; and recycle tin, rubber, and kitchen fats. Because the military had priority, the federal government promoted "meatless days" for civilians, but in the 1940s, few Americans knew any vegetarian recipes other than simple macaroni and cheese dishes. Advice was abundant. In addition to government information programs, corporations distributed meal-planning guides and integrated helpful tips within advertisements. Magazines such as *Woman's Day*, newspapers, and radio programs kept audiences informed.

> Jessie Young, the "radio homemaker" of Iowa station KMA, broadcasting from her own kitchen, suggested recipes like Marbled Macaroni with tomato sauce and Spam, and Mock Hamburgers made of oatmeal and eggs flavored with onions and sage and cooked in tomato juice. Billie Burke, better known as the Good Witch in "The Wizard of Oz," played a point-perplexed housewife talking to guest authorities from government and industry about the latest food information on a weekly radio program called "Fashions in Rations."
>
> (McFeely 1994, 112–113)

Consumption and production roles blurred as women took war jobs, tended Victory Gardens, and learned the almost forgotten art of home canning. Because

(a)

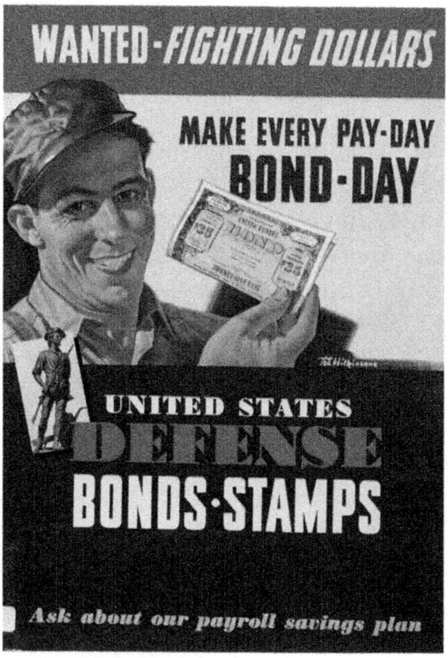

(b)

(c)

Figure 7.12 Posters for Buying War Bonds, 1942.

Sources: (a) Lawrence B. Smith for U.S. Department of the Treasury, 1942 (b) Wilkinsons for U.S. Department of the Department of the Treasury, 1942 (c) U.S. Government Printing Office, 1942.

of a shortage of workers, laundry and dry cleaning services became scarcer, forcing some women to wash more clothes at home (Williams 1943/1972). Half of all households with domestic servants lost their help (Campbell 1984).

Other media in addition to posters bombarded the consumer home front with messages. Newspapers and magazines published numerous articles on frugal consumption, and private companies printed booklets on home canning and better meal planning (Ward 1994a, 184–185). Scriptwriters incorporated conservation and other war themes into popular radio comedies, such as *Fibber McGee and Molly* (Nelson 1991). In conjunction with the waste fats salvage campaign, Walt Disney made his third wartime film, "Out of the Frying Pan into the Firing Line," for the Conservation Division of the War Production Board (Ward 1994a, 174). In the 1943 RKO movie *Tender Comrade*, airplane factory worker Jo Jones (played by Ginger Rogers) lambasted a woman who bragged about her hoarding skills and, for good measure, joined other women in denouncing a neighborhood black market butcher (Fyne 1994). Superman encouraged his comic strip readers to buy bonds, and a number of film and radio stars appeared at mammoth bond rallies (Bailey 1977).

Much commercial advertising included appeals to frugal consumption. This practice varied from simply inserting the minuteman logo for war bond drives to using frugality as the main copy theme. The American Gas Association, Texaco, and Greyhound all encouraged customers to change behaviors to avoid unnecessary use of gas and gasoline. The Bell Telephone System ran a particularly impressive campaign. One ad read:

> "AN URGENT CALL FOR YOU"
> "Please do not make Long Distance telephone calls to war-busy centers unless it is really necessary."
> That helps keep the lines open for war messages and war's on the wires these days. When we can get telephone materials again we'll give you all the wires you desire. Many Thanks.
>
> (*Life* 1943a)

However, some of this advertising was clearly self-serving. Soft-Lite Lenses captioned a photo of a woman recycling an old iron as follows: "Good work, Madam.... But wait! Do the glasses you're wearing belong in the scrap heap too?" (*Life* 1943b), while Lane Home Furniture, a maker of cedar hope chests, declared: "CONSERVE! Buy War Bonds! SAVE WOOLENS in a Lane!" (*Life* 1943c). The ownership of hope or dowry chests, in which unmarried young women stored clothing and household linens in anticipation of marriage, had a long tradition in America. Established in 1912, Lane sold thousands of hope chests during World War II. An ad from 1946 with actress Shirley Temple as the celebrity endorser persuaded GIs to buy them for their sweethearts for Valentine's Day (*Life* 1945).

American Tobacco stretched credibility when it proclaimed "Lucky Strike Green Has Gone to War!" Ostensibly, the need for camouflage paint was the reason for changing the package color of its flagship brand from dark green to white. However, previous company research had shown that the dark green pack had never been very appealing anyway (Sobel 1978). At the beginning of the War, some politically conservative admen were none too keen about helping the Roosevelt Administration (Fox 1984). However, threats from Congress to ban advertising for the duration led the industry to form the War Advertising Council in 1942, composed of representatives from ad agencies, the media, and business, to coordinate public service campaigns for the war effort and improve public relations with the home front (Fox 1975; Stole 2012). Bailey (1977) estimates that the industry contributed approximately $400 million in space, time, and services for war-related public service advertising.

A few years ago I purchased on eBay a scrapbook of World War II-era greeting cards as source material for a history of a small bookstore my parents owned and operated in Chicago at the time (Witkowski 2009). One card referred to food rationing and shortages. It featured a cartoon drawing of a white-haired man seated at a table set with just three peas and a pork chop on his plate. The folksy lines read: "HAPPY BIRTHDAY We may be eatin' less these days.... BUT GOL-DANG – What the dickens!" (Figure 7.13). This good-natured acceptance

Figure 7.13 World War II Birthday Card, *c.*1942–1945. (Publisher: W&W T7113 Made in U.S.A.).

Source: Author's collection.

of small deprivations concurred with the upbeat tone of most other wartime frugality campaigns and with consumer recollections of the period (Witkowski and Hogan 1999). Not since the nonimportation movement of the 1760s and 1770s, and certainly never since, were appeals to resist consumption and to be frugal disseminated so widely in American society by so many and with such visual imagination and intensity.

Consumer response to these campaigns was impressive. Americans recycled 538 million pounds of waste fats, 23 million tons of paper, and 800 million pounds of tin. They also planted 50 million Victory Gardens (Fox 1975, 54). When asked by a Gallup poll in the fall of 1943 "Did you or your family put up (home can) any cans or jars of food this year?" 75 percent of respondents answered "yes" (Gallup 1972, 364). Witkowski and Hogan (1999) found similar percentages when we questioned people's memories of World War II in Southern California. Nearly three-quarters of the informants said they either planted or had easy access to homegrown fruits and vegetables. Some canned their excess, some just gave it away, and some did both. At the national level, the government kept inflation under control. After rising 12 percent in 1941 and 1942, food prices increased just 4 percent over the remainder of the War. Finally, all seven of the war bond drives met their ever-increasing targets. Approximately $135 billion in bonds were sold during the War. The largest share went to banks, insurance companies, and corporations, but individuals accounted for $36 billion in Series E bond purchases. Children alone bought more than $1 billion in defense stamps and small denomination bonds (Bailey 1977).

Some hoarding occurred at the beginning of the War, and throughout the conflict, favoritism, price compliance problems, and varying degrees of black market activities were not unknown. *Business Week* magazine reported how some department stores played their own game of rationing by first filling the orders of their best charge customers (Casdorph 1989). In 1944, the OPA investigated several thousand businesses and found that 57 percent were violating price controls. Wristwatches sold for as much as $50 above ceiling prices (Casdorph 1989). Black markets for consumer goods became widespread, but most transactions were between private individuals, not large-scale dealing. People traded straight pins, radio tubes, cooking utensils, garbage can lids, and used vacuum cleaners. At worst, some consumers bought counterfeit ration stamps from racketeers (Bailey 1977). Nevertheless, the awareness that millions of American men and women in the service were risking their lives overseas kept illicit buying and selling from getting too far out of hand.

Summary

From 1930 to 1945 significant domestic and international events disrupted American consumer culture. The Great Depression reduced the incomes and spending of many households and pushed some people to the brink of starvation. Frugality in consumption was not universal, for the Depression did not diminish everyone's lifestyle, but thriftiness typified families across the nation, across social class, and across ethnic and racial groups. Then, in World War II, the federal government prioritized production of war materiel, thus interrupting the supply of consumer durables, and its rationing schemes controlled the consumption of foods, gasoline, and other nondurables. War jobs were plentiful and wages the highest in years, but with limited spending opportunities, home front consumers saved money and instead bought War Bonds.

Over the 15 years of this period, outside events imposed resistance to consumption. However, consumers organized resistance of their own. Millions flaunted Prohibition until Repeal, product-testing outfits held companies to account while championing marketplace prudence, and satirical journalism questioned the marketing infrastructure of consumer culture. African Americans boycotted stores to advance their rights to work and consume and woman's groups urged boycotts of imported Japanese silk to oppose the brutal invasion of China. Indeed, whether during the Depression or the War, women who often were at the forefront of the nation's consumer culture managed anti-consumption activities. In the early 1940s forms of non-consumption – economizing, recycling, planting Victory gardens, complying with rationing, and buying War Bonds – acquired patriotic meanings. This would soon change.

8 Consumption from 1945 to 1980

The end of World War II in 1945 had a great impact upon American consumption. The deep reservoir of consumer demand caused by retrenchment during the Great Depression, and then by shortages and rationing during the War, helped drive the postwar economy. New families and new "baby boom" babies needed provisioning and businesses quickly retooled from war production to consumer goods. This demand was funded by personal savings from the war years, encouraged by generous credit terms, and given an additional promotional boost from the new medium of television. Business, labor, and government leaders agreed that future prosperity depended upon unrelenting mass consumption and this consensus firmly established, perhaps once and for all, the great American propensity for buying and having things. In effect, purchasing was transformed into a civic responsibility – good consumers became good citizens (Cohen 2003). Large numbers of Americans dropped the ethos of Great Depression retrenchment and World War II home front frugality and re-embraced what Cross (2000), Ewen (1976), Twitchell (1999), and many other observers have contended is the deepest and most durable ideology of twentieth century America: consumerism.

The next section reviews the macro-economic context of consumption, the development of television as a medium for entertainment and advertising, and the rise of suburban shopping centers as a major locus for browsing and purchasing. Then, the section on meaning explores "populuxe" expressions of mass luxury and their influence on product design, and also revisits the topic of youth culture consumption introduced in Chapter 6. The threads of gender range from Tupperware parties and male anxieties in the 1950s to recounting how the accepted postwar household consumption assignments became contested in the 1960s and 1970s with the rise of the feminist movement. Multiple threads of consumer resistance characterize this period. They included popular critiques of affluence, racially charged consumer sit-ins and boycotts during the Civil Rights movement, rejectionist practices of the 1960s counterculture, and a new focus on environmental concerns in the 1970s. This section also examines boycotts in support of farm laborers and gay rights, and how smoking cannabis gained new traction as a symbol of consumer resistance to authority, or "the Man" as we used to say.

Material Life and the Market

With de-mobilization and budget cuts after World War II, the economy contracted for several years, but in 1950 embarked on more than two decades of impressive growth, excluding temporary setbacks in 1954 and 1958. Over the entire 35-year period covered in this chapter, the nominal GDP of the United States, $228.2 billion ($2217.8 billion in 2009 dollars) in 1945, grew to $2862.5 billion ($6450.4 billion) in 1980, while nominal per capita GDP of $1631 ($15,850) increased to $12,570 ($28,325), almost doubling in real terms (Johnston and Williamson 2017). The population grew from 132,164,569 in the 1940 census to 226,542,199 in 1980 (U.S. Bureau of the Census 2016a). As Figure 9.1 in the next chapter illustrates, inequality declined during this era of strong unionization and high taxes on the very wealthy. The top marginal income tax rate was 91 percent from 1953 to 1961. The economy remained strong through the 1960s, but in the 1970s economic growth began to stall, while inflation started to accelerate, leading to the popularity of the new portmanteau word "stagflation." The U.S. stock market tanked in 1973 and 1974 due in part to accelerating inflation and to the collapse of the "Bretton Woods" international monetary exchange system so arduously crafted by the Allies at the namesake New Hampshire conference held in July 1944 (Conway 2014).

Two oil shocks contributed to the economic malaise. The first, an embargo by the Organization of Arab Petroleum Exporting Countries in response to American support of Israel in the 1973 Yom Kippur War, lasted from October 1973 to March 1974. The price of oil quadrupled and American consumers suffered the indignities of gasoline shortages, odd/even rationing, and long lines at the pump. Because of now more expensive petroleum imports, the U.S. balance of trade started running a deficit in 1976, and has generally done so ever since. The second shock, caused by a reduced global supply of oil in the wake of the 1979 Iranian Revolution, led to a doubling in prices and, again, to shortages, panic buying, and long lines at gasoline stations. For the first time, a broad segment of Americans began to take energy conservation seriously, which provided a market opening for the more fuel-efficient vehicles imported from Japan. Some groups, such as American car manufacturers, their suppliers, and autoworkers, began nursing resentments toward Japan and its products.

Life in the 1950s often has been remembered with affection and much was indeed positive. Americans longed to have a single-family home and the Federal Housing Authority helped them realize their dreams by extending low-interest loans to veterans. Massive new suburban developments composed mostly of single-family homes, ringed cities and expanded ever outward. In New Jersey, for example, the proportion of single-family homes in the state's housing stock mushroomed from 7 percent in 1950 to 64 percent ten years later (Cohen 2003). In 1956, President Dwight D. Eisenhower (1890–1969) signed the Federal Aid Highway Act, which intensified construction of the Interstate Highway System. This big investment in infrastructure helped connect the population, encouraged demand for car travel, supported the trucking industry, and, according to proponents, even improved national defense capabilities. However, the 1950s were far less of a good thing for some segments of American society. Widespread racism and segregation, such as exclusionary housing covenants, afflicted African Americans and other minorities until the passage of the 1965 Civil Rights Act. Even then, forms of repression continued until 1980 and, for that matter, well into our final period to be discussed in the next chapter.

After World War II, television rapidly emerged as a powerful new medium for entertainment and advertising (Barnouw 1976). RCA had tested the technology in the mid-1930s and made a few transmissions from the New York World's Fair in 1939. RCA also unveiled new television studios at Rockefeller Plaza for its NBC (National Broadcasting Company) subsidiary. Within a few months, the rival CBS (Columbia Broadcasting System) started broadcasting from its new TV studios in Grand Central Station. The Federal Communications Commission (FCC) put further commercialization on hold during World War II, but started issuing new broadcasting licenses in 1945. By July 1946, 26 new licenses had been granted and that summer RCA put its black-and-white sets on the market. New television stations were soon established across the country and NBC and CBS started showing regularly scheduled programs in 1946–1947 season. A third network, DuMont, also began operation at this time, but it lacked the financial resources of its much larger competitors and eventually ceased all operations in 1956. The ABC television network debuted in 1948, but for many years lacked the coverage of NBC and CBS. Between 1948 and 1952 the FCC put a freeze on new station licenses in order to work out interference problems – some TV stations were in too close proximity – and to allocate channels along the VHF and UHF frequencies (Barnouw 1976).

The three radio networks transferred their business model to television where it remained dominant throughout the period under discussion. This system dated to 1928 when its major elements – discrete programs sponsored by advertising and distributed for free to large audiences by networks of company owned and independent stations – became fully realized (Spalding 1963). In television, it went largely unchallenged until 1976 when Ted Turner launched the first basic cable network from his superstation in Atlanta now known as WTBS. Television in the 1950s attracted very large audiences and, because the number of channels was limited in many markets, a popular program, such as *The Ed Sullivan Show* (1948–1971), *I Love Lucy* (1951–1957), or *Gunsmoke* (1955–1975), would garner very high ratings and share. On January 19, 1953, some 44 million people tuned into the episode where Lucy gave birth to "Little Ricky," many more than watched the inauguration of President Dwight D. Eisenhower the following day. When and where it became available, early television snatched audiences away from radio and motion pictures. The exciting new medium gave people reason to stay at home and so temporarily reduced book sales and library lending, taxi and jukebox receipts, and restaurant and nightclub attendance. By poaching established radio stars, television forced radio to replace network comedies and dramas with more diversified music and local sports programming. Television could be huge for advertisers. Hazel Bishop, a lipstick maker, had yearly revenues of $50,000 when it started advertising on TV in 1950. By 1952 its sales had rocketed to $4,500,000 (Barnouw 1976, 114). Women were the most important target audience, especially on daytime television (Stole 2003). Children also became enamored with the new medium (Figure 8.1).

On the retail end, suburban shopping centers became prominent in the 1950s. A shopping center or shopping mall is a privately developed space hosting multiple stores that are easily accessible to shoppers. The Cleveland Arcade, built in 1890, was one of the first shopping centers in America and, by the way, a top shelf example of late Victorian architecture. In the 1920s and 1930s, branch department stores and smaller shopping centers opened in outlying city neighborhoods and in older bedroom communities. With the massive suburbanization of the country after World War II, the shopping center format flourished (Figure 8.2). Many were open-air, but by the late 1950s a number of enclosed malls were being built along with larger assemblages known as regional shopping centers. By 1957, the U.S. had 940 shopping centers and by 1976 their number had grown to 17,520 (Cohen 2003, 258). With convenient locations and ample parking, shopping centers took customers away from central business districts in

Figure 8.1 Father Reading, Two Children Viewing Television, July 12, 1950. The photographer undoubtedly staged this picture since the children are watching a test pattern, not a program. Photograph by Hilda Kassell, East 53rd St., New York City.

Source: Library of Congress, Prints & Photographs Division, Washington, D.C.

Figure 8.2 Shopping Center, Great Neck, Long Island, New York, December 1, 1951. Photograph by Gottscho-Schleisner, Inc.

Source: Library of Congress, Prints & Photographs Division, Washington, D.C.

large cities and from main street retailers in smaller towns. As Cohen (2003) observed, developers also sought to replicate urban downtowns, but in a more sanitized version with a good mix of retail, usually anchored by one or more large department stores, and without the urban blights of homeless people, prostitutes, and the poor. Shopping centers were relentlessly middle-class and very white for the most part. By the 1970s they had become a much-favored place to spend one's leisure time.

Populuxe and Youth Culture

As McCracken (1988) theorized, the symbolic meanings of possessions continued to evolve in tandem with larger shifts in the culturally constituted world. Although product associations with nationalistic identities and forms of refinement continued to be in play, these long-standing threads seemed relatively muted during the postwar period. Americans had invested enough lives and treasure for the sake of patriotism and its symbols during World War II and the Korean War. Veterans tended to be reticent about their War experiences. Later, when the War in Vietnam escalated and political opposition mounted, patriotic symbols acquired a very negative valence in some circles. By the end of the 1960s many young people wore articles of clothing decorated with the stars and stripes in order to mock patriotism rather than celebrate it. At the extreme, angry Vietnam War protesters burned American flags and their draft cards. Similarly, the drive for self-improvement remained part of American culture and companies promoted refinement when they detected a market opportunity. Hugh Hefner's *Playboy* magazine, first issued in December 1953 with iconic actress Marilyn Monroe (1926–1962) on the cover, instructed its readers on the fine arts of urban sophistication and seduction. Yet, like patriotic meanings, old threads of refinement were relatively subdued and later even acquired some negatives of their own when they became targets for opposition to conventional mores. The "hippie" counterculture of the late 1960s, which emphasized being cool, tolerant, and "natural," did not pursue refinement in any traditional sense based on social class aspirations.

Mainstream American consumption did have cultural consistency. Throughout the 1950s and into the 1960s suburban living attracted many people from the cities and ethnic neighborhoods to vast new housing tracts (Cohen 2003). They furnished their detached single-family homes with the new mass-market consumer goods that had been pouring out of factories. Thomas Hine (1986) coined the word "Populuxe" to represent the consumption style, attitudes, and aesthetics that dominated the decade from 1954 until 1964. Shorthand for popular luxury, the term may seem self-contradicting, but it aptly expresses the American Zeitgeist, the spirit of the times: "During the Populuxe decade, the objects people could buy took on a special exaggerated quality. They celebrate confidence in the future, the excitement of the present, the sheer joy of having so much" (Hine 1986, 4). Many of these products were made of new types of plastic through new injection molding technologies. Blaszczyk (2009, 188) observed how "plastic's growing ubiquity and disposability introduced the idea that consumer goods – once valued a family keepsakes – could be discarded and replaced." As will be discussed below, critics in the 1950s began to scorn this spreading throwaway mentality.

Populuxe ideas influenced residential and commercial architecture, interior décor, and product design. Southern California was arguably its epicenter and cultural beacon. Since the 1930s futuristic mid-century modern homes and Streamline Moderne commercial structures had been built in and around Los Angeles and Palm Springs. Then in 1949 architect John Lautner (1911–1994) created "Googie" architecture through his design of a coffee shop by that name in West Hollywood. Googie, like other manifestations of the Populuxe aesthetic, drew inspiration from the car culture, jet airplanes, the space race, and atomic energy. Known for its upswept roofs, starburst motifs, parabolas, and boomerangs, the style hit its stride in the 1950s, spread across the country, and continued to be popular for motels, coffee houses, gasoline stations, bowling alleys, and drive-in theaters into the early 1960s (Figure 8.3). The architecture of the original Tomorrowland (1955), part of Disneyland in Anaheim, and the rendering

Figure 8.3 Googie Architecture: Norms Restaurant on La Cienega Boulevard, Los Angeles, 1957. Photo taken January 31, 2009.

Source: Wikimedia Commons.

Figure 8.4 Space Age Design: The Iconic 1957 Chevrolet Bel Air Convertible.

Source: Chevrolet Factory Photo.

of *The Jetsons* (1962–1963) animated television sitcom exemplified the Googie style. Populuxe decade furniture featured spindly legs and simplified lines. Among the most important designers were Charles Eames (1907–1978) and his wife "Ray" Eames (1912–1988). The couple moved from St. Louis to Los Angeles in the 1940s and commenced designing iconic lounge chairs and other furniture built from molded plywood, plastic resin, and wire mesh and manufactured by Herman Miller, Inc. in Zeeland, Michigan. High end Danish modern furniture fit the Populuxe aesthetic and soon had many imitators. American automobiles exhibited space age design when fitted with exaggerated tailfins that lent a dynamic, aeronautic feel (Figure 8.4). Portable radios, television sets, and phonographs also sported clean new looks, while household appliances acquired push button features.

Processed foods joined the national march toward the future. Manufacturer's advertising promoted their supposed healthfulness and especially their convenience. In her analysis of cookbooks from the 1950s, Jessamyn Neuhaus (1999, 533) found that "Recipes from the postwar years emphasized ease in preparation, and relied heavily on brand-name products and prepackaged foods. In several books, virtually every soup recipe consisted entirely of adding extra ingredients to canned soup." Jell-O, the trade name of a gelatinous dessert first introduced in 1897, became ubiquitous in American kitchens and women used it to make congealed or molded salads where grated carrots, pineapples, nuts, and cottage and cream cheeses were encased within brightly colored Jell-O rings. Swanson's TV Dinners, introduced in 1953, were my personal favorite Populuxe food. Fried chicken was the best, but I sometimes ate the turkey. The meals came on an aluminum tray divided into four compartments, the largest for the meat and the smaller ones for the mashed potatoes, vegetable medley, and cooked fruits. When my parents went out for an evening, I would fetch one from the freezer, take the tray out of the cardboard box, pop into the preheated oven at 425° for about 18 minutes, remove and peel back the foil to expose the chicken for a crispy skin, and then bake seven more minutes. After removing the foil, I would take it to a folding TV tray table (printed fiberglass top with aluminum legs) I had set up in our den and then ate the salty repast while watching a program. As I write more than 50 years later, I can still recall the Swanson's aromas and slightly metallic tastes.

Populuxe products and consumption rituals also had an indirect political meaning that could be wrapped around Cold War ideology and competition with communism and the Soviet Union. In her article, "One Nation Over Coals: Cold War Nationalism and the Barbecue," Kristin Matthews (2009) anchored the meaning of this popular form of outdoor cookery in the political. "Anointed an inherently American activity by advertisers, authors, and politicians alike, barbecue permeated the nationalistic discourse and socio-cultural consciousness of the immediate postwar period" (Matthews 2009, 8). Barbecue created national unity, at least for the white, suburban middle class. African Americans and the poor were left out of the picture. Populuxe as political propaganda reached its zenith in the famous 1959 "kitchen debate" in Moscow between Soviet Premier Nikita

Khrushchev (1894–1971) and U.S. Vice President Richard M. Nixon (1913–1994). "Nixon seemed to be making a stand for American values right in the setting that was most meaningful to Americans, in the heart of the suburban house – the modern push-button kitchen" (Hine 1986, 130). Consumerism was construed as not just a right, but also a civic duty for Americans in their fight against communism.

Populuxe styles did not appeal to everyone and a substantial market existed for traditional homes and colonial revival décors (see interior in Figure 8.6). As mentioned in the Preface and Acknowledgements, my own parents redid our home in the early 1960s with middle market Ethan Allen interpretations of early American furniture. These pieces fit the architectural style of the house and conveyed a sense of homeyness (see McCracken 1989a) that my mother in particular very much wanted. The cultural resonance of modernity and futurism as product meanings waned after the Kennedy assassination in 1963 and with the ramping up of civil rights demonstrations and, ominously, the Vietnam War. At the end of the 1960s and into the 1970s, the environmental movement raised new questions about just what the future might bring. Mid-century modern styles in furniture and accessories fell out of favor for several decades until enthusiastic collectors, decorators, and retro-minded retailers rediscovered them in the early twenty-first century.

In the 1950s and 1960s American youth became more conspicuous in sheer numbers and in their cultural prominence, especially with regards to consumption. As discussed previously, youth had been a recognizable cultural category and target market since the early twentieth century (Hollander and Germain 1992). With increasing postwar affluence a broader segment of young people found themselves with discretionary income earned through part- and full-time jobs and received from parents as gifts or regular allowances. Definitions of generational start and finish dates are debatable, but overall two broad cohorts participated in the new subcultures of youth consumption. The "silent generation" consisted of Americans born between about 1927 and 1945, essentially those who had not yet reached adulthood during the Great Depression and World War II. The younger ones, the war babies born between 1939 and 1945, entered their teenage years in the 1950s and by decade's end constituted a $10 billion market (*Life* 1959). Historian Richard Pells (2014) has argued that war babies occupied the forefront of the American popular culture revolution of the 1960s and 1970s. Then came the larger "baby boom" (my generation) born between 1946 and 1964. This cohort influenced macro consumption from the outset due to its sheer size and consequent demand for baby foods, clothing, toys, schools, and much more. The title and subhead of an article in *Life* (1958) said it all: "Rocketing Births: Business Bonanza. In Its Kids, U.S. Has a Recession Remedy." The boomers' influence as a consuming youth culture reached its crescendo in the late 1960s and into the 1970s.

Youth became embedded in 1950s' fashion, automobiles, and rock and roll music. Young men expressed themselves through denim jeans, sneakers, and, for the athletically talented, high school and college letterman sweaters and jackets (Figure 8.5). Young women wore full skirts and sweaters and sometimes

Figure 8.5 High School Varsity Ensemble, *c.*1953–1955. Wool letterman jacket by Harley Davidson Sporting Goods Company (1955), denim jeans by Levi Strauss (1953), and shoes by unknown U.S. maker (1955).

Source: Photo taken by author April 9, 2016 at *Reigning Men: Fashion in Menswear, 1715–2015*, Los Angeles County Museum of Art.

tight-fitting pedal pushers, now called Capri pants. Encouraged by *Hot Rod* magazine (first issued in 1948) some teens chopped old cars and installed powerful V-8 engines for cruising, scooping the loop, and street racing. The best example, of course, was the dazzling 1932 Ford yellow deuce coupe featured in the iconic movie *American Graffiti* (1973). On the music scene, a young television host named Dick Clark (1929–2012) took *American Bandstand* national in 1957. This afternoon program featured teenagers dancing to top 40 tunes and rating records, as well as the artists lip-syncing their latest singles. It introduced rock and roll to many Americans who also began to listen on small, portable transistor radios sold by Japan's Sony Corporation in the late 1950s. A youth culture clearly existed and, all in all, it conveyed relatively positive meanings despite the obsession of some critics with the attraction of young whites to black rhythm and blues once known as "race music" and with minor acts (by later standards) of teenage juvenile delinquency popularized in films such as *The Blackboard Jungle* (1955) and *Rebel Without a Cause* (1955). As in the larger consumer culture, rampant peer pressure and conformity were also troubling.

Matters changed greatly in the latter 1960s and into the 1970s. Many young people strived to differentiate themselves from older generations by wearing in various proportions long hair, beards, psychedelic floral colors, bell-bottomed trousers, beads, and sandals. Their comportment offended many Americans including some relatives of mine who disparaged the attire and perceived hygiene of protesters at the 1968 Democratic National Convention in Chicago rather than listening to their anti-war message. Circa 1970 we used to refer to those who sported the whole sartorial ensemble as "freaks." They were perceived to be anti-Vietnam War, sexually liberated, pot smokers, and in fact many did fit the stereotype. Other boomers were known as "straights." The term straight did not refer to sexual orientation, but rather to people who were more conventional in their dress and more conservative in their political and social attitudes. Youthful but rebellious styles in dress, tastes in music, and political attitudes permeated the culture.

Gender Roles Accepted, and Questioned

In the postwar 1940s and into the 1950s, millions of American women abandoned the social activism and workplace engagement of the Great Depression and World War II and returned to more traditional familial roles, or at least what they and society thought was traditional. Husbands typically took jobs in offices and factories in an era when one paycheck could support a family, finance a house mortgage, and afford an automobile. Their wives gave birth to the baby boomers and stayed at home raising them, cooking meals, cleaning the house, and driving around town to procure groceries and household goods. Family purchasing roles followed this prescribed division of labor. Based on data collected by the University of Michigan Survey Research Center, Harry Sharp and Paul Mott (1956) and Elizabeth Wolgast (1958) reported decision-making patterns for different purchase categories according to whether they were more husband dominant, wife dominant, or shared equally. Husbands had greater say about buying automobiles, but wives had more influence about food spending, money and bills, and household furnishings. Decisions in other categories, such as choices of vacations and housing, were more likely to be shared. Sharp and Mott's (1956) data came from metropolitan Detroit, then a formidable manufacturing city, whereas Wolgast (1958) drew from several different national panels.

If one had to pick an iconic postwar product whose marketing and intended applications exploited prevailing norms of gender better than anything else, a good choice would be the attractive and functional plastic food containers known as Tupperware (Velazquez 2014). Inventor Earl Silas Tupper (1907–1983) created a new form of injection-molded polyethylene and in 1947 received a patent for an innovative closure mechanism, the airtight "Tupper seal." He founded his own plastics company and began selling his line through hardware and department stores. Tupperware was an aesthetically pleasing, high quality yet inexpensive product that received numerous media mentions, such as coverage in a 1947 special issue of the reputable home interiors magazine, *House Beautiful*. Yet, female buyers showed only a modest interest in the product. These consumers had had too many negative experiences with the cracking, peeling, and otherwise disintegrating plastic products rushed to market in the 1940s (Bax 2010; Clarke 1999).

Enter the inimitable Brownie Wise (1913–1992). She had organized a social networking marketing system for Tupperware in Kissimmee, Florida that quickly exceeded local store sales (Kealing 2008). Duly impressed, Tupper hired Wise as vice president for Tupperware Home Parties Inc. (THP) in 1951. THP's business model was based upon a multi-level marketing system that employed ordinary homemakers rather than professional salespeople. Dealers recruited friends to host home "Tupperware parties" where the dealers would explain and demonstrate the product to their fellow housewives (Figure 8.6). Tupperware was withdrawn from conventional retailing and sold only through parties. Sales jumped from two million dollars in 1952 to ten million in 1957 (Bax 2010).

Figure 8.6 Brownie Wise Leads a Tupperware Party, *c.*1950s. Note the very upscale setting with colonial revival décor. Not everyone in the 1950s wanted modernism in their homes.

Source: Brownie Wise Papers, Archives Center, National Museum of American History.

The home party sales system had been developed in the 1920s and was used by Stanley Home Products where Brownie Wise had learned it (Clarke 1999; Kealing 2008). Practical for areas underserved by conventional retailing, home parties leveraged the traditional norms of female sociability that American women had been practicing as far back as the Colonial period when they would gather together for the pursuit of spinning, sewing, and other domestic arts (Ulrich 2001). Dealers always demonstrated the "Tupperware burp," the technique for creating an airtight seal, and encouraged everyone to touch and handle the products. To break the ice, as it were, attendees participated in party games where they could win Tupperware trinkets. Adding some theoretical distinctions, Clarke (1999, 108) describes the scene as follows:

> In addition to serving as a highly rarefied sales forum, the party acted as a ritual ceremony that, while focusing on Tupperware products, was filled with social significance among maker, buyer, and user. The structure of the party plan system blurred the theoretical boundaries of several identifying categories such as domesticity and commerce, work and leisure, friend and colleague, consumer and employee.

Home parties could be held in the morning as part of suburban "kaffeeklatsch" culture, the quiet time for a second cup after husbands went to work and the children had been sent off to school. Parties accompanied female dominated events such as bridal showers, housewarmings, community bake and rummage sales.

With its capability to better organize kitchen storage space and to economize by preserving leftovers for additional meals, Tupperware as a tangible good contributed to cultural ideals of female homemaking competence and efficiency preached by the Beecher sisters in the nineteenth century and Christine Frederick and many other home economists in the early twentieth (Vincent 2003). Tupperware sales also enabled the dealers, who tended to be lower middle or working class, to earn some spending or "pin" money and to contribute to the overall household budget. Although more than 20 million married women were in the workforce in 1955, they received much scorn from conservative critics, such as the National Catholic Life Conference, who accused them of deserting their homes and young children (Bax 2010). As part-time Tupperware dealers, women could satisfy social dictates and yet still work. Alas, Brownie Wise and Earl Tupper had a falling out and Tupper fired her in 1958, in part because he resented her relentless self-promotion including an autobiography she published in 1957 (Clarke 1999).

Tupperware often played a supporting role in the all-American barbecue culture discussed in the previous section. Beyond the reaffirmation of Cold War social and political ideals, barbecuing reversed, at least momentarily, prevailing domestic gender assignments. On the suburban patio, a more public space than the inside kitchen, husbands stood tall and proud. Wearing large chef aprons, they minded the meats, while their wives did the prep work and cleanup. Barbecue themed texts and advertisements played up the age-old image of men as hunters who, sharpened spits and edge tools at the ready, cooked the animal kill over a sizzling fire for the family group to devour (Matthews 2009; Neuhaus 1999; Sobal 2005). As discussed in Chapter 2, the association between meat and maleness would remain a powerful trope more than 50 years later in the early twenty-first century (Rozin *et al.* 2012).

Men's affinity for barbecue culture posturing could be interpreted as a response, both symbolic and behavioral, to looming threats to their masculinity posed by business corporations and public bureaucracies that had become even more stifling than those of the late 1890s discussed in Rotundo (1993). The postwar period saw the emergence of a literature suggesting something of a crisis in American masculinity. David Riesman in *The Lonely Crowd* (1950) described how the traditional "inner-directed" man succumbed to the accommodating "outer directed" sort valued by the corporate world. C. Wright Mills' *White Collar: The American Middle Classes* (1951) explored how the marketing mentality inexorably led to a "personality market" and potential self-alienation. William H. Whyte in his influential *The Organization Man* (1956) lamented the acceptance of corporate collectivism at the expense of rugged individualism. Many of the ideas in these books echoed Ayn Rand's vividly famous novel, *The Fountainhead* (1943), wherein architect Howard Roark battled obsequious conformity to achieve his superior personal vision. Theory and fiction are one matter; actual feelings of male panic in the period are quite another. Many men of the time probably did not feel threatened by developments in the workplace.

Assertive women could also be a source of male anxiety and the trope of the submissive, often henpecked husband already had been meandering about the cultural milieu for a number of years. For example, in the long running cartoon strip, *Blondie*, husband Dagwood Bumstead and his boss Mr Dithers routinely found themselves outmaneuvered by their wives. In the scripted comedy, *The Adventures of Ozzie and Harriet* (1952–1966), father Ozzie Nelson repeatedly had to resolve contradictions between his patriarchal instincts and his wife's domestic competence. James Gilbert, the author of *Men in the Middle: Searching for Masculinity in the 1950s* (2005, 162–163), concluded that Ozzie explored the 1950s' "paradox of masculinity: a man espousing ideas he thinks he believes in while struggling to fit into a new world of women and children, youth culture, togetherness, mass media, and consumer values." Cheesy films such as *The Incredible Shrinking Man* (1957) and *The Attack of the 50 Foot Woman* (1958) may have channeled male paranoia (Figure 8.7).

In a fascinating *Look* magazine article entitled "The American Male: Why Do Women Dominate Him," author J. Robert Moskin (1958, 80) opined with alarm

> It is certain that, as women grow even more numerous and more dominant, we will have to invent new meanings and myths for maleness in America, because, as psychiatrist Dr. Iren J. Roselyn warns, "we are drifting toward a social structure made up of he-women and she-men."

Men coped, in part, via their consumption activities. They drank in commuter train bar cars, watched televised baseball at home, played golf on weekends, and

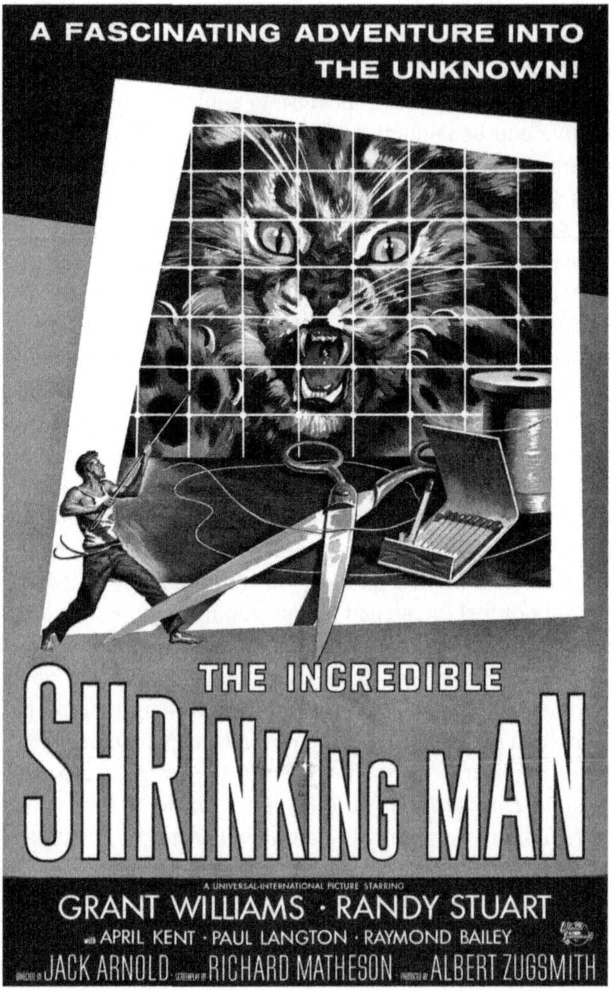

Figure 8.7 The Incredible Shrinking Man Theatrical Release Poster, 1957. Poster by Reynold Brown (1917–1991).

Source: Wikimedia Commons.

went on all-male fishing trips. In their private moments some took advantage of the visual world created by *Playboy* magazine. At work, their expense accounts paid for meals at fancy restaurants and, when traveling, for spacious suites and lavish entertaining, not unlike scenes in the television series *Mad Men*. Moskin's article seemingly focused on the lives of upper middle-class men like himself (he was Senior Editor at *Look* magazine at the time) and his allegations of declining male potency and a homosexual "flight from masculinity" (80) lack credibility in the present day. Still, he was quite prescient about threats to manliness given the even larger social changes that would be afoot in decades to come. The thread of American males compensating for real and perceived emasculation will be picked up again in the next chapter.

One gendered feature of the cult of domesticity 1950s' style differentiated it from the earlier Victorian version in the nineteenth-century. This was the expectation that both men and women should contribute to home repair and maintenance rather than hire outsiders. The phrase "do-it-yourself" had been used occasionally since it first appeared in 1912, but the idiom received much greater prominence when the June 2, 1952 issue of *Business Week* proclaimed the 1950s "the age of do-it-yourself" (Gelber 1997). This norm assumed ownership of a single-family home since renters and apartment dwellers usually had neither the space nor the incentive to perform these activities. Male householder roles and masculine virtues became attached to the new electric power tools manufacturers offered. Historian Steven Gelber contrasted the late nineteenth- to early twentieth-century "masculine domesticity" described by Margaret Marsh (1988) with 1950s' "domestic masculinity":

> Unlike masculine domesticity, which had men doing jobs that had once belonged to women, domestic masculinity was practiced in areas that had been the purview of professional (male) craftsmen, and therefore retained the aura of pre-industrial vocational masculinity. The two concepts are complementary, but the introduction of the idea of domestic masculinity recognizes the creation of a male sphere *inside* the house.
>
> (Gelber 1997, 73)

We need to bear in mind, however, that not every household in previous eras was in a position to hire outside craftsmen. Settlers on the frontier, farmers living in distant rural areas, and many working-class families by necessity had to rely on their own skills in the manual arts. So Gelber may have overstated the distinction. Still, suburbia did keep men at home and involved more of them in do-it-yourself activities. For some, this was leisurely recreation and productive consumption more than necessity, especially when they had their own basement, garage, or workshop in which to putter. This thread will be followed further in the next chapter.

The dominant cultural ideal in the 1950s and 1960s – repeated endlessly in consumer magazines and portrayed memorably in situation comedies such as *Leave It to Beaver* (1957–1963) – envisioned middle and upper class women as competent yet unpaid, stay-at-home "consumption managers" dependent upon a male breadwinner's income (Galbraith 1973). Based on data collected in 1968, Robert Ferber and Lucy Chao Lee (1974) conceptualized the role of the "family financial officer (FFO)," the person or persons who, like Galbraith's consumption manager, paid the bills, kept track of expenditures, and decided on how to spend discretionary funds. Within their very middle-American sample drawn from the small cities of Decatur and Peoria, Illinois, the authors found that the FFO role was filled by wives about a third of time, by both spouses jointly about a third of time, and by husbands about one quarter of the time.

Betty Friedan's highly influential book, *The Feminine Mystique* (1963), challenged this orthodoxy and helped spark a new wave of feminism where the accepted gendering of postwar household consumption roles became highly problematic. Friedan (1921–2006) described how many women, particularly those like her who were middle class and educated, felt relegated to a status of just being housewives. They lived their lives through their children, linked their identities to those of their husbands, and had these role definitions imposed by a manipulative media culture serving business interests. Some women turned to alcohol while doing household chores, even using Tupperware to freeze strong daiquiris (Clarke 1999, 111). Friedan lambasted advertisers and motivation researchers, such as the unnamed Ernest Dichter she had interviewed, who manipulated women's insecurities to keep them in the kitchen (Horowitz 2004). Marketers were "guilty of persuading housewives to stay at home, mesmerized in front of a television set, their nonsexual human needs unnamed, unsatisfied, drained by the sexual sell into the buying of things" (Friedan 1963, 218). With her manifesto in place, Friedan went on to co-found the National Organization for Women (NOW) in 1966. This group became a spear point for the broader feminist movement as it fought to establish new norms legitimating careers and outside work for women and new thinking about a wide range of power relationships between men and women. The introduction of oral contraceptives around this time also helped liberate American women. Approved for contraception by the Food and Drug Administration in 1962, within three years 6.5 million women were taking them. On the pill, women could better pursue their educational and career goals without fear of pregnancy and, if they chose, enjoy a more open attitude toward sex.

Companies quickly coopted elements of the cultural redefinition of gender roles. In 1968, for example, Philip Morris introduced a thinner cigarette for women named Virginia Slims. Its ad agency, Leo Burnett, created print ads and television commercials – cigarette advertising on U.S. TV and radio was not banned until after January 1, 1971 – that juxtaposed vignettes of women in the early twentieth century being hassled for smoking with the freedom counterparts enjoyed in the late 1960s and 1970s (O'Keefe and Pollay 1996). These images (see UCSF 2006 in the reference list for link to a 1969 compilation video) and the campaign slogan, "You've come a long way, baby," bound the brand to a commercialized version of feminism and women's liberation. Virginia Slims gained market share through the 1970s and 1980s, but faced an identity crisis in the 1990s when its aspirational image lost relevance to a new generation of young women (Toll and Ling 2005).

The highly successful advertising campaign for Charlie brand perfume, launched by Revlon in February 1973, also capitalized on this cultural shift. Charlie ads featured gorgeous model Shelley Hack as a liberated woman, striding confidently through New York City and other locations wearing chic Ralph Lauren pantsuits (Bird, Caldwell, and DeFanti 2011). The classy TV commercials featured a memorable tune sung by jazz pianist Bobby Short and, in another version, by popular crooner Mel Tormé, nicknamed, much to his annoyance,

"The Velvet Fog." An intended message for the working women in the target audience was that they, like Charlie, had the wherewithal to buy her own fragrances and did not have to wait for a man's gift or husband's permission. More broadly, the incomes of newly and fully employed women could enhance their economic power within the household unit. This trend accelerated in the 1970s when more and more women entered the labor force to help their families maintain living standards threatened by stagnating male incomes (U.S. Bureau of the Census 2016a).

Getting the husbands of working wives to contribute more to housework remained a challenge, but one new product helped in a small way by re-gendering coffee-making, a simple chore usually performed by women. As Rebecca Shrum (2012) explained in her delightful article, "Selling Mr. Coffee: Design, Gender, and the Branding of a Kitchen Appliance," Americans had been brewing their java with electric pumping percolators since early in the twentieth century (Shrum 2012). These small, metal appliances were convenient to operate, but imparted a bitter taste since the boiling water tended to over-extract the coffee grounds. To some extent, this brewing problem was mitigated by prevailing taste. Americans had become accustomed to drinking weak coffee when they had to economize during the Great Depression and cope with shortages and rationing during World War II. Then, in the 1940s, coffee companies started substituting cheaper robusta coffee beans for the better quality arabica variety. The famous 1962 Maxwell House slogan created by legendary adman David Ogilvy, "tastes as good as it smells," was a dubious claim despite the clever photography and catchy theme song in the commercials. America was a coffee disaster zone (trust me, I was there) and women sometimes received the blame. A 1934 a print advertisement for Chase and Sanborn depicted a husband physically assaulting his wife for bad coffee, a stunt repeated in a 1959 "Chock full o' Nuts" ad (Shrum 2012). On television, commercials for Procter & Gamble's Folgers Coffee featured a matronly Swedish immigrant neighbor, named Mrs. Olson, who repeatedly spared young wives spousal reproach and worse by dispensing patronizing coffee advice. The campaign ran from 1965 to 1986.

In 1972 an Ohio-based company, North American Systems, introduced Mr. Coffee, the first electric-drip coffeemaker for home use. Made from plastic with a faux wood-grained panel, Mr. Coffee combined the heating element and the drip-and-filter in the same device. It was easy to use and delivered somewhat better tasting coffee. Though more expensive than percolators, Mr. Coffee and its drip machine imitators quickly captured a large share of the market. The explicit male gendering of a brand used mostly by women was not unusual. Masculine brand names or personas had been applied to other household products, the best example being the launch in 1958 of Mr. Clean liquid cleaner and its bald, but muscular cartoon trade character. Mr. Coffee reinforced this angle in 1973 by hiring baseball great Joe DiMaggio (1914–1999) to be the brand spokesman. As a celebrity endorser, DiMaggio transferred his masculinity to the product by association (McCracken 1989b), but in a series of commercials he directly instructed men on how to use the system and make coffee themselves

(Shrum 2012). Societal mores concerning housework were changing, albeit slowly. According to one longitudinal (and cross-national) time-use study (Sayer 2010), American women in 1965 spent 213 minutes per day on routine housework, compared to 19 minutes by men. In 1975, the relative minutes spent were 156 and 25 and, in 1985, 145 and 52 minutes respectively.

The feminist movement of the 1960s and 1970s stimulated a great deal of scholarly work on women, society, and culture in the field of American history, in the social sciences, and in consumer research. Studies of purchasing influence and consumption began to add new variables reflective of these larger social changes. For example, Robert Green and Isabella Cunningham (1975) investigated how purchasing decisions varied according to whether their respondents, 257 married women in Houston, were classified as conservatives, moderates, or liberals. The conservatives held attitudes then identified with the traditional role of women, whereas the liberals had then-contemporary role perceptions. The moderates vacillated or did not have strongly held positions. Not unexpectedly, across ten decision areas the liberal wives made more purchasing decisions. In the mid-1970s, Alladi Venkatesh (1980) conducted a similar survey of 333 women in Syracuse, New York. Using a feminism scale, he grouped the respondents into traditionalists, moderates, and feminists and then showed how they differed across different consumption areas, such as fashion and personal appearance and frozen foods. His feminists were younger, better educated, and more independent within the household. They also were more self-confident, less prone to television viewing, and more attentive to international news.

Critics, Civil Rights, and Cannabis (Part I)

Familiar threads of moralistic anti-consumption thought can be found throughout much of the postwar period (Witkowski 2010a). Writers of the 1950s identified and criticized the excesses of post-war consumer culture. In *The Affluent Society*, for example, influential Harvard economist John Kenneth Galbraith (1958) complained about the manipulation of demand by big business, and the overemphasis on private consumption to the detriment of the quality of public services. Unlike most other critics, Galbraith (1908–2006) floated specific policy proposals, above all, a national tax on consumption. Muckraking journalist Vance Packard (1914–1996) published, in rapid succession, three very popular books that criticized consumerism and the commercial and emulative forces that drove it. In *The Hidden Persuaders* (1957), he exposed the use of motivational research and the alleged subliminal tactics by advertisers to induce consumer desire. Next, in *The Status Seekers* (1959), Packard explored American social class stratification and how it was expressed through consumption choices in foods and dining patterns, book and magazine reading, and hobbies, entertainment, and other pastimes. In *The Waste Makers* (1960), Packard took on seductive packaging, planned obsolescence, and the throwaway psychology of the masses. These books all made the *New York Times* best-seller list (Hawes 2016) and reached a wide audience.

The scathing analyses of Galbraith, Packard, and Betty Friedan did suffer from one serious flaw: they focused on the downsides of affluence among the white, middle classes, but neglected the more severe afflictions of poverty upon blacks and rural whites (Horowitz 2004). This one-sided view of consumption changed following the 1962 publication of *The Other America: Poverty in the United States* by democratic socialist writer Michael Harrington (1928–1989). Harrington showed just how invisible the poor had become and spoke of a "culture of poverty" that made economic and social mobility extremely difficult to achieve. He called for a federal "war on poverty," a tagline for programs advocated by President Lyndon Baines Johnson (1908–1973) and enacted through the Economic Opportunity Act of August 1964.

Moral sermonizing continued into the 1960s. In *Unsafe at Any Speed* (1965) then 31-year-old attorney Ralph Nader attacked America's premier industry for producing automobiles that unnecessarily endangered drivers and passengers. Galbraith, Packard, and Friedan had all derided autos as problematic symbols of excessive consumer culture, but Nader's book made a scathing direct assault that contrasted paltry industry outlay on safety with massive expenditures on stylistic changes and advertising. General Motors inadvertently assisted Nader when it hired private investigators to gather information on him. This ham-fisted ploy was exposed and led to Congressional hearings on auto safety and the passage of the National Transportation and Motor Vehicle Safety Act in September 1966. GM also settled with Nader for damages, which enabled him to launch consumer advocacy groups still active at this writing. In the meantime, Reverend Martin Luther King, Jr. (1929–1968) railed against excessive materialism, desire, and riotous living in some of his sermons and writings. This message was not always well-received among African Americans fighting for jobs and equal access to the marketplace, and so by the 1960s King shifted his focus to "the gap between black poverty and white prosperity" (Horowitz 2004, 182).

The 1950s produced alternative subcultures at odds with the conformity of Populuxe infused suburbia so attractive to the country at large. "Beat Generation" writers and poets including William S. Burroughs (1914–1997), Allen Ginsberg (1926–1997), and Jack Kerouac (1922–1969) questioned runaway capitalism and, in general, kept their distance from the materialistic consumer culture (Shi 1985). "Beatniks" became a favorite media stereotype soon appropriated and amplified for advertising and entertainment purposes. Young cats sported goatees, wore berets, played bongo drums, and dug the modern jazz style dubbed Bebop, while their chicks were pictured in tight black turtlenecks, leotards, and sunglasses. The lovable character Maynard G. Krebs (played by Bob Denver) on the TV comedy series *The Many Loves of Dobie Gillis* (1959–1963) embodied the key beatnik traits of eccentricity and work avoidance. The 1959 MGM film noir, *The Beat Generation*, sensationalized a much darker side of the beatnik scene and, perhaps appropriately, lost money at the box office (Figure 8.8).

A decade or so later, hippies and other highly committed adopters of the late 1960s counterculture practiced alternatives to conventional consumerism via

Figure 8.8 The Beat Generation Theatrical Release Poster, 1959. Poster by Reynold Brown (1917–1991).

Source: Wikimedia Commons.

experiments with drugs, communal living, and other forms of studied rejection of their parents' suburban values. Two books from the period captured the moment: *The Making of a Counter Culture: Reflections on the Technocratic Society and Its Youthful Opposition* by Theodore Roszak (1969) and *The Greening of America* by Charles A. Reich (1970). Both authors saw the counterculture in terms of a new consciousness. Roszak (1969, xii) argued that

> the interests of our college-age and adolescent young in the psychology of alienation, oriental mysticism, psychedelic drugs, and communitarian experiments comprise a cultural constellation that radically diverges from values and assumptions that have been in the mainstream of our society at least since the Scientific Revolution of the seventeenth century.

Reich (1970), whose book became a best seller, discussed three types of consciousness or worldviews that existed in the 1960s. The traditional Consciousness I, defined as the getting ahead outlook of farmers, small businessmen, and workers, originated in the nineteenth century and continued as a strong strain within American culture. Consciousness II, the values of an organizational society, reigned supreme from the 1930s through the 1950s, and remained potent in the 1960s. Consciousness III was the new generation who felt betrayed by their elders and craved liberation from social imperatives, such as "a dreary corporate job, a ranch-house life" (Reich 1970, 220). This book promised an American revolution in consciousness, but such was not to be.

Marine biologist and nature writer, Rachel Carson (1907–1964), strung a new thread of resistance on the loom of consumption when, in 1962, she published *Silent Spring*. This alarming book greatly raised awareness of the environmental consequences of American affluence. Carson presented a litany of poisons, such as DDT and other pesticides and herbicides, whose industrial overuse had entered the food chain and threatened many species including the nation's symbol, the bald eagle. She also indicted suburban development and consumer culture for the threats presented to health and well-being. The chemical industry launched a furious attack on her claims, and for half a century ultra-conservatives have denied her findings (Oreskes and Conway 2010), but she was able to get her word out through a 1963 CBS documentary *The Silent Spring of Rachel Carson*. Women, in particular, were a receptive audience for her message (Horowitz 2004). Environmental concerns received a further powerful fillip in 1968 with the publication of *The Population Bomb* by Stanford biology professor Paul R. Ehrlich. In contrast to Carson's evocation of nature's beauty and transcendence, Ehrlich presented an apocalyptic view of environmental degradation caused by ever-growing populations (Horowitz 2004).

The first Earth Day, celebrated April 22, 1970, marked the emergence of an environmental movement in the U.S. (Figure 8.9) that reasserted the need for a consumption conservation ethos in order to protect the planet from pollution and other afflictions (Fritsch 1974). Numerous private sector companies and nonprofit organizations, like the National Recycling Coalition founded in 1978, took initiatives to promote recycling, reduced energy consumption, and solid waste management, while many state governments and public utilities became leaders in promoting the conservation of resources such as water and electricity. The purely environmental concerns of the early 1970s were soon joined by worries about over-dependence on foreign oil, a point brought home to American drivers by the Arab oil embargo of 1973–1974 and by the Iranian revolution of 1979. In 1975, Congress enacted CAFE (Corporate Average Fuel Economy) standards to

Figure 8.9 Girl Scout in Canoe, Picking Trash Out of the Potomac River During Earth Week, April 22, 1970. Photograph by Thomas J. O'Halloran.

Source: Library of Congress, Prints & Photographs Division, Washington, D.C.

boost national fuel efficiency. CAFE regulations have been highly controversial. Opposed by auto and energy interests and anti-regulatory "free market" ideologues, Congress did not seriously overhaul the 1975 legislation until December 2007. Controlling demand through higher federal gasoline taxes, the approach favored by most economists, has found virtually no support among ideologically tax adverse politicians in Washington.

Resistance to racist Jim Crow laws and business practices that sought to control access to sites of consumption, or to stifle it outright, took on major significance in the postwar era. The previous two chapters reviewed African-American boycotts and other organized resistance during the first decade of the twentieth century and again during the 1930s. After World War II, black consumers in the South still could not eat in many public restaurants, stay in many hotels and motels, and rent apartments and buy homes where they chose. Blacks in other parts of the country faced similar, albeit less overt, restrictions on their consumption. Access to housing, for example, was blocked by restrictive codes and covenants. Black resistance as part of the burgeoning Civil Rights movement of the 1950s and 1960s undoubtedly generated some of the most dramatic battles over consumption in American history. Above all stands the Montgomery, Alabama bus boycott. The following summary draws from Friedman's (1999) extended account.

On Thursday, December 1, 1955, police arrested Rosa Parks (1913–2005) for refusing to give up her seat to a white man. Parks, a black political activist and an NAACP secretary, had been ejected from a bus back in the 1940s because she did not comply with orders from the white driver. By 1955, tensions over local buses had been mounting and her arrest ignited a firestorm of protest. A model for how to resist had been established two years earlier in Baton Rouge, Louisiana. In that city, following a boycott that cost the bus company dearly, an agreement was reached to partially desegregate the buses. In Montgomery, the black Women's Political Council organized a boycott for Monday, December 5, and distributed 50,000 handbills to promote it. That Monday very few blacks rode the buses, causing a huge loss of revenue for the bus company. At an afternoon meeting, activists formed a new organization, the Montgomery Improvement Association, to continue the boycott and invited a young black minister with superb oratory skills, the Reverend Martin Luther King, Jr., to lead it. The bus company summarily rejected demands for change within the existing segregation laws and soon police were harassing black carpools. Someone bombed Dr. King's house on January 30, 1956. A month later a grand jury returned indictments against 90 boycott leaders for conspiracy, but the NAACP took the case to federal court, which ruled bus segregation illegal, a decision upheld by the U.S. Supreme Court on November 13, 1956. Federal marshals served copies of the ruling to Montgomery officials and thus ended the city's bus segregation. The Montgomery bus boycott had lasted 382 days ending December 21, 1956. It energized the Civil Rights movement and its battles against Jim Crow laws that suppressed other forms of African-American consumption.

From 1958 to 1960, young black people and white sympathizers participated in another tactic of resistance to consumer segregation – the sit-in. In Wichita, Kansas, Oklahoma City, Richmond, Virginia, Nashville, Tennessee, Atlanta, Georgia, and other cities activists occupied seats at "whites only" lunch counters in department stores and refused to leave until service was desegregated. A particularly noteworthy sit-in occurred on February 1, 1960 at an F.W. Woolworth store in Greensboro, North Carolina. Initiated by four black college students, the sit-in soon drew hundreds of supporters. The reaction from white customers was brutal, to say the least, but their hostility was captured on film, disseminated nationwide, and thus generated further support for the movement. On July 25, 1960, after suffering financial losses, the Greensboro Woolworth's started serving blacks at its lunch counter. Today the former Woolworth's houses the International Civil Rights Center and Museum and, in recognition of this iconic demonstration, a section of the original lunch counter is on display at the Smithsonian National Museum of American History in Washington, D.C.

Other examples of consumer resistance in this period include the California grape boycott of 1965 to 1970 and the 1977 to 1980 boycott of Florida oranges. Outsider groups initiated both actions to forward their rights and social recognition. In September 1965 Filipino farm workers went out on strike because they were not being paid the federal minimum wage. Chicano labor organizer Cesar Chavez (1927–1993) came to their assistance and soon strikes broke out at major grape farms across California. In November 1965 a consumer boycott targeting specific companies began. Because the growers confused consumers by switching labels, a total boycott of California table grapes started in January 1968. To publicize the boycott, Chavez adopted the nonviolent tactics of India's Mahatma Gandhi and, among other activities, organized a 250-mile march to Sacramento in March 1966 followed by a 25-day hunger strike in February 1968. By 1969 some 17 million Americans were refusing to buy table grapes and Gallo wine. Grape shipments decreased by a third and the agribusiness companies suffered significant losses. Eventually, the growers signed contracts with the new United Farmworkers of America and in July 1970 the strikes, pickets, and boycotts ended (Weeks 2008). This episode of consumer resistance was relatively successful, in part, because it had a strong leader who could reach out to concerned consumers. Cesar Chavez has become an iconic figure for Mexican Americans and his birthday, March 31, is celebrated as an official holiday in California and several other states.

In January 1977, the Dade County Commission of Miami, Florida, passed an ordinance outlawing discrimination against gays and lesbians in the workplace and in the housing market. Christian and other assorted homophobes immediately began campaigning to repeal the ordinance. They were led by Anita Bryant who was a former Miss Oklahoma beauty queen, a successful pop singer, and, since 1969, a spokesperson for the Florida Citrus Commission. Bryant founded an anti-gay group, Save Our Children, and enlisted the support of local newspapers and the Florida Citrus Commission. The ordinance was repealed in June 1977, which triggered the boycott of Florida oranges and orange juice. The boycott found very limited support outside the LGBT community and liberal activists and the offending ordinance was not repealed until 1998. Although Florida citrus crops maintained sales, their spokeswoman suffered great ridicule and reproach. Anita Bryant's career turned south and in 1980 the Florida Citrus Commission fired her for the opprobrium she had brought upon the industry and to the state (Hayes 2013). This boycott had limited immediate impact upon orange consumption, and did not change the political situation much in Florida, but in the longer run it brought greater attention to LGBT rights and presaged the great cultural shift in how this group came to be perceived in the twenty-first century by the majority of Americans.

As early as the seventeenth century, when some New Englanders flaunted sumptuary laws, Americans have resisted various regulations over what and how they may consume. In the mid-1960s the smoking of marijuana became a widespread form of outsider resistance to a consumption prohibition that has had great legal, political, and social consequences. Cannabis had a long history in America. From the early 1600s, hemp, a non-intoxicating strain of cannabis, had been widely planted for use in clothing, yarn, and paper and, being relatively saltwater resistant, for weaving rope and sailcloth. At the time of the Civil War, hemp was the third most valuable cash crop in the U.S. after cotton and tobacco, but its importance gradually waned as cotton displaced it for use in textiles and wood pulp became the standard for paper. The plant also had therapeutic uses as a folk remedy. In the late nineteenth and early twentieth centuries, pharmaceutical companies sold numerous tinctures (cannabis dissolved in alcohol) for the treatment of dozens of ailments and conditions, ranging from corns to neuralgia to the afflictions of menopause. Smoking cannabis via hand-rolled cigarettes (joints, reefers, and doobies, among many other pet synonyms) for recreational purposes did not begin to catch on until perhaps the 1910s when the practice accompanied Mexico immigrants spreading across the western states. Around the same time, marijuana use came from the West Indies to Gulf of Mexico port cities – Houston, Galveston, and New Orleans – and later flowed up the Mississippi (Bonnie and Whitebread 1974). In the 1920s reefers became popular among black Jazz musicians (Lee 2012; Sloman 1998).

Turn of the century progressives concerned with moral issues, such as drinking, prostitution, and gambling, added cannabis to their prohibitionist wish list and began to create public sentiment against the drug until, in 1914, the New York City Sanitary Laws prohibited cannabis. States began to follow suit and by 1933 a total of 33 had prohibited its use (Bonnie and Whitebread 1974). The hundreds of newspapers controlled by William Randolph Hearst (1863–1951) ran stories associating black, Mexican, and West Indian pot users with heinous criminal activities and these wicked meanings were transferred to cannabis (Humphreys 2010; McCracken 1986). Given that cannabis smoking was perceived to be prevalent amongst Mexican and African Americans in an era of extreme racial prejudice, it comes as no surprise that dominant whites, their political representatives, and law enforcement interests would opt for its criminalization. Apparently, they had learned little from the failure of Prohibition a few years earlier. The anti-cannabis campaigning of the 1930s resulted in the Marihuana Tax Act of 1937, the federal law that effectively made possession and transfer illegal throughout the U.S. New laws in the 1950s imposed even harsher punishments for possession.

Nevertheless, some people resisted this prohibition and an underground cannabis marketing system served their demand. In the 1950s and early 1960s, smoking dope was generally limited to brown and black people, musicians and entertainers, and some outsider whites, such as the beat writer Jack Kerouac and the poet provocateur Allen Ginsberg who agitated for pot (Figure 8.10). For poor minorities, cannabis consumption eased the drudgery of hard lives with limited choices. Musicians thought it enhanced their playing. For the beats, it had a more transcendental meaning, a link to some high European literary traditions (Sloman 1998). As Figure 8.11 suggests, the prevalence of marijuana smoking was not insignificant and interdicting supply chains kept narcotics agents busy.

Then, the plant acquired new meaning among a vast new market. In the mid-1960s, cannabis became a popular recreational drug among young people, counter-culture types, and Vietnam War protesters. Middle-class college students quickly learned that the cannabis they consumed was not anywhere near as destructive as the substance vilified by law enforcement orthodoxy. Indeed, for most consumers smoking pot was enjoyable and harmless. Equally important, cannabis became a symbol of political protest and opposition to an establishment

Figure 8.10 Allen Ginsberg "POT IS FUN," *c.*1964.

Source: From poster based on photo by Benedict J. Fernandez.

that for many years had lied both about weed and the war in Southeast Asia. This insurgent association undoubtedly further alienated cannabis from the establishment, and made it a totem in America's long-standing "culture wars." Ironically, upwards of 50 percent of the enlisted men serving in Vietnam tried the potent strains available (Sloman 1998). For these often conservative, patriotic, and working-class soldiers, cannabis became a palliative for coping with their arduous situation. Fifty years on, people who came of age in the 1960s were more supportive of legalization than those who grew up in the previous generation (Geiger 2016).

By the late 1960s activist elements in the cannabis community were engaging in what would become a decades long crusade to resist social condemnation and oppressive government prosecution and to support efforts for decriminalization

Figure 8.11 Narcotics Agents with over 400 lbs of Marijuana, 1963. *World Telegram & Sun* photo by Ed Ford.

Source: Library of Congress, Prints & Photographs Division, Washington, D.C.

and legalization. The movement enjoyed some initial success in the 1970s. Despite the Nixon administration's "war on drugs," public approval of legalization began to increase (Motel 2014). In 1973, the state of Oregon made possession of less than an ounce a mere $100 fine and two years later Alaska decriminalized possession for personal use. Decriminalization and wider acceptance took some of the local heat off consumers and small dealers, but did not substantially change the cannabis marketing system and the product assortments it made available. Laws at the federal level and in many states remained harshly punitive of those caught possessing and selling the substance and public opinion turned against cannabis legalization during the 1980s when "just say no" became the policy slogan of the Reagan administration (Motel 2014). The movement for the legitimization of cannabis had stalled, its sales and possession remained illegal, and resistance through consumption stayed risky. The story of consumers defying cannabis prohibition in America was far from over, however, and it will be continued in the next chapter.

Summary

After the conclusion of World War II, the economy shrank for a few years due to budget cuts and a mild recession in 1948, but by 1950 strong growth had resumed and American consumption finally returned to the exuberance that had characterized it before the Great Depression. The lively new medium of television and commercials and the development of ever-larger suburban shopping centers simultaneously motivated and satisfied consumer demand for new products. Not until the 1970s, when faced with challenges from gasoline shortages, stagflation, and economic malaise, did American consumers experience a rough patch and contemplate existential doubts about the future.

The generally positive meanings of modernity and youth associated with possessions in the 1950s came under assault in the late 1960s with rising environmental concerns and a highly critical counterculture. Similarly, the feminist movement of the 1960s challenged the valorization of gendered homemaking and consumption management and instead turned national attention to issues of women's work and career opportunities. Numerous intellectuals, muckraking journalists, beatniks, and hippies criticized excessive private consumption, but threads of action also became manifest. From the 1950s into the 1970s resistance to market and labor discrimination based on race, ethnicity, and sexual orientation took the form of significant boycotts and sit-ins. Starting in the 1960s the previously covert opposition to cannabis prohibition took the form of more widespread, open, and, within some circles, socially sanctioned consumption.

9 American Consumption since 1980

The year 1980 has been chosen as the start date for our final era because about this time three major political, economic, and technological trends came into force that would have great bearing upon American consumption in the following decades. First, the election of Ronald Reagan (1911–2004) as President in November 1980 marked the ascendancy of neoliberal or "free market" thinking and policy in American life (Smith 2012). The tax cuts and deregulation of his and succeeding administrations would be among the factors that fueled a rise in income inequality and, hence, disparities in consumption. Second, with the economic reforms championed by Deng Xiaoping, the People's Republic of China began to open itself to outside ideas and investment and within three decades had become the workshop for the world of consumer goods. Global trade and investment grew inexorably until the Great Recession started about the third quarter of 2008 and globalization paused. Third, the debut of the Apple II computer in 1978 and the IBM PC in 1981 suggests 1980 as a reasonable start date for the information technology revolution whose products and services have had great impact on how and what Americans consume, and by whom.

This chapter will begin with the usual overview of a few economic, political, and social contexts of consumption. The threads of meaning will then reveal how firearms, automobiles, and other goods have become embroiled in the nation's increased political polarization. The gender section will address the thread of men and masculinity, and then explore gendered divisions in the consumption of technology and social media. Threads of resistance to be discussed will include voluntary simplicity and related opposition to consumerism, boycotts organized by conservatives, and the contested field of cannabis consumption.

Material Life and the Market

The nominal GDP of the United States in 1980, nearly three trillion dollars ($2,862,500 million or $6,450,400 million in 2009 dollars), had grown by 2015 to nearly 18 trillion ($17,942,900 or $16,345,000 in 2009 dollars). Nominal 1980 per capita GDP of $12,570 ($28,325 in 2009 dollars) increased by 2015 to $55,774 ($50,808) (Johnston and Williamson 2017). The near doubling of per capita GDP seems impressive, but being an average of GDP divided by population, the metric disguises rising inequality. The U.S. census counted 226,542,199 Americans in 1980 and the Bureau of the Census estimated 323,745,538 on January 1, 2017 (U.S. Bureau of the Census 2016a, 2017).

The material well being of American consumers was not something to be taken lightly, as postwar politicians generally recognized. In the mid-1960s during the escalation of the War in Vietnam, President Lyndon Johnson did not ask the public to sacrifice financially because he believed the nation simultaneously could afford to fight communism in Southeast Asia and to build a "Great Society" at home. After the terrible events of September 11, 2001, President George W. Bush asked people to continue spending as usual in order to help revive an already sluggish economy. In contrast, the earnest, cardigan-sweater-wearing speeches President Jimmy Carter delivered in the 1970s, which advocated plain living, energy conservation, and lowered expectations, did not help him much at the ballot box in 1980. Voters had had enough with oil shortages and stagflation and, instead, opted for change through Ronald Reagan's politics of early-morning optimism. Generally lower taxes, robust consumer spending financed by rising levels of household debt, and, after 2000, record federal budget deficits fueled economic growth until the bubble burst in 2008 with the onset of the Great Recession, whose consequences for consumption still remain profound at this writing.

Any discussion of relatively recent consumption history risks making premature assessments about the past, but the growth of income and wealth inequality since 1980 seems particularly noteworthy. Figure 9.1 shows the Gini coefficient, a measure of income inequality among all families in the U.S. economy from 1947 to 2015. The higher the coefficient, the greater is the inequality. The chart shows an overall decline from 1947 to 1969, a small increase in the 1970s, and a much faster rise after 1980. As mentioned in this chapter's introduction, the 1980s launched an era of ascendant neoliberal politics and accelerating globalization. Under the influence of conservative ideology, Congress delivered and presidents signed tax cuts for corporations and wealthy individuals that inexorably led, among other factors, to greater income and wealth inequality. Globalization provided consumers with lower prices, but because of international competition in traded industries, along with waves of immigrants willing to work for less, many Americans saw their jobs sent offshore and their wages undermined. These forces appear to have fueled the rise in inequality, although technological innovation (e.g., robotics, the Internet) and social developments (e.g., decline in unionization) also have been suggested as contributory factors.

This post-1980 trend contrasts starkly with the decreasing levels of income inequality that started during the Great Depression and New Deal of the 1930s and continued through both Democrat and Republican administrations until the presidency of Ronald Reagan. Greater inequality in income and wealth has exaggerated differences among classes of consumers where a small minority patronizes luxury boutiques and a much larger group shops at Walmart and Dollar General stores. Since consumer spending drives about 70 percent of the U.S.

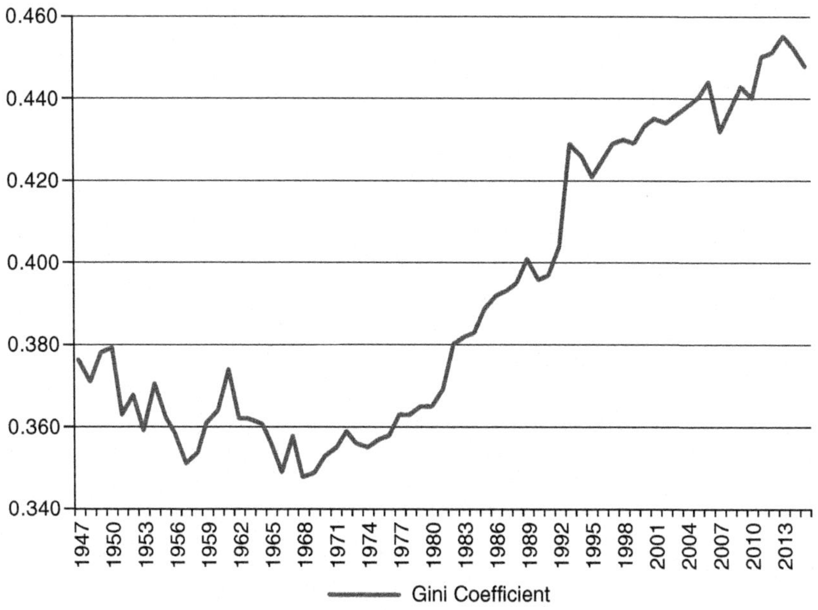

Figure 9.1 U.S. Gini Coefficient as Indicator of Inequality, 1947–2015.

Source: U.S. Bureau of the Census, Historical Income Tables Families, Table F-4.

economy, some analysts attributed the relatively slow recovery from the Great Recession to weak demand among the bottom 95 percent. Incomes were too low and, unlike previously, could no longer be propped up by working longer hours, finding jobs for spouses, and taking on more household debt as was possible after 1982 when interest rates headed downward and mortgages could be refinanced (Cynamon, Fazzari, and Setterfield 2014).

Also of import during the first two decades of this period was the growth of what might be called "consuming alone." More and more Americans chose to live by themselves, drive their own cars, watch their personal TVs, and eat their meals at the times most convenient for their hectic schedules (Cross 2000; Putnam 2001). In his influential book, *Bowling Alone*, Robert Putnam (2001) lamented the loss of social connections and capital caused by such solo consumption. Two different ideologies of individualism have been in play. "Free market" (so-called) political propaganda, not to mention massive amounts of commercial advertising, have encouraged Americans to put primacy on their supposed consumer sovereignty (Schwarzkopf 2011), rather than on community needs and collective consumption requiring more taxation (Galbraith 1958). However, a part of the 1960s' counterculture ethos also stressed the individual's right to do what he or she pleased (e.g., smoking pot and having sex), as long as the behavior did not harm someone else. Together, these two strands of thought arguably have produced a kind of hyper-individualism in American culture.

The rise of consumer individualism may have slowed and possibly reversed in the new millennium. Young people have been living longer at home with their parents and have shown less interest in owning their own automobiles (*The Economist* 2012). New services, such as Zipcar where people rent cars by the hour or day, may further encourage this countertrend. Indeed, consumers' entire relationship with possessions may be changing. In their research on elite professionals who travel internationally and relocate from country to country, authors Fleura Bardhi, Giana Eckhardt, and Eric Arnould (2012) found evidence of what they termed "liquid relationships." Their informants showed temporary attachments to things, stressed the use-value rather than identity marking through goods, and preferred light and portable objects. These "global nomads" have been relatively small in number, but their attitudes may be a harbinger of a more general trend among more and more Americans toward having liquid relationships with personal possessions. In addition, Russell Belk (2010) has contended that consumer researchers seriously neglected the study of alternative sharing phenomena, a bias potentially making individual centered consumption in the U.S. appear more prevalent than it really had been all along. Perhaps, but a number of commentators have characterized the rapt attention paid to smart phones and other electronic kit as still further evidence of thorough self-absorption.

Buy Partisan

From the time of the early republic, Americans have expressed feelings of national identity through their purchase of products featuring patriotic symbols and heroes, and images of their burgeoning country. They also bought political memorabilia, such as the Staffordshire plate commemorating President William Henry Harrison in Figure 4.4 and the National Recovery Act ephemera shown in Figure 7.3. The inclination toward such meanings may have diminished somewhat after World War II, but regained momentum with the 1976 Bicentennial celebration, the inauguration of Ronald Reagan in 1981, and the easy victory against Iraq in the 1991 Persian Gulf War. Ten years later the devastating events on 9/11 unleashed a massive outpouring of patriotic purchasing. Within hours of the attacks ending, millions of Americans started to fly flags from their homes, cars, and trucks. They then bought more: "Wal-Mart sold 116,000 flags on that Tuesday and 250,000 on Wednesday, compared with 6400 and 10,000 on the same days a year earlier" (Barnes 2001). When the going got tough, Americans went shopping to allay their pain and grieving. Later, they went to war in Iraq, which consumed an enormous amount of the nation's treasure, material and human.

In the latter part of the 1970s consumer goods started to take on new meanings that reflected the deep left vs. right cleavages in politics and culture that had opened in the 1960s over civil rights, the Vietnam War, youth counterculture, environmentalism, and pro-choice feminism. The passage of the Voting Rights Act of 1965 precipitated a white racial backlash in the country, especially among conservative Southerners who deserted the more progressive Democratic Party. Formerly known as "Yellow Dog Democrats," they voted for the overtly racist Alabama Governor George Wallace (1919–1998), who ran as the American Independent Party candidate for president in the 1968 election, and later turned Republican, thus moving the GOP to the right and anchoring it in the South. Nationwide, unrelenting propaganda emanating from conservative think tanks, such as the American Enterprise Institute and the Heritage Foundation, disseminated right wing ideology amplified further by incendiary talk radio, above all the bombast emanating from popular host Rush Limbaugh, and through the reporting and commentary on television's Fox News (Smith 2012). Meanwhile, by losing its conservative wing, the Democratic Party became more liberal (i.e., more progressive) on average even though its most successful national politicians, Presidents Bill Clinton and Barack Obama, have tended to be mildly left-leaning centrists. The ideological divisions between Democrats and Republicans widened between 1994 and 2014. According to the Pew Research Center (2014),

> 92% of Republicans are to the right of the median Democrat, and 94% of Democrats are to the left of the median Republican. Partisan animosity has increased substantially over the same period. In each party, the share with a highly negative view of the opposing party has more than doubled since 1994.

The divide in the political culture began to be transferred to products, above all into firearms. An ever-popular American consumer durable, guns started becoming highly politicized in 1977 at the annual convention of the National Rifle Association (NRA) in Cincinnati. Gun rights activists ousted the moderately conservative incumbent leadership, which had stressed the interests of hunters and target shooters, and installed new executives strongly opposed to gun control laws and willing to fight for pro-gun rights in the political arena. In 1980, for the first time ever, the NRA endorsed a presidential candidate, Ronald Reagan, and subsequently the Republican Party has pretty much done the gun lobby's bidding. By the 1990s an anti-government, absolutist fringe favoring the abolition of all gun controls had emerged in the militia movement that found support among many sympathetic gun owners (Burbick 2006; Winkler 2011). At the 2000 NRA convention, then president Charlton Heston (1923–2008) hoisted a reproduction flintlock long rifle and declaimed with his actor's fine voice that presidential candidate Al Gore, who had been portrayed as an opponent of gun rights, could take it "from my cold, dead hands."

After the December 16, 2012 slaying of 20 small children and six adults at Sandy Hook Elementary School, record numbers of Americans went shopping for more firearms, flocking to gun stores and shows in late December and into January 2013 (Witkowski 2013). Some worried that President Obama would order new gun restrictions, a fear constantly ginned up by the NRA, but political action was unlikely and, indeed, little occurred at the federal level. Buying assault rifles, whose sales had been banned from 1994 to 2004 by federal law, became a favored way to express opposition to Obama. The gun industry has referred to this as "political sales" (Spitzer 2015, A17). CCT research (see Canniford 2011) provides an alternative explanation: The gun tribe assembled to reenact rituals of consumption and solidarity in the face of bad publicity from firearms violence. Often hosting private, unregulated sales of firearms and serving as places for vending extreme right wing and misogynist bumper stickers and other assorted ephemera, American gun shows have displayed a troubling culture all their own (Burbick 2006; Wintemute 2007, 2009).

Interestingly, some gun advocates have framed their politics as a consumer rights issue and many have equated unfettered gun purchasing and the public bearing of arms with freedom from government overreach. Federal laws have been passed that, in effect, protect gun manufacturers and distributors from lawsuits and restrict research on gun violence. In red (i.e., Republican leaning) states, accommodating legislatures and governors enacted laws favoring concealed and open carry and have expanded the sites, including churches, college campuses, some public buildings, and even bars and restaurants (see Figure 9.2),

Figure 9.2 Open Carry Gun Consumption, September 24, 2011. Man with 9 mm handgun in a Burger King restaurant, Eagle, Colorado.

Source: Wikimedia Commons.

where such consumption can be practiced (Valentine 2016). America's gun culture has aggressively recruited consumers through text and images imprinted on T-shirts, hoodies, posters, mouse pads, and coffee mugs (Witkowski 2013). Visual theorists refer to this hailing practice as interpellation (Sturken and Cartwright 2002) or appellation (Rose 2012). Whatever one thinks of the social sanity of this dogged pursuit of consumer gun rights, the political success of the movement has provided remarkable support for the polarizing assertion of American exceptionalism.

Political meanings have also been assigned to different types of motor vehicles. At the start of the new millennium, sport utility vehicles, and especially General Motors' Hummer brand, became political lightning rods (Luedicke, Thompson, and Giesler 2010; Neil 2008; Witkowski 2010a). Forces from the left disapproved of the sheer excess – their size made them visually prominent, noisy, and an intimidating nuisance to other drivers – and deplored their poor fuel economy and adverse environmental consequences. Forces on the right scoffed at the claims of the critics and, in turn, hurled insults at hybrids and subsidized electric cars as being ploys of the Obama Administration. The Hummer owners interviewed in Luedicke, Thompson, and Giesler (2010) portrayed their critics as un-American, unpatriotic, freedom-hating hypocrites who themselves contributed to global warming by living in large homes and jetting around the world. These informants saw their kind as rugged individualists, high achievers, and, when they owned businesses, as job creators. Some tried to help their communities in times of peril, when their staunch vehicles might come in handy, through a brand community named HOPE (Hummer Owners Prepared for Emergencies). Unfortunately for the Hummeristas, General Motors discontinued the brand in 2010 after suffering weak sales caused by the Great Recession and high fuel prices. However, plenty more supersized vehicle models remained on the market and sold well.

Right wing pundits appeared to back off a bit from deriding environmentally friendly vehicles after the introduction of more new electric models and *Motor Trend* magazine naming the Chevrolet Volt its "Car of the Year" in 2011. Although some conservatives bought liberal vehicles to obtain California clean air decals for access to carpool lanes, and some on the left purchased gas-guzzlers for various personal reasons, auto partisan meanings remained firmly affixed overall. Democrats were more prone to drive small, fuel-efficient vehicles, whereas Republicans favored SUVs and pick-up trucks (Strategic Vision 2012). Early in the twenty-first century, some folks highly annoyed by liberals, President Obama, and the Environmental Protection Agency formed a small consumption subculture that came right out of the "Only in America" folder. Mostly youngish, white male "coal rollers" retrofitted their diesel trucks so that they could spew out clouds of black smoke at the flick of a switch in case a fuel-efficient Toyota Prius or an even greener bicycle rider happened to appear nearby. Some even stuck "Prius Repellent" stickers on their bumpers (Tabuchi 2016). As David Weigel (2014) observed,

> The motivation for political coal rolling is roughly the same one that gets people buying guns and ammo after mass shootings. The expectation, every time, is that liberals will capitalize on the shootings to ban guns, so it's time to stock up.

Sustainable consumption practices seemed to invite anti-environmental contrariness. After the World Wildlife Fund launched the "Earth Hour" – an annual turning off of electricity for 60 minutes intended to call awareness to sustainability and build the environmental movement – in 2007, the Competitive Enterprise Institute, a libertarian outfit in Washington D.C., promoted a Human Achievement Hour that encouraged energy consumption to celebrate progress and simultaneously expose the pointlessness of Earth Hour (CEI 2016; Earth Hour 2016).

Technology further accelerated the attribution of political meaning in 2014 when a company called Spend Consciously introduced an app fittingly named "Buy Partisan." Like a nutritional label for political values, this software enabled consumers to determine whether the source of any given product leaned Democrat or Republican. While shopping users could scan a barcode with their smart phone camera, or search by individual company name or specific product, and the program would report the ideological leanings of the company as measured by the political donations of boards of directors, chief executive offices, employees, and political action committees (*Economist* 2014; Nicks 2014).

One highly charged and long simmering political battle over the meaning of things came to a head in 2015. On June 17, a young white supremacist named Dylann Roof murdered nine black Methodists in a church in Charleston, South Carolina. Roof's website showed pictures of him holding the Confederate battle flag of the Army of Northern Virginia, the familiar St. Andrew's cross filled with the stars of the 11 secessionist states. To many Southerners, this flag has represented regional pride and respect for the valor of their ancestors, but to critics it has been an offensive emblem of white racism and the evil institution of slavery. An onslaught of sharp condemnation of Confederate flag displays in public places prompted South Carolina to remove the flag from its State House grounds. Big retailers including Walmart, Sears, Kmart, and Amazon quickly pulled Confederate themed merchandise from their shelves and online stores, and the following year the Southern Baptist Convention repudiated the flag and called on member churches to discontinue its display (Gorman 2016; Phipps 2015).

The meaning of the Confederate flag had evolved considerably over time. For many years after Lee's surrender at Appomattox, the flag was respectfully unfurled at Confederate memorials to commemorate the Lost Cause, but was otherwise kept out of politics and popular culture. Some soldiers and sailors in World War II and the Korean War displayed the flag, but a major movement of meaning occurred in 1948 when Southern Democrats opposed to President Truman's Civil Rights legislation appropriated it for their segregationist cause. These "Dixiecrats" firmly established a link between the flag and white supremacy (Springer 1993) or, in the words of sports management professor Joshua

Newman (2007, 267), "a marker of White space and separatist ideology." About the same time as the Dixiecrat rebellion, rebel flags appeared on Southern college campuses and for decades became a fixture at their football games and, in general, were deeply entangled with Southern sport culture such as NASCAR racing (Newman 2007). In the 1950s and 1960s, as the Civil Rights movement gathered moral force and gained national attention, the brandishing of confederate flags by whites became more pronounced, ominously so at Ku Klux Klan rallies. Black Americans objected strongly to the rebel flag craze, but most of the country was not paying close attention (Coski 1996). In a 2015 CNN poll conducted after the Charleston shooting, 57 percent of the national sample believed the flag was a symbol of regional pride, just two points below the percentage in a similar poll taken in 2000. Less educated whites were more likely to assign the Southern pride meaning than more educated respondents. In the South, 75 percent of white respondents described the flag as representing Southern pride, whereas 72 percent of African Americans called it a symbol of racism (Agiesta 2015).

The Confederate flag did not just acquire charged political associations. It gained additional layers of meaning through commercialization and cultural references. Printed on trucker caps, T-shirts, belt buckles, bikini tops and bottoms, beach towels, blankets, and many more fashion goods, the flag and its image were widely sold (Figure 9.3). Several Southern states made it an option for

Figure 9.3 Selling Confederate Flags and Heritage, October 23, 2015. Photo of roadside stand in Princeton, West Virginia by Carol M. Highsmith.

Source: Library of Congress, Prints & Photographs Division, Washington, D.C.

customizing automobile license plates. Fans of the top-rated television series, *The Dukes of Hazzard* (1979–1985), will remember the Confederate flag painted on the roof of the orange 1969 Dodge Charger dubbed "General Lee." Affable, "good ol' boy" cousins Bo and Luke Duke roared around fictional Hazzard County, Georgia in this vehicle. They constantly upset the schemes of the rich, powerful, and deliciously corrupt county commissioner, Jefferson Davis "Boss" Hogg, and his bumbling and crooked brother-in-law, Sheriff Roscoe P. Coltrane. For the show's viewing audience, as well as many consumers of flag-themed merchandise, the Confederate icon likely symbolized a more generalized impulse to rebel against authority. I watched the show myself and, perhaps naively, never gave the flag much thought. However, for some people, especially black Americans, the meaning of white supremacy was not far below the surface. Although the surviving stars later denied the rooftop flag having any racist connotations, in 2015 the Viacom channel, TV Land, pulled reruns of *The Dukes of Hazzard* from its schedule, while Warner Bros. Consumer Products stopped selling *Dukes* merchandise showing the flag, above all, die cast models of the General Lee (Kaplan 2015). As of this writing (March 2017), General Lee cars and other collectibles with the flag could be found for sale on eBay. Numerous online stores still sell Confederate flag bikinis and men's swimsuits. For me, personally, the semiotic valence of the Confederate flag has swung from neutral indifference to decidedly negative.

Gender and Compensatory Consumption

For 250 years following first settlement, American men generally had the upper hand in purchasing influence. They controlled household finances, made credit arrangements with local stores and overseas merchants, and did much of the family shopping. Women utilized their own female trading networks, laboriously engaged in production/consumption activities, and, in some households, probably wielded more power due to force of personality, strategic male acquiescence, and other factors. But overall, the preponderance of decision-making favored men. In the middle of the nineteenth century, women acquired greater consumer agency in the domestic sphere (Blaszczyk 2009; Slater 1997; Strasser 1982; Witkowski 2004), and this trend continued through the Gilded Age and into the twentieth century when, by the 1920s and certainly by the 1950s, the balance of power in household decision-making, in the aggregate, was shared by men and women (Sharp and Mott 1956; Wolgast 1958). These patterns remained relatively stable for more than a half a century, perhaps with the consumption balance of power gradually tilting more toward women. A national telephone poll conducted in July 2008 asked 1260 respondents who were married or living as a couple about four decision areas: choosing shared weekend activities, buying major things for the home, deciding what to watch on television, and managing household finances. In 43 percent of all couples the woman made decisions in more areas than the man. Men made more decisions in 26 percent of the couples and 31 percent of couples split decision-making equally (Pew Research Center 2008).

American men experienced a difficult period after 1980. Because of technological advances (e.g., robotics) and globalization (e.g., offshoring of production), many well-paying manufacturing jobs disappeared. Male incomes stagnated, especially for less educated men who faced competition from immigrants. In 1980, the median income for full-time male workers was $52,466 in 2014 dollars, but only $51,456 in 2014. Male mean incomes improved, growing from $58,658 to $71,184, but this metric indicates rising inequality where those at the top did very well compared to lower income males and thus pulled up the average. Although women still earned far less than men, the income gap was closing. The 1980 median income for full-time female workers was $31,718 in 2014 dollars and $40,797 in 2014. Their comparable mean income figures, $34,837 and $51,463, also suggested mounting inequality (all income data from U.S. Bureau of the Census 2015). American women became increasingly better educated and by 2009/2010 accounted for 62 percent of all associate's degrees, 57.4 percent of all bachelor's, 62.6 percent of all master's, and 53.3 percent of all doctorates granted (Aud *et al.* 2012). An analysis by the Pew Research Center reported that by 2011, in 40.4 percent of American households with children under 18, the mother was either the sole or primary breadwinner (Wang, Parker, and Taylor 2013). The researchers also found that in 22.5 percent of these households, mothers earned more than the fathers.

Various pundits and gender theorists discussed how these developments threatened the masculinity of American men, especially in their role as traditional family breadwinners (Kimmel 1996, 2013). According to the masculine overcompensation thesis, men react to gender insecurities by demonstrating their masculinity in extreme ways. Two lines of theory support this thesis:

> First, masculinity is both more narrowly defined (making masculinity more easily threatened) and socially valued (making men more motivated to recover it) than femininity. Second, theories of identity, which argue that individuals tend to react to feedback that threatens valued identities with overcompensation, enacting attitudes and behaviors associated with the identity to a more extreme extent than they would have in the absence of threats.
>
> (Willer *et al.* 2013, 982)

Robb Willer and his colleagues marshaled support for the overcompensation thesis through three laboratory experiments and, to gain external validity, an additional large-scale (N=2210) field study. Men whose masculinity was threatened expressed greater support for war, showed more homophobia and pro dominance attitudes, and endorsed beliefs in male superiority. In one of the experiments, male subjects whose gender identity was questioned also reported greater interest in purchasing an SUV and being willing to pay more for it compared to men whose identity was not questioned. Female participants whose gender identity was threatened showed no difference in SUV desirability and willingness to pay or, for that matter, on any other dependent variable, from women whose gender identity was not threatened.

This SUV finding suggests that in compensation for their emasculation, American men may have been turning to their possessions and consumption activities for self-definition. This was not a new phenomenon. Rotundo (1993) and Kimmel (1996) have speculated that this was how men at the turn of the twentieth century coped with female inroads into formerly all-male offices, and Moskin (1958) gave examples from the 1950s of reactive male consumption patterns. In the early twenty-first century, Holt and Thompson (2004) dubbed this proposition the "compensatory consumption thesis" and explained it as follows:

> men have invested more and more of their identity work into consumption, where they have more degrees of freedom to shroud themselves in the symbolic cloaks of autonomy. Men use the plasticity of consumer identity construction to forge atavistic masculine identities based upon an imagined life of self-reliant, premodern men who lived outside the confines of cities, families, and work bureaucracies.
>
> (Holt and Thompson 2004, 426)

During the 2008 presidential primary campaign, candidate Barack Obama broadly articulated a variant of this thesis when he casually remarked that people in small towns in Pennsylvania and across the Midwest, where jobs had been vanishing for 25 years, "get bitter, and they cling to guns, religion" (potus08blog 2008). He received considerable flak for his remark being elitist and had to apologize for using the wrong language. Still, he was neither the first nor the last to talk of gun ownership as a substitute for lost social and economic standing.

Holt and Thompson (2004) maintained that compensatory consumption was implicit in two ethnographic studies carried out in the 1990s on largely male subcultures. In the first, John Schouten and James McAlexander (1995) immersed themselves for three years (1990 to 1993) among Harley-Davidson riders to understand the adoption of a biker persona, or temporary alter ego, and the deviant meanings that identity entailed. Riding motorcycles, they learned, symbolized freedom from containment. The Harley subculture encouraged expressions of open machismo – T-shirts proclaimed "Real Men Wear Black" – and a degree of sexual license. Schouten and McAlexander (1995, 55) speculated

> Some informants give the impression that they are engaged in something akin to performance art for the mere fun of it. There is indeed a Halloween-ish aspect of playing biker that is amusing and enjoyable. Others, however, take the machismo more seriously, as if they have something to prove by it. In either case, indulgence in an overtly masculine subculture may function (for men at least) to compensate for some self-doubt in an area of supposed male competency.

The company has leveraged the outlaw stereotypes that film, television, and other media had attributed to bikers, while selling factory-made "choppers" to affluent sorts and sponsoring the Harley Owners Group (HOG) and its rallies.

In another alleged ethnography of compensatory consumption, Russell W. Belk and Janeen Costa (1998, 221) studied how men (and some women and children) reenacted the lives of nineteenth-century mountain communities. Between 1990 and 1994, the authors attended 13 rendezvous events in Colorado, Utah, Montana, and Wyoming and interviewed about 50 participants. They also visited mountain supply stores and weddings and conducted eight in-depth interviews in the homes of mountain men and their families. These late twentieth century mountain men adopted period-appropriate grooming, clothing, and manners and, when at a rendezvous, lived in tepees or tents with as few modern conveniences as possible. Obtaining the right stuff for living simply was costly and often assembled over a period of years. Whether this subculture represented compensatory consumption was debatable. Although Belk and Costa (1998) referred in their article to "rugged, raucous, masculine individualism" (221) and "masculine virility" (228), the authors did not posit compensatory consumption as an underlying factor. They interpreted this subculture through theories of consumption fantasy that drew from history as well as the myth making of novels, films, and television. Fantasies, however, can be a response to threatened masculinity and western themed symbols and props have served this purpose since the late 1800s (Kimmel 1996).

Just as it is unscientific to attribute any one weather event to global warming, characterizing the particular behavior of any one man (or woman) as compensatory consumption is dubious. If a male gun owner, coal roller, Harley rider, or mountain man re-enactor has above average income and education and remains the primary family breadwinner, would he have reason to feel his masculinity was threatened? Holt and Thompson (2004) themselves thought the thesis failed to capture the full range of male identity work. However, regardless of his personal circumstances, even very favorable ones in terms of career, home life, and socioeconomic status, a man may still perceive a self-identity threat. Willer *et al.* (2013, 1000) found just such perceptions in responses to their survey's central independent variable, in which male [female] respondents were asked if they agreed with the statement "Recent changes in our society often disadvantage men [women]." From a macro, historical perspective, many small, individual experiences and petty resentments may accumulate over time to produce a larger discourse disseminated person-to-person and amplified by various media. Certain types of consumption behavior, say, owning a gun or driving an SUV, can become legitimated as socially acceptable responses to perceived threats to masculinity. Male compensatory consumption should perhaps be understood on a societal level, rather than as an individual characteristic.

The previous chapter gave a brief account of the popularity of male do-it-yourself (DIY) activities in the 1950s. CCT researchers label this behavior "productive consumption" and throughout the late twentieth century and into the twenty-first much of it transpired within manly spaces – basements, garages, and workshops – inside or adjacent to the home. In the 1990s, the term "mancaves" entered public conversation after being mentioned in John Gray's (1992) popular self-help relationship guide, *Men Are from Mars, Women Are from Venus.*

Furnished in straight male décor, mancaves (aka manspaces) were areas for productive consumption, such as fixing and building things, as well as venues for the manly arts of recreation, such as playing video games and watching sports programming on television, often with other men. Popular culture references abounded, above all the television show *Home Improvement* (1991–1999) where star Tim Allen played a stereotypical American male who hosted a show-within-a-show called *Tool Time*. Consumer culture writer James Twitchell and photographer Kenneth Charles Ross (2006) documented mancaves and related out-of-home retreats for men in their photo essay, *Where Men Hide*. In 2007 the DIY Network started programming a home renovation reality series called *Man Caves* where each episode features a custom remodeling job for a guy and his hobbies. In the CCT literature, Ristio Moisio and Mariam Beruchashvili (2016) published an article, "Mancaves and Masculinity," based on interviews with 49 suburban American men in a medium-sized midwestern city. The authors explained these in-home masculine spaces as therapeutic enclaves rather than sites for compensatory consumption. Their respondents described how they used mancaves to find refuge from work and the family, but also as special places for bonding with sons and male friends. A photo of a mancave in Los Angeles appears in Figure 9.4.

Figure 9.4 Oakland Raiders Themed Mancave, November 9, 2014. Photo taken in Los Angeles.

Source: Courtesy of Risto Moisio and Mariam Beruchashvili.

Some American males have avoided forms of consumption they perceive as having feminine associations. By the 1990s sustainability researchers had established a link between gender and environmentally friendly attitudes, choices, and behaviors. Women cared more about the environment. They exhibited more overall concern than men, and especially when greater risk was involved (e.g., from a nuclear reactor accident), and when local environmental issues were at stake (Davidson and Freudenburg 1996). A nationwide online poll of 1005 adults conducted in December 2014 by an advocacy law firm (Tiller, LLC 2014) found that American women, compared to men, were more likely to show concern about increasing global warming (64 percent vs. 52 percent), to look for opportunities to go green (87 percent vs. 78 percent), and to feel guilty about not leading a more eco-friendly lifestyle (53 percent vs. 42 percent). Part of these differences could be explained by political motives in that Republican leaning men might deny global warming for ideological reasons. In 2015 and 2016, Aaron R. Brough and his colleagues (Brough *et al.* 2016) conducted a series of studies largely using American undergraduates as respondents. The authors found that both males and females associated greenness with femininity. Through an experimental manipulation of gender cues, they also established that threats to masculinity resulted in men being less likely to choose green products. This last finding was consistent with the compensatory consumption hypothesis.

Since 1980, as in past eras, the gendered threads of some brands and product consumption became entangled and contested. For example, a neat follow-up to the Harley-Davidson study by Schouten and McAlexander (1995) – this time with Diane Martin as lead author (see Martin, Schouten, and McAlexander 2006) – re-analyzed the original ethnographic data from the perspective of feminist theories and then augmented the research with further participant observation and interviews with female bikers. Wondering how women coped with the hyper-masculinity of the biker world, the authors discovered that female riders often felt empowered mastering riding skills and resisting male domination. They took control of their own bodies, made their own assessments of risk, and enjoyed subverting conventional notions of femininity. And many just had fun riding their motorcycles.

A final example of gender fluidity developed in the consumption of computer and information technologies. After 1980, about when personal computers and other IT products started to come to market in a big way, American men usually were the most informed and enthusiastic consumers. In the early twenty-first century, however, social media gained a big following among younger American women. A national telephone poll conducted between March 17 and April 12, 2015 by the Pew Research Center found that among Internet users, 77 percent of women versus 66 percent of men used Facebook; 44 percent of women versus 16 percent of men used Pinterest; and 31 percent of women versus 24 percent of men used Instagram. Male Internet users were slightly more likely than women to use LinkedIn (26 versus 25 percent) and Twitter (25 versus 21 percent) (Duggan 2015). Perhaps the long-standing norms of female sociability, evident from the spinning and weaving get-togethers in the colonial era to the Tupperware home parties of the 1950s, remained in force in the new millennium, though now expressed virtually.

Simplicity, Boycotts, and Cannabis (Part II)

Familiar threads of resistance persisted during this final period. The voluntary simplicity movement, which first emerged during the 1970s (Leonard-Barton 1981), rebranded earlier ideas of living plain and avoiding all-consuming materialism (Shi 1985). In the 1980s and 1990s numerous newspaper and magazine articles, book-length anti-consumption guides, and a modest selection of scholarly analyses instructed readers about the meaning and practice of varying degrees of voluntary simplicity (Dominguez and Robin 1992; Elgin 1993; Etzioni 1998; Schor 1998; St. James 1996). Along the lines of earlier anti-consumption debates, this movement was faulted for focusing on individual consumers and their personal lifestyle choices, rather than advocating collective action to reform larger political processes (Maniates 2002). In effect, the discourse resisting consumption echoed neoliberal ideology, which celebrated individual responsibility.

In the 1990s anti-consumption activists held national conferences (Maniates 2002) and formed networks of local consciousness-raising groups, called "simplicity circles" (Andrews 1997; Thompson 1998). Estimates of the number of converts varied, but the U.S. total was probably in the millions. Simplifiers tended to be in the middle quintile in terms of household income, and were more educated than the average American (Maniates 2002). Unlike the working poor, who have always been saddled with involuntary simplicity by necessity, simplifiers had enough control over their economic lives to rearrange their work schedules or, if need be, to change jobs. For many of its proponents, voluntary simplicity had as much to do with the time pressures and pace of life dictated by a highly competitive and marketized economy as it had with overconsumption of material things.

Communitarian sociologist and public intellectual Amitai Etzioni (1998) distinguished between "downshifters," who refrained from buying some consumer goods, such as a new car every few years, but otherwise maintained a consumerist lifestyle; "strong simplifiers," who gave up significant income and, hence, some goods and services for discretionary time and leisure; and "the simple living movement," people who adjusted entire life patterns motivated by a coherently articulated philosophy. Deirdre Shaw and Terry Newholm (2002) referred to this last group as "ethical consumers" because their buyer behaviors and lifestyles are shaped by moral concerns about the environment, fair trade practices, and animal rights. However, the term ethical consumer has not been used frequently in the U.S., perhaps indicating weaker social consensus over its meaning. John Lastovicka and his colleagues (1999, 96) found the frugal empirically "less susceptible to interpersonal influence, less materialistic, less compulsive in buying, and more price and value conscious." Interestingly, their frugality scale was not related statistically to their measure of "ecocentricity" or environmental concern.

In 1989 Kalle Lasn and Bill Schmalz founded the Adbusters Media Foundation and then, two years later, debuted *Adbusters* magazine, whose subtitle was "The Journal of the Mental Environment," to espouse a humorously dissident ideology of anti-consumption and resistance. Based in Vancouver, but with about two-thirds of its readers in the United States, this quarterly magazine, along with companion books, videos, and a website, advocated grassroots activities to resist the hegemony of the dominant consumerist system (Bordwell 2002; Lasn 1999; Rumbo 2002). The tactic known as "culture jamming" created "counter-messages that hacked into a corporation's own method of communication to send a message starkly at odds with the one that was intended" (Klein 1999, 281). Parodies of Joe Camel (a sickly "Joe Chemo") and Absolut Vodka (a limp bottle of "Absolut Impotence") provided a critical "perspective by incongruity" (Bordwell 2002, 247). *Adbusters* tried to place (usually without success, save for a few spots on CNN) "uncommercials" or "subvertisements" with anti-consumption messages on network television. It also has promoted an annual "TV Turnoff Week," "World Car-Free Day," and a "Buy Nothing Day" on the Friday after Thanksgiving, the busiest shopping day of the year in the United States. *Adbusters* encouraged company and industry boycotts and, following the precedent set by *Ballyhoo* magazine in the 1930s, discussed guerilla tactics like defacing outdoor advertising, now known as "billboard liberation." *Adbuster* memes, such as the corporate American flag in Figure 9.5, continued to be deployed into the twenty-first century.

In a similarly subversive vein, the 2007 film *What Would Jesus Buy?* addressed tensions between Christmas as a religious holiday and Christmas as a

Figure 9.5 Protester Holding *Adbusters* Corporate American Flag at the Second Inauguration of President George W. Bush, January 20, 2005. Photo by Jonathan MacIntosh.

Source: Wikimedia Commons.

commercial proposition. This entertaining documentary recounted the 2005 cross-country trek of the "Reverend Billy" (a character created by actor Bill Talen) and "The Church of Stop Shopping" gospel choir as these musicians and performance artists stage agitprop events at the Mall of America, Walmart headquarters, Disneyland, and other retail venues (see Figure 9.6). This troupe has exploited long-standing American religious social types – the loquacious, big-haired preacher and rocking, gospel singers – to ridicule excessive consumption,

Figure 9.6 Reverend Billy and the Church of Stop Shopping, March 10, 2007. Photo by Mason Wendell. Protesting Starbucks in Austin, Texas.

Source: Wikimedia Commons.

a harbinger of the "shopocalypse." Like *Adbusters*, Reverend Billy has deployed the media and formats of contemporary consumer culture in an attempt to undermine it.

In the Fall of 2002, a small group of concerned Christians calling itself "The Evangelical Environmental Network" (EEN) launched a media campaign built around the headline "What Would Jesus Drive?" An advertisement published on their website and in *Christianity Today* juxtaposed an image of Jesus at prayer with a photo of freeway congestion (Figure 9.7). The copy attacked car pollution

Figure 9.7 "What Would Jesus Drive?" 2002.

Source: Witkowski 2010a.

for the illness and death it causes – the elderly, poor, sick, and young being the most afflicted – and for its contribution to global warming. The appeal concluded as follows:

> Transportation is now a moral choice and an issue for Christian reflection. It's about more than engineering – it's about ethics. About obedience. About loving our neighbor. So what would Jesus drive? We call upon America's automobile industry to manufacture more fuel-efficient vehicles. And we call upon Christians to drive them. Because it's about more than vehicles – it's about values.
>
> (Cited in Witkowski 2010a)

This rhetoric did not explicitly accuse owners of gas-guzzlers of immorality, for not loving their neighbors as themselves, but the implication was not far below the surface. In the tradition of stewardship theology, the EEN argument emphasized unity with nature, in contrast with a dominionism stance, which accords humans mastery over nature (Landrum, Tomaka, and McCarthy 2016). In the politicized American context, this debate has differentiated the religious left (stewardship) from the religious right (dominionism). At this writing, the original campaign website appears dormant, but the ministry continues at www.creationcare.org and on Facebook. Current EEN President and CEO, Reverend Mitch Hescox co-authored with Paul Douglas in 2016 a book they called *Caring for Creation: An Evangelical's Guide to Climate Change and a Healthy Environment.*

Less strident frugality appeals appeared in more mainstream media. The PBS documentary, "Affluenza," and its sequel "Escape from Affluenza," diagnosed an "epidemic of over-consumption" and provided viewers with teaching and program guides for changing consumer behavior (Affluenza 1998). Bill Maher (2002), a habitually caustic humorist and television host, wrote *When you Ride ALONE you Ride with Bin Laden,* a book that reworked the visual style of World War II posters in order to question American consumption habits in the aftermath of 9/11. Yet, these frugality discourses have also been coopted and commoditized. Books on voluntary simplicity and sustainability have been an apparently successful cottage industry. Two glossy, advertising-intensive magazines launched in 2000, *Simplicity* and *Real Simple*, fostered a postmodern kind of branded simplicity where resistance becomes actualized through consumerism (Maniates 2002). In 2002, *Advertising Age* voted *Real Simple* its "Magazine of the Year." Frugality metamorphosed into hyper real farce in late 2003 when the Fox TV reality show, "The Simple Life," garnered high ratings by staging the travails of heiress Paris Hilton and her sidekick Nicole Richie, two shallow, pampered consumers, who had been assigned to live and work with an Altus, Arkansas farm family. A confrontation between state-of-the-art indulgence and more traditional virtues became a platform for mass entertainment sponsored by consumer products companies.

Chapter 2 discussed the annual Burning Man festival of art and anti-consumption in the Nevada desert (Kozinets 2002). The Occupy Wall Street movement of 2011–2012, where mostly young protesters camped for weeks in dozens of urban public spaces across the U.S., shared many of the same impulses as Burning Man attendees. Occupy activism resonated with millennials facing poor job prospects and firmly established the notion of the "1 percent" versus the "99 percent" within American political discourse. However, the reluctance of young activists to engage in party politics and vote their interests at the time greatly diluted the impact of the movement. In contrast, older, white, conservatives, who have been dubbed the "Tea Party," have voted early and often and have participated in a variety of partisan events. Even if some of them questioned consumption trends and cared about the natural world, they still empowered right-wing politicians who denied global warming, trashed the Environmental Protection Agency, and generally supported unbridled corporate capitalism.

As revealed in the earlier discussion of the antebellum nonintercourse movement, where Southerners called for boycotts of Northern manufacturers and retailers in order to make a point about preserving their slave system, not all consumption resistance has been left-leaning politically and environmentally friendly. For example, in 1977 the Reverend Donald Wildmon from Tupelo, Mississippi formed the National Federation for Decency – renamed the American Family Association (AFA) in 1988 – to combat excessive sex, violence, and coarseness on television. Jiggle shows and ostensibly immoral comedies, like *Charlie's Angels* and *Three's Company*, annoyed this Methodist minister. In 1980, he teamed up with Jerry Falwell (1933–2007), a Southern Baptist pastor, televangelist, and conservative political commentator, to form a new organization called the Coalition for Better Television (CBTV). Wildmon instructed CBTV volunteers to monitor prime-time shows and threatened boycotts of companies advertising on offensive programs. Major corporations capitulated to this pressure in 1981 and withdrew advertising from some shows. Wildmon's group next turned on the NBC network and its owner, RCA, but boycotts carried out in 1982 appear to have been ineffective (Friedman 1999). Wildmon and Falwell had a falling out and CBTV disbanded in 1982, but the AFA continued to threaten and carry out boycotts against a number of companies during the 1980s and up to the present. One of the better-known campaigns targeted the Walt Disney Company in 1996 for its "gay friendly" policies toward employees and theme park visitors and for broadcasting, on the Disney-owned ABC network, the comedy series *Ellen* (1994–1998) whose eponymous lead character, multi-talented Ellen DeGeneris, came out as a lesbian. In April 2016, the AFA, now led by Donald's son Tim Wildmon, promoted a boycott against Target for its policy of allowing transgender team members (i.e., workers) and guests (i.e., customers) to use restrooms and fitting rooms that correspond with their gender identity (Wildmon 2016). Perhaps as a backlash against the 2015 Supreme Court decision legalizing gay marriage, not to mention the extensive media coverage of transgender people and issues, bathroom use became a hot issue in 2016. Legislation in North Carolina and elsewhere restricting bathroom access to the sex recorded on a person's birth certificate triggered retaliatory boycotts against these states from companies, private groups, some government bodies, and the LGBT community.

Picking up the fibers of cannabis, after 1980 the repression of its consumption – not to mention its continued public demonization largely for reasons of cultural belligerence, ideological rigidity, and political expediency – was met by spirited resistance from pot consumers and product innovation from their suppliers. Government interdiction of cannabis smuggled from Mexico and Colombia led domestic growers in northern California and the Pacific Northwest to ramp up production. Law enforcement activities also drove improvements in marijuana cultivation. With the help of inventive growers in the Netherlands, new strains of *cannabis sativa* were developed and existing types of *cannabis indica*, which grew at higher latitudes, became more potent through experiments in breeding. Techniques of indoor cultivation also improved and suppliers started making available better lamps, fertilizers, and other home gardening equipage for enthusiasts. Most important of all, cannabis activists started making a powerful case for supplying medical marijuana to AIDS patients. Despite the continued refusal of most law enforcers, government officials, and politicians to acknowledge that cannabis had medical benefits, direct observation showed that smoking pot could mitigate the wasting syndrome that accompanied AIDS, as well as the severe nausea caused by chemotherapy and protease-inhibitor drugs. Emotions ran high in the gay community and highly motivated cannabis buyers' clubs were formed in San Francisco to supply the growing numbers of AIDS patients (Lee 2012).

On November 5, 1996 California voters approved Proposition 215, the first successful medical cannabis initiative in the United States. This eventually resulted in a new, quasi-legal marketing system where most anyone with a state driver's license could obtain a medical doctor's recommendation and then purchase the product from a medical marijuana collective's storefront dispensary, or simply have it delivered. This did not come easily. State and local officials dragged their feet and erected procedural barriers and it took a good decade before the people's will was being put into effect (Lee 2012). Eventually other states followed suit and after the 2016 presidential election a total of 28 states and the District of Columbia (D.C.) had passed similar laws, but only 17 and D.C. allowed dispensaries selling combustibles (NCSL 2016). With a few exceptions (e.g., Arizona, Alaska, Montana), medical marijuana states lean blue (vote for the Democratic Party). As of January 1, 2017, 16 states and the District of Columbia had passed laws decriminalizing marijuana meaning, in effect, that first-time possession of small amounts for personal consumption is treated like a minor traffic violation (NORML 2017a). After the 2016 election, eight states also had legalized cannabis for recreational purposes.

The spread of cannabis legalization may have created an aura of inevitability that further swayed public opinion in its direction. Figure 9.8 charts findings from public opinion surveys conducted by the Pew Research Center starting in 1969. Public support for marijuana legalization increased dramatically after 1990 and reached 57 percent in 2016 (Geiger 2016). Polls by Gallup have yielded similar results over this period with 60 percent of the 2016 respondents agreeing that marijuana should be legalized, the highest percentage in 47 years.

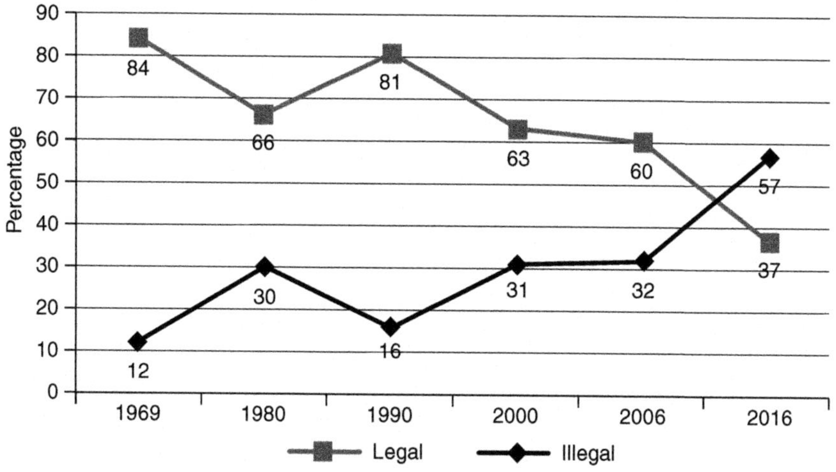

Figure 9.8 Percentage of Americans Saying Marijuana Should Be Made Legal, 1969–2016.
Source: Adapted from Geiger 2016.

Support was stronger among younger cohorts and among political independents and Democrats (Swift 2016). Still other polls corroborate these results (see list at NORML 2017b).

This evolving public opinion can be explained by social cognition theory where people acquire knowledge by observing the actions of others and whether they are successful or a failure (Bandura 1986). Parallels can be drawn between attitudes toward cannabis and with rapidly changing feelings about homosexuals and gay marriage. When more and more people came to know and interact with gay persons, stigmatization began to ease. Then more homosexuals came out of the closet, further bolstering their cause. Similarly, as people learned to live with medical marijuana dispensaries and completely legal (at the state level) pot shops, and as more smokers admitted their indulgence, the marketing and consumption of cannabis became normalized. The connection with gay rights is not glib. The gay community was quite open to cannabis early on and became fiercely supportive, especially in San Francisco, when it became a palliative for surviving HIV/AIDS. This politically active subculture had much in common with the cannabis crowd:

> Advocates for gay rights and marijuana legalization believed in the same basic principle – that people should not be punished for personal lifestyle matters that are nobody's business but their own. The two issues were analogous in many ways. Like homosexuals who remained in the closet, pot smokers often hid the fact that they used marijuana for fear of being ostracized by their neighbors, coworkers, or disapproving family members.
>
> (Lee 2012, 225)

Media coverage assisted this process of social learning. Reporting on cannabis spiked after voters in Colorado and Washington states legalized recreational growing, sale, and consumption in 2012. The mainstream *Denver Post* started hosting a column called "The Cannabist" with two full-time staffers and 12 freelance contributors (Kelly 2014). In the summer of 2014 the august *New York Times* ran a series of six commentaries on cannabis and, at their conclusion, the editorial board at long last endorsed its legalization for people over the age of 21 (*New York Times* 2014). Much like in the case of casino gambling discussed by Humphreys (2010), generally favorable media coverage legitimized cannabis marketing and consumption.

Although many cannabis supporters have come to believe that it is just a matter of time before legalization becomes the norm, upward trending support could be reversed. Powerful social actors have long had vested interests in the suppression and criminalization of cannabis consumption and have harbored deep-seated animosities toward the substance and its users. These actors have included American culture warriors, religious conservatives, law enforcement and criminal justice personnel, and the country's enormous prison industrial complex. The latter two entities rely on anti-cannabis laws for part of their funding, both directly from government budgets and, more controversially, through state and federal asset forfeiture laws where law officers can confiscate property assumed to be related to drug dealing. Manufacturers of prescription opioids, such as Purdue Pharma, the maker of the widely abused painkiller Oxycontin, have sponsored groups taking a hard line against marijuana but a relatively relaxed approach to prescription drug abuse (Fang 2014). The present exuberance of cannabis vendors and consumers may grate the sensibilities of these prohibitionist actors and thus may provoke a backlash. Early in the twentieth century, pundit H.L. Mencken famously wrote an epigram describing a venerable streak in the American character: "Puritanism: The Haunting Fear that Someone, Somewhere, May be Happy" (Mencken 1949, 624).

Summary

The American economy pulled out of a mild recessionary period during the early 1980s and then grew fairly steadily until 2008–2009 when the Great Recession hit hard. Subsequent GDP expansion has been continuous, but modest. Working-class people have struggled for decades to maintain their standard of living in the face of job losses. Since the late 1990s less educated whites have experienced rising midlife mortality rates due to alcohol abuse, drug overdoses, and suicide. This "sea of despair" may have been aggravated by an erosion of social support in the form of stable marriages and labor unions (*The Economist* 2017). Meanwhile, the young millennial cohort has endured diminished career aspirations, the repayment of student loans, and living with their parents. In most years since 1980 income inequality has risen, which may have added to the distress of less fortunate consumers. Ideological and real world trends toward individualism have affected consumption choices, but in the new millennium a culture of sharing may be on the rise.

As in the more distant past, the threads of meaning, gender, and resistance have been intertwined in our final period. Partisan meanings have permeated guns, motor vehicles, and other possessions. The Confederate battle flag has been deployed as a symbol of Southern heritage, but also has been reviled as an emblem of slavery and contemporary racism. Goods with right leaning associations have been purchased and used predominantly, though not exclusively, by men. These same goods also may have become symbolic vessels for male compensatory consumption for real and perceived threats to masculinity. *Adbusters* and the Reverend Billy have advocated subversive forms of resistance, whereas Burning Man and the Occupy movement adopted more communal opposition. All kinds of interests, including groups from the religious right, have launched boycotts against brands, stores, and the media. Finally, cannabis activists for many years have belied the unmotivated stoner stereotype by working diligently toward their goals of legal medical and recreational pot consumption.

10 Conclusion

This book provides a thumbnail sketch of the American consumption history. It does not claim to be a comprehensive history and, regrettably, does not do full justice to the richness and excitement of the topic. However, it does offer a theoretically informed account. The first two chapters ground the subsequent narrative in consumption historiography and in the intellectual history of consumer research and consumer culture theory. Chapters 3 through 9 then follow, from the seventeenth century to the present, three complex phenomena: the meaning of possessions, the gender of consumption, and the expression of consumer resistance. This concluding chapter first presents three historical timelines that recap the many milestones in meaning, gender, and resistance previously described. It then discusses how consumption threads can be analyzed through their cultural continuities and change. The chapter next suggests additional cultural threads worthy of fuller scrutiny and draws a few implications of this history for CCT research.

Timelines, Continuities, and Change

Timelines are excellent visual aids for quickly reviewing and learning about historical developments. Timelines come in many varieties, but after several unsatisfying experiments with different layouts, I concluded it best to create separate timelines for meaning, gender, and resistance as shown in Figures 10.1, 10.2, and 10.3. Note that the first 150 years of colonial history are compressed into one time interval. As argued in Chapter 3, American consumption did not really start ramping up materially until the middle of the eighteenth century. The term "milestone" refers to the approximate time when threads of ideas and actions take place. Though most dates have an associated consumption milestone, some do not. In particular, the early nineteenth century appears rather threadbare in terms of gender and resistance.

One way to analyze cultural threads historically is to distinguish between what about them has stayed reasonably the same over time and what has not. Take, for instance, the meanings attributed to possessions. Some of these threads have had long histories. Possessions in all eras have symbolized deeply personal and familial attachments. Since the middle of the eighteenth century, Americans

Milestones in Meaning

1600	
1750	Consumers pursue refinement through possessions and activities
1760	Imports of luxury goods leads to trade deficits and personal debt
1770	American made goods acquire patriotic associations
1780	
1790	Images and objects begin to convey national identity and pride
1800	Greater emphasis placed on cleanliness and personal care products
1810	
1820	Staffordshire pottery features images of America
1830	Imported swords include patriotic motifs and eagle pommels
1840	Lithographic prints disseminate American scenes and Victorian values
1850	Mormons goods carry sacred, material, personal, familial, and communal meanings
1860	
1870	Parlors, hall furnishings, and knickknacks signify middle-class values
1880	Trade cards convey meanings ranging from childhood innocence to overt racism
1890	National brands increasingly become vessels of meaning
1900	
1910	Colonial revival movement favors elite, nativist heritage
1920	Advertising stresses modernity, youth, and sex appeal
1930	Hobbies help economically distressed to build self-esteem
1940	
1950	Mass luxury, futurism, and youth subculture characterize 1950s
1960	Confederate flag symbolizes southern heritage for some, white racism to others
1970	
1980	Partisan meaning increasingly permeates guns, motor vehicles, and other goods
1990	
2000	After 9/11 attack, Americans display patriotism through consumption
2010	
2020	

Figure 10.1 Threads of Meaning Timeline, 1600s to Present.

have used their homes, halls, and public rooms, furnishings and décor, clothing and bearing, and other goods and services to demonstrate their personal refinement, to differentiate themselves in terms of social status and cultural preeminence, and to otherwise build personal and group identities through goods. By the early nineteenth century national pride was expressed in the purchasing of swords, ceramic tableware, and lithographic prints that incorporated patriotic symbols (the flag, the bald eagle, lady liberty, Columbia) and images of cities, the landscape, and folk heroes (Washington, Franklin, Jefferson). Forms of such patriotic consumption have continued to more recent times, such as during the 1976 Bicentennial and after September 11, 2001 when great numbers of Americans bought and displayed patriotic emblems. Twentieth-century goods, their branding, and rituals of consumption introduced notions of youth and modernity. These are just some of the broad historical continuities in the meaning of things.

Milestones in Gender

1600	Settlers import ideology of male supremacy coded into law
1750	Wives maintain separate, female networks of exchange
1760	Elite males buy household items from London on behalf of their families
1770	Women participate in nonimportation movement
1780	Husband-dominated marriages start to become less popular
1790	"Republican mother" ideal of virtue gains social approval
1800	Evidence of women shopping alone, with female companions, and with spouses
1810	
1820	
1830	
1840	
1850	Genre artists paint consumption as having a female inflection
1860	Victorian "cult of domesticity" emerges
1870	Sharpshooting embodies manliness
1880	Shopping and consumption increasingly gendered as a female activity
1890	Department stores entice women and invite kleptomania; bicycling craze peaks
1900	Males engage in bodybuilding, hunting, and spectator sports
1910	Women's fashions change greatly during and after Word War I
1920	Women targeted by greeting card, tobacco, and home appliance industries
1930	Great Depression undercuts male breadwinning role
1940	Women manage home front consumption
1950	Suburban males barbecue meats and engage in do-it-yourself activities
1960	Feminists question gendered production and consumption roles
1970	Virginia Slims and Charlie coopt feminism; Mr. Coffee genders drip brewing
1980	Men experience economic difficulties after 1980
1990	Men turn to possessions and consumption activities for self-definition
2000	"Mancave" meme gets traction in popular culture
2010	Women avidly consume social media
2020	

Figure 10.2 Threads of Gender Timeline, 1600s to Present.

Nevertheless, the specific meanings associated with possessions, as well as the transmission processes themselves, often have been in flux. The culturally constituted world changes – as Grant McCracken (1986, 72) implied when he carefully referred to cultural categories in "contemporary" and "present day" North America – and as new meanings have arisen, they have been transferred to goods and services. For example, the previous chapter described the expanding partisan divide endemic to late twentieth and early twenty-first century American culture and society. Less educated white males have become the chief bearers of conservative, anti-government ideology and this tribal political identity arguably has become embedded in the purchase and brandishing of firearms. Several institutions, namely the advertising and fashion systems (McCracken 1986), journalists framing meanings (Humphreys 2010), and interest groups representing gun owners, have transmitted meaning into firearms. Guns in America may always have had associations with conservative virility in the form of

Milestones in Resistance

1600	New Englanders enact and break sumptuary laws during 1600s
1750	Revivalist preachers and theologians stress simple living
1760	Nonimportation movement begins in 1765
1770	Boston Tea Party in 1773 and Revolutionary War 1775–1781
1780	
1790	
1800	
1810	
1820	Reverend Lyman Beecher preaches “Christian simplicity”
1830	Anti-slavery “free produce” stores founded
1840	Supporters of slavery advocate “nonintercourse” with abolitionists
1850	Emerson and Thoreau endorse “transcendental simplicity”
1860	
1870	Women’s Christian Temperance Union founded in 1874
1880	The word “boycott” coined; thousands of small boycotts break out
1890	Veblen and other critics lambast the leisure class
1900	Meat boycotts occur in northern cities; streetcar boycotts take place in southern cities
1910	Wealthier African Americans adopt marketplace activism
1920	Mass resistance to Prohibition; thrift movement in full swing
1930	*Ballyhoo* subversion; boycotts of businesses not hiring African Americans; silk boycott
1940	U.S. government promotes frugal consumption during World War II
1950	Critiques of consumerism; civil rights boycotts and sit-ins; Beat Generation opposition
1960	Rise of counterculture; California grape boycott; mass resistance to cannabis laws
1970	First Earth Day fuels environmental movement; Florida orange boycott over gay rights
1980	Voluntary simplicity movement receives media attention
1990	Religious right boycotts stores and television programs friendly to gays
2000	*Adbusters*, Reverend Billy, and other subversives question consumption
2010	Occupy Wall Street movement 2011–2012; first states legalize marijuana in 2012
2020	

Figure 10.3 Threads of Resistance Timeline, 1600s to Present.

hunters, sharpshooters, and soldiers, but this connection greatly intensified as the National Rifle Association (NRA) became a far more politically strident and right leaning after 1976 (Witkowski 2013).

Moreover, the countless goods and services that acquire meaning will themselves be transformed in many ways over time. Clothing fashions, materials, and means of production and distribution have changed throughout American history. Having been intentionally bred, genetically modified, seriously altered through processing, and constantly packaged in new ways for a good century and a half, the foods we eat in the twenty-first century bear scant resemblance to those in the eighteenth. In the realm of American firearms, the single-shot, flintlock ignition muskets and pistols in use during the framing of the Second Amendment to the U.S. Constitution evolved into far deadlier assault rifles and semi-automatic pistols two centuries later. Plus, new products and brands, such as the innovative Glock semi-automatic pistol (Barrett 2013), were invented, marketed, and eventually filled with meaning.

Finally, the rituals of consumption that transmit meaning from things to consumers have also been in motion. Rising standards of hygiene have, for example, made daily bathing the norm and, in so doing, have created opportunities for marketing personal care products. In the late twentieth century, consuming individually and often alone became more common, although in the twenty-first sharing may be on the increase. In the world of American gun culture, the epicenters of market exchange are no longer predominantly within main street hardware and sporting goods stores, but have migrated to well-attended periodic gun shows and auctions (Burbick 2006; Wintemute 2007, 2009).

The history of gender and consumption in America can similarly be interpreted as having threads of continuity as well as instances of change. One long strand has pointed toward greater gender equality in family decision-making, while another led to increasing female dominance in the management of household consumption. Male dominated in the colonial and early national eras, domestic purchasing and consumption became increasingly feminized in the second half of the nineteenth century and throughout much of the twentieth. Companies responded to and abetted this evolution by making shopping and store environments suitable for women, and by developing and marketing products expressly for female consumers. Male consumption occupied specific niches within the home (libraries, billiard rooms, dens, garages) and was conducted outside the home at sports venues and drinking establishments. The threats to American masculinity brought about by industrialization and modernity gathered force in the late nineteenth century and, in somewhat different form, reemerged in the 1950s. Both episodes appear to have influenced male consumption practices. Around the turn of the new millennium male status and manliness became even more problematic as posited by the male overcompensation (Willer *et al.* 2013) and compensatory consumption theses (Holt and Thompson 2004).

Anti-consumption thought and outright resistance have shown broad continuities in motives (religious, philosophical, political) and in behavioral expressions (targeted boycotts, voluntary simplicity, defiance of prohibitions). Take moralistic critiques of consumption. Critical theology and rhetoric stretch back to the seventeenth century and through regulatory and normative means social actors have made repeated efforts to "protect" American consumers from themselves by controlling and sometimes prohibiting alcohol, tobacco, soft and hard drugs, gambling, prostitution, and any number of additional perceived vices (Hollander 1984). Starting with progressive reformers in the early twentieth century, the consumer movement has championed the rights of buyers and has protected them from infringements by companies through educational campaigns, litigation, and government regulation (Herrmann and Mayer 1997). The publishing of inflammatory critiques of the advertising, branding, and many other marketing mix abuses perpetrated on American buyers by corporations has been a cottage industry for quite some time (see, e.g., Galbraith 1958; Klein 1999; Packard 1957, 1959, 1960).

Yet, by the twentieth century, the strong traditions of social criticism and resistance to materialistic consumer culture among Protestants had greatly diminished, while Catholics and Jews focused more on assimilation than on their prophetic traditions (Leach 1994). Some evangelicals have asked "What Would Jesus Drive?" but this theology has been more than matched by environmentally unfriendly dominionist preaching. Although religious rituals (fasting, observing a Sabbath) sometimes dictated short-term consumption sacrifices, few faiths have made such practices a total lifestyle choice. For over 200 years, the majority of American faithful have seemed quite content to let their consumerist and religious lives coexist peacefully (Witkowski 2010a). In an interesting interpretive twist, Jackson Lears (1994, 7) maintained that the Protestant ethos of self-control could often give way to a more emotional religiosity that then, in turn, paved the way for an eroticization of goods. This may be connected with the success of the dominionist "prosperity gospel" in America. In this theology believing Christians have been entitled to enjoy well-being and material success provided they have made the appropriate donation (tithing has been recommended) to a church or television ministry. These beliefs, which have been frequently criticized by other Christian groups, have a history with roots that can be traced back to the late nineteenth century.

Additional Cultural Threads

The bundles of cultural threads considered herein have undoubted importance, but still constitute just one fragment of the larger fabric of American consumption history. Many of the CCT topics and perspectives outlined in Arnould and Thompson (2005, 2015) lend themselves to substantive (actual things and events) and/or intellectual (development of thought) historical research. For example, consumption rituals ranging from daily acts of hygiene and grooming to rites of passage like birthdays, graduations, weddings, and funerals to important holidays like Valentine's Day, Thanksgiving, and Christmas have all changed over time (Bushman and Bushman 1988; Schmidt 1991). New consumption histories of these and many more rituals, which draw from and build upon theoretically driven CCT studies, beg to be researched and written about.

Different American demographic subcultures – racial, ethnic, religious, sexual orientation, and age-based – have had their own consumption histories with distinctive threads of meaning, gender, and resistance. They have not been totally ignored in this book, but should be explored in much greater depth. For example, anthropologist Bruce Tharp (2007) has conducted ethnographic investigations of the Amish in northeastern Indiana. He looked into the valued possessions of this religious subculture and how the meanings attributed to material things have been influenced by the larger American culture of consumption. Regarding LGBT subcultures, marketing historian Blaine Branchik (2007) content analyzed the depiction of gay men in print advertising from 1917 to 2004. He found evidence of targeted recognition early on, but also ridicule and scorn for many decades until the 1990s when portrayals finally became cutting edge and eventually more respectful. Historical research opportunities are plentiful.

Similarly, far more could be said about the history of social class and the problems faced by poor consumers living among affluence. Ronald Hill and his colleagues have examined homeless women and the meanings they have assigned to their special possessions (Hill and Stamey 1990; Hill 1991). Though data sources may be sparse, more on the history of consumption among the disadvantaged is surely worth pursuing. At this writing in Spring 2017, the issue of immigration from Mexico and Middle Eastern countries has become especially controversial. Thus, new histories of immigrant groups and their acculturation as American consumers would be desirable and have the advantage of being able to draw concepts from prior CCT oriented research on the topic, such as the good work of Lisa Peñaloza (1994).

CCT researchers have surveyed specific brand and broader consumption communities and tribes (Belk and Costa 1998; Canniford 2011; Schouten and McAlexander 1995), but how these groupings have evolved over time, and what meanings they have transferred to their possessions, should be promising avenues for future historical research. Take, for example, the iconic Winchester brand of lever action rifles. Evidence suggests that plains Indians may have formed a Winchester community (or consumer tribe as it were) soon after the brand name appeared in 1866. Military historian Alexander Rose (2008, 7) observed how "By the 1870s, Indians were among the repeater's most zealous fans, and were widely (but falsely) believed to be better armed than the soldiers sent to fight them." I have seen half a dozen photos from the 1870s and 1880s depicting Native Americans cradling Winchester rifles. In the 1890s still another oppressed minority group, African Americans, may have aspired to form a Winchester brand community. Southern whites were inflicting horrific violence upon blacks and so gave them every reason to arm themselves. Fiery black journalists such as Ida B. Wells (1862–1931), encouraged them to buy Winchesters. Commenting on incidents of blacks resisting lynching with arms, Wells (1892, 23) wrote:

> The lesson this teaches and which every Afro-American should ponder well, is that a Winchester rifle should have a place of honor in every black home, and it should be used for that protection which the law refuses to give.

Many years later, in 1977, brand aficionados formed the Winchester Arms Collectors Association (WACA). WACA currently has about 2000 members who, according to WACA's mission statement, "are devoted to the preservation, understanding and collecting of Winchester firearms and related products as well as the role these products had in forging America's heritage" (Winchester Arms Collectors Association 2017). Photos on the group's website indicate that this incarnation of the Winchester brand community consists mostly of white males. The guns now stand as a marker of white heritage. Many other brand and consumption communities also have had long, polysemic histories well worth recounting.

Implications for Consumer Culture Theory

What does this book have to say to consumer culture theory researchers? The most obvious lesson is to simply acknowledge that consumption phenomena, their supporting ideologies, and their critical opposition, have histories that may very well have bearing on present day behavior and how we think about it. In America, for instance, expressing refinement through goods dates to the mid-eighteenth century, communicating national identity to the early federal period, associating brands with youth and modernity to the early twentieth, and purchasing things based on partisanship to at least the 1970s. CCT researchers need to be historically curious and learn about past antecedents of the specific consumption phenomenon being investigated. Historical knowledge can expand theoretical perspectives by illuminating additional dimensions of consumption phenomena not readily apparent or perhaps, like sharing phenomena (Belk 2010) or assumptions about gender (Bristor and Fischer 1993), given short shrift by prevailing ideologies.

Equally important, history teaches us that theories may be restricted to a given time and place. Stated differently, CCT researchers should remember that their thinking, the data they collect, and how they analyze and write it up for publication are historically determined. For example, McCracken's (1986) theory of the movement of meaning from the culturally constituted world to consumer goods and then to consumers themselves was situated within the advertising and fashion systems of late, twentieth century North America. As this book has shown, meanings can flow into possessions without these elaborate institutional transmitters, as they did in the case of the mid-nineteenth century Mormon pioneers ably studied by Belk (1992). Similarly, most CCT researchers in the early twenty-first century have a much different understanding of gender and resistance than did consumers during their grandparents' generation and earlier.

While writing this book and reviewing the CCT literature on meaning, gender, and resistance, I was reminded how most theoretically driven studies may eventually lose their relevance as the literature moves on to trendy new topics and theories. When I was a graduate student in the mid-1970s, expectancy value models (beliefs, attitude, intentions, and behavior) and attribution theories were all the rage in consumer research, but they became far less prominent in subsequent decades and of relatively minor concern in CCT circles. Feminist thought has challenged many assumptions and biases in the social sciences and in historical writing (Bristor and Fischer 1993). Thus, the study of female bikers by Martin, Schouten, and McAlexander (2006) explicitly challenged the theory posited in the earlier research of Schouten and McAlexander (1995). Well over a century ago the German Historical School warned that any generalizations about society – and this would definitely include much analysis within CCT, as well as in the larger field of consumer research – may be evanescent because of social, cultural, and technological change (Fullerton 1987).

However, some CCT research might pass into a second life as evidence useful for consumption historians. For example, Kozinets' (2002) report on Burning

Man festival ideologies and Kozinets and Handelman's (2004) enquiry into consumer activist identities made theoretical contributions when originally published. But their research may also have future value as documentation of discourses and activities pertaining to consumption resistance around the turn of the new millennium. In years to come the theoretical contribution of CCT studies may become attenuated, even passé, as the literature moves on to greener pastures, but their historical value as documents may possibly continue to grow. Take heart, CCT mavens! Consumption historians in the future will see to it that your hard work will be remembered, especially when it was based on solid empirical evidence.

That said, redeploying CCT research as a primary source data for consumption history has its limitations. First, the phenomena investigated often have been relatively obscure and attracted few consumers at their time. For example, the mountain men re-enactors meticulously researched by Belk and Costa (1998) comprised a very small subculture within American life at the time. The authors' rich description of these men, their families, their accoutrements, and their sociability revealed much of human interest that presented theoretical implications for fantasy consumption. However, the specific activities under investigation were not characteristic of the lives of most American men in the early 1990s when the ethnography was conducted. Second, some CCT research has drawn from such small samples that its historical generalizability may be problematic. Craig Thompson (1996) deftly reported the experiences of just seven professional working mothers and Douglas Holt and Thompson (2004) essentially boiled their empirical data down to long interviews with just two American men. Further, in both studies the authors ultimately filtered the voices of their respondents by selecting data they (and their reviewers) deemed to be of most theoretical interest. Thus, these scholarly interpretations will be admissible, but not particularly robust historical evidence. They indicate ranges of consumption experience, but not their frequency. In this consumption historian's humble opinion, data taken from larger survey samples or from more extensive ethnographic research would be preferable as primary data sources.

References

Abelson, Elaine S. (1989), *When Ladies Go A-Thieving: Middle-Class Shoplifters in the Victorian Department Store*, Oxford, UK: Oxford University Press.

ACR (2016), "ACR History," www.acrwebsite.org/web/about-acr/acr-history.aspx.

Affluenza (1998), Public Broadcasting Service, www.pbs.org/kcts/affluenza/home.html.

Agiesta, Jennifer (2015), "Poll: Majority Sees Confederate Flag as Southern Pride Symbol, Not Racist," CNN Politics, (July 2), http://edition.cnn.com/2015/07/02/politics/confederate-flag-poll-racism-southern-pride/.

American Home Economics Association (1909), "Announcement" and "Lake Placid Conference on Home Economics, 1899–1908," *The Journal of Home Economics*, 1 (February), 1–6.

Ames, Kenneth L. (1978), "Meaning in Artifacts: Hall Furnishings in Victorian America," *Journal of Interdisciplinary History*, 9 (1), 19–46.

Ames, Kenneth L. (1985), "The Stuff of Everyday Life: American Decorative Arts and Household Furnishing," in *Material Culture: A Research Guide*, ed. Thomas J. Schlereth, Lawrence, KS: The University Press of Kansas, 79–112.

Andrews, Cecile (1997), *The Circle of Simplicity: Return to the Good Life*, New York: Harper Perennial.

Andrews, Charles Mclean (1918/1968), *The Boston Merchants and the Nonimportation Movement*, New York: Russell & Russell.

Armes, Ethel, ed. (1935/1968), *Nancy Shippen: Her Journal Book*, New York: Benjamin Bloom.

Arnould, Eric J. and Craig J. Thompson (2005), "Consumer Culture Theory (CCT): Twenty Years of Research," *Journal of Consumer Research*, 31 (March), 868–882.

Arnould, Eric J. and Craig J. Thompson (2015), "Introduction: Consumer Culture Theory: Ten Years Gone (and Beyond)," in *Research in Consumer Behavior*, Vol. 17, ed. Anastasia E. Thyroff, Jeff B. Murray, and Russell W. Belk, Bingley, UK: Emerald Group Publishing Limited, 1–21.

Aronson, Sidney H. (1952), "The Sociology of the Bicycle," *Social Forces*, 30 (3), 305–312.

Atwan, Robert, Donald McQuade, and John W. Wright (1979), *Edsels, Luckies, & Frigidaires: Advertising the American Way*, New York: Dell Publishing Co., Inc.

Aud, Susan, William Hussar, Frank Johnson, Grace Kena, Erin Roth, Eileen Manning, Xiaolei Want, and Jijun Zhang (2012), *The Condition of Education*, Washington, D.C: U.S. Department of Education, National Center for Educational Statistics, http://nces.ed.gov/pubs2012/2012045.pdf.

Bader, Louis (1939), "Consumers and Chain-Store Taxation," *Journal of Retailing*, 15 (December), 115–119.

Bailey, Ronald H. (1977), *The Home Front: U.S.A.*, Alexandria, VA: Time-Life Books.

Baker Chuck (2016), "The Brownie Camera Page," www.brownie-camera.com/.

Ballyhoo (1938), "Jap Number," (May).

Bandura, Albert (1986), *Social Foundations of Thought and Action: A Social Cognitive Theory*, Englewood Cliffs, NJ: Prentice-Hall.

Banks, Seymour (1950), "The Relationship Between Preference and Brands," *Journal of Marketing*, 15 (2), 145–157.

Baragwanath, Albert K. (1978), *100 Currier and Ives Favorites*, New York: Crown Publishers, Inc.

Bardhi, Fleura, Giana Eckhardt, and Eric J. Arnould (20012), "Liquid Relationship to Possessions," *Journal of Consumer Research*, 39 (October), 510–529.

Barendsen, Joyce P. (1983), "Wallace Nutting, An American Tastemaker: The Pictures and Beyond," *Winterthur Portfolio*, 18 (2/3), 187–212.

Barnard, Malcolm (2001), *Approaches to Understanding Visual Culture*, New York: Palgrave.

Barnes, Julian E. (2001), "A Nation Challenged: Proud Spirits; As Demand Soars, Flag Makers Help Bolster Nation's Morale," *New York Times*, (September 23), www.nytimes.com/2001/09/23/business/nation-challenged-proud-spirits-demand-soars-flag-makers-help-bolster-nation-s.html.

Barnouw, Erik (1976), *Tube of Plenty: The Evolution of American Television*, New York: Oxford University Press.

Barrett, Paul M. (2013), *Glock: The Rise of America's Gun*, New York: Broadway Paperbacks.

Bartels, Robert (1962), *The Development of Marketing Thought*, Homewood, IL: Richard D. Irwin.

Barth, Fredrik, ed. (1969), *Ethnic Groups and Boundaries: The Social Organization of Culture Difference*, Boston, MA: Little, Brown and Company.

Baugher, Sherene and Robert W. Venables (1987), "Ceramics as Indicators of Status and Class in Eighteenth-Century New York," in *Consumer Choice in Historical Archaeology*, ed. Suzanne M. Spencer-Wood, New York: Plenum, 31–53.

Bax, Christina E. (2010), "Entrepreneur Brownie Wise: Selling Tupperware to America's Women in the 1950s," *Journal of Women's History*, 22 (2), 171–180.

Bayton, James A. (1958), "Motivation, Cognition, Learning: Basic Factors in Consumer Behavior," *Journal of Marketing*, 22 (3), 282–289.

Beard, Fred and Anna Klyueva (2010), "George Washington Hill and the 'Reach for a Lucky …' Campaign," *Journal of Historical Research in Marketing*, 2 (2), 148–165.

Becher, Tony and Paul R. Trowler (2001), *Academic Tribes and Territories: Intellectual Enquiry and the Culture of Disciplines* (Second Edition), Buckingham, UK: Open University Press.

Belk, Russell W. (1986), "Art versus Science as Ways of Generating Knowledge about Materialism," in *Perspectives on Methodology in Consumer Research*, eds. David Brinberg and Richard J. Lutz, New York: Springer-Verlag, 31–53.

Belk, Russell W. (1988), "Possessions and the Extended Self," *Journal of Consumer Research*, 15 (2), 139–168.

Belk, Russell W. (1991), "The History and Development of the Consumer Behavior Odyssey," in *Highways and Buyways: Naturalistic Research from the Consumer Behavior Odyssey*, ed. Russell W. Belk, Provo, UT: Association for Consumer Research, 1–12.

Belk, Russell W. (1992), "Moving Possessions: An Analysis Based on Personal Documents from the 1847–1869 Mormon Migration," *Journal of Consumer Research*, 19 (December), 339–361.

Belk, Russell W. (1996), *Collecting in a Consumer Society*, London and New York: Routledge.

Belk, Russell W. (2010), "Sharing," *Journal of Consumer Research*, 36 (February), 715–734.

Belk, Russell W. (2011), "Examining Markets, Marketing, Consumers, and Society through Documentary Films," *Journal of Macromarketing*, 31 (4), 403–409.

Belk, Russell W. (2014), "The Labors of the Odysseans and the Legacy of the Odyssey," *Journal of Historical Research in Marketing*, 6 (3), 379–404.

Belk, Russell W. and Janeen Costa (1998), "The Mountain Man Myth: A Contemporary Consuming Fantasy," *Journal of Consumer Research*, 25 (December), 218–240.

Belk, Russell W. and Richard W. Pollay (1985), "Images of Ourselves: The Good Life in Twentieth Century Advertising," *Journal of Consumer Research*, 11 (March), 887–897.

Beller, Andrea H. and D. Elizabeth Kiss (1999), "On the Contribution of Hazel Kyrk to Family Economics," paper presented at the Society for the Advancement of Behavioral Economics, San Diego, CA.

Bellesiles, Michael A. (2000), *Arming America: The Origins of a National Gun Culture*, New York: Vintage Books.

Benson, Susan P. (1986) *Counter Cultures: Saleswomen, Managers, and Customers in American Department Stores, 1890–1940*. Urbana, IL: University of Illinois Press.

Betsky, Celia (1985), "Inside the Past: The Interior and the Colonial Revival in American Art and Literature, 1860–1914," in *The Colonial Revival in America*, ed. Alan Axerod, New York: W.W. Norton, 241–277.

Bilkey, Warren J. (1953), "A Psychological Approach to Consumer Behavior Analysis," *Journal of Marketing*, 18 (1), 18–25.

Bird, Deirdre, Helen Caldwell, and Mark DeFanti (2011), "A Fragrance to Empower Women: The History of 'Charlie,'" in *Marketing History: Voyaging to the New World: Proceedings of the 15th Biennial Conference on Historical Analysis and Research in Marketing*, ed. Leighann C. Neilson, Hamden, CT: Quinnipiac University, 217–219.

Black, Mary (1973), *Old New York in Early Photographs, 1853–1901* (Second Revised Edition), New York: Dover Publications, Inc.

Blakey, Roy G. (1920), "American's New Conception of Thrift: Foreword," *Annals of the American Academy of Political and Social Science*, 87, 1–3.

Blaszczyk, Regina L. (2000), *Imagining Consumers: Design and Innovation from Wedgwood to Corning*, Baltimore, MD: The Johns Hopkins University Press.

Blaszczyk, Regina L. (2009), *American Consumer Society, 1865–2005: From Hearth to HDTV*, Wheeling, IL: Harlan Davidson, Inc.

Blocker, Jack S. (2006), "Did Prohibition Really Work? Alcohol Prohibition as a Public Health Innovation," *American Journal of Public Health*, 96 (2), 233–243.

Blum, John Morton (1976), *V WAS FOR VICTORY: Politics and American Culture During World War II*, San Diego, CA: Harcourt Brace Jovanovich.

Bolton-Smith, Robin and William H. Truettner (1973), *Lilly Martin Spencer, 1822–1902: The Joys of Sentiment*, Washington, D.C.: Smithsonian Institution Press.

Bonnie, Richard J. and Charles H. Whitebread, II (1974), *The Marihuana Conviction: A History of Marihuana Prohibition in the United States*, Charlottesville, VA: University Press of Virginia.

Boorstin, Daniel J. (1973), *The Americans: The Democratic Experience*, New York: Random House.

Bordwell, Marilyn (2002), "Jamming Culture: Adbusters' Hip Media Campaign Against Consumerism," in *Confronting Consumption*, eds. Thomas Princen, Michael Maniates, and Ken Conca, Cambridge, MA: MIT Press, 237–253.

Borgerson, Janet L. and Jonathan E. Schroeder (2002), "Ethical Issues of Global Marketing: Avoiding Bad Faith in Visual Representation," *European Journal of Marketing*, 36 (5/6), 570–594.

Borgerson, Janet L. and Jonathan E. Schroeder (2006), "The Pleasures of the Used Text: Revealing Traces of Consumption," in *Consuming Books: The Marketing and Consumption of Literature*, ed. Stephen Brown, London: Routledge, 46–59.

Borgerson, Janet L. and Jonathan E. Schroeder (2017), *Designed for Hi-Fi Living: The Vinyl LP in Midcentury America*, Cambridge, MA: MIT Press.

Bose, Christine E. (1987), "Dual Spheres," in *Analyzing Gender: A Handbook of Social Science Research*, eds. Beth B. Hess and Myra M. Ferree, Newbury Park, CA: SAGE Publications, 267–285.

Branchik, Blaine J. (2007), "Pansies to Parents: Gay Male Images in American Print Advertising," *Journal of Macromarketing*, 27 (1), 38–50.

Branchik, Blaine J. and Judy Foster Davis (2009), "Marketplace Activism: A History of the African American Elite Market Segment," *Journal of Macromarketing*, 29 (1), 37–57.

Breazeale, Kenon (1994), "In Spite of Women: *Esquire* Magazine and the Construction of the Male Consumer," *Signs*, 20 (1), 1–22.

Bredhoff, Stacey (1994), *Powers of Persuasion: Poster Art from World War II*, Washington, D.C.: National Archives Trust Fund Board.

Breen, T.H. (1986), "An Empire of Goods: The Anglicization of Colonial America, 1690–1776," *Journal of British Studies*, 25 (October), 467–499.

Breen, T.H. (1988), " 'Baubles of Britain': The American and Consumer Revolutions of the Eighteenth Century," *Past and Present*, 119 (May), 73–105.

Breen, T.H. (2004), *The Marketplace of Revolution: How Consumer Politics Shaped American Independence*, New York: Oxford University Press.

Breward, Christopher (2015), *The Culture of Fashion: A New History of Fashionable Dress*, Manchester: Manchester University Press.

Bridenbaugh, Carl (1950), *The Colonial Craftsman*, New York: New York University Press.

Bridenbaugh, Carl (1955), *Cities in Revolt: Urban Life in America, 1743–1776*, London: Oxford University Press.

Bridges, Madeline S. (1893), "Wheels and Wheels," *Outing* (September), 460, https://babel.hathitrust.org/cgi/pt?id=umn.319510009255562;view=1up;seq=474.

Bristor, Julia M. and Eileen Fischer (1993), "Feminist Thought: Implications for Consumer Research," *Journal of Consumer Research*, 19 (March), 518–536.

Brough, Aaron R., James E.B. Wilkie, Jingjing Ma, Mathew S. Isaac, and David Gal (2016), "Is Eco-Friendly Unmanly? The Green-Feminine Stereotype and Its Effect on Sustainable Consumption," *Journal of Consumer Research*, 43 (4), 567–582.

Bullock, Steven C., and Sheila McIntyre (2012), "The Handsome Tokens of a Funeral: Glove-Giving and the Large Funeral in Eighteenth-Century New England," *William and Mary Quarterly*, 69 (2), 305–346.

Bunker, Nick (2014), *An Empire on the Edge: How Britain Came to Fight America*, New York: Vintage Books.

Burbick, Joan (2006), *Gun Show Nation: Gun Culture and American Democracy*, New York: The New Press.

Burke, Peter (2001), *Eyewitnessing: The Uses of Images as Historical Evidence*, Ithaca, NY: Cornell University Press.

Burks, Jean M. (1986), *Birmingham Brass Candlesticks*, Charlottesville, VA: University of Virginia Press.

Bushman, Richard L. (1992), *The Refinement of America: Persons, Houses, Cities*, New York: Alfred A. Knopf.

Bushman, Richard L. and Claudia L. Bushman (1988), "The Early History of Cleanliness in America," *The Journal of American History*, 74 (4), 1213–1238.

Campbell, Colin (1987), *The Romantic Ethic and the Spirit of Modern Consumerism*, New York: Basil Blackwell.

Campbell, D'Ann (1984), *Women at War with America: Private Lives in a Patriotic Era*, Cambridge, MA: Harvard University Press.

Canniford, Robin (2011), "A Typology of Consumption Communities," in *Research in Consumer Behavior*, Vol. 13, eds. Russell W. Belk, Kent Grayson, Albert M. Muniz, and Hope J. Schau, Bingley, UK: Emerald Group Publishing Limited, 57–75.

Carpenter, Charles H., Jr. (1985), "The Tradition of the Old: Colonial Revival Silver for the American Home," in *The Colonial Revival in America*, ed. Alan Axelrod, New York: W.W. Norton, 139–158.

Carr, Lois Green and Lorena S. Walsh (1980), "Inventories and the Analysis of Wealth and Consumption Patterns in St. Mary's County, Maryland, 1658–1777," *Historical Methods*, 13 (Spring), 81–104.

Carson, Rachel (1962), *Silent Spring*, Boston, MA: Houghton Mifflin.

Carver, T.N. (1920), "The Relation of Thrift to Nation Building," *Annals of the American Academy of Political and Social Science*, 87, 4–8.

Casdorph, Paul D. (1989), *Let the Good Times Roll: Life at Home in America During World War II*, New York: Paragon House.

Cashman, Sean Dennis (1993), *America in the Gilded Age: From the Death of Lincoln to the Rise of Theodore Roosevelt* (Third Edition), New York: New York University Press.

CEI (2016), Competitive Enterprise Institute, (April 25), https://cei.org.

Chandler, Alfred D. Jr. (1977), *The Visible Hand: The Managerial Revolution in American Business*, Cambridge, MA: The Belknap Press of Harvard University Press.

Chase, Stuart (1925), *The Tragedy of Waste*, New York: Grosset & Dunlap.

Chase, Stuart and F.J. Schlink (1927), *Your Money's Worth: A Study in the Waste of the Consumer's Dollar*, New York: The Macmillan Company.

Child, Lydia Maria (1833), *The American Frugal Housewife*, Boston, MA: Carter, Hendee, and Co. (reprinted by Applewood Books, Bedford, MA, n.d.).

CIA (2017), *The World Factbook*, US Central Intelligence Agency, www.cia.gov/library/publications/the-world-factbook/geos/us.html.

Clark, H. Nichols B. (1988), *Francis W. Edmonds: American Master in the Dutch Tradition*, Washington, D.C.: Smithsonian Institution Press for the Amon Carter Museum.

Clarke, Alison J. (1999), *Tupperware: The Promise of Plastic in 1950s America*, Washington, D.C. and London: Smithsonian Institution Press.

Clemens, Paul G.E. (2005), "The Consumer Culture of the Middle Atlantic, 1760–1820," *William and Mary Quarterly*, 62 (4), 577–624.

Cohen, Joanna (2014), "Promoting Pleasure as Political Economy: The Transformation of American Advertising, 1800 to 1850," *Winterthur Portfolio*, 48 (2/3), 163–189.

Cohen, Lizabeth (2003), *A Consumers' Republic: The Politics of Mass Consumption in Postwar America*, New York: Knopf.

Conn, Steve (2015), "Heritage Is Not History," *philly.com, The Inquirer/Daily News*, (July 10), www.philly.com/philly/blogs/thinktank/313315391.html.

Conway, Ed (2014), *The Summit: Bretton Woods, 1944: J.M. Keynes and the Reshaping of the Global Economy*, New York: Pegasus Books.

Cook, Noble David (1998), *Born to Die: Disease and New World Conquest, 1492–1650.* New York: Cambridge University Press.

Cooper, Troy (2014), "'You Can Fool Some of the People Some of the Time': Perspective by Incongruity in Ballyhoo Magazine, 1931–1932," unpublished dissertation, Department of Communication, College of Liberal Arts and Sciences, University of Illinois, Urbana, IL 61801.

Copeland, Melvin T. (1923), "Relation of Consumers' Buying Habits to Marketing Methods," *Harvard Business Review*, 1 (3), 282–289.

Coski, John M. (1996), "The Confederate Battle Flag in American History and Culture," *Southern Cultures*, 2 (2), 195–231.

Cott, Nancy F. (1977), *The Bonds of Womanhood: "Women's Sphere" in New England, 1780–1835*, New Haven, CT: Yale University Press.

Cowan, Ruth Schwartz (1983), *More Work for Mother: The Ironies of Household Technology from the Open Hearth to the Microwave*, New York: Basic Books.

Crawford, Anthony R., ed. (1979), *Posters of World War I and World War II in the George C. Marshall Research Foundation*, Charlottesville, VA: University of Virginia Press.

Cross, Gary (2000), *An All-consuming Century: Why Commercialism Won in Modern America*, New York: Columbia University Press.

Cruikshank, Jeffrey L. and Arthur W. Schultz (2010), *The Man Who Sold America: The Amazing (but True!) Story of Albert D. Lasker and the Creation of the Advertising Century*, Boston, MA: Harvard Business Review Press.

Curti, Merle (1967), "The Changing Concept of 'Human Nature' in the Literature of American Advertising," *The Business History Review*, 41 (4), 335–357.

Cushion, John P. (1976), *Pottery & Porcelain Tablewares*, New York: Morrow.

Cutler, David and Grant Miller (2005), "The Role of Public Health Improvements in Health Advances: The Twentieth-Century United States," *Demography*, 42 (1), 1–22.

Cynamon, Barry Z., Steven Fazzari, and Mark Setterfield eds. (2014), *After the Great Recession: The Struggle for Economic Recovery and Growth*, New York: Cambridge University Press.

Davidson, Debra J, and William R. Freudenburg (1996), "Gender and Environmental Risk Concerns: A Review and Analysis of Available Research," *Environment and Behavior*, 28 (3), 302–339.

Davies, Andrea (2011), "Voices Passed," *Journal of Historical Research in Marketing*, 3 (4), 469–485.

Davis, Harry L. (1970), "Dimensions of Marital Roles in Consumer Decision Making," *Journal of Marketing Research*, 7 (2), 168–177.

Davis, Harry L. (1971), "Measurement of Husband-Wife Influence in Consumer Purchase Decisions," *Journal of Marketing Research*, 8 (3), 305–312.

de Grazia, Victoria (1996), "Introduction," in *The Sex of Things: Gender and Consumption in Historical Perspective*, eds. Victoria de Grazia with Ellen Furlough, Berkeley, CA: University of California Press, 1–24, 151–161, 275–286.

Deák, Gloria-Gilda (1976), *American Views: Prospects and Vistas*, New York: The Viking Press and The New York Public Library.

Demos, John (1970), *A Little Commonwealth: Family Life in Plymouth Colony*, London: Oxford University Press.

Detweiler, Susan Gray (1982), *George Washington's Chinaware*, New York: Abrams.

Deutsch, Tracey (2010), *Building a Housewife's Paradise: Gender, Politics, and American Grocery Stores in the Twentieth Century*, Chapel Hill, NC: The University of North Carolina Press.

Dichter, Ernest (1947), *The Psychology of Everyday Living*, New York: Barnes and Noble.

Dichter, Ernest (1960), *Strategy for Desire*, Garden City, NY: Doubleday.

Doerflinger, Thomas M. (1986), *A Vigorous Spirit of Enterprise: Merchants and Economic Development in Revolutionary Philadelphia*, Chapel Hill, NC: University of North Carolina Press.

Dolan, J.R. (1964), *The Yankee Peddlers of Early America*, New York: Bramhall House.

Dominguez, Joseph and Vicki Robin (1992), *Your Money or Your Life*, New York: Viking.

Dow, George Francis (1927/1967), *The Arts & Crafts in New England, 1704–1775*, New York: Da Capo Press.

Dower, John W. (1986), *War Without Mercy: Race and Power in the Pacific War*, New York: Pantheon Books.

Downing, Andrew Jackson (1842/1981 from 1873 edition), *Victorian Cottage Residences*, Mineola, NY: Dover Publications.

Downing, Andrew Jackson (1850/1968), *The Architecture of Country Houses*, New York: Da Capo Press.

Dreiser, Theodore (1900), *Sister Carrie*, New York: Bantam Books.

Dröge, Cornelia, Roger Calantone, Madhu Agrawal, and Robert Mackoy (1993), "The Consumption Culture and Its Critiques: A Framework for Analysis," *Journal of Macromarketing*, 13 (2), 32–45.

Duggan, Maeve (2015), "Mobile Messaging and Social Media 2015, Pew Research Center," (August 19), www.pewinternet.org/2015/08/19/mobile-messaging-and-social-media-2015/.

Earth Hour (2016), "About Us," www.earthhour.org/about-us.

Ebert, Roger (2005), "Great Movie: Top Hat," (October 23), www.rogerebert.com/reviews/great-movie-top-hat-1935.

Eckhardt, Giana M. and Anders Bengtsson (2010), "A Brief History of Branding in China," *Journal of Macromarketing*, 30 (3), 210–221.

Economist, The (2012), "The Future of Driving: Seeing the Back of the Car," (September 22), www.economist.com/node/21563280.

Economist, The (2014), "BuyPartisan: Voting with Your Wallet," (September 13), 38.

Economist, The (2017), "Deaths of Despair," (March 25), 67.

Ehrlich, Paul R. (1968), *The Population Bomb*, New York: Ballantine Books.

Eighmey, John and Sela Sar (2007), "Harlow Gale and the Origins of the Psychology of Advertising," *Journal of Advertising*, 36 (4), 147–158.

Elgin, Duane (1993), *Voluntary Simplicity*, New York: Morrow.

Elliott, Richard and Andrea Davies (2006), "Using Oral History in Consumer Research," in *Handbook of Qualitative Research Methods in Marketing*, ed. Russell W. Belk, Cheltenham, UK: Edward Elgar Publishing, 244–254.

Ellis, Joseph J. (2004), *His Excellency: George Washington*, New York: Alfred A. Knopf, Inc.

Engel, James F., David T. Kollat, and Roger D. Blackwell (1968), *Consumer Behavior*, New York: Holt, Rinehart, and Winston.

Etzioni, Amitai (1998), "Voluntary Simplicity: Characterization, Select Psychological Implications, and Societal Consequences," *Journal of Economic Psychology* 19 (5), 619–643.
Evans, Emory G. (1962), "Planter Indebtedness and the Coming of the Revolution in Virginia," *William and Mary Quarterly*, 19 (October), 511–533.
Evans, Sara M. (1989), *Born for Liberty: A History of Women in America*, New York: The Free Press.
Ewen, Stuart (1976), *Captains of Consciousness: Advertising and the Social Roots of the Consumer Culture*, New York: McGraw-Hill Book Company.
Fales, Martha Gandy (1974), *Joseph Richardson and Family, Philadelphia Silversmiths*, Middleton, CT: Wesleyan University Press.
Fang, Lee (2014), "The Real Reason Pot Is Still Illegal," *The Nation*, (July 1), www.thenation.com/article/180493/anti-pot-lobbys-big-bankroll?page=0,0.
Ferber, Robert (1955), "On the Reliability of Purchase Influence Studies," *Journal of Marketing*, 19 (3), 225–232.
Ferber, Robert and Lucy Chao Lee (1974), "Husband-Wife Influence in Family Purchasing Behavior," *Journal of Consumer Research*, 1 (June), 43–50.
Fernie, Eric, ed. (1995), *Art History and Its Methods: A Critical Anthology*, London: Phaidon.
Firat, Fuat (1987), "Historiography, Scientific Method, and Exceptional Historical Events," in *Advances in Consumer Research*, Vol. 14, eds. Melanie Wallendorf and Paul F. Anderson, Provo, UT: Association for Consumer Research, 435–438.
Fischer, Eileen and Stephen J. Arnold (1990), "More than a Labor of Love: Gender Roles and Christmas Gift Shopping," *Journal of Consumer Research*, 17 (December), 333–345.
Fleming, E. McClung (1974), "Artifact Study: A Proposed Model," *Winterthur Portfolio*, 9 (Spring), 153–161.
Forget, Evelyn (1996), "Margaret Gilpin Reid: A Manitoba Home Economist Goes to Chicago," *Feminist Economics*, 2 (3), 1–16.
Fox, Frank W. (1975), *Madison Avenue Goes to War: The Strange Military Career of American Advertising, 1941–45*, Provo, UT: Brigham Young University Press.
Fox, Stephen (1984), *The Mirror Makers: A History of American Advertising and Its Creators*, New York: William Morrow.
Frederick, Christine (1929), *Selling Mrs. Consumer*, New York: The Business Bourse.
Friedan, Betty (1963), *The Feminine Mystique*, New York: Dell Publishing Co., Inc.
Friedman, Monroe (1999), *Consumer Boycotts: Effecting Change Through the Marketplace and the Media*, New York and London: Routledge.
Friedman, Walter A. (2004), *Birth of a Salesman: The Transformation of Selling in America*, Cambridge, MA and London: Harvard University Press.
Fritsch, Albert J. (1974), *The Contrasumers: A Citizen's Guide to Resource Conservation*, New York: Praeger Publishers.
Foucault, Michel (1972) "The Discourse on Language," trans. Rupert Swyer, appendix to *The Archaeology of Knowledge*, New York: Pantheon.
Fullerton, Ronald A. (1987), "Historicism: What It Is, and What It Means for Consumer Research," in *Advances in Consumer Research* Vol. 14, eds. Melanie Wallendorf and Paul Anderson, Provo, UT: Association for Consumer Research, 431–434.
Fullerton, Ronald A. (1988), "How Modern is Modern Marketing: Marketing's Evolution and the Myth of the 'Production Era,'" *Journal of Marketing*, 52 (January), 108–125.
Fullerton, Ronald A. (2007), "Psychoanalyzing Kleptomania," *Marketing Theory*, 7 (4), 335–352.

Fullerton, Ronald A. (2011), "Historical Methodology: The Perspective of a Professionally Trained Historian Turned Marketer," *Journal of Historical Research in Marketing*, 3 (4), 436–448.

Fullerton, Ronald A. and Girish N. Punj (2004), "Shoplifting as Moral Insanity: Historical Perspectives on Kleptomania," *Journal of Macromarketing*, 24 (1), 8–16.

Fyne, Robert (1994), *The Hollywood Propaganda of World War II*, Metuchen, NJ: The Scarecrow Press, Inc.

Galbraith, John Kenneth (1958), *The Affluent Society*, New York: Mentor Books.

Galbraith, John Kenneth (1973), *Economics & the Public Purpose*, Boston, MA: Houghton Mifflin.

Gallup, George H. (1972), *The Gallup Poll: Public Opinion 1935–1971, Volume One 1935–1948*, New York: Random House.

Garrett, Elisabeth Donaghy (1983), "The American Home, Part II: Lighting Devices and Practices," *The Magazine Antiques*, (February), 408–417.

Garrett, Elisabeth Donaghy (1990), *At Home: The American Family 1750–1870*, New York: Harry N. Abrams.

Geiger, Abigail (2016), "Support for Marijuana Legalization Continues to Rise," Pew Research Center, (October 12), www.pewresearch.org/fact-tank/2016/10/12/support-for-marijuana-legalization-continues-to-rise/.

Geissler, L.R. (1917), "Association-Reactions Applied to Ideas of Commercial Brands of Familiar Articles," *Journal of Applied Psychology*, 1 (3), 275–290.

Gelber, Steven M. (1997), "Do-It-Yourself: Constructing, Repairing and Maintaining Domestic Masculinity," *American Quarterly*, 49 (1), 66–112.

Gilbert, James (2005), *Men in the Middle: Searching for Masculinity in the 1950s*, Chicago, IL: University of Chicago Press.

Gilmore, Russell S. (1999), "'Another Branch of Manly Sport': American Rifle Games, 1840–1900," in *Guns in America: A Reader*, eds. Jan E. Dizard, Robert Merrill Muth, and Stephen P. Andrews, New York: New York University Press, 105–121.

Glickman, Lawrence B. (2004), "'Buy for the Sake of the Slave': Abolitionism and the Origins of American Consumer Activism," *American* Quarterly, 56 (4), 889–912.

Glickman, Lawrence B. (2005), "'Make Lisle the Style': The Politics of Fashion in the Japanese Silk Boycott, 1937–1940," *Journal of Social History*, 38 (3), 573–608.

Glickman, Lawrence B. (2009), *Buying Power: A History of Consumer Activism in America*, Chicago, IL and London: The University of Chicago Press.

Gluck, Sherna A. (1987), *Rosie the Riveter Revisited: Women, the War, and Social Change*, Boston, MA: Twayne Publishers.

Goodwin, Doris Kearns (2005), *Team of Rivals: The Political Genius of Abraham Lincoln*, New York: Simon & Schuster Paperbacks.

Goodwin, Doris Kearns (2013), *The Bully Pulpit: Theodore Roosevelt, William Howard Taft, and the Golden Age of Journalism*, New York: Simon & Schuster.

Gordon, Jean and Jan McArthur (1985), "American Women and Domestic Consumption, 1800–1920," *Journal of American Culture*, 8 (Fall), 35–46.

Gordon, Robert J. (2016), *The Rise and Fall of American Growth: The U.S. Standard of Living Since the Civil War*, Princeton, NJ and Oxford, UK: Princeton University Press.

Gorman, Steve (2016), "U.S. Southern Baptists Formally Repudiate Confederate Flag," *The Huffington Post*, (June 15), www.huffingtonpost.com/entry/southern-baptists-confederate-flag_us_57610aa5e4b0df4d586e9983.

Gottesman, Rita S. (1938/1970), *The Arts and Crafts of New York, 1726–1776*, New York: Da Capo Press.

Gottlieb, Moshe (1973), "The Anti-Nazi Boycott Movement in the United States: An Ideological and Sociological Appreciation," *Jewish Social Studies*, 35 (3/4), 198–227.

Gray, John (1992), *Men Are from Mars, Women Are from Venus: A Practical Guide for Improving Communications and Getting What You Want in Your Relationships*, New York: HarperCollins.

Green, Harvey (1992), *The Uncertainty of Everyday Life, 1915–1945*, New York: Harper-Collins Publishers, Inc.

Green, Robert T. and Isabella C.M. Cunningham (1975), "Feminine Role Perception and Family Purchase Decisions," *Journal of Marketing Research*, 12 (3), 325–332.

Gunderson, Joan R. and Gwen Victor Gampel (1982), "Married Women's Legal Status in Eighteenth-century New York and Virginia," *William and Mary Quarterly*, 39 (January), 114–134.

Gusfield, Joseph R. (1963), *Symbolic Crusade: Status Politics and the American Temperance Movement*," Urbana, IL: University of Illinois Press.

Gusfield, Joseph R. (1967), "Moral Passage: The Symbolic Process in Public Designations of Deviance," *Social Problems*, 15 (2), 175–188.

Haire, Mason (1950), "Projective Techniques in Marketing Research," *Journal of Marketing*, 14 (5), 649–656.

Hale, Grace Elizabeth (1998), *Making Whiteness: The Culture of Segregation in the South, 1890–1940*, New York: Pantheon Books.

Harper's Weekly (1874), "The International Rifle Match," (October 10), 838.

Harper's Weekly (1886), "The Root of the Problem," (May 8), 293.

Harrington, Michael (1962), *The Other America: Poverty in the United States*, New York: Macmillan.

Harris, Neil (1981), "The Drama of Consumer Desire," in *Yankee Enterprise: The Rise of the American System of Manufactures*, eds. Otto Mayr and Robert C. Post, Washington, D.C.: Smithsonian Institution Press, 189–216.

Harrison, Robert L. III, Ann Veeck, and James W. Gentry (2011), "A Life Course Perspective of Family Meals Via the Life Grid Method," *Journal of Historical Research in Marketing*, 3 (2), 214–233.

Haulman, Kate (2005), "Fashion and the Culture Wars of Revolutionary Philadelphia," *William and Mary Quarterly*, 62 (4), 625–662.

Hawes (2016), "Adult New York Times Best Seller Listings," Hawes Publications (May 13), www.hawes.com/pastlist.htm.

Hayes, Christen Boas (2013), "Florida Gay Rights Activists Boycott Orange Juice, 1977–1980," *Global Nonviolent Action Database*, (September 22), https://nvdatabase.swarthmore.edu/content/florida-gay-rights-activists-boycott-orange-juice-1977-1980.

HDR (1998), "Consumption from a Human Development Perspective," *Human Development Report 1998*, New York and Oxford, UK: Oxford University Press, 38–45.

Heckscher, Morrison H. (1985), *American Furniture in the Metropolitan Museum of Art, Late Colonial Period: The Queen Anne and Chippendale Styles*, New York: The Metropolitan Museum of Art and Random House.

Henning, Robert A. and Terrence H. Witkowski (2013), "The Advertising of E. Remington & Sons: The Creation of an Iconic Brand, 1854–1888," *Journal of Historical Research in Marketing*, 5 (4), 418–448.

Henretta, James A. (1973), *The Evolution of American Society, 1700–1815: An Interdisciplinary Analysis*, Lexington, MA: D.C. Heath.

Henretta, James A. (1984), "Wealth and Social Structure," in *Colonial British America: Essays in the New History of the Early Modern Era*, eds. Jack P. Greene and J.R. Pole, Baltimore, MD: The Johns Hopkins University Press, 262–289.

Herlihy, David V. (2004), *Bicycle: The History*, New Haven, CT and London: Yale University Press.

Herrmann, Robert O. (1970), "Consumerism: Its Goals, Organizations and Future," *Journal of Marketing*, 34 (4), 55–60.

Herrmann, Robert O. and Robert N. Mayer (1997), "U.S. Consumer Movement: History and Dynamics," in *Encyclopedia of the Consumer Movement*, ed. Stephen Brobeck, Santa Barbara, CA: ABC-CLIO, 584–601.

Hescox, Mitch and Paul Douglas (2016), *Caring for Creation: An Evangelical's Guide to Climate Change and a Healthy Environment*, Bloomington, MN: Bethany House Publishers.

Hill, Ronald Paul (1991), "Homeless Women, Special Possessions, and the Meaning of Home: An Ethnographic Case Study," *Journal of Consumer Research*, 18 (December), 298–310.

Hill, Ronald Paul, Elizabeth C. Hirschman, and John F. Bauman (1997), "Consumer Survival During the Great Depression: Reports from the Field," *Journal of Macromarketing*, 17 (Spring), 107–127.

Hill, Ronald Paul and Mark Stamey (1990), "The Homeless in America: An Examination of Possessions and Consumption Behaviors," *Journal of Consumer Research*, 17 (December), 303–321.

Hills, Patricia (1974), *The Painters' America: Rural and Urban Life, 1810–1910*, New York: Praeger.

Hine, Thomas (1986), *Populuxe*, New York: Alfred A. Knopf.

Hine, Thomas (1995), *The Total Package: The Evolution and Secret Meanings of Boxes, Bottles, Cans, and Tubes*, Boston, MA: Little, Brown.

Hirschman, Elizabeth C. and Morris B. Holbrook (1982), "Hedonic Consumption: Emerging Concepts, Methods and Propositions," *Journal of Marketing*, 48 (Summer), 92–101.

Holbrook, Morris B. and Elizabeth C. Hirschman (1982), "The Experiential Aspects of Consumption: Consumer Fantasies, Feelings, and Fun," *Journal of Consumer Research*, 9 (September), 132–140.

Hollander, Stanley C. (1984), "Sumptuary Legislation: Demarketing by Edict," *Journal of Macromarketing*, 4 (1), 4–16.

Hollander, Stanley C. (1986), "The Marketing Concept: A Déjà vu," in *Marketing Management Technology as a Social Process*, ed. George Fisk, New York: Praeger, 3–29.

Hollander, Stanley C. and Richard Germain (1992), *Was There a Pepsi Generation before Pepsi Discovered It? An Historical Approach to Youth-Based Age Segmentation*, Lincolnwood, IL: NTC Business Books for the American Marketing Association.

Hollander, Stanley C. and Glenn S. Omura (1989), "Chain Store Developments and Their Political, Strategic, and Social Interdependencies," *Journal of Retailing*, 65 (Fall), 299–325.

Hollander, Stanley C., Kathleen M. Rassuli, D.G. Brian Jones, and Laura F. Dix (2005), "Periodization in Marketing History," *Journal of Macromarketing*, 25 (June), 32–41.

Holt, Douglas B. and Craig J. Thompson (2004), "Man-of-Action Heroes: The Pursuit of Heroic Masculinity in Everyday Consumption," *Journal of Consumer Research*, 31 (2), 425–440.

Homeland Security (2013), *Yearbook of Immigration Statistics*, U.S. Department of Homeland Security, www.dhs.gov/publication/yearbook-immigration-statistics-2013-lawful-permanent-residents.

Horowitz, Daniel (1985), *The Morality of Spending: Attitudes Toward the Consumer Society in America, 1875–1940*, Baltimore, MD and London: Johns Hopkins University Press.

Horowitz, Daniel (2004), *The Anxieties of Affluence: Critiques of American Consumer Culture, 1939–1979*, Amherst and Boston, MA: University of Massachusetts Press.

Horowitz, Roger and Arwen Mohun (1998), "Introduction," in *His and Hers: Gender, Consumption, and Technology*, eds. Roger Horowitz and Arwen Mohun, Charlottesville, VA and London: University Press of Virginia, 1–6.

Horwitz, Elinor Lander (1976), *The Bird, the Banner, and Uncle Sam: Images of America in Folk and Popular Art*, Philadelphia, PA and New York: J.P. Lippincott Company.

Hosmer, Charles B., Jr. (1965), *Presence of the Past: A History of the Preservation Movement in the United States before Williamsburg*, New York: G.P. Putnam's Sons.

Hosmer, Charles B., Jr. (1985), "The New England, or 'Olde Tyme,' Kitchen Exhibit at Nineteenth-Century Fairs," in *The Colonial Revival in America*, ed. Alan Axelrod, New York: W.W. Norton, 159–183.

Howard, John A. and Jagdish N. Sheth (1969), *The Theory of Buyer Behavior*, New York: John Wiley & Sons, Inc.

Hoyt, Elizabeth Ellis (1928), *The Consumption of Wealth*, New York: The Macmillan Company.

Humphreys, Ashlee (2010), "Semiotic Structure and the Legitimation of Consumption Practices: The Case of Casino Gambling," *Journal of Consumer Research*, 37 (3), 490–510.

Hyland, Peter (2005), *The Herculaneum Pottery: Liverpool's Forgotten Glory*, Liverpool: National Museums Liverpool and Liverpool University Press.

Hyman, Paula E. (1980), "Immigrant Women and Consumer Protest: The New York City Kosher Meat Boycott of 1902," *American Jewish History*, 70, 91–105.

Jay, Robert (1987), *The Trade Card in Nineteenth Century America*, Columbia, MO: University of Missouri Press.

Jobe, Brock and Myrna Kaye (1984), *New England Furniture: The Colonial Era*, Boston, MA: Houghton Mifflin.

Johns, Elizabeth (1991), *American Genre Painting: The Politics of Everyday Life*, New Haven, CT: Yale University Press.

Johnson, Nicholas (2014), *Negroes and the Gun: The Black Tradition of Arms*, Amherst, NY: Prometheus Books.

Johnston, Louis and Samuel H. Williamson (2017), "What Was the U.S. GDP Then?" Measuring Worth, www.measuringworth.com/datasets/usgdp/result.php.

Jones, Alice Hanson (1980), *Wealth of a Nation to Be: The American Colonies on the Eve of the Revolution*, New York: Columbia University Press.

Jones, D.G. Brian and Alan J. Richardson (2007), "The Myth of the Marketing Revolution," *Journal of Macromarketing*, 27 (1), 15–24.

Kaplan, Madeline (2015), "'Dukes of Hazzard' Pulled from TV Land Schedule Amid Confederate Flag Controversy," *The Huffington Post*, (July 2), www.huffingtonpost.com/2015/07/01/dukes-of-hazzard-tv-land-pulled_n_7706752.html.

Karababa, Eminegül and Güliz Ger (2011), "Early Modern Ottoman Coffeehouse Culture and the Formation of the Consumer Subject," *Journal of Consumer Research*, 37 (5), 737–760.

Karlsen, Carol F. and Laurie Crumpacker, eds. (1984), *The Journal of Esther Edwards Burr, 1754–1757*, New Haven, CT: Yale University Press.

Kassarjian, Harold H. (1994), "Scholarly Traditions and European Roots of American Consumer Research," in *Research Traditions in Marketing*, eds. Gilles Laurent, Gary L. Lilien, and Bernard Pras, Boston, MA: Kluwer Academic Publishers, 265–279.

Kassarjian, Harold H. and Ronald C. Goodstein (2010), "The Emergence of Consumer Research," in *The SAGE Handbook of Marketing Theory*, eds. Pauline Maclaran, Michael Saren, Barbara Stern, and Mark Tadajewski, London: Sage Publications, Ltd., 59–73.

Kassarjian, Harold H. and Thomas S. Robertson (1968), *Perspectives in Consumer Behavior*, Glenview, IL: Scott, Foresman and Company.

Katona, George (1951), *Psychological Analysis of Economic Behavior*, New York: McGraw-Hill Book Company, Inc.

Katona, George (1960), *The Powerful Consumer*, New York: McGraw-Hill Book Company.

Katona, George (1964), *The Mass Consumption Society*, New York: McGraw-Hill Book Company.

Katz, Elihu and Paul F. Lazarsfeld (1955), *Personal Influence: The Part Played by People in the Flow of Mass Communications*, New York: The Free Press.

Kealing, Bob (2008), *Tupperware Unsealed: Brownie Wise, Earl Tupper, and the Home Party Pioneers*, Gainesville, FL: University Press of Florida.

Kelly, David (2014), "All the News That's Fit to Smoke," *Los Angeles Times* (December 22), A8.

Keith, Robert J. (1960), "The Marketing Revolution," *Journal of Marketing*, 24 (January), 35–38.

Kimmel, Michael S. (1994), "Consuming Manhood: The Feminization of American Culture and the Recreation of the American Male Body, 1832–1920," *Michigan Quarterly Review*, 33 (1), 7–36.

Kimmel, Michael S. (1996), *Manhood in America: A Cultural History*, New York: The Free Press.

Kimmel, Michael S. (2013), *Angry White Men: American Masculinity at the End of an Era*, New York: Nation Books.

Klein, L.R. and J.B. Lansing (1955), "Decisions to Purchase Consumer Durable Goods," *Journal of Marketing*, 20 (2), 109–132.

Klein, Naomi (1999), *No Logo: Taking Aim at the Brand Bullies*, New York: Picador USA.

Koehn, Nancy F. (2001), *Brand New: How Entrepreneurs Earned Consumers' Trust from Wedgwood to Dell*, Boston, MA: Harvard Business School Press.

Kotchemidova, Christina (2005), "Why We Say 'Cheese': Producing the Smile in Snapshot Photography," *Critical Studies in Media Communication*, 22 (1), 2–25.

Kotler, Philip (1972), "What Consumerism Means for Marketers," *Harvard Business Review*, 50 (May–June), 48–57.

Kozinets, Robert V. (2002), "Can Consumers Escape the Market? Emancipatory Illuminations from Burning Man," *Journal of Consumer Research*, 29 (1), 20–38.

Kozinets, Robert V. and Jay M. Handelman (2004), "Adversaries of Consumption: Consumer Movements, Activism, and Ideology," *Journal of Consumer Research*, 31 (3), 691–704.

Kuhn, Thomas S. (1970), *The Structure of Scientific Revolutions* (Second Edition, Enlarged), Chicago, IL: The University of Chicago Press.

Kulikoff, Allan (1986), *Tobacco and Slaves: The Development of Southern Cultures in the Chesapeake, 1680–1800*, Chapel Hill, NC: University of North Carolina Press.

Kumcu, Erdogan (1987), "An Historical Perspective Framework to Study Consumer Behavior and Retailing Systems," in *Advances in Consumer Research*, Vol. 14, eds. Melanie Wallendorf and Paul F. Anderson, Provo, UT: Association for Consumer Research, 439–441.

Kyrk, Hazel (1923), *A Theory of* Consumption, Boston, MA and New York: Houghton Mifflin Company.

Kyrk, Hazel (1933), *Economic Problems of the Family*, New York: Harper & Brothers Publishers.

Kyrk, Hazel (1953), *The Family in the American Economy*, Chicago, IL: University of Chicago Press.

Kyrk, Hazel (1939), "The Development of the Field of Consumption," *Journal of Marketing*, 4 (1), 16–19.

Ladik, Daniel, Francois Carrillat, and Mark Tadajewski (2015), "Belk's (1988) 'Possessions and the Extended Self' Revisited," *Journal of Historical Research in Marketing*, 7 (2), 184–207.

Laermans, Rudi (1993), "Learning to Consume: Early Department Stores and the Shaping of the Modern Consumer Culture (1860–1914)," *Theory, Culture & Society*, 10, 79–102.

Laird, Pamela Walker (1998), *Advertising Progress: American Business and the Rise of Consumer Marketing*, Baltimore, MD: The Johns Hopkins University Press.

Landrum, Nancy E. Connor Tomaka, and John McCarthy (2016), "Analyzing the Religious War of Words Over Climate Change," *Journal of Macromarketing*, 36 (4), 471–482.

Lantz, Herman R., Margaret Britton, Raymond Schmitt, and Eloise C. Snyder (1968), "Pre-Industrial Patterns in the Colonial Family in America: A Content Analysis of Colonial Magazines," *American Sociological Review*, 33 (June), 413–426.

Larkin, Jack (1988), *The Reshaping of Everyday Life: 1790–1840*, New York: Harper & Row.

Lasn, Kalle (1999), *Culture Jam: The Uncooling of America™*, New York: Eagle Brook.

Last, Jay T. (2005), *The Color Explosion: Nineteenth-Century American Lithography*, Santa Ana, CA: Hillcrest Press.

Lastovicka, John L., Lance A. Bettencourt, Renée Shaw Hughner, and Ronald J. Kuntze (1999), "Lifestyle of the Tight and Frugal: Theory and Measurement," *Journal of Consumer Research*, 26, (1), 85–98.

Lavin, Marilyn (1995), "Creating Consumers in the 1930s: Irna Philips and the Radio Soap Opera," *Journal of Consumer Research*, 22 (1), 75–89.

Lavin, Marilyn and Thomas J. Archdeacon (1989), "The Relevance of Historical Method for Marketing Research," in *Interpretive Consumer Research*, ed. Elizabeth C. Hirschman, Provo, UT: Association for Consumer Research, 60–68.

Leach, William R. (1984), "Transformations in a Culture of Consumption: Women and Department Stores, 1890–1925," *Journal of American History*, 71 (September), 319–342.

Leach, William R. (1994), *Land of Desire: Merchants, Power, and the Rise of a New American Culture*, New York: Pantheon Books.

Lears, T.J. Jackson (1983), "From Salvation to Self-Realization: Advertising and the Therapeutic Roots of the Consumer Culture, 1880–1930," in *The Culture of Consumption: Critical Essays in American History, 1880–1980*, eds. Richard Wightman Fox and T.J. Jackson, Lears, New York: Pantheon Books, 1–38, 213–218.

Lears, T.J. Jackson (1994), *Fables of Abundance: A Cultural History of Advertising in America*, New York: Basic Books.

Le Beau, Bryan F. (2007), "Art in the Parlor: Consumer Culture and Currier and Ives," *The Journal of American Culture*, 30 (1), 18–37.

Lebergott, Stanley (1993), *Pursuing Happiness: American Consumers in the Twentieth Century*, Princeton, NJ: Princeton University Press.

Lee, Martin A. (2012), *Smoke Signals: A Social History of Marijuana – Medical, Recreational, and Scientific*, New York: Scribner.

Leiss, William, Stephen Kline, and Sut Jhally (1986), *Social Communication in Advertising: Persons, Products, & Images of Well Being*, Toronto and New York: Methuen.

Leonard-Barton, Dorothy (1981), "Voluntary Simplicity Lifestyles and Energy Conservation," *Journal of Consumer Research*, 8 (December), 243–252.

Levine, Bruce (2013), *The Fall of the House of Dixie: The Civil War and the Social Revolution That Transformed the South*, New York: Random House.

Levy, Sidney J. (1959), "Symbols for Sale," *Harvard Business Review*, 37 (4), 117–124.

Levy, Sidney J. (1981), "Interpreting Consumer Mythology: A Structural Approach to Consumer Behavior," *Journal of Marketing*, 45 (3), 49–61.

Lewis, Jan (1987), "The Republican Wife: Virtue and Seduction in the Early Republic," *William and Mary Quarterly*, 44 (July), 689–721.

Life (1943a), "Bell Telephone System," (January 4), 3.

Life (1943b), "Soft-Lite Lenses," (February 1), 3.

Life (1943c), "Lane Cedar Hope Chest," (February 1), 8.

Life (1945), "Lane Cedar Hope Chest," (January 29), 61.

Life (1958), "Rocketing Births: Business Bonanza," (June 15), 83–89.

Life (1959), "A New, $10 Billion Power: The U.S. Teen-Age Consumer," (August 31), 78–85.

Lindgren, James and Justin L. Heather (2002), "Counting Guns in Early America," *William & Mary Law Review*, 43 (5), 1777–1842.

Lindquist, David P. and Caroline C. Warren (1993), *Colonial Revival Furniture*, Radnor, PA: Wallace-Homestead Book Company.

Lockridge, Kenneth A. (1974), *Literacy in Colonial New England*, New York: Norton.

Low, George S. and Ronald A. Fullerton (1994), "Brands, Brand Management, and the Brand Manager System: A Critical-Historical Evaluation," *Journal of Marketing Research*, 31 (2), 173–190.

Lubar, Steven (1998), "Men/Women/Production/Consumption," in *His and Hers: Gender, Consumption, and Technology*, eds. Roger Horowitz and Arwen Mohun, Charlottesville, VA and London: University Press of Virginia, 7–37.

Lubin, David (1993), "Lilly Martin Spencer's Domestic Genre Painting in Antebellum America," in *American Iconology: New Approaches to Nineteenth-Century Art and Literature*, ed. David C. Miller, New Haven, CT: Yale University Press, 135–162.

Luedicke, Marius K., Craig. J. Thompson, and Markus Giesler (2010), "Consumer Identity Work as Moral Protagonism: How Myth and Ideology Animate a Brand-mediated Moral Conflict," *Journal of Consumer Research*, 36 (6), 1016–1032.

Lupton, Ellen (1993), *Mechanical Brides: Women and Machines from Home to Office*, New York: Cooper-Hewitt National Museum of Design, Smithsonian Institution, and Princeton Architectural Press.

Lynd, Robert S. and Helen Merrell Lynd (1929), *Middletown: A Study of Contemporary American Culture*, New York: Harcourt, Brace and Company.

Lynd, Robert S. and Helen Merrell Lynd (1937), *Middletown in Transition: A Study of Cultural Conflicts*, New York: Harcourt, Brace and Company.

Lysaker, Richard L. and Joseph E. Bradley (1957), "What Is a Pictorial Projective Technique," *Journal of Marketing*, 21 (3), 339–340.

Maher, Bill (2002), *When You Ride ALONE You Ride with Bin Laden: What the Government SHOULD be Telling us to Help Fight the War on Terrorism*, Beverly Hills, CA: New Millennium Press.

Maier, Pauline (1973), *From Resistance to Revolution: Colonial Radicals and the Development of American Opposition to Britain, 1765–1776*, New York: Vintage.

Main, Gloria L. (1975), "Probate Records as a Source for Early American History," *William and Mary Quarterly*, 32 (1), 89–99.

Main, Gloria L. (1982), *Tobacco Colony: Life in Early Maryland, 1650–1720*, Princeton, NJ: Princeton University Press.

Main, Gloria L. (1994), "Gender, Work, and Wages in Colonial New England," *William and Mary Quarterly*, 51 (1), 39–66.

Main, Jackson Turner (1965), *The Social Structure of Revolutionary America*, Princeton, NJ: Princeton University Press.

Maniates, Michael (2002), "In Search of Consumptive Resistance: The Voluntary Simplicity Movement," in *Confronting Consumption*, eds. Thomas Princen, Michael Maniates, and Ken Conca, Cambridge, MA: The MIT Press, 199–235.

Mann, Maybelle (1977), *Francis William Edmonds: Mammon and Art*, New York: Garland Publishing, Inc.

Marchand, Roland (1985), *Advertising the American Dream: Making Way for Modernity, 1920–1940*, Berkeley, CA: University of California Press.

Marchand, Roland (1994), "Suspended in Time: Mom-and-Pop Groceries, Chain Stores, and National Advertising during the World War II Interlude," in *Produce and Conserve, Share and Play Square: The Grocer and the Consumer on the Home-Front Battlefield during World War II*, ed. Barbara McLean Ward, Portsmouth, NH: Strawbery Banke Museum, 117–139.

Marling, Karal Ann (1988), *George Washington Slept Here: Colonial Revivals and American Culture, 1876–1986*, Cambridge, MA: Harvard University Press.

Marsh, Margaret (1988), "Suburban Men and Masculine Domesticity, 1870–1915." *American Quarterly*, 40 (2), 165–186.

Martin, Ann Smith (1993), "Makers, Buyers, and Users: Consumerism as a Material Culture Framework," *Winterthur Portfolio*, 28 (2/3), 141–157.

Martin, Diane M., John W. Schouten, and James H. McAlexander (2006), "Claiming the Throttle: Multiple Femininities in a Hyper-Masculine Subculture," *Consumption, Markets and Culture*, 9 (3), 171–205.

Masten, April F. (2004), "*Shake Hands?* Lilly Martin Spencer and the Politics of Art," *American Quarterly*, 56 (2), 348–394.

Matherly, Walter J. (1942), "The Development of Consumer Economics," *Southern Economic Journal*, 9 (1), 53–61.

Matthews, Kristin L. (2009), "One Nation Over Coals: Cold War Nationalism and the Barbecue," *American Studies*, 50 (3/4), 5–34.

McCabe, James D. (1876), *The Illustrated History of the Centennial Exposition*, Philadelphia, PA: The National Publishing Company.

McCracken, Grant (1986), "Culture and Consumption: A Theoretical Account of the Structure and Movement of the Cultural Meaning of Consumer Goods," *Journal of Consumer Research*, 13 (June), 71–84.

McCracken, Grant (1988), *Culture and Consumption: New Approaches to the Symbolic Character of Consumer Goods and Attitudes*, Bloomington, IN: Indiana University Press.

McCracken, Grant (1989a), "'Homeyness': A Cultural Account of One Constellation of Consumer Goods and Meanings," in *Interpretive Consumer Research*, ed. Elizabeth C. Hirschman, Provo, UT: Association for Consumer Research, 168–183.

McCracken, Grant (1989b), "Who Is the Celebrity Endorser? Cultural Foundations of the Endorsement Process," *Journal of Consumer Research*, 16 (December), 310–321.

McCusker, John J. (1999), "Measuring Colonial Gross Domestic Product: An Introduction," *William and Mary Quarterly*, 56 (1), 3–8.

McCusker, John J. and Russell R. Menard (1985), *The Economy of British America, 1607–1789*, Chapel Hill, NC: The University of North Carolina Press.

McFadden, Margaret (2003), "'WARNING – Do Not Risk Federal Arrest by Looking Glum!': *Ballyhoo* Magazine and the Cultural Politics of Early 1930s Humor," *The Journal of American Culture*, 26 (1), 124–133.

McFeely, Mary Drake (1994), "The War in the Kitchen," in *Produce and Conserve, Share and Play Square: The Grocer and the Consumer on the Home-Front Battlefield during World War II*, ed. Barbara McLean Ward, Portsmouth, NH: Strawbery Banke Museum, 105–116.

McKearin, Helen and Kenneth M. Wilson (1978), *American Bottles & Flasks and Their Ancestry*, New York: Crown Publishers, Inc.

McKendrick, Neil, John Brewer, and J.H. Plumb, eds. (1982), *The Birth of a Consumer Society: The Commercialization of Eighteenth-Century England*, Bloomington, IN: Indiana University Press.

McMahon, Theresa S. (1925), *Social and Economic Standards of Living*, Boston, MA: D.C. Heath and Company.

McNair, Malcolm P. (1957), "Melvin T. Copeland," *Journal of Marketing*, 22 (2), 181–184.

Meir, August and Elliott Rudwick (1969), "The Boycott Movement Against Jim Crow Streetcars in the South, 1900–1906," *Journal of American History*, 55 (4), 756–775.

Meir, August and Elliott Rudwick (1973), "Negro Boycotts of Segregated Streetcars in Virginia, 1904–1907," *The Virginia Magazine of History and Biography*, 81 (4), 479–487.

Mencken, H.L. (1949), *A Mencken Chrestomathy*, New York: Alfred P. Knopf.

Merriam-Webster (2017a), "Meaning," www.merriam-webster.com/dictionary/meaning.

Merriam-Webster (2017b), "Gender" and "Gendered," www.merriam-webster.com/dictionary/gender.

Milbank, Caroline Rennolds (2000), "'Ahead of the World:' New York City Fashion," in *Art and the Empire City: New York, 1825–1861*, eds. Catherine Hoover Voorsanger and John K. Howat, New York: The Metropolitan Museum of Art, 243–257.

Mills, C. Wright (1951), *White Collar: The American Middle Classes*, New York: Oxford University Press.

Minneapolis Fed (2017), "CPI Calculator Information," Federal Reserve Bank of Minneapolis, www.minneapolisfed.org/community/teaching-aids/cpi-calculator-information/consumer-price-index-1800.

Miron, Jeffrey A. and Jeffrey Zweibel (1991), "Alcohol Consumption During Prohibition," *American Economic Review*, 81 (2), 242–247.

Moisio, Risto, Eric J. Arnould, and James W. Gentry (2013), "Productive Consumption in the Class-Mediated Construction of Domestic Masculinity: Do-It-Yourself (DIY) Home Improvement in Men's Identity Work," *Journal of Consumer Research*, 40 (August), 298–316.

Moisio, Risto and Mariam Beruchashvili (2016), "Mancaves and Masculinity," *Journal of Consumer Culture*, 16 (3), 656–676.

Mokyr, Joel (2000), "'More Work for Mother?' Knowledge and Household Behavior, 1870–1945," *The Journal of Economic History*, 60 (1), 1–41.

Monkhouse, Christopher (1983), "The Spinning Wheel as Artifact, Symbol, and Source of Design," in *Victorian Furniture*, ed. Kenneth L. Ames, Philadelphia, PA: Victorian Society of America, 155–172.

Montgomery Ward (1895), *Montgomery Ward & Co. Catalogue and Buyer's Guide 1895, 2008 Unabridged Facsimile Edition*, New York: Skyhorse Publishing.

Moore, Karl and Susan Reid (2008), "The Birth of the Brand: 4000 Years of Branding," *Business History*, 50 (4), 419–432.

Morgan, Edmund S. (1967), "The Puritan Ethic and the American Revolution," *William and Mary Quarterly*, 24 (4), 3–43.

Mosher, Max (2012), "Window Dressing: The Art and Artists," *Utne Reader* (March/April), www.utne.com/media/window-dressing-zm0z12mazsie.aspx?PageId=1#axzz2ye9EYBtr.

Moskin, J. Robert (1958), "The American Male: Why Women Dominate Him?" *Look*, (February 4), 77–80.

Moskowitz, Marina (2004), *Standard of Living: The Measure of the Middle Class*, Baltimore, MD: Johns Hopkins University Press.

Motel, Seth (2014), "6 Facts About Marijuana," Pew Research Center, (November 5), www.pewresearch.org/fact-tank/2014/11/05/6-facts-about-marijuana/.

Mukerji, Chandra (1983), *From Graven Images: Patterns of Modern Materialism*, New York: Columbia University Press.

Munsinger, Gary M., Jean E. Weber, and Richard W. Hansen (1975), "Joint Home Purchasing Decisions by Husbands and Wives," *Journal of Consumer Research*, 1 (4), 60–66.

Murdoch, David Hamilton (2001), *The American West: The Invention of a Myth*, Reno and Las Vegas, NV: University of Nevada Press.

Music Trade Review, The (1916), "Opening of the Palatial New Home of Lyon & Healy," (July 19), reprinted by Mechanical Music Registration Project, www.mechanicalmusicpress.com/registry/empress/empress_p01_lyon-healy.htm.

Musser, Charles (1990), *The Emergence of Cinema: The American Screen to 1907*, New York: Charles Scribner's Sons.

Nader, Ralph (1965), *Unsafe at Any Speed: The Designed-in Dangers of the American Automobile*, New York: Grossman.

NARA (1994), *Powers of Persuasion: Poster Art from World War II*, online sample from more extensive exhibit by National Archives and Records Administration, (May 1994 to February 1995), www.archives.gov/exhibits/powers_of_persuasion/powers_of_persuasion_home.html.

Nash, Gary B. (1979), *The Urban Crucible: Social Change, Political Consciousness, and the Origins of the American Revolution*, Cambridge, MA: Harvard University Press.

NCSL (2016), "State Medical Marijuana Laws," National Conference of State Legislatures (November 11), www.ncsl.org/research/health/state-medical-marijuana-laws.aspx.

Neil, Dan (2008), "Hummer: Requiem for a Heavyweight?," *Los Angeles Times* (June 7), C1, C2.

Nelson, Christina H. (1980), "Transfer-Printed Creamware and Pearlware for the American Market," *Winterthur Portfolio*, 15 (Summer), 93–115.

Nelson, Derek (1991), *The Posters That Won the War*, Osceola, WI: Motorbooks International.

Nettels, Curtis P. (1963), *The Roots of American Civilization*, New York: Appleton-Century-Crofts.

Neuhaus, Jessamyn (1999), "The Way to a Man's Heart: Gender Roles, Domestic Ideology, and Cookbooks in the 1950s," *Journal of Social History*, 32 (3), 529–555.

New York Times (2014), "Repeal Prohibition, Again," (July 26), www.nytimes.com/interactive/2014/07/27/opinion/sunday/high-time-marijuana-legalization.html.

Newman, Joshua I. (2007), "Old Times There Are Not Forgotten: Sport, Identity, and the Confederate Flag in the Dixie South," *Sociology of Sport Journal*, 24 (3), 261–282.

Nicosia, Franco M. (1966), *Consumer Decision Processes: Marketing and Advertising Implications*, Englewood Cliffs, NJ: Prentice-Hall, Inc.

Nicks, Denver (2014), "Meet the App That Helps You Put Your Money Where Your Mouth Is," *Time* (September 23), http://time.com/3418502/shopping-beer-buypartisan-politics/.

NORML (2017a), "State Laws," http://norml.org/laws.

NORML (2017b), "National Polls," National http://norml.org/library/national-legalization-polls.

Norton, Mary Beth (1980), *Liberty's Daughters: The Revolutionary Experience of American Women, 1750–1800*, Boston, MA: Little, Brown and Company.

Norton, Mary Beth (2016), "The Seventh Tea Ship," *William and Mary Quarterly*, 73 (4), 681–710.

Nystrom, Paul H. (1929), *Economic Principles of Consumption*, New York: The Ronald Press Company.

Officer, Lawrence H. and Samuel H. Williamson (2017), "Computing 'Real Value' Over Time with a Conversion Between U.K. Pounds and U.S. Dollars, 1774 to Present," MeasuringWorth, www.measuringworth.com/exchange/.

O'Keefe, Anne Marie and Richard W. Pollay (1996), "Deadly Targeting of Women in Promoting Cigarettes," *Journal of the American Medical Women's Association*, 51 (1/2), 67–69.

Okrent, Daniel (2010), *Last Call: The Rise and Fall of Prohibition*, New York: Scribner.

O'Leary, Elizabeth L. (1996), *At Beck and Call: The Representation of Domestic Servants in Nineteenth-Century American Painting*, Washington, D.C.: Smithsonian Institution Press.

Olton, Charles S. (1975), *Artisans for Independence: Philadelphia Mechanics and the American Revolution*, Syracuse, NY: Syracuse University Press.

Orbach, William (1982), "Shattering the Shackles of Powerlessness: The Debate Surrounding the Anti-Nazi Boycott of 1933–41," *Modern Judaism*, 2 (2), 149–169.

Oreskes, Naomi and Erik M. Conway (2010), *Merchants of Doubt: How a Handful of Scientists Obscured the Truth on Issues from Tobacco Smoke to Global Warming*, New York: Bloomsbury Press.

Packard, Vance (1957), *The Hidden Persuaders*, New York: David McKay.

Packard, Vance (1959), *The Status Seekers*, New York: David McKay.

Packard, Vance (1960), *The Waste Makers*, New York: Pocket Books.

Page, Ida Lillian (1929), "The Cross Roads Cigarette Advertisements in Magazines," *Education*, 50 (September), 57–59.

Palamountain, Joseph Cornwall (1955), *The Politics of Distribution*, Cambridge, MA: Harvard University Press.

Palmer, Arthur Judson (1956), *Riding High: The Story of the Bicycle*, New York: E.P. Dutton.

Parsons, Elizabeth (2014), "Pioneering Consumer Economist: Elizabeth Ellis Hoyt (1893–1980)," *Journal of Historical Research in Marketing*, 5 (3), 334–350.

Patten, Simon N. (1901), *Consumption of Wealth*, Philadelphia, PA: University of Pennsylvania.

Paulson, Erika L. and Mary E. Schramm (2017), "Electric Appliance Advertising: The Role of the Good Housekeeping Institute," *Journal of Historical Research in Marketing*, 9 (1), 41–65.

PBS Online (2004), "John Wanamaker," *They Made America*, WGBH Boston, www.pbs.org/wgbh/theymadeamerica/whomade/wanamaker_lo.html.

Peck, Amelia (2000), "The Products of Empire: Shopping for Home Decorations in New York City," in *Art and the Empire City: New York, 1825–1861*, eds. Catherine Hoover Voorsanger and John K. Howat, New York: The Metropolitan Museum of Art, 259–285.

Pells, Richard (2014), *War Babies: The Generation That Changed America*, La Vergne, TN: Cultural History Press.

Peñaloza, Lisa (1994), "Atravesando Fronteras/Border Crossings: A Critical Ethnographic Study of the Consumer Acculturation of Mexican Immigrants," *Journal of Consumer Research*, 21 (June), 32–53.

Pendergrast, Mark (2000), *For God, Country, and Coca-Cola: The Definitive History of the Great American Soft Drink and the Company That Makes It*, New York: Basic Books.

Perkins, Edwin J. (1988), *The Economy of Colonial America*, New York: Columbia University Press.

Perkins, Elizabeth A. (1991), "The Consumer Frontier: Household Consumption in Early Kentucky," *Journal of American History*, 78 (September), 486–510.

Peters, Harry T. (1942), *Currier & Ives: Printmakers to the American People*, Garden City, New York: Doubleday, Doran & Co., Inc.

Petty, Ross D. (1995), "Peddling the Bicycle in the 1890s: Mass Marketing Shifts into High Gear," *Journal of Macromarketing*, 15 (1), 32–46.

Petty, Ross D. (1997), "Women and the Wheel," *Cycle History: Proceedings of the 7th International Cycle History Conference*, ed. Rob van der Plas, San Francisco, CA: Cycle Publishing/Van der Plas Publications, 112–133.

Petty, Ross D. (2011), "The Codevelopment of Trademark Law and the Concept of Brand Marketing in the United States before 1946," *Journal of Macromarketing*, 31 (1), 85–99.

Petty, Ross D. (2012), "From Label to Trademark: The Legal Origins of the Concept of Brand Identity in Nineteenth Century America," *Journal of Historical Research in Marketing*, 4 (1), 129–153.

Pew Research Center (2008), "Women Call the Shots at Home; Public Mixed on Gender Roles in Jobs," Pew Research Social and Demographic Trends (September 25), www.pewsocialtrends.org/2008/09/25/women-call-the-shots-at-home-public-mixed-on-gender-roles-in-jobs/.

Pew Research Center (2014), "Political Polarization in the American Public," Pew Research Center for the People and the Press, (June 12), www.people-press.org/2014/06/12/political-polarization-in-the-American-public/.

Phipps, Claire (2015), "Walmart Removes Confederate Flag Merchandise from Stores," *Guardian*, (June 23), www.theguardian.com/us-news/2015/jun/23/walmart-removes-confederate-flag-merchandise-from-stores.

Piott, Steven L. (1981), "Missouri and the Beef Trust: Consumer Action and Investigation, 1902," *Missouri Historical Review*, 76 (1), 31–52.

Pollay, Richard W. (1985), "The Subsiding Sizzle: A Descriptive History of Print Advertising, 1900–1980," *Journal of Marketing*, 49 (3), 24–37.

Pollay, Richard W. (1987), "Insights into Consumer Behavior from Historical Studies of Advertising," in *Advances in Consumer Research*, Vol. 14, eds. Melanie Wallendorf and Paul Anderson, Provo, UT: Association for Consumer Research, 447–450.

Pollay, Richard W. (2011), "Biographic and Bibliographic Recollections Re: Collections and Contributions," *Journal of Historical Research in Marketing*, 3 (4), 507–527.

Pope, Daniel (1983), *The Making of Modern Advertising*, New York: Basic Books.

Porter, Glenn and Harold C. Livesay (1971), *Merchants and Manufacturers: Studies in the Changing Structure of Nineteenth-Century Marketing*, Baltimore, MD: Johns Hopkins Press,

Potter, David M. (1954), *People of Plenty: Economic Abundance and the American Character*, Chicago, IL: University of Chicago Press.

Potus08blog (2008), "Barack Obama's Small Towns Guns and Religion Comments," (April 11), www.youtube.com/watch?v=DTxXUufI3jA.

Presbrey, Frank (1929), *The History and Development of Advertising*, Garden City, NY: Doubleday.

Prown, Jules David (1980), "Style as Evidence," *Winterthur Portfolio*, 15 (Spring), 197–210.

Prown, Jules David (1982), "Mind in Matter: An Introduction to Material Culture Theory and Method," *Winterthur Portfolio*, 17 (Spring), 1–19.

Putnam, Robert D. (2001), *Bowling Alone: The Collapse and Revival of American Community*, New York: Touchstone.

Rand, Ayn (1943), *The Fountainhead*, Indianapolis, IN: Bobbs-Merrill Company.

Randel, William Peirce (1973), *The American Revolution: Mirror of a People*, Maplewood, NJ: Hammond.

Rassuli, Kathleen M. and Stanley C. Hollander (1986), "Desire – Induced, Innate, Insatiable?" *Journal of Macromarketing*, 6 (2), 4–24.

Rassuli, Kathleen M. and Stanley C. Hollander (1987), "Comparative History as a Research Tool in Consumer Behavior," in *Advances in Consumer Research*, Vol. 14, eds. Melanie Wallendorf and Paul F. Anderson, Provo, UT: Association for Consumer Research, 442–446.

Rawls, Walton (1979), *The Great Book of Currier & Ives' America*, New York: Abbeville Press.

Reich, Charles A. (1970), *The Greening of America*, New York: Random House.

Renouard, Joe (2007), "The Predicaments of Plenty: Interwar Intellectuals and American Consumerism," *The Journal of American Culture*, 30 (1), 54–67.

Resseguie, Harry E. (1964), "A.T. Stewart's Marble Palace – The Cradle of the Department Store," *New York Historical Society Quarterly* 48, (April), 131–162.

Rhoads, William B. (1977). *The Colonial Revival*, New York: Garland Publishing.

Richardson, Alan J. (2008), "Strategies in the Development of Accounting History as an Academic Discipline," *Accounting History*, 13 (August), 247–280.

Richins, Marsha L. (1994a), "Valuing Things: The Public and Private Meanings of Possessions," *Journal of Consumer Research*, 21 (December), 504–521.

Richins, Marsha L. (1994b), "Special Possessions and the Expression of Material Values," *Journal of Consumer Research*, 21 (December), 522–533.

Riesman, David (1950), *The Lonely Crowd: A Study of the Changing American Character*, New Haven, CT: Yale University Press.

Ritchie, Donald A. (1995), *Doing Oral History*, New York: Twayne Publishers.

Robinson, Eric (1987), "Matthew Boulton and Josiah Wedgwood, Apostles of Fashion," in *Business in the Age of Reason*, eds. R.P.T. Davenport-Hines and Jonathan Liebenau, London: Frank Cass, 98–114.

Rook, Dennis W. (1985), "The Ritual Dimension of Consumer Behavior," *Journal of Consumer Research*, 12 (3), 251–264.

Roosens, Eugeen (1995), "Interest Groups with a Noble Face," in *Marketing in a Multicultural World: Ethnicity, Nationalism, and Cultural Identity*, eds. Janeen Arnold Costa and Gary J. Bamossy, Thousand Oaks, CA: SAGE Publications, Inc, 126–141.

Rorabaugh, W.J. (1979), *The Alcoholic Republic: An American Tradition*, Oxford, UK: Oxford University Press.

Rorty, James (1934), *Our Master's Voice*, New York: John Day.

Rose, Alexander (2008), *American Rifle: A Biography*, New York: Delacorte Press.

Rose, Gillian (2012), *Visual Methodologies: An Introduction to Researching with Visual Materials*, London: Sage Publications.

Roszak, Theodore (1969), *The Making of a Counter Culture: Reflections on the Technocratic Society and its Youthful Opposition*, Garden City, NY: Doubleday, Inc.

Roth, Rodris (1964), "The Colonial Revival and "Centennial Furniture," *The Art Quarterly*, 27 (1), 57–81.

Rothwell, N.D. (1955), "Motivation Research Revisited," *Journal of Marketing*, 20 (2), 150–154.

Rotundo, E. Anthony (1993), *American Manhood: Transformations in Masculinity from the Revolution to the Modern Era*, New York: Basic Books.

Rozin, Paul, Julia M. Hormes, Myles S. Faith, and Brian Wansink (2012), "Is Meat Male? A Quantitative Multimethod Framework to Establish Metaphoric Relationships," *Journal of Consumer Research*, 39 (October), 629–643.

Rumbo, Joseph D. (2002), "Consumer Resistance in a World of Advertising Clutter: The Case of Adbusters," *Psychology & Marketing*, 19, (2), 121–126.

Rutherford, Janice Williams (2003), *Selling Mrs. Consumer: Christine Frederick and the Rise of Household Efficiency*, Atlanta, GA: University of Georgia Press.

Ryan, Mary P. (1975), *Womanhood in America: From Colonial Times to the Present*, New York: Franklin Watts.

Salmon, Marylynn (1982), "Women and Property in South Carolina: The Evidence from Marriage Settlements, 1730 to 1830," *William and Mary Quarterly*, 39 (October), 655–685.

Sandlin, Jennifer A. and Jamie L. Callahan (2009), "Deviance, Dissonance, and Détournement: Culture Jammers' Use of Emotion in Consumer Resistance," *Journal of Consumer Culture*, 9 (1), 79–115.

Savitt, Ronald (1980), "Historical Research in Marketing," *Journal of Marketing*, 44 (Fall), 52–58.

Sayer, Liana C. (2010), "Trends in Housework," in *Dividing the Domestic: Men, Women, and Household Work in Cross-National Perspective*, eds. Judith Treas and Sonja Brobnic, Stanford, CA: Stanford University Press, 19–40.

Scanlon, Jennifer (1995), *Inarticulate Longings: The Ladies' Home Journal, Gender, and the Promises of Consumer Culture*, New York and London: Routledge.

Schlesinger, Arthur M. (1917/1957), *The Colonial Merchants and the American Revolution*, New York: Frederick Ungar.

Schmidt, James M. (2009), *Lincoln's Labels: America's Best-Known Brands and the Civil War*, Roseville, MN: Edinborough Press.

Schmidt, Leigh Eric (1991), "The Commercialization of the Calendar: American Holidays and the Culture of Consumption, 1870–1930," *The Journal of American History*, 78 (December), 887–916.

Schoelwer, Susan Prendergast (1985), "Curious Relics and Quaint Scenes: The Colonial Revival at Chicago's Great Fair," *The Colonial Revival in America*, ed. Alan Axelrod, New York: W.W. Norton, 184–216.

Scholten, Catherine M. (1977), "On the Importance of the Obstetric Art: Changing Customs of Childbirth in America, 1760–1825," *William and Mary Quarterly*, 34 (July), 426–444.

Schor, Juliet B. (1998), *The Overspent American: Upscaling, Downshifting, and the New Consumer*, New York: Basic Books.

Schouten, John W. (1991), "Life Among the Winnebago," in *Highways and Buyways: Naturalistic Research from the Consumer Behavior Odyssey*, ed. Russell W. Belk, Provo, UT: Association for Consumer Research, 13.

Schouten, John W. and James H. McAlexander (1995), "Subcultures of Consumption: An Ethnography of the New Bikers," *Journal of Consumer Research*, 22 (June), 43–61.

Schroeder, Fred E.H. (1998), "*Say Cheese!* The Revolution in the Aesthetics of Smiles," *Journal of Popular Culture*, 32 (2), 103–145.

Schroeder, Jonathan E. and Janet L. Borgerson (1998), "Marketing Images of Gender: A Visual Analysis," *Consumption, Markets and Culture*, 2 (2), 161–201.

Schroeder, Jonathan E. and Detlev Zwick (2004), "Mirrors of Masculinity: Representation and Identity in Advertising Images," *Consumption, Markets and Culture*, 7 (1), 21–52.

Schudson, Michael (1984), *Advertising, The Uneasy Persuasion*, New York: Basic Books, Inc.

Schudson, Michael (1991), "Delectable Materialism: Were the Critics of Consumer Culture Wrong All Along?," *The American Prospect*, 5 (Spring), 26–35.

Schwarzkopf, Stefan (2011), "The Consumer as 'Voter,' 'Judge,' and 'Jury': Historical Origins and Political Consequences of a Marketing Myth," *Journal of Macromarketing*, 31 (1), 8–18.

Scott, Linda M., Jason Chambers, and Katherine Sredl (2006), "The Monticello Correction: Consumption in History," in *Handbook of Qualitative Research Methods in Marketing*, ed. Russell W. Belk, Cheltenham, UK: Edward Elgar Publishing, 219–229.

Scott, Walter Dill (1903), *The Theory of Advertising*, Boston, MA: Small, Maynard.

Scott, Walter Dill (1908), *The Psychology of Advertising*, Boston, MA: Small, Maynard.

Sears, Roebuck and Company (1897), *1897 Sears Roebuck & Co. Catalogue, 2007 Facsimile Edition*, New York: Skyhorse Publishing.

Seaton, Beverly (1985), "A Pedigree for a New Century: The Colonial Experience in Popular Historical Novels, 1890–1910," in *The Colonial Revival in America*, ed. Alan Axelrod, New York: W.W. Norton, 278–293.

Seifried, Chad S. and Ari de Wilde (2014), "Building the Garden and Making Arena Sports Big Time: 'Tex' Rickard and His Legacy in Sports Marketing," *Journal of Macromarketing*, 34 (4), 452–470.

Shammas, Carole (1978), "Constructing a Wealth Distribution from Probate Records," *Journal of Interdisciplinary History*, 9 (2), 297–307.

Shammas, Carole (1982a), "How Self-Sufficient Was Early America?," *Journal of Interdisciplinary History*, 13 (Autumn), 247–272.

Shammas, Carole (1982b), "Consumer Behavior in Colonial America," *Social Science History*, 6 (Winter), 67–86.

Sharp, Harry and Paul Mott (1956), "Consumer Decisions in the Metropolitan Family," *Journal of Marketing*, 23 (October), 149–156.

Shaw, Deirdre and Terry Newholm (2002), "Voluntary Simplicity and the Ethics of Consumption," *Psychology & Marketing*, 19 (2), 167–185.

Sherry, John F., Jr. (1983), "Gift Giving in Anthropological Perspective," *Journal of Consumer Research*, 10 (2), 157–168.

Shi, David E. (1985), *The Simple Life: Plain Living and High Thinking in American Culture*, New York: Oxford University Press.

Shrum, Rebecca K. (2012), "Selling Mr. Coffee: Design, Gender, and the Branding of a Kitchen Appliance," *Winterthur Portfolio*, 46 (4), 271–298.

Shumway, David R. and Ellen Messer-Davidow (1991), "Disciplinarity: An Introduction," *Poetics Today*, 12 (Summer), 201–225.

Simmel, Georg (1904/1957), "Fashion," *The American Journal of Sociology*, 62 (6), 541–558.

Sinclair Andrew (1962), *Prohibition: The Era of Excess*, Boston, MA: Little, Brown and Company.

Sitikoff, Harvard (1994), "The American Home Front," in *Produce and Conserve, Share and Play Square: The Grocer and the Consumer on the Home-Front Battlefield during World War II*, ed. Barbara McLean Ward, Portsmouth, NH: Strawbery Banke Museum, 36–56.

Slater, Don (1997), *Consumer Culture and Modernity*, Cambridge, UK: Polity Press.

Sloman, Larry "Ratso" (1998), *Reefer Madness: The History of Marijuana in America*, New York: St. Martin's Press.

Slotkin, Richard (1992), *Gunfighter Nation: The Myth of the Frontier in Twentieth-Century America*, New York: Atheneum.

Smith, Hedrick (2012), *Who Stole the American Dream?* New York: Random House.

Smith, Ruth Ann and David S. Lux (1993), "Historical Method in Consumer Research: Developing Causal Explanations of Change," *Journal of Consumer Research*, 19 (4), 595–610.

Snyder, Jeffrey B. (1995), *Historical Staffordshire: American Patriots and Views*, Atglen, PA: Schiffer Publishing Ltd.

Sobal, Jeffery (2005), "Men, Meat, and Marriage: Models of Masculinity," *Food and Foodways*, 13 (1/2), 135–158.

Sobel, Robert (1978), *They Satisfy: The Cigarette in American Life*, Garden City, NY: Anchor Books.

Spalding, John W. (1963), "1928: Radio Becomes a Mass Advertising Medium," *Journal of Broadcasting*, 8 (1), 31–44.

Spellman, Susan V. (2016), *Cornering the Market: Independent Grocers and Innovation in American Small Business*, New York: Oxford University Press.

Spira, S.F. (2001), *The History of Photography as Seen Through the Spira Collection*, New York: Aperture.

Spitzer, Robert J. (2015), "Why Assault Rife Sales Are Booming," *Los Angeles Times* (June 12), A17.

Springer, Chris (1993), "The Troubled Resurgence of the Confederate Flag," *History Today*, 43 (June), 7–9.

Spruill, Julia Cherry (1938/1972), *Women's Life and Work in the Southern Colonies*, New York: Norton.

Stearns, Peter N. (2001), *Consumerism in World History: The Global Transformation of Desire*, London and New York: Routledge.

Stebbins Jr., Theodore E., Carol Troyen, and Trevor J. Fairbrother (1983), *A New World: Masterpieces of American Painting, 1760–1910*, Boston, MA: Museum of Fine Arts.

Steckel, Richard H. (1999), "Nutritional Status in the Colonial American Economy," *William and Mary Quarterly*, 56 (1), 31–52.

Stevenson, Katherine Cole and H. Ward Jandl (1986), *Houses by Mail: A Guide to Houses from Sears, Roebuck and Company*, Washington, D.C.: The Preservation Press.

Steward, O.M. (1904), "Richmond's Jim Crow Cars," *The Richmond Planet* (April 30), http://chroniclingamerica.loc.gov/lccn/sn84025841/1904-04-30/ed-1/seq-1/.

Stigler, George J. (1954), "The Early History of Empirical Studies of Consumer Behavior," *The Journal of Political Economy*, 62 (2), 95–113.

Stillinger, Elizabeth (1980), *The Antiquers*, New York: Alfred A. Knopf.

St. James, Elaine (1996), *Living the Simple Life: A Guide to Scaling Down and Enjoying More*, New York: Hyperion.

Stole, Inger L. (2003), "Televised Consumption: Women, Advertisers and the Early Daytime Television Industry," *Consumption, Markets and Culture*, 6 (1), 65–80.

Stole, Inger L. (2006), *Advertising on Trial: Consumer Activism and Corporate Public Relations in the 1930s*, Urbana, IL: University of Illinois Press.

Stole, Inger L. (2012), *Advertising at War: Business, Consumers, and Government in the 1940s*, Urbana, IL: University of Illinois Press.

Strasser, Susan (1982), *Never Done: A History of American Housework*, New York: Henry Holt and Company.

Strasser, Susan (1989), *Satisfaction Guaranteed: The Making of the American Mass Market*, New York: Pantheon Books.

Strategic Vision (2012), "Democrat vs. Republican: Who's Buying What Car?" (March 29), www.businesswire.com/news/home/20120329005040/en/Democrat-vs.-Republican-Who's-Buying-Car-Answers.

Sturken, Marita and Lisa Cartwright (2002), *Practices of Looking: An Introduction to Visual Culture*, Oxford, UK: Oxford University Press.

Swiencicki, Mark A. (1998), "Consuming Brotherhood: Men's Culture, Style and Recreation as Consumer Culture, 1880–1930," *Journal of Social History*, 31 (4), 773–808.

Swift, Art (2016), "Support for Legal Marijuana Use Up to 60% in U.S.," Gallup Poll Social Series, (October 19), www.gallup.com/poll/196550/support-legal-marijuana.aspx?g_source=POLITICS&g_medium=topic&g_campaign=tiles.

Tabuchi, Hiroko (2016), "'Rolling Coal' in Diesel Trucks, to Rebel and Provoke," *New York Times*, (September 5), A1, A11.

Tadajewski, Mark (2006), "Remembering Motivation Research: Toward an Alternative Genealogy of Interpretive Consumer Research," *Marketing Theory*, 6 (4), 429–466.

Tadajewski, Mark (2013), "Promoting the Consumer Society: Ernest Dichter, the Cold War, and FBI," *Journal of Historical Research in Marketing*, 5 (2), 192–211.

Tadajewski, Mark (2014), "Helen Woodward and Hazel Kyrk: Economic Radicalism, Consumption Symbolism and Female Contributions to Marketing Theory and Advertising Practice," *Journal of Historical Research in Marketing*, 5 (3), 385–412.

Taylor, Jason E. (2007), "Buy Now! Buy Here!: The Rise and Fall of the Patriotic Blue Eagle Emblem, 1933–1935," *Essays in Economic & Business History*, Vol. 25, 117–130.

Teitelman, S. Robert, Patricia A. Halfpenny, and Ronald W. Fuchs II (2010), *Success to America: Creamware for the American Market*, Woodbridge, UK: Antique Collectors' Club.

Tharp, Bruce M. (2007), "Valued Amish Possessions: Expanding Material Culture and Consumption," *The Journal of American Culture*, 30 (1), 38–53.

The Met (2016), "About the Met," Metropolitan Museum of Art, www.metmuseum.org/about-the-met.

Thompson, Bob (1998), "Consumed," *Washington Post Magazine*, (December 20), W10–15, W25–30.

Thompson, Craig J. (1996), "Caring Consumers: Gendered Consumption Meanings and the Juggling Lifestyle," *Journal of Consumer Research*, 22 (March), 388–407.

Thompson, Craig J. and Gokcen Coskuner-Balli (2007), "Countervailing Market Responses to Corporate Co-Optation and the Ideological Recruitment of Consumption Communities," *Journal of Consumer Research*, 34 (2), 135–152.

Thompson, Paul (1988), *The Voice of the Past: Oral History*, Oxford, UK: Oxford University Press.

Thoreau, Henry David (1854/1971), *Walden; Or, Life in the Woods*, Princeton, NJ: Princeton University Press.

Tiller, LLC (2014), "Nationwide Survey Finds: Americans Believe Environmental Issues Pose Greater Long-Term Threat to Their Health and Well-Being Than Terrorism or Global Epidemics like Ebola," (December), www.prnewswire.com/news-releases/nationwide-survey-finds-Americans-believe-environmental-issues-pose-greater-long-term-threat-to-their-health-and-well-being-than-terrorism-or-global-epidemics-like-ebola-300014118.html.

Time (1931), "Hooey," (December 14), 44.

Tipple, John (1959), "The Anatomy of Prejudice: Origins of the Robber Baron Legend," *Business History Review*, 33 (4), 510–523.

Toll, Benjamin A. and Pamela M. Ling (2005), "The Virginia Slims Identity Crisis: An Inside Look at Tobacco Marketing to Women," *Tobacco Control*, 14 (June), 172–180.

Tunis, Edwin (1965), *Colonial Craftsmen and the Beginnings of American Industry*, New York: Thomas Y. Crowell.

Twede, Diana (1997), "Uneeda Biscuit: The First Consumer Package?," *Journal of Macromarketing*, 17 (2), 82–88.

Twede, Diana (2012), "The Birth of Modern Packaging: Cartons, Cans and Bottles," *Journal of Historical Research in Marketing*, 4 (2), 245–272.

Twitchell, James B. (1999), *Lead Us into Temptation: The Triumph of American Materialism*, New York: Columbia University Press.

Twitchell, James B. and Kenneth Charles Ross (2006), *Where Men Hide*, New York: Columbia University Press.

UCSF (2006), "Virginia Slims Commercials, 1969 September, Philip Morris," Truth Tobacco Industry Documents, University of California San Francisco (June 16, 2006), www.industrydocumentslibrary.ucsf.edu/tobacco/docs/#id=yhyd0111.

Ulrich, Laurel Thatcher (1976), "Virtuous Women Found: New England Ministerial Literature, 1668–1735," *American Quarterly*, 28 (Spring), 20–40.

Ulrich, Laurel Thatcher (1982), *Good Wives: Image and Reality in the Lives of Women in Northern New England, 1650–1750*, New York: Alfred A. Knopf.

Ulrich, Laurel Thatcher (1990), *A Midwife's Tale: The Life of Martha Ballard, Based on Her Diary, 1785–1812*, New York: Vintage Books.

Ulrich, Laurel Thatcher (1998), "Wheels, Looms, and the Gender Division of Labor in Eighteenth-Century New England," *William and Mary Quarterly*, 55 (1), 3–38.

Ulrich, Laurel Thatcher (2001), *The Age of Homespun: Objects and Stories in the Creation of an American Myth*, New York: Vintage Books.

U.S. Bureau of the Census (1976), *Historical Statistics of the United States: Colonial Times to 1970*, New York: Basic Books.

U.S. Bureau of the Census (2015), "Historical Income Tables: People," (September 15), www.census.gov/hhes/www/income/data/historical/people/.

U.S. Bureau of the Census (2016a), "History: Fast Facts," www.census.gov/history/www/through_the_decades/fast_facts/.

U.S. Bureau of the Census (2016b), "Table 4. Population: 1790 to 1990," www.census.gov/population/censusdata/table-4.pdf

U.S. Bureau of the Census (2017), "Population," (January 1), www.census.gov/topics/population.html.

Valentine, Matt (2016), "Tallying the Costs of Open Carry," *The Atlantic*, (January 23), www.theatlantic.com/politics/archive/2016/01/open-carry-laws/436665/.

van Velzen, Susan (2003), "Hazel Kyrk and the Ethics of Consumption," in *Toward a Feminist Philosophy of Economics*, eds. Drucilla K. Barker and Edith Kuiper, Abingdon, UK: Routledge, 38–55.

Vanderbilt, Tom (1996), "It's a Wonderful (Simplified) Life," *Nation*, (January 22), 20.

Veblen, Thorstein (1899/1953), *Theory of the Leisure Class*, New York: New American Library.

Velazquez, Alyssa (2014), "Tupperware: An Open Container During a Decade of Containment," *Women's History Magazine*, 74 (Spring), 19–26.

Venkatesh, Alladi (1980), "Changing Roles of Women – A Life-Style Analysis," *Journal of Consumer Research*, 7 (September), 189–197.

Vincent, Susan (2003), "Preserving Domesticity: Reading Tupperware in Women's Changing Domestic, Social and Economic Roles," *The Canadian Review of Sociology and Anthropology*, 40 (2), 171–196.

Wagner, Charles (1904), *The Simple Life*, New York: McClure, Phillips & Co.

Walker, Robert H. (1971), *Life in the Age of Enterprise*, New York: Capricorn Books.

Wang, Wendy, Kim Parker, and Paul Taylor (2013), "Breadwinner Moms," Pew Research Center, Social & Economic Trends, (May 29), www.pewsocialtrends.org/2013/05/29/breadwinner-moms/.

Ward, Barbara McLean, ed. (1994a), *Produce and Conserve, Share and Play Square: The Grocer and the Consumer on the Home-Front Battlefield during World War II*, Portsmouth, NH: Strawbery Banke Museum.

Ward, Barbara McLean, ed. (1994b), "A Fair Share at a Fair Price: Rationing, Resource Management, and Price Controls during World War II," in *Produce and Conserve, Share and Play Square: The Grocer and the Consumer on the Home-Front Battlefield during World War II*, ed. Barbara McLean Ward, Portsmouth, NH: Strawbery Banke Museum, 79–103.

Watkins, George P. (1915), *Welfare as an Economic Quantity*, Boston, MA: Houghton Mifflin Co.

Watson, Alan D. (1981), "Women in Colonial North Carolina: Overlooked and Underestimated," *North Carolina Historical Review*, 58 (January), 1–22.

Weeks, Maurice (2008), "U.S. Farmworkers in California Campaign for Economic Justice (Grape Strike), 1965–70," *Global Nonviolent Action Database*, (August 14; updated by Lindsay Carpenter August 3, 2011), https://nvdatabase.swarthmore.edu/content/us-farmworkers-california-campaign-economic-justice-grape-strike-1965-70.

Weigel, David (2014), "Rolling Coal," *Slate*, (July 3), www.slate.com/articles/news_and_politics/politics/2014/07/rolling_coal_conservatives_who_show_their_annoyance_with_liberals_obama.html.

Wells, Ida B. (1892), *Southern Horrors: Lynch Law in All Its Phases*, The New York Age Print, www.gutenberg.org/ebooks/14975.

Wells, William D. (1956), "Is Motivation Research Really an Instrument of the Devil?," *Journal of Marketing*, 21 (2), 196–198.

Wells, William D. (1991), "Preface," in *Highways and Buyways: Naturalistic Research from the Consumer Behavior Odyssey*, ed. Russell W. Belk, Provo, UT: Association for Consumer Research, iii.

Wengrow, David (2008), "Prehistories of Commodity Branding," *Current Anthropology*, 49 (1), 7–34.

Westfall, Ralph L., Harper W. Boyd, Jr., and Donald T. Campbell (1957), "The Use of Structured Techniques in Motivation Research," *Journal of Marketing*, 22 (2), 134–139.

Wharton, Edith (1905), *The House of Mirth*, New York: Charles Scribner's Sons.

Wharton, Edith (1921), *The Age of Innocence*, New York: D. Appleton and Company.

Wharton, Edith and Ogden Codman, Jr. (1897/1997), *The Decoration of Houses*, New York: W.W. Norton.

Whittaker, Frederick (1876), "The Story of Creedmoor," *The Galaxy: A Magazine of Entertaining Reading*, 22 (August), 258–267.

Whyte, William H. (1956) *The Organization Man*, New York: Simon & Schuster.

Wiebe, G.D. (1958), "Is It True What Williams Say about Motivation Research?," *Journal of Marketing*, 22 (4), 408–411.

Wildmon, Tim (2016), "Sign the Boycott Target Pledge!" American Family Association, www.afa.net/the-stand/press-releases/2016/04/sign-the-boycott-target-pledge/#disqus_thread.

Willer, Robb, Bridget Conlon, Christabel L. Rogalin, and Michael T. Wojnowicz (2013), "Overdoing Gender: A Test of the Masculine Overcompensation Thesis," *American Journal of Sociology*, 118 (4), 980–1022.

Williams, Faith M. (1943/1972), "The Standard of Living in Wartime," in *The American Family in World War II*, ed. Ray H. Abrams, New York: Arno Press and New York Times, 117–127.

Williams, Hermann Warner (1973), *Mirror to the American Past: A Survey of American Genre Painting, 1750–1900*, Greenwich, CT: New York Graphic Society.

Williams, Robert J. (1957), "Is It True What They Say About Motivation Research?" *Journal of Marketing*, 22 (2), 125–133.

Williamson, Samuel H. (2016), "Purchasing Power of Money in the United States from 1774 to Present," *Measuring Worth*, www.measuringworth.com/ppowerus/.

Winchester Arms Collectors Association (2017), "About," http://winchestercollector.org/about/.

Winkler, Adam (2011), *Gun Fight: The Battle Over the Right to Bear Arms in America*, New York: W.W. Norton & Company.

Wintemute, Garen J. (2007), "Gun Shows Across a Multistate American Gun Market: Observational Evidence of the Effects of Regulatory Policies," *Injury Prevention*, 13 (3), 150–155.

Wintemute, Garen J. (2009), "Inside Gun Shows: What Goes on When Everybody Thinks Nobody's Watching, Sacramento, CA: Violence Prevention Research Program, UC Davis School of Medicine," http://ucdmc.ucdavis.edu/newsroom/images/Wintemute_gun_study9-2009/IGS5web.pdf.

Witkowski, Terrence H. (1989), "Colonial Consumers in Revolt: Buyer Values and Behavior During the Nonimportation Movement, 1764–1776," *Journal of Consumer Research*, 16 (September), 216–226.

Witkowski, Terrence H. (1991), "Promise Them Anything: A Cultural History of Cigarette Advertising Health Claims," *Journal of Current Issues and Research in Advertising*, 13 (2), 393–409.

Witkowski, Terrence H. (1994), "Data Sources for American Consumption History: An Introduction, Analysis, and Application," in *Research in Marketing: Explorations in the History of Marketing*, Supplement 6, eds. Jagdish Sheth and Ronald A. Fullerton, Greenwich, CT: JAI Press, Inc., 167–182.

Witkowski, Terrence H. (1996), "Farmers Bargaining: Buying and Selling as a Subject in American Genre Painting, 1835–1868," *Journal of Macromarketing*, 16 (Fall), 84–101.

Witkowski, Terrence H. (1998), "The Early American Style: A History of Marketing and Consumer Values," *Psychology and Marketing*, 15 (March), 125–143.

Witkowski, Terrence H. (1999), "The Early Development of Family Purchasing Roles in America, 1750–1840," *Journal of Macromarketing*, 19 (December), 104–114.

Witkowski, Terrence H. (2003), "World War II Poster Campaigns: Preaching Frugality to American Consumers," *Journal of Advertising*, 32 (Spring), 69–82.

Witkowski, Terrence H. (2004), "Re-Gendering Consumer Agency in Mid-Nineteenth-Century America: A Visual Understanding," *Consumption, Markets, and Culture*, 7 (September), 261–283.

Witkowski, Terrence H. (2009), "General Book Store in Chicago, 1938–1947: Linking Neighborhood to Nation," *Journal of Historical Research in Marketing*, 1 (1), 93–121.

Witkowski, Terrence H. (2010a), "A Brief History of Frugality Discourses in the United States," *Consumption, Markets and Culture*, 13 (September), 235–258.

Witkowski, Terrence H. (2010b), "The Marketing Discipline Comes of Age, 1934–1936," *Journal of Historical Research in Marketing*, 2 (November), 370–396.

Witkowski, Terrence H. (2013), "The Visual Politics of U.S. Gun Culture," in *Research in Consumer Behavior*, Vol. 15, eds. Russell W. Belk, Linda Price, and Liza Peñaloza, Bingley, UK: Emerald Group Publishing Limited, 3–23.

Witkowski, Terrence H. (2016a), "Mythical Moments in Remington Brand History," *Culture and Organization*, 22 (1), 44–66.

Witkowski, Terrence H. (2016b), "A History of Consumption in the United States," in *The Routledge Companion to Marketing History*, eds. D.G. Brian Jones and Mark Tadajewski, London and New York: Routledge, 41–60.

Witkowski, Terrence H. and Ellen Hogan (1999), "Home Front Consumers: An Oral History of California Women During World War II," in *Marketing History: The Total Package*, eds. Peggy Cunningham and David Bussiere. East Lansing: Michigan State University, 151–164.

Witkowski, Terrence H. and D.G. Brian Jones (2006), "Qualitative Historical Research in Marketing," in *Handbook of Qualitative Research Methods in Marketing*, ed. Russell W. Belk, Cheltenham, UK: Edward Elgar Publishing, 70–82.

Witkowski, Terrence H. and D.G. Brian Jones (2016), "Historical Research in Marketing: Literature, Knowledge, and Disciplinary Status," *Information & Culture: A Journal of History*, 51 (3), 399–418.

Witzel, Michael Karl (1993), *The American Drive-In*, Osceola, WI: Motorbooks International.

Wolfe, Frank E. (1920), "Organized Labor's Attitude toward the National Thrift Movement," *Annals of the American Academy of Political and Social Science, Vol. 87: The New American Thrift*, 50–51.

Wolgast, Elizabeth H. (1958), "Do Husbands or Wives Make the Purchasing Decisions?" *Journal of Marketing*, 23 (October), 151–158.

Woloch, Nancy (1984), *Women and the American Experience*, New York: A.A. Knopf.

Woods, Walter A. (1960), "Psychological Dimensions of Consumer Decision," *Journal of Marketing*, 24 (3), 15–19.

Wyand, Charles S. (1937), *The Economics of Consumption*, New York: The Macmillan Company.

Yi, Yun-Ae (1996), "Margaret G. Reid: Life and Achievements," *Feminist Economics*, 2 (3), 17–36.

Young, William H. and Nancy K. Young (2002), *The 1930s*, Westport, CT: Greenwood Press.

Zimmerman, Carle C. (1936), *Consumption and Standards of Living*, New York: D. Van Nostrand Company.

Zober, Martin (1956), "Some Projective Techniques Applied to Marketing Research," *Journal of Marketing*, 20 (3), 262–268.

Zuckerman, Mary Ellen (2014), "Martha Van Rensselaer and the *Delineator*'s Homemaking Department," *Journal of Historical Research in Marketing*, 5 (3), 370–384.

Index

Page numbers in **bold** denote figures.